# Common Praise

# Common Praise

### ANGLICAN CHURCH OF CANADA

## Anglican Book Centre
### Toronto, Canada

Published 1998

Anglican Book Centre
600 Jarvis Street
Toronto, Ontario
Canada M4Y 2J6

**Canadian Cataloguing in Publication data**

Main entry under title:

Common Praise

Includes index.
ISBN 1-55126-204-5

1. Anglican Church of Canada—Hymns. 2. Hymns, English—Canada.
I. Anglican Church of Canada

M2133.C685 1998          782.27' 1713          C98-931451-0


**Printed and bound in Canada by Transcontinental Printing Inc.**
**First Printing, 1998**

# Contents

# Preface

*Common Praise* is the fourth hymn book authorized by General Synod for Anglicans in Canada. It succeeds *The Book of Common Praise* of 1908, *The Book of Common Praise (Revised)* of 1938, and *The Hymn Book* of 1971 which was produced jointly with the United Church of Canada. The present book appears following a period of intense change: new translations of the Bible; new forms of worship; new lectionaries; new styles of language and music in worship; shifts in sensitivity to the ways in which language can exclude or include; increased awareness of and contact with other cultures, races, languages, and religious denominations. It also comes after a period of unparalleled creativity in both words and music for congregational song. So many new texts have been written in the past 30 years that people have spoken of a "hymn explosion." New musical styles in a variety of popular idioms have become familiar, as has music from the Taizé and Iona communities, and from Africa, Asia, and South America, not to mention tunes recovered from American folk hymnody. *Common Praise* makes much of this new material readily available to Canadian Anglicans while preserving valued expressions from the past. In accord with the fluidity of the tradition of hymn singing and the practice of the compilers of hymn books in every period, some older texts have been altered so that they may continue to be sung in the present and in years to come.

The origins of the present book lie in a proposal made at General Synod in 1983 immediately after the adoption of *The Book of Alternative Services*. After three years of discussion and refinement a resolution was prepared for presentation in 1986. This resolution, adopted by the National Executive Council, called for a hymn book which would contain material both new and old, which would draw on a wide variety of styles and traditions, which would complement the Common Lectionary, and which would be couched in language as inclusive as possible. In 1992 the General Synod extended this mandate to interpret the word "inclusive" in terms of theology, languages, music, and cultural heritage in addition to gender.

Previous hymn books were prepared in the expectation that each would, for a period of time, be the only one in common use in the church. The experience of the past 25 years has made it clear that an authorized hymn book is now better regarded as a rich core resource, and that some congregations may wish to supplement it with other hymns and service music drawn from the immense treasury of material old and new now available.

There are certain obvious changes in the way in which the material in this book is presented. Most of the words are placed between the staves of the music so that it will be easier to read both at once. In addition to the usual indexes are new ones: an index of music for children and youth, an index of scriptural associations, and one which draws attention to hymns which may be substituted for parts of the liturgy. Guitar chords are provided for many hymns. Although the book is conceived mainly for use in congregations, homes, and conferences where English is the primary language of worship, some of the texts are available in aboriginal languages, in French, in Spanish, and in other tongues.

Based for the most part on texts in *The Book of Alternative Services* (1985), the service music has been prepared with the needs of congregations with modest musical resources in mind. Merbecke's music for the Holy Eucharist, first made widely available to Canadians in Healey Willan's arrangement in the 1938 hymnbook, has been slightly adapted for use with *The Book of Alternative Services*. Most of the other music, whatever the source of its composition, has arisen from the experience and use of various local congregations in Canada.

In the prefatory material to *The Book of Common Praise* of 1908 is a statement that it was to be "understood that nothing in this Hymnal contained shall be construed as an authoritative pronouncement upon any doctrinal question, or interpreted as impugning or varying any of the articles or standards of the Church as set forth in the solemn declaration prefixed to the Constitution of this Synod." Similar statements are affixed to the books of 1938 and 1971 and the principle applies equally to the present collection.

## Hymn Book Task Force

| | | |
|---|---|---|
| George Black,<br>   Task Force convener | Kenneth Hull,<br>   Music Subcommittee convener | Brian Ruttan<br>Peter Walker |
| John Campbell | Lawrence McErlean | Patrick Wedd |
| Walter Deller | Thelma-Anne McLeod, SSJD | |
| Paul Gibson | Kate Merriman | |
| Desmond Hunt* | Louise Peters    * served during part of the project | |

## Ecumenical Partners
John Ambrose, United Church of Canada
Donald Anderson, Presbyterian Church in Canada
Andrew Donaldson, Presbyterian Church in Canada
Fred Kimball Graham, United Church of Canada

## Service Music Working Group
Brigid Coult, convener
David Millard
Steven Morgan
Michael Murray
Bryn Nixon

## Staff
Jo Abrams, project coordinator; Alyson Barnett-Cowan, director, Faith Worship, and Ministry; Sharon L. Beckstead, proofreader; Michael Du Maresq, copyright clerk; Paul Gibson, project manager; Melva Treffinger Graham, copy editor; Jo-Ann Listro, program assistant; Robert Maclennan, publishing manager; Elizabeth Phinney, proofreader; Doug Tindal, director, Information Resources.

Major contributions were made by people across the country, including Ben Arrcak, Ann Bemrose Fetter, Jim Boles, Rachael Boles, Jeffrey Campbell, Michael Capon, Cheryl Kristolaitis, Barbara Liotscos, Iain Luke, Kathy McClellan, Paul Murray, Elaine Pudwell, Eileen Scully, and many others who searched the hymn books of other denominations and traditions for new hymns, assisted in indexing, and examined the music for both suitability and error. The Canadian Bible Society typeset the texts of hymns in First Nations' languages which appear in syllabics. Thanks are due to these and many others who contributed to the complex totality of this book.

## Copyright Permissions
Binary Editions
Donald Anderson, Andrew Donaldson, Diane Strickland, Virginia Lovering.

## Typesetting
Selah Publishing Co., Inc.
David Schaap, Virginia Schaap, Lawrell D. Arnold, Bethlyn D. Burrows, Lynn Dennison, Percival W. Gazlay II, Roy Hopp, Lonnie Kulick, and James Lorenz.

## Cover Design
Saskia Rowley

## Suggestions for Worship Planners

*Common Praise* is organized in sections which correspond to the time of day, frequent acts of worship, the Christian year, and various themes and topics of faith and devotion. However, this does not mean that every hymn in each section is suitable on every such occasion and with every congregation. Nor does it mean that hymns which are associated with a certain occasion cannot be used at other times. The book has been organized to provide hints and suggestions, but great flexibility in use is not only possible but desirable.

The editors have provided a number of indexes to help planners choose hymns creatively and with sensitivity to the style and culture of each congregation. A biblical index will help planners choose hymns which complement the readings assigned or chosen for the occasion. Such hymns do not need to repeat the lection in question, nor even precede or follow it immediately, but could at appropriate points in the liturgy resonate with the tones and vibrations of the same theme.

The subject index is best consulted after the theme or themes of the occasion or moment have been clearly identified.

Since children are full members of the worshipping community, it was felt that having a separate section called "Hymns for Children" would have implied that such hymns were inappropriate for adults and other hymns were inappropriate for children. Instead, an index of hymns which are likely to appeal strongly to children has been provided to facilitate selection of these hymns. Worship planners may also find it useful to check the hymns they have identified in other ways against this index, to ensure that in congregations where children are active participants at least one such hymn is provided in each liturgical celebration as frequently as possible.

In the lower left corner of the first page of each item there is information about the source of the words and music, and copyright information when it applies. The following abbreviations are used.

| | | | | | |
|---|---|---|---|---|---|
| acc. | accompaniment | coll. | collected by | perc. | percussion |
| adapt. | adapted (by) | desc. | descant by | ref. | refrain |
| admin. | administered (by) | Eng. | English | rev. | revised |
| alt. | altered (by) | fauxb. | fauxbourdon | st. | stanza(s) |
| altern. | alternative | fl. | flute | tpt. | trumpet |
| arr. | arranged by | Fr. | French | tr. | translated (by) |
| attrib. | attributed to | harm. | harmonization (by) | trad. | traditional |
| cent. | century | Ltd. | Limited | transc. | transcribed (by) |
| Co. | Company | para. | paraphrased (by) | vers. | versified (by) |

When a brief introduction to a hymn or song is sufficient, introduction marks ⌐ ¬ are provided as a suggestion to the organist or other musicians.

Service Music is provided for the eucharist and other liturgical texts. Each element in the Service Music section is numbered in a scheme which is continuous with the rest of the book, to make it as easy to announce each setting of each liturgical text as the hymns themselves. Worship planners should be flexible and innovative in choosing music, combining music from different settings in one liturgical celebration if that is desired. Hymns which are metrical versions of a number of liturgical texts are identified in the Subject Index (see, for instance, Exsultet; Give rest, O Christ, to your servants; Glory to God; Song of Simeon; Song of Mary); and so are hymns which may be substituted for some liturgical texts.

# Hymns

# 1 Holy, Holy, Holy, Lord God Almighty

*Descant*

4 Ho - - - ly, Lord God al - might - y!

1 Ho - ly, ho - ly, ho - ly, Lord God al - might - y!
2 Ho - ly, ho - ly, ho - ly! All the saints a - dore thee,
3 Ho - ly, ho - ly, ho - ly! Though the dark - ness hide thee,
4 Ho - ly, ho - ly, ho - ly, Lord God al - might - y!

All thy works shall praise thy name;

Ear - ly in the morn - ing our song shall rise to thee:
cast - ing down their gold - en crowns a - round the glass - y sea;
though our sin - ful hu - man gaze thy glo - ry may not see,
All thy works shall praise thy name in earth and sky and sea;

ho - - - - ly, mer - ci - ful and might - y,

ho - ly, ho - ly, ho - ly, mer - ci - ful and might - y,
cher - u - bim and ser - a - phim fall - ing down be - fore thee,
on - ly thou art ho - ly; there is none be - side thee,
ho - ly, ho - ly, ho - ly, mer - ci - ful and might - y,

Text: Reginald Heber (1783–1826), alt.
Music: John Bacchus Dykes (1823–1876); desc. Godfrey Hewitt (1909– ) ©.

Irregular
NICAEA

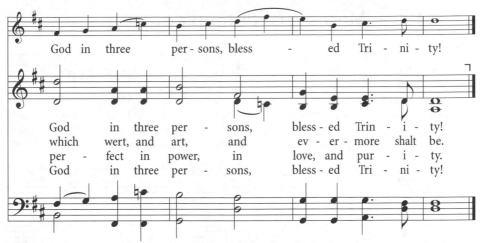

God in three per-sons, bless-ed Tri-ni-ty!

God in three per-sons, bless-ed Trin-i-ty!
which wert, and art, and ev-er-more shalt be.
per-fect in power, in love, and pur-i-ty.
God in three per-sons, bless-ed Tri-ni-ty!

## Plains Cree text

1 ᐃ ᑲᐊᓂᑌᔪᐤ, ᑌᐹᔨᒋᑳᔪᐤ
ᐁᐳᐨ ᑳᑭᓛᐸ ᑯ ᓂᑯᒧᐢᑌᑎᐣ
ᐃ ᑲᐊᓂᑌᔪᐤ, ᑳᓛᐗᑎᓭᔪᐤ
ᐃ ᓂᐢᑐ ᐊᔭᔭᐣ ᐹᔪᐠ ᒪᓂᑐ.

1 Ka Kunatiseyun, Tāpāyichikāyun
Wepuch kākisāpa ku nikumostatin
Ka Kunatiseyun, Kāsāwatiseyun
Ka nisto uyayan pāyuk Manito.

2 ᐃ ᑲᐊᓂᑌᔪᐤ ᐅᐲᒫᒋᐦᐅᐅᐗᐣ
ᑭ ᐸᐸᑌᐢᑕᐠᐗᐣ ᐃᐢᐱᒥᐠ ᑭᓯᑯᐠ
ᐊᔨᒋ ᑭᑫᔪᐤ ᐋᑯᑐ ᐊᐣᑫᓗᐠ
ᐃᑫᑳ ᑭᔪ ᒪᓂᑑᐁᔪᐣ.

2 Ka Kunatiseyun opimachihoowuk
Ke putupestakwak ispimik kesikok
Usiche kukeyow ākotu angeluk
Kakekā keyu Mānitooweyun.

3 ᐃ ᑲᐊᓂᑌᔪᐤ ᑎᐱᐢᑲᐠ ᐋᔭᔪᐣ
ᐋᑐ ᐊᔨᓭᔨᓀᐤ ᐋᑲ ᐋ ᐗᐳᒥᐢᐠ
ᑭᔪ ᐱᑯ ᐃ ᒧᒥᑐᓀᐠᑯᑐᒧᐣ
ᒧᐢᑯᐃᓭᐏᐣ, ᓵᑭᐦᐃᐚᐏᐣ.

3 Ka Kunatiseyun tipiskak āyayun
Atu uyiseyinew āka ā wapumisk
Keyu piko ka mumitonèkutumun
Muskuwisewin, sakihiwāwin.

4 ᐃ ᑲᐊᓂᑌᔪᐤ, ᓭᔪᑲᑎᓭᔪᐤ
ᒥᓯᐚ ᐊᑐ ᓄᐠᐩᐣ ᑭᐟ ᐊᐧᑐᐢᑳᐏᐣ
ᐃ ᑲᐊᓂᑌᔪᐤ, ᑳᓛᐗᑎᓭᔪᐤ
ᐃ ᓂᐢᑐ ᐊᔭᔭᐣ ᐹᔪᐠ ᒪᓂᑐ.

4 Ka Kunatiseyun, Seyokatiseyun
Misiwā ittu nokwun ket utoskāwin
Ka Kunatiseyun, Kāsāwatiseyun
Ka nisto uyayun pāyuk Munito.

Tr. John Alexander Mackay (1838–1923).

## Naskapi text

1 ᓂᔾ ᒋᔕᒪᐣᑐ, ᐃ ᐸᔭᒋᔀᐃᐣ,
ᒫᐗᐨ ᒋ ᔓᑲᑎᔑᐣ, ᒋ ᒋᔕᐗᑎᔑᐣ,
ᒋᒋᔕᐸ ᒋ ᐃ ᓂᑲᒧᐢᑕᑎᓇᐣ
ᒋᔕᒪᐣᑐᐤ, ᓇᐢᑐᐸᐃᑯᐃᐣ.

1 Chiya chishamantu, ka payachishiin,
Mawach chi shukatishin, chi chishawatishin,
Chichishapa chi ka nikamustatinan
Chishamantu, nastupaikuin.

2 ᐃ ᐸᔭᒋᔑᐃᐣ, ᒋ ᒋᐢᑕᒋᒥᒀᐨ
ᒋᒋ ᐊᐣᒋᓈᐨ ᑭᔭ ᐸᔭᒋᔑᔑᐚᐨ;
ᒋ ᐸᒋᔑᓄᐢᑕᒀᐨ ᐊᐢᐱᐢᒋᐢᑎᔑᐃᐣ,
ᒋᔾ, ᒧᐢ ᐊᑌᐃᐣ, ᒋᔕᒪᓂᑐᐤ.

2 Ka payachishiin, chi chistachimikwach
Chichi anchinach kiya payachishishiwach;
Chi pachishinustakwach ashpischistishiin,
Chiy, mush atain, chishamanitu.

3 ᐃ ᐸᔭᒋᔑᐃᐣ, ᐊᔑᓇᑯᔑᐃᐣ
ᐃ ᐅᒫᒋᐟᐚᐏᐣ ᓇᒪ ᒋ ᐗᐸᑕᒼ:
ᐋᐧ ᐸᐃᑯᐃᐣ ᓇᐢᑎᐦ ᔕᐹᓇ
ᐋᑲ ᐃᔾᐢ ᐊᔑ ᓄᑕᔑᐃᐣ.

3 Ka payachishiin, ashinakushiin
Ka umachitwawinit nama chi wapatam:
Akwa paikuin nastiich shapwana
Aka wiyast ashi nutashiin.

4 ᐃ ᐸᔭᒋᔑᐃᐣ, ᒋ ᔓᒐᔨᑎᐏᐣ
ᓄᐠᐗᐣ ᒋᒋᒋᔑᑯᐨ, ᐊᐢᒋᐨ ᑭᔭ ᓂᐱᐨ;
ᒥᑐᐣ ᒋ ᔓᑲᑎᔑᐣ, ᓇᐢᐨ ᒋ ᔕᒋᐚᐣ
ᒋᔕᒪᓂᑐᐤ, ᓇᐢᑐᐸᐃᑯᐃᐣ.

4 Ka payachishiin, chi shuchayitiwin
Nukwan chichichishikuch, aschich kiya nipich;
Mitun chi shukatishin, nasch chi shachiiwan
Chishamantu, nastupaikuin.

## Inuktitut text

1 ᐃᔭᕐᖁᖂᓄᑦᑐᔪᐊᑦ
ᐊᑦᓂᐅᐅᑦᑎᑦ,
ᐅᓚᒻᒪᓄᖅ ᖃᐳᑕᒫᑦ
ᓂᖅᐅᔅᖃᑦᑕᓂᔅᓘ:
ᐃᔭᕐᖁᖂᓄᑦᑐᔪᐊᑦ
ᐊᓵᖅᐳᒍᖅᖂᑦᑎᑦ,
ᐃᔅᐊᔅ ᔫᑎ
ᐱᖃᓗᔫᓛᕐᑐᑦ.

2 ᐃᔭᕐᖁᖂᓄᑦᑐᔪᑎᑦ
ᓇᓴᐃᐊᔅᖃᑦᑎᑦ,
ᐅᔭᒍᓛᖂ ᖅᑲᖅᑯᐳ-
ᓚᔅᔅᔭᐊᑎᓗᔅᖃᑐᖅᑲᖅ,
ᖅᑲᔅᕆᐊᔅᖃᑦᑎᑦ,
ᔫᓪᖃᑦᑎᑦᐊᔅᖃᑎᑦ,
ᐊᑎᐅᖅᑐᑎᑦ
ᐃᓯᔅᒫᖅᑐᓂᐠᒍ.

3 ᐃᔭᕐᖁᖂᓄᑦᑐᔪᐊᑦ
ᔫᓪᖃᔅᔭᖅᑐᑎᑦᒍ,
ᑕᖅᑐᖀᓄᒐᑦᓇᓄᒐᑦ
ᖅᑲᐳᔅᔭᒃᖀᖅᓇᑦᖅᑐᑎᒍ
ᔫᑎ ᓂᖅᐅᔅᖃᖀᐊᑦ
ᐊᖂᒐ ᐃᐃᓇᔅᔾ,
ᔫᑎᑦᖁ ᓇᐊᖅᓴᖀ-
ᓛᑎᒍᔅ ᐃᐃᔅᐨ.

4 ᐃᔭᕐᖁᖂᓄᑦᑐᔪᐊᑦ
ᔫᑎᑎᐊᐅᑐᔅᑎᑦᒍ,
ᐃᓵᐊᔅ ᑭᕆᐊᑦ
ᐊᑦᓂᐅᐊᔅᔫᖃᑎᑦ,
ᐃᐊᖀᑦ ᑕᐸᓚᖂᔅᐨᒍ
ᑲᑕᓚᔅᕐᔭᐊᑦ
ᓂᐱᖅᐩ ᐊᔭᖅᔅᖃᑐᔅᒍ
ᓂᖅᐅᔫᖃᖀᖅᐨᑦ.

Tr. Benjamin T.
Arreak (1947– ) ©.

Tr. Joseph Guanish (1931– ) ©. Adapt. from Eastern Cree, William Gladstone Walton
(1867–1948) and Daisy Alice Spencer Walton (1873–1948). © *Anglican Book Centre.*

# 2  When Morning Gilds the Skies

1 When morn-ing gilds the skies, my heart, a-wak-ing, cries: "May
2 When-e'er the sweet church bell peals o-ver hill and dell, may
3 In heaven's e-ter-nal bliss the love-liest strain is this: may
4 To God, the Word, on high, the hosts of an-gels cry: "May

Je-sus Christ be praised!" A-like at work and prayer to
Je-sus Christ be praised! O hark to what it sings, as
Je-sus Christ be praised! The powers of dark-ness fear when
Je-sus Christ be praised!" Let mor-tals, too, up-raise their

Je-sus I re-pair: "May Je-sus Christ be praised!"
joy-ous-ly it rings: may Je-sus Christ be praised!
this sweet chant they hear: may Je-sus Christ be praised!
voice in hymns of praise: "May Je-sus Christ be praised!"

5 Let earth's wide circle round
in joyful notes resound:
"May Jesus Christ be praised!"
Let air and sea and sky
from depth to height reply:
"May Jesus Christ be praised!"

6 Be this, while life is mine,
my canticle divine:
may Jesus Christ be praised!
Be this the eternal song
through all the ages on:
may Jesus Christ be praised!

Text: *Katolisches Gesangbuch*, Würzburg, 1828; tr. Edward Caswall (1814–1878), alt.
Music: Joseph Barnby (1838–1896).

666 666
LAUDES DOMINI

# Morning Has Broken

1 Morn - ing has bro - ken like the first morn - ing;
2 Sweet the rain's new fall sun - lit from heav - en,
3 Mine is the sun - light! Mine is the morn - ing

black - bird has spo - ken like the first bird.
like the first dew - fall on the first grass.
born of the one light E - den saw play!

Praise for the sing - ing! Praise for the morn - ing!
Praise for the sweet - ness of the wet gar - den,
Praise with e - la - tion, praise ev - ery morn - ing,

Praise for them, spring - ing fresh from the Word!
sprung in com - plete - ness where his feet pass.
God's re - cre - a - tion of the new day!

Text: Eleanor Farjeon (1881–1965). © David Higham Associates Ltd.
Music: Melody Gaelic trad.; arr. C. Richard Hunt (1930– ) ©.

55 54D
BUNESSAN
*Alt. settings and lower key 287, 445*

# O God, Creation's Secret Force

1 O God, creation's secret force, yourself unmoved, all motion's source, you, from the morn till evening's ray, through all its changes guide the day:

2 grant us, when this short life is past, the glorious evening that shall last; that, by a holy death attained, eternal glory may be gained.

3 Almighty Father, hear our cry through Jesus Christ, our Lord most high, whom with the Spirit we adore forever and forevermore.

Text: Ambrose of Milan (340–397); st. 1–2, tr. John Mason Neale (1818–1866), alt.;
    st. 3, tr. James Waring McCrady (1938– ) ©.
Music: Melody *Rheinfelsisches Deutsches Catholisches Gesangbuch*, Augsburg, 1666; harm. *Orgelbuch zum*
    *Gesangbuch der Evangelisch-Reformierten Kirchen der Deutschsprachigen Schweiz*, 1926.

LM
O HEILAND, REISS

# Christ Whose Glory Fills the Skies

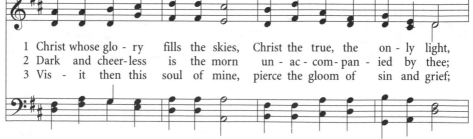

1 Christ whose glory fills the skies, Christ the true, the only light,

2 Dark and cheerless is the morn unaccompanied by thee;

3 Visit then this soul of mine, pierce the gloom of sin and grief;

Text: Charles Wesley (1707–1788).
Music: Melody *Geystliche Gesangk Buchleyn*, 1524;
    adapt. and harm. William Henry Havergal (1793–1870), alt.

77 77 77
RATISBON

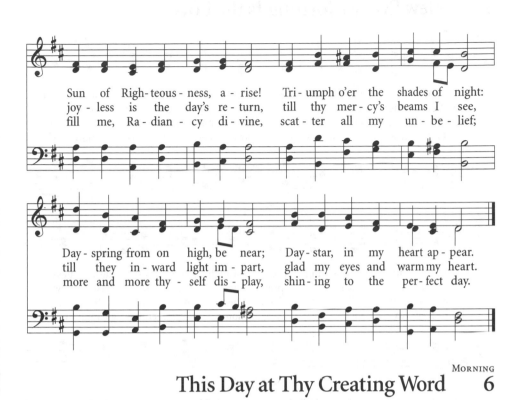

Sun of Right-teous - ness, a - rise! Tri - umph o'er the shades of night:
joy - less is the day's re - turn, till thy mer - cy's beams I see,
fill me, Ra - dian - cy di - vine, scat - ter all my un - be - lief;

Day - spring from on high, be near; Day - star, in my heart ap - pear.
till they in - ward light im - part, glad my eyes and warm my heart.
more and more thy - self dis - play, shin - ing to the per - fect day.

## This Day at Thy Creating Word

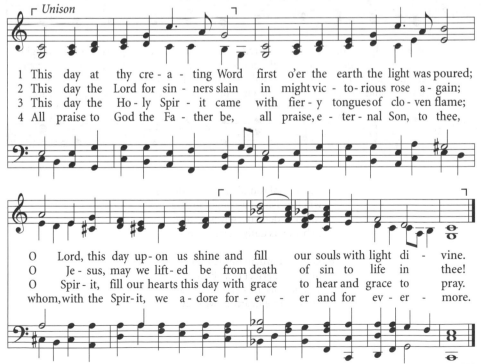

*Unison*

1 This day at thy cre - a - ting Word first o'er the earth the light was poured;
2 This day the Lord for sin - ners slain in might vic - to - rious rose a - gain;
3 This day the Ho - ly Spir - it came with fier - y tongues of clo - ven flame;
4 All praise to God the Fa - ther be, all praise, e - ter - nal Son, to thee,

O Lord, this day up - on us shine and fill our souls with light di - vine.
O Je - sus, may we lift - ed be from death of sin to life in thee!
O Spir - it, fill our hearts this day with grace to hear and grace to pray.
whom, with the Spir - it, we a - dore for - ev - er and for ev - er - more.

Text: William Walsham How (1823–1897), alt.
Music: Henry G. Ley (1877–1962). © 1936 Ascherberg, Hopwood and Crew Ltd. Chappell Music Ltd. London.

LM
RUSHFORD

# 9 Today I Awake

1 To - day I a - wake and God is be - fore me. At
2 To - day I a - rise and Christ is be - side me. He
3 To - day I af - firm the Spir - it with - in me at
4 To - day I en - joy the Trin - i - ty round me, a -

night, as I dreamt, he sum - moned the day; for
walked through the dark to scat - ter new light. Yes,
wor - ship and work, in strug - gle and rest. The
bove and be - neath, be - fore and be - hind; the

God nev - er sleeps, but pat - terns the morn - ing with
Christ is a - live, and beck - ons his peo - ple to
Spir - it in - spires all life which is chang - ing from
Mak - er, the Son, the Spir - it to - geth - er— they

slith - ers of gold or glo - ry in grey.
hope and to heal, re - sist and in - vite.
fear - ing to faith, from bro - ken to blest.
called me to life and call me their friend.

Text and music: John L. Bell (1949– ).
© 1989 WGRG The Iona Community (Scotland).
Used by permission of G.I.A. Publications, Inc., exclusive agent.

56 55D
SLITHERS OF GOLD

*Unison*

1 We, the Lord's peo - ple, heart and voice u - nit - ing, praise him who
2 This is the Lord's house, home of all his peo - ple, school for the
3 This is the Lord's day, day of God's own mak - ing, day of cre -
4 In the Lord's ser - vice bread and wine are of - fered, that Christ may

called us out of sin and dark - ness in - to his own light,
faith - ful, ref - uge for the sin - ner, rest for the pil - grim,
a - tion, day of re - sur - rec - tion, day of the Spir - it,
take them, bless them, break, and give them to all his peo - ple,

that he might a - noint us a roy - al priest - hood.
ha - ven for the wea - ry; all find a wel - come.
sign of heav - en's ban - quet, day for re - joic - ing.
his own life im - part - ing, food ev - er - last - ing.

Text: John E. Bowers (1923– ), alt. ©.
Music: Melody *Antiphoner*, Paris, 1681; harm. Derek Holman (1931– ) ©.

11 11 11 5
CHRISTE SANCTORUM

# Blessed Be the God of Israel

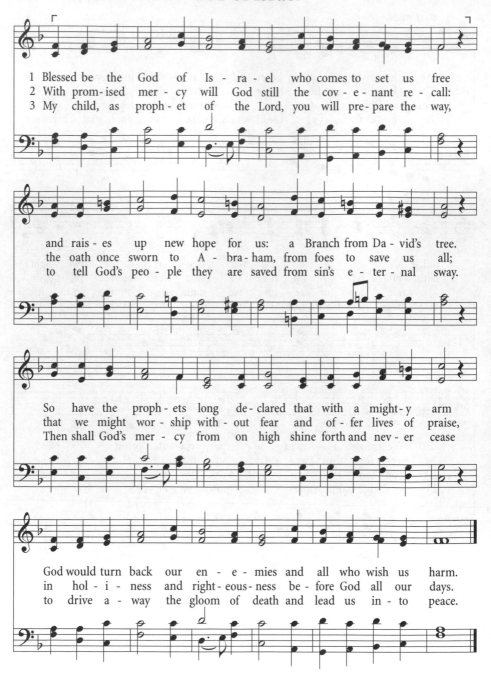

1 Blessed be the God of Is - ra - el who comes to set us free
2 With prom - ised mer - cy will God still the cov - e - nant re - call:
3 My child, as proph - et of the Lord, you will pre - pare the way,

and rais - es up new hope for us: a Branch from Da - vid's tree.
the oath once sworn to A - bra - ham, from foes to save us all;
to tell God's peo - ple they are saved from sin's e - ter - nal sway.

So have the proph - ets long de - clared that with a might - y arm
that we might wor - ship with - out fear and of - fer lives of praise,
Then shall God's mer - cy from on high shine forth and nev - er cease

God would turn back our en - e - mies and all who wish us harm.
in hol - i - ness and right - eous - ness be - fore God all our days.
to drive a - way the gloom of death and lead us in - to peace.

Text: *Song of Zechariah* (Luke 1.68–79); para. Carl P. Daw, Jr. (1944– ).
*Para. © 1989 Hope Publishing Co.*
Music: Dorothy Howell Sheets (1915– ) ©.

CMD
SONG OF ZACHARIAS

*Unison*

1 We bless you, God of Is - ra - el;
2 You prom - ised through the proph - ets' word
3 This child will go be - fore the Lord,
4 Your ten - der love, like ear - ly dawn,

you come to set your peo - ple free.
to save your peo - ple from their foes;
the van - guard of Mes - si - ah's way,
her - alds the day of end - less peace;

In Je - sus, born of Da - vid's line,
in free - dom they will wor - ship you,
preach - ing for - give - ness full and free—
the dark - ness of death's shad - ow fades;

sal - va - tion springs for all to see.
fear - less, de - liv - ered from their woes.
the pre - lude to God's per - fect day.
your jus - tice reigns, and will not cease.

Text: *Song of Zechariah* (Luke 1.68–79); para. Paul Gibson (1932– ) ©.
Music: Melody *Antiphoner*, Rouen, 1728; harm. Ralph Vaughan Williams (1872–1958).
*Harm. © Oxford University Press.*

LM
ST. VENANTIUS
*Alt. setting 163, 214*

# 13  O Gladsome Light, O Grace

1 O glad-some light, O grace of God the Fa-ther's face,
2 As day fades in - to night, we see the eve-ning light,
3 To you of right be - longs all praise of ho-ly songs,

the e - ter - nal splen-dour wear-ing; ce - les - tial, ho-ly, blest,
our hymn of praise out - pour-ing, Fa - ther of might un - known,
O Son of God, life - giv - er; you, there-fore, O Most High,

our Sav - iour Je - sus Christ, joy - ful in your ap - pear-ing.
Christ, his in - car - nate Son, and Ho - ly Spirit, a - dor - ing.
the world will glo - ri - fy, and shall ex - alt for ev - er.

Text: *Phos hilaron*, Greek hymn (200?); tr. Robert Seymour Bridges (1844–1930).
*Tr. © Oxford University Press.*
Music: Melody Geneva, 1551; harm. Claude Goudimel (1514–1572) and others.

667 667
NUNC DIMITTIS

# O Gracious Light, Lord Jesus Christ

1 O gracious Light, Lord Jesus Christ, in you the
2 Now sunset comes, but light shines forth; the lamps are
3 Worthy are you of endless praise, O Son of

Father's glory shone. Immortal, holy,
lit to pierce the night. Praise Father, Son, and
God, life-giving Lord; wherefore you are through

blest is he, and blest are you, his holy Son.
Spirit: God who dwells in the eternal light.
all the earth and in the highest heaven adored.

Text: *Phos hilaron*, Greek hymn (200?); para. F. Bland Tucker (1895–1984).
*Para. © 1985 The Church Pension Fund.*
Music: Thomas Tallis (1505?–1585).

LM
TALLIS'S CANON
*Lower key 664*

# 15 Light of the World, in Grace and Beauty

Light of the world, in grace and beau - ty, mir - ror of God's e -
ter - nal face, trans - par - ent flame of love's free du - ty,
you bring sal - va - tion to our race. Now as we see the
lights of eve - ning we raise our voice in hymns of praise:
wor - thy are you of end - less bless - ing,

Text: *Phos hilaron*, Greek hymn (200?); para. Paul Gibson (1932– ) ©.  
Music: Melody Strasbourg, 1545; Geneva, 1551; harm. Ralph Vaughan Williams (1872–1958).  
*Harm. © Oxford University Press.*

98 98D  
RENDEZ À DIEU  
*Lower key and alt. setting 165, 316*

sun of our night, lamp of our days.

## O Light, Whose Splendour Thrills

1 O Light, whose splen - dour thrills and glad - dens with ra - diance
2 as twi - light hov - ers near at sun - set, and lamps are
3 In all life's bril - liant, time - less mo - ments, let faith - ful

bright - er than the sun, pure gleam of God's un - end - ing
lit, and chil - dren nod, in eve - ning hymns we lift our
voic - es sing your praise, O Son of God, our life - be -

glo - ry, O Je - sus, blest A - noint - ed One;
voic - es to Fa - ther, Spir - it, Son: one God.
stow - er, whose glo - ry light - ens end - less days.

Text: *Phos hilaron*, Greek Hymn (200?); para. Carl P. Daw, Jr. (1944– ).
*Para. © 1989 Hope Publishing Co.*
Music: Melody Strasbourg, 1545.

98 98
LES COMMANDEMENS
*Alt. tune* ST. CLEMENT *29*

# Christ, Mighty Saviour

1 Christ, might-y Sav-iour, Light of all cre-a-tion, you make the
2 Now comes the day's end as the sun is set-ting: mir-ror of
3 There-fore we come now, eve-ning rites to of-fer, joy-ful-ly
4 Give heed, we pray you, to our sup-pli-ca-tion: that you may
5 Though bod-ies slum-ber, hearts shall keep their vig-il, for-ev-er

day-time ra-di-ant with sun-light and to the night give
day-break, pledge of res-ur-rec-tion; while in the heav-ens,
chant-ing ho-ly hymns to praise you, with all cre-a-tion
grant us par-don for of-fen-ces, strength for our weak hearts,
rest-ing in the peace of Je-sus, in light or dark-ness

glit-ter-ing a-dorn-ment, stars in the heav-ens.
choirs of stars ap-pear-ing hal-low the night-fall.
join-ing hearts and voic-es sing-ing your glo-ry.
rest for ach-ing bod-ies, sooth-ing the wea-ry.
wor-ship-ping our Sav-iour now and for-ev-er.

Text: *Phos hilaron*, Greek hymn (200?); para. Mozarabic (10th cent.);
tr. Alan G. McDougall (1895–1964); rev. Anne K. LeCroy (1930– ) ©. *Tr.* © *1982 The Church Pension Fund.*
Music: Melody Poitiers, 1746; harm. Healey Willan (1880–1968). *Harm. © Estate of Healey Willan.*

11 11 11 5
ISTE CONFESSOR

# O Laughing Light, O First-Born of Creation  18

1 O laugh-ing Light, O First-born of cre-a-tion, ra-diance of
2 Day's light is fra-gile; your light is e-ter-nal. We look to
3 Light of the world, O Je-sus, you are wor-thy! Giv-er of

glo-ry, light from light be-got-ten, God self-re-veal-ing,
you, our light with-in the shad-ow. We sing to you, Cre-
life and Child of God, we praise you! Hear as the un-i-

ho-ly, bright, and bless-ed: you shine up-on us.
a-tor, Christ, and Spir-it; you shine be-fore us.
verse pro-claims your glo-ry! You shine a-mong us.

Text: *Phos hilaron*, Greek hymn (200?); para. Sylvia G. Dunstan (1955–1993).
*Para.* © *1991 G.I.A. Publications, Inc.*
Music: John R. Van Maanen (1958– ) ©.

11 11 11 5
PHOS HILARON
*Alt. tune* ISTE CONFESSOR 17

# 19 The Duteous Day Now Closes

1 The du-teous day now clos-es, each flower and tree re-pos-es, shade creeps o'er wild and wood: let us, as night is fall-ing, on God our mak-er call-ing, give thanks and bless the Giv-er good.

2 Now all the heaven-ly splen-dour breaks forth in star-light ten-der from myr-iad worlds un-known; and we, this mar-vel see-ing, for-get our self-ish be-ing for joy of beau-ty not our own.

3 Though long our mor-tal blind-ness has missed God's lov-ing kind-ness and plunged us in-to strife; yet when life's day is ov-er, shall death's fair night dis-cov-er the fields of ev-er-last-ing life.

Text: Paul Gerhardt (1607–1676); tr. Robert Seymour Bridges (1844–1930), alt.
*Tr. © Oxford University Press. Alt. with permission.*
Music: Melody German (15th. cent.); adapt. Heinrich Isaac (1450?–1517);
    adapt. and harm. Johann Sebastian Bach (1685–1750).

776 778
INNSBRUCK

# Day Is Done, But Love Unfailing

1 Day is done, but love un-fail-ing dwells ev-er here;
2 Dark de-scends, but light un-end-ing shines through our night;
3 Eyes will close, but you un-sleep-ing watch by our side;

shad-ows fall, but hope, pre-vail-ing, calms ev-er-y fear.
you are with us, ev-er lend-ing new strength to sight.
death may come, in love's safe keep-ing still we a-bide.

God, our mak-er, none for-sak-ing, take our hearts, of love's own mak-ing;
One in love, your truth con-fess-ing, one in hope of heav-en's bless-ing,
God of love, all e-vil quell-ing, sin for-giv-ing, fear dis-pell-ing,

watch our sleep-ing, guard our wak-ing, be al-ways near.
may we see, in love's pos-sess-ing, love's end-less light!
stay with us, our hearts in-dwell-ing, this ev-en-tide.

Text: James Quinn, SJ (1919– ) ©. *Used by permission of Selah Publishing Co., Inc., North American Agent.*
Music: Melody Welsh trad.; harm. *The English Hymnal,* 1906, alt.

84 84 888 4
AR HYD Y NOS
*Lower key 30, 259*

# 21 Come, Holy Ghost

*Refrain*

Come, Holy Ghost, soon we should be sleep-ing.
Come, come, Holy Ghost,
Come, Holy Ghost, Holy Ghost,
Come, Holy Ghost, to ev-

*Last time*

Glad-den ev-ery heart en-trust-ed to your keep-ing.
glad-den ev-ery heart en-trust-ed to your keep-ing.
glad-den ev-ery heart en-trust-ed to your keep-ing.
ery heart en-trust-ed to your keep-ing.

1 Now the day is done, thanks for all it brought us, for
2 Bless the ones we love, bless the ones we wea-ry, and
3 Let our bod-ies rest, free our minds for dream-ing, and

Oh_____ Oh_____ 1 For
Oh_____ Oh_____ 2 and
3 and

Text: John L. Bell (1949– ) and Graham Maule (1958– ).
Music: Melody Scottish trad.; arr. The Iona Community (Scotland).
*Text and arr. © 1989 WGRG The Iona Community (Scotland). Used by permission of G.I.A. Publications, Inc., exclusive agent.*

56 67 with refrain
AYE WAUKIN O

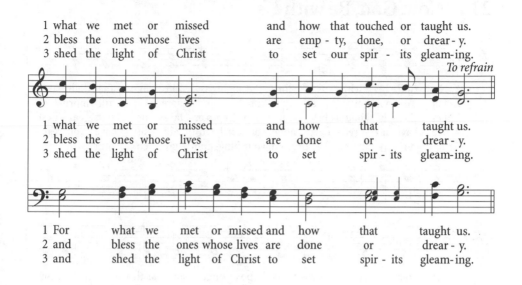

1 what we met or missed and how that touched or taught us.
2 bless the ones whose lives are emp - ty, done, or drear - y.
3 shed the light of Christ to set our spir - its gleam-ing.

*To refrain*

1 what we met or missed and how that taught us.
2 bless the ones whose lives are done or drear - y.
3 shed the light of Christ to set spir - its gleam-ing.

1 For what we met or missed and how that taught us.
2 and bless the ones whose lives are done or drear - y.
3 and shed the light of Christ to set spir - its gleam-ing.

## Now from the Altar of My Heart  22

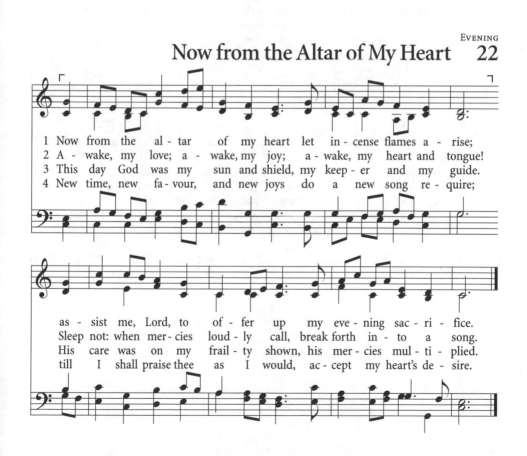

1 Now from the al - tar of my heart let in - cense flames a - rise;
2 A - wake, my love; a - wake, my joy; a - wake, my heart and tongue!
3 This day God was my sun and shield, my keep - er and my guide.
4 New time, new fa - vour, and new joys do a new song re - quire;

as - sist me, Lord, to of - fer up my eve - ning sac - ri - fice.
Sleep not: when mer - cies loud - ly call, break forth in - to a song.
His care was on my frail - ty shown, his mer - cies mul - ti - plied.
till I shall praise thee as I would, ac - cept my heart's de - sire.

Text: John Mason (1645?–1694).
Music: Attrib. Charles Collignon (1725–1785).

CM
UNIVERSITY

## 23 Now, God, Be with Us

1 Now, God, be with us, for the night is clos - ing; the light and
2 Let e - vil thoughts and spir - its flee be - fore us; till morn-ing's
3 Let ho - ly thoughts be ours when sleep o'er - takes us; our ear - liest
4 We have no ref - uge; none on earth to aid us save you, Cre -
5 Your ho - ly name be praised, your king-dom giv - en, your will be

dark - ness are of your dis - pos - ing, and 'neath your shad - ow
dawn - ing, watch, Pro - tec - tor, o'er us; in soul and bod - y
thoughts be yours when morn-ing wakes us, serv - ing you on - ly,
a - tor, who your own have made us; but your dear pres - ence
done on earth as 'tis in hea - ven; keep us, for - give us,

here to rest we yield us, for you will shield us.
from all harm de - fend us; your an - gels send us.
and in all our do - ing your praise pur - su - ing.
will not leave them lone - ly who seek you on - ly.
and from ill de - liv - er us now and ev - er.

Text: Petrus Herbert (?–1571); tr. Catherine Winkworth (1827–1878), alt.
Music: Melody Philippe Goibaud Dubois (1626–1696);
    harm. Ralph Vaughan Williams (1872–1958). *Harm. © Oxford University Press.*

11 11 11 5
CHRISTE FONS JUGIS

1 A - bide with me: fast falls the e - ven - tide;
2 Swift to its close ebbs out life's lit - tle day;
3 I need thy pres - ence ev - ery pass - ing hour;
4 I fear no foe with thee at hand to bless;
5 Hold thou thy cross be - fore my clos - ing eyes;

the dark - ness deep - ens; Lord, with me a - bide.
earth's joys grow dim, its glo - ries pass a - way;
what but thy grace can foil the tempt - er's power?
ills have no weight, and tears no bit - ter - ness.
shine through the gloom, and point me to the skies;

When oth - er help - ers fail, and com - forts flee,
change and de - cay in all a - round I see:
Who like thy - self my guide and stay can be?
Where is death's sting? Where, grave, thy vic - to - ry?
heaven's morn - ing breaks, and earth's vain shad - ows flee:

Help of the help - less, O
O thou, who chang - est not,
Through cloud and sun - shine, Lord, a - bide with me.
I tri - umph still, if thou
in life, in death, O Lord,

Text: Henry Francis Lyte (1793–1847).
Music: William Henry Monk (1823–1889).

10 10 10 10
EVENTIDE

# 25 Glory to Thee, My God, This Night

1 Glo - ry to thee, my God, this night for all the
2 For - give me, Lord, for thy dear Son, the ill that
3 O may my soul on thee re - pose, and may sweet
4 When in the night I sleep - less lie, my soul with
5 Praise God, from whom all bless - ings flow; praise God, all

bless - ings of the light; keep me, O keep me,
I this day have done, that with the world, my -
sleep mine eye - lids close, sleep that shall me more
heaven - ly thoughts sup - ply; let no ill dreams dis -
crea - tures here be - low; praise God a - bove, ye

King of kings, be - neath thine own al - might - y wings.
self, and thee, I ere I sleep at peace may be.
vig - orous make to serve my God when I a - wake.
turb my rest, no powers of dark - ness me mo - lest.
heaven - ly host; praise Fa - ther, Son, and Ho - ly Ghost.

Text: Thomas Ken (1637–1711), alt.
Music: Thomas Tallis (1505?–1585).

LM
TALLIS'S CANON
*Lower key 664*

1 To you be-fore the close of day, Cre - a - tor
2 Save us from trou - bled, rest - less sleep; from all ill
3 A health - y life we ask of you: the fire of
4 Al - might - y Fa - ther, hear our cry through Je - sus

of all things, we pray that, in your sav - ing
dreams your chil - dren keep. So calm our minds that
love in us re - new, and when the dawn new
Christ, our Lord most high, whom with the Spir - it

con - stan - cy, our guard and keep - er you would be.
fears may cease and rest - ed bod - ies wake in peace.
light will bring, your praise and glo - ry we shall sing.
we a - dore for - ev - er and for ev - er - more.

Text: Latin (6th cent.); st. 1–3, *The Hymnal 1982*, alt. St. 1–3 © *The Church Pension Fund.*
St. 4. James Waring McCrady (1938– ) ©.
Music: Plainsong, Mode 8; harm. Healey Willan (1880–1968). © *Estate of Healey Willan.*

LM
TE LUCIS

## 29 The Day Thou Gavest

*Descant*

5 So be it, Lord! Thy throne shall nev-er, like

1 The day thou gav - est, Lord, is end - ed; the
2 We thank thee that thy church un - sleep-ing, while
3 As o'er each con - ti - nent and is - land the
4 The sun that bids us rest is wak - ing thy
5 So be it, Lord! Thy throne shall nev - er, like

earth's proud em - pires, pass a - way; thy

dark - ness falls at thy be - hest. To
earth rolls on - ward in - to light, through
dawn leads on an - oth - er day, the
faith - ful 'neath the west - ern sky, and
earth's proud em - pires, pass a - way; thy

Text: John Ellerton (1826–1893), alt.
Music: Clement Cotterill Scholefield (1839–1904); desc. Kenneth Hull (1952– ) ©.

98 98
St. Clement

king - dom stands and grows for - ev - er, till

thee our morn - ing hymns as - cend - ed; thy
all the world her watch is keep - ing, and
voice of prayer is ne - ver si - lent, nor
hour by hour fresh lips are mak - ing thy
king - dom stands and grows for - ev - er, till

all thy crea - tures own thy sway.

praise shall sanc - ti - fy our rest.
rests not now by day or night.
dies the strain of praise a - way.
won - drous do - ings heard on high.
all thy crea - tures own thy sway.

# 30 God, that Madest Earth and Heaven

1 God, that mad-est earth and heav-en, dark-ness and light;
2 Guard us wak-ing, guard us sleep-ing, and, when we die,

who the day for toil hast giv-en, for rest, the night;
may we in thy might-y keep-ing all peace-ful lie:

may thine an-gel-guards de-fend us, slum-ber sweet thy mer-cy
when the last dread call shall wake us, do not thou our God for-

send us, ho-ly dreams and hopes at-tend us, this live-long night.
sake us, but to reign in glo-ry take us with thee on high.

Text: St.1, Reginald Heber (1783–1826); st.2, Richard Whately (1787–1863).
Music: Melody Welsh trad.; harm. *The English Hymnal*, 1906, alt.

84 84 888 4
AR HYD Y NOS
*Higher key 20*

# Saviour, Again to Thy Dear Name We Raise

1 Sav - iour, a - gain to thy dear name we raise
2 Grant us thy peace up - on our home-ward way;
3 Grant us thy peace, Lord, through the com - ing night;
4 Grant us thy peace through-out our earth - ly life,

with one ac - cord our part - ing hymn of praise.
with thee be - gan, with thee shall end the day.
turn thou for us its dark - ness in - to light.
our balm in sor - row, and our stay in strife.

We stand to bless thee ere our wor - ship cease,
Guard thou the lips from sin, the hearts from shame,
From harm and dan - ger keep thy chil - dren free,
Then, when thy voice shall bid our con - flict cease,

then low - ly kneel - ing, wait thy word of peace.
that in this house have called up - on thy name.
for dark and light are both a - like to thee.
call us, O Lord, to thine e - ter - nal peace.

Text: John Ellerton (1826–1893).
Music: Edward John Hopkins (1818–1901).

10 10 10 10
ELLERS

# 32  Be Our Light in the Darkness

1 Be our light in the dark - ness, we ask you, O
2 Be our guest through this dark - ness, we ask you, O
3 Keep a watch through the dark - ness, we ask you, O

Lord, and in your great mer - cy de - fend us and
Lord, for the shad - ows are deepen - ing, and at hand is the
Lord, with the work - ers who keep us se - cure while we

keep us from the per - ils and dan - gers this night may af -
eve - ning, and our hearts need you here for a light on our
sleep, and the mourn - ers who weep, and the watch - ful who

ford, for the sake of Christ Je - sus whose love nev - er leaves us;
road. May the word that is spo - ken and the bread that is bro - ken
guard. Give the wea - ry sweet rest, take the ill to your breast, rouse

*Each stanza is a metrical version of a collect for Evening*
*Prayer or Compline and may be used separately as sung prayers.*

Text: Arthur Charles Lawson (1941– ) ©.
Music: Patrick Wedd (1948– ) ©.

Irregular
LAWSON

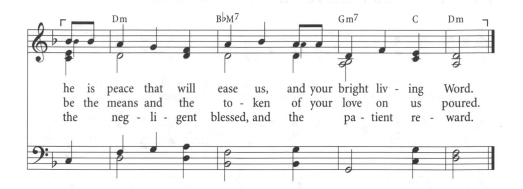

he is peace that will ease us, and your bright liv - ing Word.
be the means and the to - ken of your love on us poured.
the neg - li - gent blessed, and the pa - tient re - ward.

## We Praise You, Father, for Your Gift 33

1 We praise you, Fa - ther, for your gift of dusk and
2 With - in your hands we rest se - cure, in qui - et
3 Your glo - ry may we ev - er seek in rest, as

night - fall o - ver earth, fore - shad - ow - ing the
sleep our strength re - new; yet give your peo - ple
in ac - tiv - i - ty, un - til its full - ness

mys - ter - y of death that leads to end - less day.
hearts that wake in love to you, un - sleep - ing Lord.
is re - vealed, O source of life, O Trin - i - ty.

Text: Benedictine Nuns of Malling Abbey ©.
Music: Jane Manton Marshall (1924– ). © 1984 G.I.A. Publications, Inc.

LM
JACOB

# 36 Now There Is No Male or Female

1 Now there is no male or fe-male, now there is no free or slave,
2 Cru-ci-fied with Christ the Sav-iour, bap-tized in his ho-ly death,
3 Death has no do-min-ion o'er him, so for us death holds no power;

now there is no Jew or Gen-tile in the earth Christ died to save.
and as Christ was raised to glo-ry we have new life on this earth.
life's own wa-ters now have marked us born to God this ver-y hour.

Christ has set us free for free-dom: we no more sing slav-ery's creed;
Power of wa-ter and God's nam-ing, turn-ing us from dark to light,
From this mo-ment and for-ev-er dead to sin, a-live to Christ,

old sub-mis-sions can-not claim us, Christ has set us free in-deed.
joins us to those who, be-fore us, ran the race and fought the fight.
born of wa-ter and the Spir-it, now in Christ we find our life.

Text: Lynette Miller (1943– ) ©.
Music: Melody *Gesangbuch*, Trier, 1695.

87 87D
OMNI DIE

# We'll Sing in the Morning 37

*Unison*

1 We'll sing in the morn-ing a song of cre-a-tion, of
2 We'll sing in the noon-time a song of re-demp-tion: how
3 We'll sing in the eve-ning a song of your pas-tures, of

your breath that stirs up the wa-ters to birth; and
Naa-man was cleansed in the flow of your grace; how,
riv-ers that glad-den the ci-ty of God; and

here at the fount of Christ's mer-cy we join you, co-
when we were sick, in our sin you re-leased us to
when we ar-rive on the bank of our Jor-dan, you'll

heirs of heaven and stew-ards of your gra-cious earth.
laugh in health and dance in love be-fore your face.
help us through its cold by fords your saints have trod.

Text: Ian Sowton (1929– ) ©.
Music: Melody A. Emmet Adams; arr. John Campbell (1950– ) ©.
*Melody © 1994 Hal Leonard Corp.*

12 11 12 12
THE BELLS OF ST. MARY'S

# 40   O Spirit of the Living God

1 O Spirit of the living God, in all the
2 Give tongues of fire and hearts of love to preach the
3 Be darkness at thy coming, light; confusion,
4 O Spirit of the Lord, prepare all the round
5 Baptize the nations; far and nigh the triumphs

fullness of thy grace, wherever human
reconciling word; give power and unction
order in thy path; souls without strength inspire
earth its God to meet; breathe thou abroad like
of the cross record; the name of Jesus

foot hath trod, descend on our rebellious race.
from above wher-e'er the joyful sound is heard.
spire with might; bid mercy triumph over wrath.
morning air, till hearts of stone begin to beat.
glorify, till every kindred call him Lord.

Text: James Montgomery (1771–1854), alt.
Music: William Knapp (1698–1768).

LM
WAREHAM
*Higher key 353*

# Spirit of God, Unleashed on Earth    41

1 Spir - it of God, un - leashed on earth with rush of
2 You came in power, the church was born; O Ho - ly
3 With burn - ing words of vic - to-ry won, in - spire our

wind and roar of flame! With tongues of fire saints
Spir - it, come a - gain! From liv - ing wa - ters
hearts grown cold with fear. Re - vive in us bap -

spread good news; earth, kin - dling, blazed her loud ac - claim.
raise new saints; let new tongues hail the ris - en Lord.
tis - mal grace, and fan our smoul - dering lives to flame.

Text: John W. Arthur (1922–1980), alt. © Mary E. Arthur.
Music: *Llyfr Tonau Cynulleidfaol*, 1859.

LM
LLEDROD (LLANGOLLEN)
*Higher key 518*

# 44  I Believe in God Almighty

1 I be-lieve in God al-might-y, Fa-ther* of all things that be,
2 I be-lieve that Je-sus suf-fered, scourged and scorned and cru-ci-fied;
3 I be-lieve in God's own Spir-it, bond-ing all the saints with-in

mak-er of the earth and hea-vens, keep-er of the sky and sea.
tak-en from the cross, was bur-ied— true life there had tru-ly died.
one church, cath-o-lic, and ho-ly, where for-give-ness frees from sin;

I be-lieve in God's Son, Je-sus, now for us both Lord and Christ,
I be-lieve that on the third day Christ was raised up from the grave,
in the bod-y's res-ur-rec-tion, for the break-ing of death's chain

of the Spir-it and of Ma-ry born to bring a-bun-dant life.
then as-cend-ed to God's right hand. He will come to judge and save.
gives the life that's ev-er-last-ing: this the faith that I have claimed.

\* or "Author"

Text: *The Apostles' Creed*; para. Sylvia G. Dunstan (1955–1993). *Para.* © *1991 G.I.A. Publications, Inc.*
Music: Melody Welsh trad. coll. Edward Jones (1752–1824), *Musical & Poetical Relicks
of the Welsh Bards*, 1784, alt.; harm. George Black (1931– ) ©.

87 87D
ARFON MAJOR

# Down Galilee's Slow Roadways   45

1 Down Gal - i - lee's slow road - ways, a stran - ger trav - elled on
2 A - ris - ing from the riv - er, he saw the hea - vens torn;
3 We too have found a road - way; it led us to this place.

from Na - za - reth to Jor - dan to be bap - tized by John.
it seemed the sky was o - pen to show the Spir - it's form.
We all have had to trav - el in search of hope and grace.

He went down to the wa - ters with sol - dier, scribe, and slave,
The ho - ly dove de - scend - ed; he heard a glo - rious voice:
But now be - side this wa - ter a - gain a voice is heard:

but there with - in the riv - er the sign was birth and grave.
"You are my own be - lov - ed—my child, my heart, my choice."
"You are my own, my cho - sen, be - lov - ed of your Lord."

Text: Sylvia G. Dunstan (1955–1993), alt. © *1991 G.I.A. Publications, Inc.*
Music: Melody Johann Steurlein (1546–1613); harm. Healey Willan (1880–1968).
*Harm. © 1959 Concordia Publishing House.*

76 76D
WIE LIEBLICH IST DER MAIEN

# 46 I Believe in God the Almighty

1 I believe in God the almight-y, Ni-na-sa-di-ki,*
and in Je-sus, the Son from heav-en, Ni-na-sa-di-ki,
2 And con-ceived by the Ho-ly Spir-it, Ni-na-sa-di-ki,
To the earth he came as a ba-by, Ni-na-sa-di-ki,
3 On the earth he lived much as we do, Ni-na-sa-di-ki,
He was cru-ci-fied, died, and bur-ied, Ni-na-sa-di-ki,

who cre-a-ted earth and the heav-ens, Ni-na-sa-di-ki.
of e-ter-nal love was be-got-ten. Ni-na-sa-di-ki.
he was born of the vir-gin Ma-ry, Ni-na-sa-di-ki.
born for us, and for our sal-va-tion, Ni-na-sa-di-ki.
and he suf-fered much un-der Pi-late, Ni-na-sa-di-ki.
he de-scend-ed down in-to hell,— Ni-na-sa-di-ki.

**Refrain**

Na-sa-di-ki, na-sa-di-ki, Ni-na-sa-di-ki.

Na-sa-di-ki, na-sa-di-ki, Ni-na-sa-di-ki.

*Translation: "I believe" (Swahili)*

Text: *The Nicene Creed* (4th cent.); para. S.C. Ochieng Okeyo (19??– ) ©.
Music: S. C. Ochieng Okeyo, (19??– ) ©.

95 95 with refrain
NASADIKI

4 On the third day, he rose triumphant, Ninasadiki,
   as was prophesied in the scriptures, Ninasadiki.
   He ascended then up to heaven, Ninasadiki,
   and shall come again in great glory, Ninasadiki.
     *Refrain*

5 He shall come once more then to judge us, Ninasadiki,
   and his kingdom shall have no ending, Ninasadiki.
   I believe in the Holy Spirit, Ninasadiki,
   I believe in the holy church, Ninasadiki.
     *Refrain*

6 I acknowledge one holy baptism, Ninasadiki,
   I believe in forgiving sinners, Ninasadiki.
   I expect one great resurrection, Ninasadiki,
   and the life of the world to come, Ninasadiki.
     *Refrain*

## We Praise You, Lord, for Jesus Christ    47

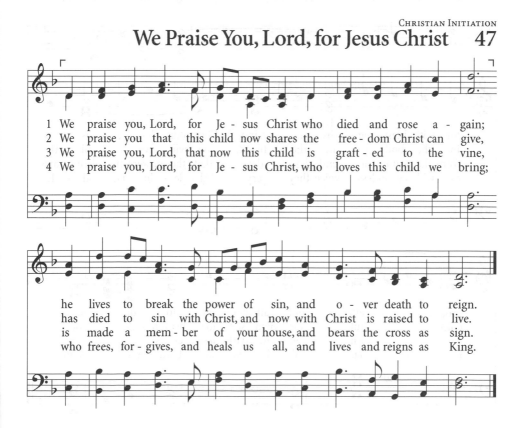

1 We praise you, Lord, for Je-sus Christ who died and rose a-gain;
2 We praise you that this child now shares the free-dom Christ can give,
3 We praise you, Lord, that now this child is graft-ed to the vine,
4 We praise you, Lord, for Je-sus Christ, who loves this child we bring;

he lives to break the power of sin, and o-ver death to reign.
has died to sin with Christ, and now with Christ is raised to live.
is made a mem-ber of your house, and bears the cross as sign.
who frees, for-gives, and heals us all, and lives and reigns as King.

Text: Judith Beatrice O'Neill (1930– ), alt., ©.
Music: Melody *Supplement to Kentucky Harmony*, 1820; harm. Russell Schulz-Widmar (1944– ).
  Harm. © 1991 Hope Publishing Co.

CM
DETROIT

# 51 Now, My Tongue, the Mystery Telling

1 Now, my tongue, the mystery telling, of the glorious
2 That last night, at supper lying with the twelve, his
3 Word made flesh, by word he maketh very bread his
4 Therefore we, before him bending, this great sacra-
5 Glory let us give, and blessing, to the Father

bod-y sing, and the blood, all price excelling,
cho-sen band, Jesus, with the law complying,
flesh to be, wine his blood for whoso taketh;
ment revere; types and shadows have their ending,
and the Son; honour, thanks, and praise addressing

which the nations' Lord and King, once on earth a-
keeps the feast its rites demand; then, more precious
and if senses fail to see, faith alone the
for the newer rite is here; faith, our outward
while eternal ages run, and the Spirit's

Text: Attrib. Thomas Aquinas (1225?–1274); tr. Edward Caswall (1814–1878), alt.
Music: Melody *Le Recueil noté*, Lyon, 1871; harm. *Songs of Praise*, 1925.

87 87 87
GRAFTON

mong us dwell-ing, shed for this world's ran-som-ing.
food sup-ply-ing, gives him-self with his own hand.
true heart wak-eth to be-hold the mys-ter-y.
sense be-friend-ing, makes our in-ward vis-ion clear.
power con-fess-ing, who from both with both is one.

## O God, Unseen Yet Ever Near  52

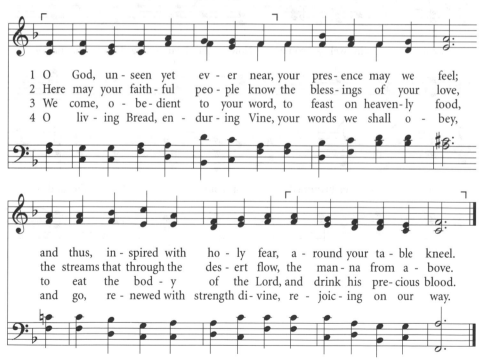

1 O God, un-seen yet ev-er near, your pres-ence may we feel;
2 Here may your faith-ful peo-ple know the bless-ings of your love,
3 We come, o-be-dient to your word, to feast on heaven-ly food,
4 O liv-ing Bread, en-dur-ing Vine, your words we shall o-bey,

and thus, in-spired with ho-ly fear, a-round your ta-ble kneel.
the streams that through the des-ert flow, the man-na from a-bove.
to eat the bod-y of the Lord, and drink his pre-cious blood.
and go, re-newed with strength di-vine, re-joic-ing on our way.

Text: Edward Osler (1798–1863); rev. *Hymns for Today's Church.* © 1982 Hope Publishing Co.
Music: John Day (1522–1584), *Psalmes*, 1562.

CM
ST. FLAVIAN

# 56 I Am the Bread, the Bread of Life

*Unison*

1 I am the bread, the bread of life; who comes to
(2) vine, the liv - ing vine; a - part from
(3) bread, and drink this wine, and as you

me will nev - er hun - ger. I am the bread,
me you can do noth - ing. I am the vine,
do, re - ceive this life of mine. All that I am,

the bread of heaven; who feeds on me will nev - er
the real vine; a - bide in me and I in
I give to you, that you may live for ev - er -

Text and music: Brian R. Hoare (1935– ). *© 1988 Hope Publishing Co.*

Irregular
PICKET WOOD

*Last time*

die.    And as you eat,    re-mem-ber me—    my bod-y
you.    And as you drink,    re-mem-ber me—    my blood was
more.

bro - ken on the tree:    my life was given    to set you
shed    up-on the tree:    my life was given    to set you

free,    and I'm a - live    for ev - er - more.    2 I am the
free,    and I'm a - live    for ev - er - more.    3 So eat this

# 57 Thou, Who at Thy First Eucharist

1 Thou, who at thy first eu - cha - rist didst pray that all thy
2 For all thy church, O Lord, we in - ter - cede: make thou our
3 So, Lord, at length when sac - ra - ments shall cease, may we be

church might be for - ev - er one, grant us at ev - ery
sad di - vi - sions soon to cease; draw us the near - er
one with all thy church a - bove, one with thy saints in

eu - cha - rist to say with long - ing heart and soul, "Thy will be
each to each, we plead, by draw - ing all to thee, O Prince of
one un - bro - ken peace, one with thy saints in one un - bound - ed

done." O may we all one bread, one bod - y be,
Peace. Thus may we all one bread, one bod - y be,
love; more bless - ed still, in peace and love to be

Text: William Henry Turton (1856–1938). © 1983 Hope Publishing Co.
Music: Orlando Gibbons (1583–1625).

10 10 10 10 10 10
SONG 1

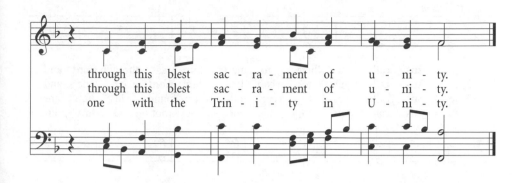

through this blest sac - ra - ment of u - ni - ty.
through this blest sac - ra - ment of u - ni - ty.
one with the Trin - i - ty in U - ni - ty.

## O Christ Was a Good Guest  58

1 O Christ was a good guest to have at the feast to
2 O Christ was a guest at Sa - mar - i - a's well, where
3 O Christ be our guest and true host at this rite, and

pledge all glad lov - ers in mirth, to charm wa - ter jars with
out - cast and cho - sen at strife were of - fered God's drink—grace
bless what you bring to our feast: bread bro - ken for us, shared

God's cheer- ful yeast, leav- ing friends with a full wed- ding's worth.
in a dry spell— sweet wa - ter still run-ning deep as life.
wine of de - light, and the flow of love's well - spring re - leased.

Text: Ian Sowton (1929– ) ©.
Music: Jeremiah Clarke (1673?–1707); arr. Edward Miller (1731–1807), alt.

11 8 10 9
BISHOPTHORPE
*Higher key 112*

# 59 Jesus Calls Us Here to Meet Him

*Unison*

1 Je - sus calls us here to meet him, as through word and
2 Je - sus calls us to con - fess him Word of life and
3 Je - sus calls us to each oth - er: found in him are
4 Je - sus calls us to his ta - ble root - ed firm in

song and prayer we af - firm God's prom - ised pres - ence where his
Lord of all, shar - er of our flesh and frail - ness, sav - ing
no di - vides. Race and class and sex and lan - guage—such are
time and space, where the church in earth and heav - en finds a

peo - ple live and care. Praise the God who keeps his prom - ise;
all who fail or fall. Tell his ho - ly hu - man sto - ry;
bar - riers he de - rides. Join the hand of friend and stran - ger;
com - mon meet - ing place. Share the bread and wine, his bod - y;

praise the Son who calls us friends; praise the Spir - it
tell his tales that all may hear; tell the world that
join the hands of age and youth; join the faith - ful
share the love of which we sing; share the feast for

Text: John L. Bell (1949– ) and Graham Maule (1958– ).
Music: Melody Gaelic trad.; adapt. and arr. The Iona Community (Scotland).
*Text and arr. © 1989 WGRG The Iona Community (Scotland). Used by permission of G.I.A. Publications, Inc., exclusive agent.*

87 87D
JESUS CALLS US

who,     a - mong   us,   to   our   hopes   and   fears   at - tends.
Christ   in   glo - ry   came   to   earth   to   meet   us   here.
and   the   doubt - er   in   their   com - mon   search   for   truth.
saints   and   sin - ners   host - ed   by   our   Lord   and   King.

# I Come with Joy 60

1 I   come   with   joy,   a   child   of   God,   for -
2 I   come   with   Chris - tians   far   and   near   to
3 As   Christ   breaks bread   and   bids   us   share,   each
4 The   spir - it   of   the   ris - en   Christ,   un -
5 To - geth - er   met,   to - geth - er   bound,   by

giv - en,   loved,   and   free,   the   life   of   Je - sus
find,   as   all   are   fed,   the   new   com - mu - ni -
proud   di - vi - sion   ends.   The   love   that made   us
seen,   but   ev - er   near,   is   in   such   friend - ship
all   that God   has   done,   we'll   go   with   joy,   to

to   re - call,   in   love   laid down   for   me.
ty   of   love   in   Christ's   com - mu - nion   bread.
makes   us   one,   and   strang - ers   now   are   friends.
bet - ter known,   a - live   a - mong   us   here.
give   the   world   the   love   that makes   us   one.

# 63 Eat This Bread, Drink This Cup

*Refrain*

Eat this bread, drink this cup, come to me and nev-er be hun-gry.

Eat this bread, drink this cup, trust in me and you will not thirst.

*Choir (humming) or keyboard*

*Cantor*

1 I am the bread of life, the

2 Your an-ces-tors ate man-na in the des-ert, but

3 Eat my flesh and drink my blood, and

4 An-y one who eats this bread, will

5 If you be-lieve and eat this bread,

Text: John 6. 35–51; para. Robert J. Batastini (1942– ) and the Taizé Community (France), 1984.
Music: Jacques Berthier (1923–1994).
EAT THIS BREAD
*Para. and music © 1984 Les Presses de Taizé. Used by permission of G.I.A. Publications, Inc., exclusive agent.*

true bread sent from the Fa - ther.

this is the bread come down from heav - en.

I will raise you up on the last day.

live for - ev - er.

you will have e - ter - nal life.

* Choose either part

Refrain

Keyboard or Guitar

G C Am D Bm Em Dsus⁴ D G D Em Bm C Dsus⁴ D G

*The refrain may be sung as an ostinato without the verses,
repeating as many times as desired. Or the refrain may be sung
at the beginning and repeated after each verse.*

# 64  Author of Life Divine

1 Author of life divine, who hast a table spread,
2 Our need-y souls sus-tain with fresh sup-plies of love,

furnished with mys-tic wine and ev-er-last-ing bread,
till all thy life we gain, and all thy ful-ness prove,

pre-serve the life thy-self hast given, pre-serve the life thy-
and, strength-ened by thy per-fect grace, and, strength-ened by thy

self hast given, and feed and train us up for heaven.
per-fect grace, be-hold with-out a veil thy face.

Text: John Wesley (1703–1791).
Music: John David Edwards (1806–1885).

66 66 888
RHOSYMEDRE

# Here, Lord, We Take the Broken Bread 65

1 Here, Lord, we take the bro - ken bread and drink the wine, be - liev - ing that by thy life our souls are fed, thy part - ing gifts re - ceiv - ing.

2 As thou hast given, so we would give our - selves for oth - ers' heal - ing; as thou hast lived, so we would live, the Fa - ther's love re - veal - ing.

*Optional flute descant*

Text: Charles Venn Pilcher (1879–1961). © *Estate of F. E.V. Pilcher.*
Music: Melody Irish; adapt. and harm. Charles Villiers Stanford (1852–1924);
fl. desc. Melva Treffinger Graham (1947– ) ©.

87 87
St. Columba
*Alt. tune DOMINUS REGIT ME 520*

# 68 We Hold the Death of the Lord

*Refrain*

We hold the death of the Lord deep in our hearts,
liv - ing;
liv - ing;
now we re - main with Je - sus the

Text and music: David Haas (1957– ). © 1983 G.I.A. Publications, Inc.

Irregular with refrain
NOW WE REMAIN

1 Once we were peo - ple a - fraid, lost in the
4 We are the pres - ence of God. This is our

2 Some - thing which we have known, some - thing we've

3 He chose to give of him - self, be - came our

# 71 Jesus, the Joy of Loving Hearts

1 Jesus, the joy of loving hearts,
2 Your truth un - changed has ev - er stood;
3 We taste of you, the li - ving bread,
4 Our rest - less spir - its long for you,
5 Jesus, for - ev - er with us stay:

true source of life, our lives sus - tain;
you res - cue those who on you call:
and long to feast up - on you still.
how - ev - er may our lot be cast,
make all our mo - ments calm and bright;

from the best bliss that earth im - parts,
to those yet seek - ing, you are good;
We drink from you, the foun - tain - head;
glad when your gra - cious smile we view,
chase the dark night of sin a - way;

Text: Latin (*Jesu, dulcedo cordium,* 12th cent.); tr. Ray Palmer (1808–1887), alt.  LM
Music: Melody Sarum plainsong, Mode 1;  CHRISTE REDEMPTOR OMNIUM
harm. Alfred Leslie Rose, SSJE (1890–1970). *Harm. © The Society of St. John the Evangelist.*

we turn un - filled to you a - gain.
to those who find you, all in all.
our thirst - y souls from you we fill.
blessed when our faith can hold you fast.
spread through the world your ho - ly light.

## Bread of Heaven, on Thee We Feed 72

1 Bread of heaven, on thee we feed, for thy flesh is food in - deed;
2 Vine of heaven, thy blood sup - plies this blest cup of sac - ri - fice;

ev - er may our souls be fed with this true and liv - ing bread,
Lord, thy wounds our heal - ing give; to thy cross we look and live:

day by day with strength sup - plied through the life of him who died.
Je - sus, may we ev - er be graft - ed, root - ed, built on thee.

Text: Josiah Conder (1789–1855).
Music: Johann Crüger (1598–1662).

77 77 77
JESU, MEINE ZUVERSICHT
Alt. tune NICHT SO TRAURIG 190

# 73 One Bread, One Body, One Lord of All

One bread, one bod-y, one Lord of all,

One bread, one bod-y, one Lord of all,

one cup of bless - ing which we bless— and

one cup of bless - ing which we bless— and

446 with refrain
ONE BREAD, ONE BODY

we, though man-y, through-out the earth,

we, though man-y, through-out the earth,

we are one bod-y in this one Lord.

we are one bod-y in this one Lord.

*Last time*

1 Gen - tile or Jew, ser - vant or free,
2 Man - y the gifts, man - y the works,
3 Grain for the fields, scat - tered and grown,

# 76 Thee We Adore, O Hidden Saviour, Thee

*Unison*

1 Thee we a - dore, O hid - den Sav - iour, thee,
2 O blest me - mo - rial of our dy - ing Lord,
3 Foun - tain of good - ness, Je - sus, Lord and God,
4 O Christ, whom now be - neath a veil we see,

who in thy sac - ra - ment dost deign to be;
who liv - ing bread to us doth here af - ford,
cleanse us, un - clean, with thy most cleans - ing blood;
may what we thirst for soon our por - tion be,

both flesh and spir - it at thy pres - ence fail,
O may our souls for - ev - er feed on thee,
in - crease our faith and love, that we may know
to gaze on thee un - veiled, and see thy face,

Text: Thomas Aquinas (1225?–1274); tr. James Russell Woodford (1820–1885), alt.
Music: Melody Mode 5, *Processionale*, Paris, 1697; harm. Margaret Drynan (1915– ) ©.

10 10 10 10
ADORO TE

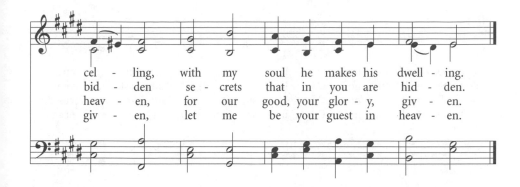

cel - ling, with my soul he makes his dwell - ing.
bid - den se - crets that in you are hid - den.
heav - en, for our good, your glor - y, giv - en.
giv - en, let me be your guest in heav - en.

## To You, O Kindly Jesus Christ    79

1 To you, O kind - ly Je - sus Christ, e -
2 With glad - ness now, my soul, break forth, for

ter - nal thanks my heart will pour, for with your bod - y
I am rich with joy's de - light. O Je - sus, in my

and your blood you feed my soul for ev - er - more.
heart you live, your love for - ev - er burn - ing bright.

Text: Thomas Hanson Kingo (1634–1703); tr. Anitra Hansen, SSJD (1936– ).
Tr. © The Sisterhood of St. John the Divine.
Music: Melody *Das ander Theil*, 1605; adapt. Johann Hermann Schein (1586–1630), alt.; harm. Johann Sebastian Bach (1685–1750).

LM
EISENACH
*Higher key and alt. setting 644*

---

yet here thy pres - ence we de - vout - ly hail.
and thou, O Christ, for - ev - er pre - cious be.
the hope and peace which from thy pres - ence flow.
the vi - sion of thy glo - ry and thy grace.

## The Son of God Proclaim    77

1 The Son of God pro - claim, the Lord of time and space;
2 Be - hold his out - stretched hands; though all was in his power,
3 He, God's cre - a - tive Word, the chur - ch's Lord and head,
4 The Lord of life and death with won - dering praise we sing;
5 We take this cup in hope: for he, who glad - ly bore

the God who bade the light break forth now shines in Je - sus' face.
he took the towel and ba - sin then, and serves us in this hour.
here bids us gath - er as his friends, and share his wine and bread.
we break the bread at his com - mand, and name him God and King.
the shame - ful cross, is risen a - gain, and reigns for ev - er - more.

Text: Basil E. Bridge (1927– ) ©.
Music: Henry Thomas Smart (1813–1879).

SM
SUNDERLAND

## 78 Deck Yourself, My Soul, with Gladness

1 Deck your-self, my soul, with glad-ness; leave the gloom-y haunts of
2 Lord, I bow be-fore you low-ly, filled with joy most deep and
3 Shin-ing Sun, my life you bright-en; Ra-diance, you my soul en-
4 Je-sus, bread of life, I pray you, let me glad-ly here o-

sad-ness. Come in-to the day-light's splen-dour, there with
ho-ly, as with trem-bling awe and wond-er all your
light-en. Joy, the best of all our know-ing, Foun-tain,
bey you; nev-er to my hurt in-vit-ed, al-ways

joy your prais-es ren-der to the Lord whose grace un-bound-ed;
might-y works I pon-der— how, by mys-ter-y sur-round-ed,
swift-ly in me flow-ing: at your feet I kneel, my Mak-er—
by your love de-light-ed: from this ban-quet let me meas-ure,

has this roy-al ban-quet found-ed; though all oth-er powers ex-
depth no one has ev-er sound-ed, none may dare to pierce un-
let me be a fit par-tak-er of this sac-red food from
Lord, how vast and deep its trea-sure; through the gifts your hands have

Text: Johann Franck (1618–1677); tr. Catherine Winkworth (1827–1878);
rev. *Hymns for Today's Church.* © 1982 Hope Publishing Co.
Music: Melody Johann Crüger (1598–1662); harm. *The English Hymnal*, 1906.

LMD
SCHMÜCKE DICH

## 80 We Hail Thee Now, O Jesus

1 We hail thee now, O Je-sus: thy pres-ence here we own,
2 We hail thee now, O Je-sus: in si-lence hast thou come,
3 We hail thee now, O Je-sus: for law and type have ceased,
4 We hail thee now, O Je-sus: for death is ev-er near,

though sight and touch have failed us, and faith per-ceives a-lone.
for all the hosts of heav-en with won-der-ment are dumb—
and thou in each com-mun-ion art sac-ri-fice and priest.
and in thy pres-ence on-ly its ter-rors dis-ap-pear.

Thy love has veiled thy glo-ry and hid thy power di-vine,
so great the con-de-scen-sion, so mar-vel-lous the love,
We make this great me-mo-rial in un-ion, Lord, with thee,
Dwell with us, liv-ing Sav-iour, and guide us through the night,

in mer-cy to our weak-ness, be-neath an earth-ly sign.
which for our sakes, O Sav-iour, have drawn thee from a-bove.
and plead thy death and pas-sion to cleanse and set us free.
till shad-ows end in glo-ry, and faith is lost in sight.

Text: Frederick George Scott (1861–1944), alt.
Music: Frederick Charles Maker (1844–1927).

76 76D
ST. CHRISTOPHER
*Alt. tune* PASSION CHORALE 198

# Father, We Thank Thee Who Hast Planted  81

1 Fa - ther, we thank thee who hast plant - ed
2 Thou, Lord, didst make all for thy plea - sure,
3 Watch o'er thy church, O Lord, in mer - cy;
4 As grain, once scat - tered on the hill - sides,

thy ho - ly name with - in our hearts.
didst give us food for all our days,
save it from e - vil; guard it still;
was in this bro - ken bread made one,

Know - ledge and faith and life im - mor - tal
giv - ing in Christ the bread e - ter - nal;
per - fect it in thy love; u - nite it,
so from all lands thy church be gath - ered

Je - sus thy Son to us im - parts.
thine is the power, be thine the praise.
cleansed and con - formed un - to thy will.
in - to thy king - dom by thy Son.

Text: Greek (110?); tr. F. Bland Tucker (1895–1984), rev. Tr. © 1985 The Church Pension Fund.  98 98
Music: Melody Strasbourg, 1545.  LES COMMANDEMENS

# 84 Lord, Enthroned in Heavenly Splendour

1 Lord, en-throned in heaven-ly splen-dour, first be-got-ten from the dead, thou a-lone, our strong de-fend-er, lift-est up thy peo-ple's head.

2 Here our hum-blest hom-age pay we; here in lov-ing rev-erence bow; here for faith's dis-cern-ment pray we, lest we fail to know thee now.

3 Though the low-liest form doth veil thee as of old in Beth-le-hem, here as there thine an-gels hail thee, branch and flower of Jes-se's stem.

4 Pas-chal Lamb, thine of-fering, fin-ished once for all when thou wast slain, in its full-ness un-di-min-ished shall for ev-er-more re-main,

5 Life-im-part-ing heaven-ly Man-na, strick-en Rock with stream-ing side, heaven and earth with loud hos-san-na wor-ship thee, the Lamb who died,

Text: George Hugh Bourne (1840–1925).
Music: Healey Willan (1880–1968). © 1994 Waterloo Music Co. Ltd.

87 87 47
ST. OSMUND

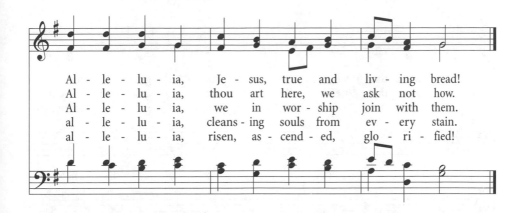

Al - le - lu - ia, Je - sus, true and liv - ing bread!
Al - le - lu - ia, thou art here, we ask not how.
Al - le - lu - ia, we in wor - ship join with them.
al - le - lu - ia, cleans - ing souls from ev - ery stain.
al - le - lu - ia, risen, as - cend - ed, glo - ri - fied!

## Shepherd of Souls, Refresh and Bless    85

1 Shep-herd of souls, re - fresh and bless your cho - sen pil - grim flock
2 We would not live by bread a - lone, but by your word of grace,
3 Be known to us in break-ing bread, but do not then de - part;
4 Lord, sup with us in love di - vine; your bod - y and your blood,

with man - na in the wil - der - ness, with wa - ter from the rock.
in strength of which we trav - el on to our a - bid - ing place.
Sav - iour, a - bide with us, and spread your ta - ble in our heart.
that liv - ing bread, that heaven-ly wine, be our im - mor - tal food.

Text: James Montgomery (1771–1854), alt.
Music: John Bacchus Dykes (1823–1876).

CM
ST. AGNES

# 86 More Than We Can Ask or Imagine

1 More than we can ask or im-a-gine, more than
2 More than we will ev-er im-a-gine, more than
3 More than we can ask or im-a-gine, more than

we can ev-er dare to dream, we are the chil-dren of
we will ev-er un-der-stand; we are sent to
we could ev-er de-sire; out of the dust God's

heav-en's cre-a-tion, God's own be-loved, each called by
walk with com-pas-sion, to live out God's love by heart and by
build-ing a king-dom, like wine from the press, like bread from the

name. And we cry, Glo-ry! Glo-ry!
hand. (Glo-ry!) (Glo-ry!)
fire.

Text: Gordon Light (1944– ).
Music: Melody Gordon Light (1944– ); arr. Andrew Donaldson (1951– ) ©.
*Text and melody © 1993 Common Cup Company.*

Irregular
WINEPRESS

## 90  How the World Longs for Your Birth

1 How the world longs for your birth, bear - ing news of
2 How the earth a - waits your seed, parched and bar - ren
3 How we ache to know your peace; wars and weap - ons
4 How our minds for heal - ing long, bro - ken bo - dies

hu - man worth; to our la - bour bring your mirth:
from our greed; now to hal - low it we need:
still in - crease; bid our fears and hate to cease:
to be strong, wound - ed hearts to learn your song:

Ma - ra - na - tha, come, Lord, come.

5 God, who sets your people free,
God, who comes, our flesh to be,
now we wait, your reign to see:
Maranatha, come, Lord, come.

6 To our darkness bring your light;
fill our longing eyes with sight.
In our lives shine ever bright:
Maranatha, come, Lord, come.

Text: Anna Briggs (1947– ) ©.
Music: Melody plainsong, adapt. Johann Walther (1496–1570), alt.;
  harm. Johann Sebastian Bach (1685–1750).

77 77
NUN KOMM, DER HEIDEN HEILAND

# People, Look East! The Time Is Near  91

1 Peo - ple, look east! The time is near of the
2 Fur - rows, be glad! Though earth is bare, one more
3 Birds, though you long have ceased to build, guard the
4 Stars, keep the watch: when night is dim one more
5 An - gels, an - nounce with shouts of mirth Christ who

crown - ing of the year. Make your house fair as you are
seed is plant - ed there: give up your strength the seed to
nest that must be filled; e - ven the hour when wings are
light the bowl shall brim, shin - ing be - yond the frost - y
brings new life to earth. Set ev - ery peak and val - ley

a - ble, trim the hearth and set the ta - ble. Peo - ple, look
nour - ish, that in course the flower may flour - ish. Peo - ple, look
fro - zen God for fledg - ing time has cho - sen. Peo - ple, look
weath - er, bright as sun and moon to - geth - er. Peo - ple, look
humm - ing with the word, the Lord is com - ing. Peo - ple, look

east and sing to - day: Love, the guest, is on the way.
east and sing to - day: Love, the rose, is on the way.
east and sing to - day: Love, the bird, is on the way.
east and sing to - day: Love, the star, is on the way.
east and sing to - day: Love, the Lord, is on the way.

Text: Eleanor Farjeon (1881–1965). © David Higham Associates Ltd.
Music: Melody French trad.; harm. Martin Shaw (1875–1958), alt. *Harm.* © Oxford University Press.

87 98 87
BESANÇON

# 96   Creator of the Stars of Night

1 Cre - a - tor of the stars of night, thy peo - ple's ev -
2 Thou, sor - rowing at the help - less cry of all cre - a -
3 When earth was near its eve - ning hour, thou didst in love's
4 At thy great name, ex - alt - ed now, all knees in low -
5 To God the Fa - ther, God the Son, and God the Spi -

er - last - ing light, Je - sus, re - deem - er of us all,
tion doomed to die, didst save our lost and guil - ty race
re - deem - ing power, like bride - groom from his cham - ber, come
ly hom - age bow; all things in heaven and earth a - dore,
rit, Three - in - One, praise, hon - our, might, and glo - ry be

hear thou thy ser - vants when they call.
by heal - ing gifts of heaven - ly grace.
forth from a mai - den moth - er's womb.
and own thee King for ev - er - more.
from age to age e - ter - nal - ly.

Text: Latin (6th cent.); tr. John Mason Neale (1818–1866), alt.
Music: Melody Sarum plainsong, Mode 4; harm. John Henry Arnold (1887–1956).
*Harm. © Oxford University Press.*

LM
CONDITOR ALME SIDERUM

# Jesus Came, the Heavens Adoring

1 Je - sus came, the heavens a - dor - ing, came with peace from
2 Je - sus comes a - gain in mer - cy, when our hearts are
3 Je - sus comes to hearts re - joic - ing, bring - ing news of
4 Je - sus comes on clouds tri - um - phant, when the heavens shall

realms on high. Je - sus came for our re - demp - tion,
bowed with care. Je - sus comes a - gain in an - swer
sins for - given. Je - sus comes in sounds of glad - ness,
pass a - way. Je - sus comes a - gain in glo - ry:

low - ly came on earth to die: al - le - lu - ia,
to our ear - nest heart - felt prayer, al - le - lu - ia,
lead - ing souls re - deemed to heaven. Al - le - lu - ia,
let us then our hom - age pay, al - le - lu - ia,

al - le - lu - ia! came in deep hu - mil - i - ty.
al - le - lu - ia! comes to save us from des - pair.
al - le - lu - ia! Now the gate of death is riven.
al - le - lu - ia! till the dawn of end - less day.

Text: Godfrey Thring (1823–1903), alt.
Music: Melody John Francis Wade (1711–1786);
    harm. attrib. Francis Vincent Novello (1781–1861), alt.

87 87 87
TANTUM ERGO (ST. THOMAS)

# 98  Hark the Glad Sound! The Saviour Comes

1 Hark the glad sound! The Sav - iour comes, the
2 Christ comes, the pris - oners to re - lease in
3 Christ comes, the bro - ken heart to bind, the
4 Our glad hos - an - nas, Prince of Peace, thy

Sav - iour pro - mised long: let ev - ery heart pre -
Sa - tan's bon - dage held; the gates of brass be -
bleed - ing soul to cure, and from the trea - sur -
wel - come shall pro - claim; and heaven's e - ter - nal

pare a throne, and ev - ery voice a song.
fore him burst; the i - ron fet - ters yield.
ies of grace to bless the hum - ble poor.
ar - ches ring with thy be - lov - ed name.

Text: Philip Doddridge (1702–1751), alt.
Music: Thomas Ravenscroft (1590?–1634?), *Whole Book of Psalmes*, 1621.

CM
BRISTOL
*Alt. tune* RICHMOND *224, 306*

# Break, Day of God, O Break 99

1 Break, day of God, O break! The night has lin-gered
2 Break, day of God, O break! The earth with strife is
3 Break, day of God, O break, like to the days a-

long. Our hearts with sigh-ing wake; we weep for
worn; the hills with thun-der shake; hearts of the
bove! Let pu-ri-ty a-wake, and faith, and

sin and wrong: O bright and morn-ing star, draw
peo-ple mourn: break, day of God, sweet day of
hope, and love. But lo! We see the bright-ening

near; O Sun of Right-eous-ness, ap-pear.
peace, and bid the shout of war-riors cease.
sky; the gold-en morn is draw-ing nigh.

Text: Henry Burton (1840–1930).
Music: Charles Steggall (1826–1905).

66 66 88
CHRISTCHURCH
Alt. setting 238

# 100 Comfort, Comfort Ye My People

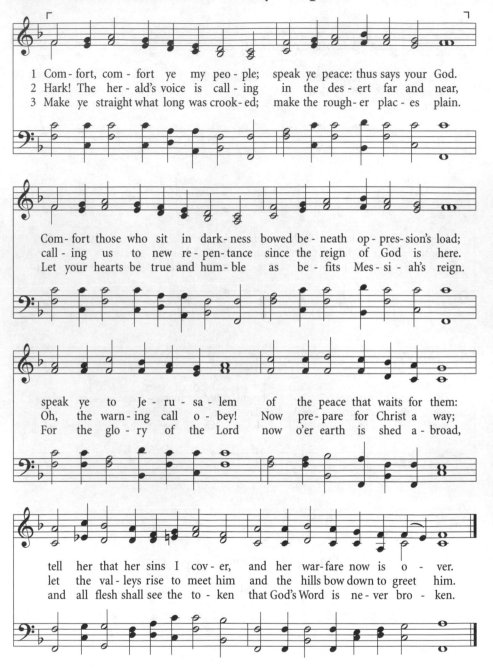

1 Com - fort, com - fort ye my peo - ple; speak ye peace: thus says your God.
2 Hark! The her - ald's voice is call - ing in the des - ert far and near,
3 Make ye straight what long was crook - ed; make the rough - er plac - es plain.

Com - fort those who sit in dark - ness bowed be - neath op - pres - sion's load;
call - ing us to new re - pen - tance since the reign of God is here.
Let your hearts be true and hum - ble as be - fits Mes - si - ah's reign.

speak ye to Je - ru - sa - lem of the peace that waits for them:
Oh, the warn - ing call o - bey! Now pre - pare for Christ a way;
For the glo - ry of the Lord now o'er earth is shed a - broad,

tell her that her sins I cov - er, and her war - fare now is o - ver.
let the val - leys rise to meet him and the hills bow down to greet him.
and all flesh shall see the to - ken that God's Word is ne - ver bro - ken.

Text: Is. 40.1–5; para. Johannes G. Olearius (1611–1684); tr. Catherine Winkworth (1827–1878), alt.    87 87 77 88
Music: Melody Geneva, 1551; harm. based on Claude Goudimel (1505–1572); rev. Alain Mabit (19??– ).    PSALM 42
Rev. © 1995 Réveil Publications.

# Hail to the Lord's Anointed  101

1 Hail to the Lord's a - noint - ed, great Da - vid's great - er Son!
2 He shall come down like show - ers up - on the fruit - ful earth,
3 Kings shall fall down be - fore him, and gold and in - cense bring;
4 O'er ev - ery foe vic - to - rious, he on his throne shall rest,

Hail, in the time ap - point - ed, his reign on earth be - gun!
and love, joy, hope, like flow - ers, spring in his path to birth.
all na - tions shall a - dore him, his praise all peo - ple sing.
from age to age more glo - rious, all - bless - ing and all - blest.

He comes to break op - pres - sion, to set the cap - tive free,
Be - fore him on the moun - tains shall peace the her - ald go,
To him shall prayer un - ceas - ing and dai - ly vows as - cend,
The tide of time shall nev - er his cov - e - nant re - move.

to take a - way trans - gres - sion, and rule in eq - ui - ty.
and right - eous - ness in foun - tains from hill to val - ley flow.
his king - dom still in - creas - ing, a king - dom with - out end.
His name shall stand for - ev - er: that name to us is Love.

Text: James Montgomery (1771–1854), alt.                                      76 76D
Music: Melody Johann Crüger (1598–1662); adapt. William Henry Monk (1823–1889).   CRÜGER

# 104  Joy Shall Come

*Unison*

Joy shall come e-ven to the wil-der-ness, and the parched

land shall then know great glad - ness; as the rose,

as the rose shall des-erts blos - som, des - erts

like a gar-den blos - som. For liv-ing springs

shall give cool wa - ter, in the des-ert streams shall

Text: Israeli trad.
Music: Melody Israeli trad.; arr. Patrick Wedd (1948– ) ©.

Irregular
JOY SHALL COME

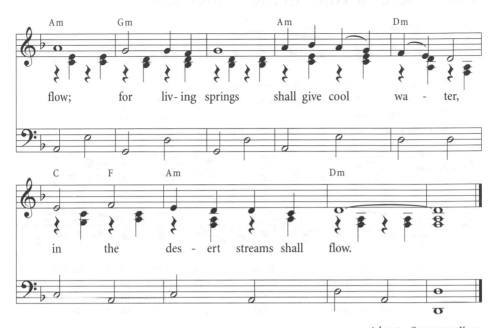

flow; for liv-ing springs shall give cool wa - ter,

in the des - ert streams shall flow.

## Where Jordan Cuts the Wilderness 105

1 Where Jor-dan cuts the wil-der-ness, a burn-ing voice now warns:
2 There comes a day of har-vest-ing the fruit of faith and love:
3 The her-i-tage of A-bra-ham means less than des-ert stones
4 Ex-ploit-ers of the poor and weak with rage and theft be done.
5 With wa-ter I bap-tize you now in read-i-ness for one

"You brood of snakes, you hy-po-crites, pre-pare! Mes-si-ah comes.
the use-less culled, the e-vil purged. Pre-pare! Mes-si-ah comes.
un-less we share our need and wealth. Pre-pare! Mes-si-ah comes.
Pre-pare the way of ho-li-ness, pre-pare! Mes-si-ah comes.
whose Spir-it bathes, whose fire re-fines—pre-pare! Mes-si-ah comes."

Text: Brian Ruttan (1947– ) ©.                                                                                    CM
Music: Melody *Sixteen Tune Settings*, Philadelphia, 1812; harm. C. Winfred Douglas (1867–1944). MORNING SONG
    Harm. © 1940, renewed 1981, The Church Pension Fund.

# 108  Hark, a Herald Voice Is Sounding

*Descant*

5 Hon - our,  glo - ry,  might, and  bless - ing  to  the

1 Hark,  a  her - ald  voice  is  soun - ding:  "Christ  is
2 Wa - kened  by  the  sol - emn  warn - ing,  let  the
3 Lo,  the  Lamb,  so  long  ex - pect - ed,  comes  with
4 that  when  next  he  comes  with  glo - ry,  and  the
5 Hon - our,  glo - ry,  might, and  bless - ing  to  the

Fa - ther  and  the  Son,  with  the  ev - er -

nigh,"  it  seems  to  say.  "Cast  a - way  the
earth - bound  soul  a - rise;  Christ  our  sun,  all
par - don  down  from  heaven;  let  us  all,  with
world  is  wrapped  in  fear,  with  his  mer - cy
Fa - ther  and  the  Son,  with  the  ev - er -

last - ing  Spir - it,  while  e - ter - nal  a - ges  run.

dreams  of  dark - ness,  O  ye  chil - dren  of  the  day!"
sloth  dis - pel - ling,  shines  up - on  the  morn - ing  skies.
deep  re - pen - tance,  pray  that  we  may  be  for - given,
he  may  shield  us,  and  with  words  of  love  draw  near.
last - ing  Spir - it,  while  e - ter - nal  a - ges  run.

Text: Latin (*Vox clare*, 10th cent.); tr. Edward Caswall (1814–1878), alt.          87 87
Music: William Henry Monk (1823–1889); desc. Alan Gray (1855–1935). *Desc.* © *Cambridge University Press.*          MERTON

low;    make straight all the crook - ed   plac - es
cay;    the   power and pomp   of   na - tions
breast;    in   pas - tures of peace you'll lead   them,
low;    make straight all the crook - ed   plac - es

where the Lord our God may go!
shall    pass like a dream a - way.
and    give to the wea - ry rest.
where the Lord our God may go!

## Prepare the Way   107

① Pre - pare the way of the Lord,   pre -

② pare the way of the Lord,   ③ and all   peo - ple will

④ see the sal - va - tion of our God.   Pre -

*May be sung as a 4-part round or canon.*

Text: Luke 3.4, 6; para. Taizé Community (France).

Music: Jacques Berthier (1923–1994). *Para. and music © 1982, 1983, 1984, Les Presses de Taizé.*
   *Used by permission of G.I.A. Publications, Inc., exclusive agent.*

77 67

PREPARE THE WAY

# 108 Hark, a Herald Voice Is Sounding

*Descant*

5 Hon - our, glo - ry, might, and bless - ing to the

1 Hark, a her - ald voice is soun - ding: "Christ is
2 Wa - kened by the sol - emn warn - ing, let the
3 Lo, the Lamb, so long ex - pect - ed, comes with
4 that when next he comes with glo - ry, and the
5 Hon - our, glo - ry, might, and bless - ing to the

Fa - ther and the Son, with the ev - er -

nigh," it seems to say. "Cast a - way the
earth - bound soul a - rise; Christ our sun, all
par - don down from heaven; let us all, with
world is wrapped in fear, with his mer - cy
Fa - ther and the Son, with the ev - er -

last - ing Spir - it, while e - ter - nal a - ges run.

dreams of dark - ness, O ye chil - dren of the day!"
sloth dis - pel - ling, shines up - on the morn - ing skies.
deep re - pen - tance, pray that we may be for - given,
he may shield us, and with words of love draw near.
last - ing Spir - it, while e - ter - nal a - ges run.

Text: Latin (*Vox clare*, 10th cent.); tr. Edward Caswall (1814–1878), alt.        87 87
Music: William Henry Monk (1823–1889); desc. Alan Gray (1855–1935). *Desc. © Cambridge University Press.*        MERTON

# When the King Shall Come Again  109

1 When the King shall come a - gain, all his power re - veal - ing,
2 In the des - ert, trees take root, fresh from God's cre - a - tion;
3 Strength-en fee - ble hands and knees; faint - ing hearts, be cheer - ful!
4 There God's high-way shall be seen where no roar - ing li - on,

splen-dour shall an - nounce his reign, life and joy and heal - ing;
plants and flowers and sweet-est fruit join the cel - e - bra - tion;
God, who comes for such as these, seeks and saves the fear - ful.
noth - ing e - vil or un - clean, walks the road to Zi - on:

earth no long - er in de - cay, hope no more frus - tra - ted,
riv - ers spring up from the earth, bar - ren lands a - dorn - ing.
Deaf ears, hear the sil - ent tongues sing a - way their weep - ing;
ran - somed peo - ple home-ward bound all your prais - es voic - ing,

this is God's re - demp - tion day long - ing - ly a - wait - ed.
Val - leys, this is your new birth; moun-tains, greet the morn - ing!
blind eyes, see the life - less ones walk-ing, run - ning, leap - ing!
see your Lord with glo - ry crowned, share in his re - joic - ing!

Text: Christopher Idle (1938– ). © 1982 Hope Publishing Co.
Music: Melody *Piae Cantiones*, 1582.

76 76D
TEMPUS ADEST FLORIDUM
*Higher key 145*

# 110 "Sleepers, Wake!" A Voice Astounds Us

1 "Sleep - ers, wake!"   A   voice as - tounds   us;   the
2 Zi - on   hears   the watch - men   sing - ing.   Her
3 Lamb   of   God,   the heavens a - dore   you;   let

shout   of   ram - part - guards sur - rounds   us:   "A -
heart   with   joy - ful   hope   is   spring - ing;   she
saints   and   an - gels   sing   be - fore   you,   as

wake,   Je - ru - sa - lem,   a - rise!"   Mid - night's peace   their
wakes   and   hur - ries through the   night.   Forth   he   comes,   her
harps   and   cym - bals   swell   the   sound.   Twelve great   pearls,   the

cry   has   bro - ken,   their   ur - gent   sum - mons
bride - groom glo - rious   in   strength of   grace,   in
ci - ty's   por - tals:   through them   we   stream to

Text: Philipp Nicolai (1566–1608); tr. Carl P. Daw, Jr. (1944– ). *Tr.* © *1982 Hope Publishing Co.*
Music: Melody Hans Sachs (1494–1576); adapt. Philipp Nicolai (1556–1608);
    adapt. and harm. Johann Sebastian Bach (1685–1750).

898D 66 4 88
WACHET AUF

# 111 Herald! Sound the Note of Judgement

1 Her - ald! Sound the note of judge-ment, warn-ing note of
2 Her - ald! Sound the note of glad-ness! Tell the news that
3 Her - ald! Sound the note of par-don! Those re-pent-ing
4 Her - ald! Sound the note of tri-umph! Christ has come to

right and wrong, turn-ing us from sin and sad-ness,
Christ is here; make a path-way through the des-ert
are for-given; God re-stores the way-ward chil-dren,
share our life, bring-ing God's own love and pow-er,

till once more we sing the song.
for the one who brings God near.
and to all new life is given.     Sound     the trum-pet!
grant-ing vic-tory in our strife.

Tell     the mes-sage! Christ     the Sav-iour     King has come!

Text: Moir A. J. Waters (1906–1980), alt. © *Estate of Moir A.J. Waters, c/o Margaret Waters.*
Music: Melody Joachim Neander (1650–1680), alt.

87 87 87
NEANDER (UNSER HERRSCHER)

# Behold! The Mountain of the Lord  112

1 Behold! The mountain of the Lord in
2 The beam that shines from Zion hill shall
3 Among the nations he shall judge, with
4 No strife shall rage, nor hostile feuds dis-

latter days shall rise on mountain tops a-
lighten every land; the king who reigns in
judgements true shall guide; his sceptre shall pro-
turb those peaceful years; to ploughshares all shall

bove the hills, and draw the wondering eyes.
Salem's towers shall all the world command.
tect the just, and quell the sinner's pride.
beat their swords, to pruning-hooks their spears.

5 No longer hosts encountering hosts
shall crowds of slain deplore;
they hang the trumpet in the hall,
and study war no more.

6 Come then, O come from every land
to worship at God's shrine;
and, walking in the radiant light,
with holy beauties shine.

Text: *Song of Peace* (Isaiah 2.2–6); para. *Scottish Paraphrases,* 1781, alt.
Music: Jeremiah Clarke (1673?–1707); arr. Edward Miller (1731–1807).

CM
BISHOPTHORPE
*Lower key 58*

# 113   Come, O Lord, and Set Us Free

*Refrain*

Come, O Lord, and set us free.

Ma - ra - na - tha.

1 Des - ert and dry land will grow green in praise;
2 Strength-en the hearts of the fear - ful and weak;
3 We have been wait - ing and long - ing for light,
4 Give us a star in the sky day and night,

Text and music: Tim Schoenbachler (1952– ), alt.
© *1976 North American Liturgy Resources (NALR). Reprinted by permission of OCP Publications.*

Irregular with refrain
MARANATHA

clay will re - joice with full bloom:
be strong; fear not, God is near,
watch - ing for signs of the Lord.
sign of your prom - ise to save.

show - ers of flow - ers given birth in dead earth; in
com - ing in pow - er and loos - ing our bonds,
"Prom - ised of a - ges," "Mes - si - ah to come,"
O - ver the moun - tains we fol - low its light,

*To refrain*

col - ours they ech - o Love's song.
set - ting the cap - tives free.
hear us, we beg you: "Come, save!"
hop - ing for sign of your life.

*To refrain*

# 114 Lo, He Comes with Clouds Descending

1 Lo, he comes with clouds de-scend-ing, once for
2 Ev-ery eye shall now be-hold him, robed in
3 Now re-demp-tion, long ex-pect-ed, see in
4 Yea, a-men, let all a-dore thee, high on

fa-voured sin-ners slain; thou-sand thou-sand
dread-ful maj-es-ty; all who set at
sol-emn pomp ap-pear; all his saints, on
thine e-ter-nal throne; Sa-viour, take the

saints at-tend-ing swell the tri-umph of his
nought and sold him, pierced, and nailed him to the
earth re-ject-ed, thrill the trum-pet sound to
power and glo-ry; claim the king-dom for thine

train: hal-le-lu-jah, hal-le-lu-jah,
tree, deep-ly griev-ing, deep-ly griev-ing,
hear: hal-le-lu-jah, hal-le-lu-jah,
own: O come quick-ly! O come quick-ly!

Text: John Cennick (1718–1755), Charles Wesley (1707–1788), Martin Madan (1726–1790), alt.
Music: Melody attrib. Thomas Olivers (1725–1799) and Martin Madan (1726–1790).

87 87 47
HELMSLEY

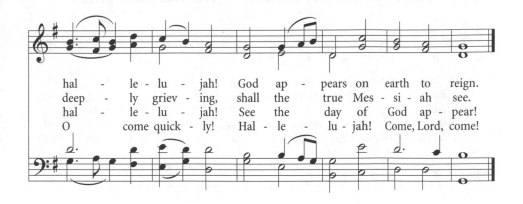

hal - le - lu - jah! God ap - pears on earth to reign.
deep - ly griev - ing, shall the true Mes - si - ah see.
hal - le - lu - jah! See the day of God ap - pear!
O come quick - ly! Hal - le - lu - jah! Come, Lord, come!

## Awake, O Sleeper, Rise from Death   115

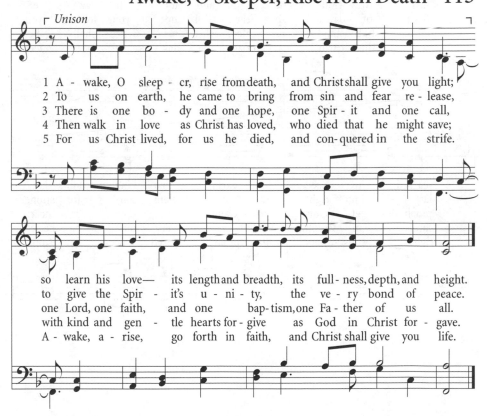

*Unison*

1 A - wake, O sleep - er, rise from death, and Christ shall give you light;
2 To us on earth, he came to bring from sin and fear re - lease,
3 There is one bo - dy and one hope, one Spir - it and one call,
4 Then walk in love as Christ has loved, who died that he might save;
5 For us Christ lived, for us he died, and con - quered in the strife.

so learn his love— its length and breadth, its full - ness, depth, and height.
to give the Spir - it's u - ni - ty, the ve - ry bond of peace.
one Lord, one faith, and one bap - tism, one Fa - ther of us all.
with kind and gen - tle hearts for - give as God in Christ for - gave.
A - wake, a - rise, go forth in faith, and Christ shall give you life.

Text: F. Bland Tucker (1895–1984), alt. © 1980 Augsburg Publishing House.
*Reprinted by permission of Augsburg Fortress.*
Music: Max B. Miller (1927– ) ©.

CM
MARSH CHAPEL

# 116 "Your Kingdom Come"—On Bended Knee

1 "Your king - dom come"— on bend - ed knee the
2 But the slow watch - es of the night not
3 And lo, al - rea - dy on the hills the
4 the day in whose clear shin - ing light all
5 when knowl - edge, hand in hand with peace, shall

pass - ing a - ges pray; and faith - ful souls have
less to God be - long, and for the ev - er -
flags of dawn ap - pear. Gird up your loins, you
wrong shall stand re - vealed, when jus - tice shall be
walk the earth a - broad— the day of per - fect

yearned to see on earth that king - dom's day.
last - ing right the si - lent stars are strong.
proph - et souls; pro - claim the day is near:
throned in might, and ev - ery hurt be healed;
right - eous - ness, the prom - ised day of God.

Text: Frederick Lucian Hosmer (1840–1929), alt.
Music: *Hymns and Sacred Poems*, Dublin, 1749.

CM
IRISH

# Lo, How a Rose E'er Blooming    117

1 Lo, how a Rose e'er bloom-ing    from ten-der    stem    hath sprung,
2 I - sai-ah 'twas fore-told it,    the Rose I    have    in mind;
3 O Flower, whose fra-grance ten - der    with sweet-ness    fills    the air,

of    Jes - se's lin-eage com - ing    as    seers of    old    have sung.
with    Ma - ry    we be-hold    it,    the    vir - gin    moth - er kind.
dis - pel in    glo-rious splen-dour    the    dark-ness    ev - ery-where;

It    came,    a    blos - som bright    a - mid the
To    show God's love    a-right,    she    bore to
true    man,    yet    ve - ry    God,    from sin    and

cold    of win - ter,    when half spent    was    the night.
us    a Sav - iour,    when half spent    was    the night.
death now save    us,    and    share our    ev - ery load.

Text: St. 1–2, German (15th cent.); tr. Theodore Baker (1851–1934).
St. 3, Friedrich Layritz (1808–1859); tr. Harriet Reynolds Krauth Spaeth (1845–1925).
Music: Melody *Alte Catholische Geistliche Kirchengesäng*, Köln, 1599; harm. Michael Praetorius (1571–1621).

76 76 6 76
ES IST EIN' ROS

# 118 O Come, All Ye Faithful

1 O come, all ye faith-ful, joy-ful and tri-um-phant, O
2 God of God, Light of Light,
3 Sing, choirs of an-gels, sing in ex-ul-ta-tion,
4 See how the shep-herds, sum-moned to his cra-dle,

come ye, O come ye to Beth-le-hem:
lo, he ab-hors not the vir-gin's womb;
sing, all ye cit-i-zens of heaven a-bove;
leav-ing their flocks, draw nigh with low-ly fear;

*Refrain*

come and be-hold him, born the king of an-gels;
ver-y God, be-got-ten not cre-a-ted:
glo-ry to God in the high-est:
we too will thith-er bend our joy-ful foot-steps;

O

come let us a-dore him, O come let us a-dore him, O

come let us a-dore him, Christ the Lord.

Text: St. 1, 2, 3, and 5, John Francis Wade (1711–1786);
st. 4, Étienne-Jean-François Borderies, 1822; st. 5a, *Thesaurus Animae Christianae*, 1850?;
st. 1, 2, 3, and 5, tr. Frederick Oakley (1802–1880); st. 4 and 5a, tr. William T. Brooke (1848–1917).

Irregular with refrain
ADESTE FIDELES

*For Christmas*
5 Yea, Lord we greet thee, born this happy morning;
 Jesus, to thee be glory given;
 Word of the Father, now in flesh appearing:
  O come…

*For Epiphany*
5a Led by the starlight, Magi, Christ adoring,
 offer him incense, gold, and myrrh;
 we to the Christ-child bring our hearts' oblations.
  O come…

**Latin text**

1 Adeste, fideles, laeti triumphantes,
 venite, venite in Bethlehem:
 natum videte regem angelorum:
 venite, adoremus Dominum.

2 Deum de Deo, lumen de lumine,
 parturit virgo mater,
 Deum verum, genitum, non factum.
 Venite, adoremus Dominum.

3 Cantet nunc hymnos chorus angelorum;
 cantet nunc aula cælestium:
 gloria in excelsis Deo!
 Venite, adoremus Dominum.

4 En grege relicto, humiles ad cunas
 vocati pastores approperant:
 et nos ovanti gradu festinemus:
 venite, adoremus Dominum.

*For Christmas*

5 Ergo qui natus die hodierna,
 Jesu, tibi sit gloria:
 Patris aeterni verbum caro factum.
 Venite, adoremus Dominum.

*For Epiphany*

5a Stella duce, Magi, Christum adorantes,
 aurum, thus, et myrrham dant munera;
 Jesu infanti cordi praebeamus.
 Venite, adoremus Dominum

Music: Melody attrib. John Francis Wade (1711–1786), alt.; harm. *The English Hymnal*, 1906.
 Ref. desc. and altern. harm. David Willcocks (1919– ). *Altern. ref. setting © 1961 Oxford University Press.*

# 119 Silent Night

Capo 1

1 Si - lent night! Ho - ly night! All is calm,
2 Si - lent night! Ho - ly night! Shep - herds quake
3 Si - lent night! Ho - ly night! Son of God,

all is bright round yon vir - gin moth - er and child.
at the sight: glo - ries stream from heav - en a - far,
love's pure light rad - iant beams from thy ho - ly face,

Ho - ly in - fant so ten - der and mild, sleep in
heav - enly hosts sing al - le - lu - ia, Christ the
with the dawn of re - deem - ing grace, Je - sus,

heav - en - ly peace, sleep in heav - en - ly peace.
Sav - iour is born, Christ the Sav - iour is born.
Lord, at thy birth. Je - sus, Lord, at thy birth.

Text: Joseph Mohr (1792–1848); tr. John Freeman Young (1820–1885).
Music: Melody Franz Xaver Gruber (1787–1863), alt.; harm. Carl H. Reinecke (1824–1910).

Irregular
STILLE NACHT

*Naskapi text*

1 ᒋᔭᐅᐤ ᐊᑎᐱᔅᑲᐧ
  ᐸᔭᒋ ᒥᔑᐧᐁ
  ᐊᐧᐋᔅᑕᐧ ᐧᐊᔅᑲ ᑲᐃᔅ ᐃᑕᐟ
  ᒪ ᑭᔭ ᐊᐧᐋᔑᔅ ᒋᔕᔅ
  ᓂᐸ ᒋᒋᔑᑯᐧ
    ᐅᒋᔭᒪᐃᐟᒍᐊ᙮

Chiyamaun atipiskach
Payachi mishiwa
Awastach waska kaish itat
Mary kiya awashish Jeshash
Nipa chichishiku
  uchiyamaitamun.

2 ᒋᔭᐅᐤ ᐊᑎᐱᔅᑲᐧ
  ᐧᐋᔅᑕᔪ ᐊᐊᑕᐧ
  ᒪᓂᔅᒑᓂᔑᐧᐃᔪᐧ
  ᐸᑕᐧᐊᐧ ᒪᐧ ᐊᓐᒑᓇ ᐊ
  ᓂᑲᒧᐃᒋ ᔕᔅ
    ᒋᔕᔅ X ᓂᑕᐧᐃᒋᐤ᙮

Chiyamaun atipiskach
Wastayu aitach
Manischanishiwiyuch
Patawach mak anchana ha
Nikamuichi shash
  Jeshash Christ nitawichiw.

3 ᒋᔕᒪᓐᑐᐤ ᐅᑯᔑᔕ
  ᔑᔭᒋᐧᐋᐃᒋ
  ᑭᔭ ᐊᐸᔭᒋᔑᐃᒋ
  ᐊᐧᐋᔑᔑᐃᒋ ᐊᐧ ᑲ
  ᑎᐸᐃᒋᒋᐊᐃᒋ,
    ᒋᔕᔅ ᐊᓂᑕᐅᒋᐟ᙮

Chishamantuw ukushisha
Shiyachiwaichi
Kiya apayachishiichi
A washishuichi an ka
Tipaichichaichi,
  Jeshash a nitauchit.

4 ᒋᔭᐅᐤ ᐊᑎᐱᔅᑲᐧ
  ᐧᐋᔅᑕᐧᐋᐤ ᐅᒑᑭᑕᐧ
  ᓂᑲᒧᑦᐧᐊᐧ ᐊᓐᒑᓇᐧ
  ᐊᓂᓄᔭ ᒋᒋᐅᒋᒪᐤ
  X ᑲᐱᒪᒋᐊᐧᐋᐟ
  ᐊᓂᑕᐅᒋᐟ ᐊᓄᐧ᙮

Chiyamaun atipiskach
Wastawaw uchakitakw
Nikamutwauch anchanach
Aninuya chicchiuchimaw
Christ ka pimachiiwat
  a nitauchit anuch.

Tr. Joseph Guanish (1931– ) ©. Adapt. from Eastern Cree
  tr. William Gladstone Walton (1867–1948)
  and Daisy Alice Spencer Walton (1873–1948).

*Kwak´wala text*

Sal̲tex̲sa ganuttex̲
Ṕad̲akida 'naxwa
Higa'am̲ k̲wak̲atida
ma'yud̲tama 'nak̲wata
ma'yud̲t̲aman's Gi'ya
Ik̲idz̲asa gananam̲

Iku̲xw da ganuttex̲
Gax̲'mi igalatsi
sa̲n's ike Gigama'ya
Nak̲i'stamas x̲a 'naxwa
Ma'yud̲t̲aman's Gi'ya
Ik̲idz̲asa gananam̲

Iku̲xw da ganuttex̲
Ma'yud̲tami x̲wa̲nukwas God
Hi'ligam̲ k̲a'an's A̲naxwa
K̲a k̲wak̲wa̲la gax̲an's lax̲a
'naxwa 'yaksa'ma
Ma'yud̲t̲amgit̲ tsa̲n's Gi'ya'.

Iku̲xw da ganuttex̲
Wiga'x̲an's amya'x̲a
Ťsa̲lwa'k̲a x̲an's Gigama'ya
K̲a wiwa'x̲bad̲zalatse'si
Ťsosis higa'ma x̲wa̲nukw
k̲a k̲iyox̲w'ide's 'yek̲ine'

Tr. Audrey Wilson (1939– )
  and Pauline Alfred (1938– ).
  © 1997 U'mista Cultural Society.

# 120   O Little Town of Bethlehem

1 O  lit - tle  town  of  Beth - le - hem, how  still  we  see  thee  lie!
2 For Christ is  born  of  Ma - ry;  and,  gath - ered  all  a - bove,
3 How  si - lent - ly,  how  si - lent - ly  the  won - drous gift  is  given
4 O  ho - ly  child  of  Beth - le - hem, de - scend to  us,  we  pray;

A - bove thy deep and  dream-less sleep the  si - lent stars go  by;
while mor - tals sleep, the  an - gels keep their watch of  won - dering love.
as  love im - parts to  hu - man hearts the  bles - sings of God's heaven!
cast  out  our  sin  and  en - ter  in;  be  born in  us  to - day.

yet  in  thy  dark streets  shi - neth the  ev - er - last - ing  light;
O  morn - ing  stars, to - geth - er  pro - claim the  ho - ly  birth,
No  ear  may hear his  com - ing; but  in  this  world of  sin,
We  hear  the  Christ - mas  an - gels the  great glad tid - ings  tell;

the  hopes and fears of  all  the years are  met  in  thee  to - night.
and  prais - es  sing  to  God the King, and  peace to  all  the earth.
where meek souls will  re - ceive him, still  the  dear Christ en - ters in.
O  come to  us,  a - bide with us,  our  Lord Em - man - u - el.

Text: Phillips Brooks (1835–1893), alt.                          86 86 76 86
Music: Lewis Henry Redner (1831–1908).                          ST. LOUIS

# O Little Town of Bethlehem 121

1 O lit-tle town of Beth-le-hem, how still we see thee lie!
2 For Christ is born of Ma - ry; and, gath-ered all a - bove,
3 How si - lent-ly, how si - lent-ly the won-drous gift is given
4 O ho - ly child of Beth-le-hem, de - scend to us, we pray;

A - bove thy deep and dream-less sleep the si - lent stars go by;
while mor-tals sleep, the an - gels keep their watch of won-dering love.
as love im-parts to hu - man hearts the bles-sings of God's heaven!
cast out our sin and en - ter in; be born in us to - day.

yet in thy dark streets shi - neth the ev - er - last - ing light;
O morn-ing stars, to - geth - er pro - claim the ho - ly birth,
No ear may hear his com - ing; but in this world of sin,
We hear the Christ-mas an - gels the great glad tid - ings tell;

the hopes and fears of all the years are met in thee to - night.
and prai - ses sing to God the King, and peace to all the earth.
where meek souls will re - ceive him, still the dear Christ en - ters in.
O come to us, a - bide with us, our Lord Em - man - u - el.

Text: Phillips Brooks (1835–1893), alt.
Music: Melody English trad.; coll. and harm. Ralph Vaughan Williams (1872–1958).
*Harm. © Oxford University Press.*

86 86 76 86
FOREST GREEN
*Alt. rhythm and higher key 427*

# 122  In the Bleak Midwinter

1 In the bleak mid-win-ter, frost-y wind made moan,
2 Our God, heaven can-not hold him, nor earth sus-tain;
3 An-gels and arch-an-gels may have gath-ered there;
4 What can I give him, poor as I am?

earth stood hard as i-ron, wa-ter like a stone;
heaven and earth shall flee a-way when he comes to reign.
cher-u-bim and ser-a-phim thronged the air;
If I were a shep-herd, I would bring a lamb;

snow had fal-len, snow on snow, snow on snow,
In the bleak mid-win-ter a sta-ble place suf-ficed the
but his moth-er on-ly in her maid-en bliss,
if I were a wise man, I would do my part; yet

in the bleak mid-win-ter, long a-go.
Lord God al-might-y, Je-sus Christ.
wor-shipped the be-lov-ed with a kiss.
what I can, I give him— give my heart.

Text: Christina Georgina Rossetti (1830–1894).
Music: Gustav Theodore Holst (1874–1934). © *Oxford University Press.*

Irregular
CRANHAM

# Once in Royal David's City  123

1 Once in roy - al Da - vid's cit - y stood a low - ly
2 He came down to earth from heav - en who is God and
3 Not in that poor low - ly sta - ble, with the ox - en

cat - tle shed, where a moth - er laid her ba - by in a
Lord of all, and his shel - ter was a sta - ble, and his
stand - ing by, we shall see him, but in heav - en, set at

man - ger for his bed. Ma - ry was that
cra - dle was a stall. With the poor and
God's right hand on high, when, like stars, his

moth - er mild, Je - sus Christ her lit - tle child.
mean and low - ly lived on earth our Sav - iour ho - ly.
chil - dren crowned all in white shall gath - er round.

Text: Cecil Frances Alexander (1818–1895), alt.
Music: Henry John Gauntlett (1805–1876).

87 87 77
IRBY

# 126 Away in a Manger

1 A - way in a man - ger, no crib for a bed,
2 The cat - tle are low - ing, the ba - by a - wakes,
3 Be near me, Lord Je - sus; I ask you to stay

the lit - tle Lord Je - sus laid down his sweet head.
but lit - tle Lord Je - sus, no cry - ing he makes.
close by me for ev - er and love me, I pray.

The stars in the bright sky looked down where he lay,
I love you, Lord Je - sus — look down from on high
Bless all the dear chil - dren in your ten - der care,

the lit - tle Lord Je - sus a - sleep on the hay.
and stay by my side un - til morn - ing is nigh.
and fit us for heav - en to live with you there.

Text: American (19th cent.).
Music: William James Kirkpatrick (1838–1921), adapt.

11 11 11 11
CRADLE SONG

# O Come, Little Children 127

1 O come, lit-tle chil-dren; O come, one and all. Look
2 He lies there be-fore you, a-sleep in the hay, with
3 A-dore like the shep-herds! Your glad voic-es raise with

in - to the man-ger in Beth-le-hem's stall; for
Ma-ry and Jo-seph to guard him and pray. The
those of the an-gels who sing in his praise. Your

there, lit-tle chil-dren, on this ho-liest night, our
won-der-ing shep-herds look in at the door, and
cho-rus will ech-o from earth to the sky, with

God sends from heav-en his Son, your de-light.
see-ing the in-fant, they kneel and a-dore.
"Glo-ry to God in his heav-en most high."

Text: Christoph von Schmid (1768–1854); tr. Edward C. Currie (?–1967), alt.   11 11 11 11
Music: Melody Johann Abraham Peter Schulz (1747–1800);   IHR KINDERLEIN, KOMMET
  harm. J. Alfred Schehl (1822–1959), alt. *Tr. and harm. © 1958 Basilian Fathers, Willis Music Co.*

# 128 The Virgin Mary Had a Baby Boy

1 The Vir - gin Ma - ry had a ba- by boy,  the
2 The an - gels sang  when the ba- by was born,  the
3 The wise  men went  where the ba- by was born,  the

Vir - gin Ma - ry had a ba- by  boy,  the Vir - gin Ma - ry had a
an - gels sang  when the ba- by was born,  the an - gels sang  when the
wise  men went  where the ba- by was born,  the wise  men went  where the

⁑ =clap (optional)

Text and music: West Indian carol; adapt. Edric Conner, *Collection of West Indian*
*Spirituals*, 1945; arr. John Barnard (1948– ).
*Text and music © 1945 Boosey & Co., Ltd., copyright renewed. Used by permission of Boosey & Hawkes, Inc.*

Irregular with refrain
THE VIRGIN MARY

ba- by boy, and they say that his name was Je - sus.
ba- by was born, and pro-claim him the Sav - iour Je - sus.
ba- by was born, and they say that his name was Je - sus.

*Refrain*

He come from the glo — ry, he come from the

glo - rious king - dom. He come from the glo — ry,

he come from the glo - rious king - dom. O

yes, be - liev - er! O yes, be - liev - er!

He come from the glo - ry, he come from the

*After st. 3*

glo - rious king - dom!

𝄶 =*clap (optional)*

# No Crowded Eastern Street  129

1 No crowd-ed east-ern street, no sound of pass-ing
2 No rock– hewn place of peace shared with the gen-tle
3 No blaze of heaven-ly fire, no bright ce-les-tial
4 No kings with gold and grain, no state-ly cam-el

feet; far to the left and far to right the
beasts, but stur-dy farm house, stout and warm, with
choir, on-ly the star-light as of old, crossed
train; yet in his pres-ence all may stand with

prai-rie snows spread fair and white; yet still to us is
sta-ble, shed, and great red barn; and still to us is
by the planes' flash, red and gold; yet still to us is
lov-ing heart and will-ing hand; for still to us is

born to-night the child, the King of glo-ry.

Text: Frieda Major (1891–1976). © St. Luke's Anglican Church, Winnipeg. Used by permission.
Music: Robert J. B. Fleming (1921–1976). © 1976 Margaret Fleming.

66 88 87
HERITAGE

# 130 Born in the Night

1 Born in the night, Ma-ry's child, a long way
2 Clear shin-ing light, Ma-ry's child, your face lights
3 Truth of our life, Ma-ry's child, you tell us
4 Hope of the world, Ma-ry's child, you're com - ing

from your home: com - ing in need,
up our way: light of the world,
God is good: prove it is true,
soon to reign: king of the earth,

Ma - ry's child, born in a bor - rowed room.
Ma - ry's child, dawn on our dar - kened day.
Ma - ry's child. Go to your cross of wood.
Ma - ry's child, walk in our streets a - gain.

Text and melody: Geoffrey Ainger (1925– ); harm. Richard D. Wetzel (1935– ).

436D
MARY'S CHILD

# Love Came Down at Christmas 131

1 Love came down at Christ - mas, love all love - ly, love di - vine;
2 Wor - ship we the God - head, love in - car - nate, love di - vine;
3 Love shall be our to - ken, love be yours and love be mine;

love was born at Christ - mas— star and an - gels gave the sign.
wor - ship we our Je - sus— what shall be our sa - cred sign?
love to God and neigh - bour, love for prayer and gift and sign.

Text: Christina Georgina Rossetti (1830–1894), rev. *Hymns for Today's Church.*
    *© 1987 Hope Publishing Co.*
Music: Reginald Owen Morris (1886–1948), alt.; harm. adapt. Fred Kimball Graham (1946– ).
    *Music and harm. adapt. © Oxford University Press.*

67 67
HERMITAGE

## 132  Of Eternal Love Begotten

1 Of e - ter - nal Love be - got - ten
2 At his Word the worlds were fram - ed.
3 O that birth for ev - er bless - ed,
4 This is he whom seers in old time
5 O ye heights of heaven, a - dore him;
6 Christ, to thee, with God the Fa - ther,

ere the worlds be - gan to be,
He com - mand - ed, it was done:
when the vir - gin, full of grace,
chant - ed of with one ac - cord,
an - gel hosts, his prais - es sing;
and, O Ho - ly Ghost, to thee,

he is Al - pha and O - me - ga,
heaven and earth and depths of o - cean
by the Ho - ly Ghost con - ceiv - ing,
whom the voic - es of the proph - ets
all do - min - ions, bow be - fore him,
hymn and chant and high thanks - giv - ing,

Text: Aurelius Clemens Prudentius (348–413?); tr. John Mason Neale (1818–1866), alt.
Music: Melody plainsong, Mode 8 (12th cent.?); adapt. *Piae Cantiones*, 1582;
harm. Healey Willan (1880–1968). *Harm. © Estate of Healey Willan.*

87 87 87 7
DIVINUM MYSTERIUM

## 133  From Heaven on High to Earth I Come

1 "From heaven on high to earth I come to bring good
2 To you this night is born a child of Ma - ry,
3 This is the Christ, God's Son most high, who hears your
4 O Lord, you have cre - a - ted all! How did you

news to ev - ery home; such news of joy to
chos - en moth - er mild; this ten - der child of
sad and bit - ter cry; he will him - self your
come to be so small, to sweet - ly sleep in

all I bring, I glad - ly now both say and sing:
low - ly birth shall be the joy of all the earth.
Sav - iour be and from all sin will set you free."
man - ger - bed where lov - ing cat - tle late - ly fed?

5 Were earth a thousand times as fair
   and set with gold and jewels rare,
   still such a cradle would not do
   to rock a prince so great as you.

6 O dearest Jesus, holy child,
   prepare a bed, soft, undefiled,
   a holy shrine, within my heart,
   that you and I need never part.

7 Glory to God in highest heaven,
   who unto us his Son has given:
   the angels sing with joyful cheer,
   and hail with us the glad new year.

Text: Martin Luther (1483–1546); tr. Catherine Winkworth (1827–1878), alt.
   St. 3–6 © 1978 Lutheran Book of Worship. *Reprinted by permission of Augsburg Fortress.*
Music: Melody *Geistliche lieder auffs new gebessert und gemehrt*, Leipzig, 1539;
   harm. Hans Leo Hassler (1564–1612).

LM
VOM HIMMEL HOCH

# While By the Sheep We Watched At Night 134

1 While by the sheep we watched at night, glad tid-ings
2 There shall be born, so he did say, in Beth-le-
3 There shall the child lie in a stall, this child who
4 This gift of God we'll cher-ish well, that ev-ery

brought an an - gel bright: how great our joy!
hem a child to - day. How great our joy! Great our
shall re-deem us all. How great our joy!
joy our hearts shall fill. How great our joy!

joy! Joy, joy, joy! Joy, joy, joy! Praise we the Lord in

heaven on high! Praise we the Lord in heaven on high!

Text: German carol (17th cent.); tr. Theodore Baker (1851–1934), alt.
Music: Melody German trad.; arr. Hugo Jüngst (1853–1923).

88 with refrain
JÜNGST

# 135 Shepherds in the Field Abiding

1 Shep - herds in the field a - bid - ing, tell us,
2 We be - held (it is no fa - ble), God in -
3 Chor - is - ters on high were sing - ing Je - sus
4 Thanks, good shep - herds, true your sto - ry; let us

when the ser - aph bright greet - ed you with
car - nate, king of bliss, swathed and cra - dled
and his vir - gin birth, heaven - ly bells the
go to Beth - le - hem. An - gels hymn the

won - drous ti - ding, what you saw and heard that night.
in a sta - ble, and the an - gel strain was this:
while a - ring - ing, "Peace, good - will to all on earth."
king of glo - ry; car - ol we with you and them.

*Refrain*

Glo - - - - - ri - a

Glo - - - - - ri - a

Text: French trad.; tr. George Ratcliffe Woodward (1848–1934), alt.
  *Tr. © Mowbray (an imprint of Cassell plc, London).*
Music: Melody French; arr. Martin Shaw (1875–1958). *Arr. © Oxford University Press.*

87 87 with refrain
IRIS

in ex - cel - sis De - o! Glo - - - - - ri - a in ex - cel - sis De - o!

Glo - - - ri - a

*Texte français*

1  Les anges dans nos campagnes
   ont entonné l'hymne des cieux;
   et l'écho de nos montagnes
   redit ce chant mélodieux:
   Gloria in excelsis Deo!

2  Bergers, pour qui cette fête?
   Quel est l'objet de tous ces chants?
   Quel vainqueur, quelle conquête
   mérite ces cris triomphants?
   Gloria in excelsis Deo!

3  Ils annoncent la naissance
   du libérateur d'Israël,
   et pleins de reconnaissance
   chantent en ce jour solennel:
   Gloria in excelsis Deo!

4  Cherchons tous l'heureux village
   qui l'a vu naître sous ses toits;
   Offrons-lui le tendre hommage
   et de nos coeurs et de nos voix:
   Gloria in excelsis Deo!

## 136 While Shepherds Watched Their Flocks

*Descant*

6 "All glo - ry be to God on high, and

1 While shep - herds watched their flocks by night all
2 "Fear not," said he, for migh - ty dread had
3 To you in Da - vid's town this day is
4 the heaven - ly babe you there shall find to

to the world be peace; good will hence - forth from

seat - ed on the ground, the an - gel of the
seized their trou - bled mind. "Glad ti - dings of great
born of Da - vid's line a Sav - iour, who is
hu - man view dis - played, all mean - ly wrapped in

heaven to earth be - gin, and ne - ver cease."

Lord came down and glo - ry shone a - round.
joy I bring to you and hu - man - kind.
Christ the Lord; and this shall be the sign:
swadd - ling bands, and in a man - ger laid."

5 Thus spake the seraph; and forthwith
appeared a shining throng
of angels praising God, who thus
addressed their joyful song:

6 "All glory be to God on high,
and to the world be peace;
good will henceforth from heaven to earth
begin, and never cease."

Text: Luke 2.8–14; para. Nahum Tate (1652–1715), alt.
Music: Melody *Whole Book of Psalmes*, 1592; desc. Craig Sellar Lang (1891–1971).
*Desc. © Novello & Co., Ltd. Reprinted by permission of Shawnee Press, Inc. (ASCAP).*

CM
WINCHESTER OLD

# What Child Is This  137

1 What child is this, who, laid to rest, on
2 Why lies he in such mean es-tate where
3 So bring him in-cense, gold, and myrrh; come,

Ma - ry's lap is sleep - ing? Whom an - gels greet with
ox and ass are feed - ing? Good Chris - tian, fear: for
peas - ant, king, to own him. The King of kings sal -

an - thems sweet, while shep - herds watch are keep - ing?
sin - ners here the si - lent Word is plead - ing.
va - tion brings; let lov - ing hearts en - throne him.

*Refrain*

This, this is Christ the king, whom shep - herds guard and an - gels sing;

haste, haste to bring him laud, the babe, the son of Ma - ry.

Text: William Chatterton Dix (1837–1898).
Music: Melody English trad.; arr. *Christmas Carols New and Old*, 1871, alt.

87 87 with refrain
GREENSLEEVES

# 138 Hark! The Herald Angels Sing

1 Hark! The her - ald an - gels sing, "Glo - ry to the new - born King, peace on earth, and mer - cy mild, God and sin - ners re - con - ciled." Joy - ful, all ye na - tions, rise, join the tri - umph of the skies;

2 Christ, by high - est heaven a - dored; Christ, the ev - er - last - ing Lord; late in time be - hold him come, off - spring of a vir - gin's womb. Veiled in flesh the God - head see; hail, the in - car - nate de - i - ty,

3 Hail, the heaven - born Prince of Peace! Hail, the Sun of Right - eous - ness! Light and life to all he brings, risen with heal - ing in his wings. Mild he lays his glo - ry by, born that we no more may die,

Text: Charles Wesley (1701–1788), alt.
Music: Felix Mendelssohn-Bartholdy (1809–1847); adapt. William Hayman Cummings (1831–1915);
altern. harm. David Willcocks (1919– ). *Altern. harm. © 1961 Oxford University Press.*

77 77D with refrain
MENDELSSOHN

with the an-gel - ic host pro - claim, "Christ is born in Beth- le - hem!"
pleased as one of us to dwell, Je - sus, our Em - man- u - el!
born to raise each child of earth, born to give us sec- ond birth.

*Refrain*

Hark! The her - ald an - gels sing, "Glo - ry to the new- born King."

*Alternate harmonization*

# 139 The First Nowell

1 The first no - well the an - gel did say
2 They look - ed up and saw a star,
3 And by the light of that same star
4 This star drew nigh to the north - west;

was to cer - tain poor shep - herds in fields as they lay,
shin - ing in the east, be - yond them far;
three wise men came from coun - try far;
o'er Beth - le - hem it took its rest,

in fields where they lay keep - ing their sheep
and to the earth it gave great light,
to seek for a king was their in - tent,
and there it did both stop and stay,

on a cold win - ter's night that was so deep.
and so it con - tin - ued both day and night.
and to fol - low the star where - ev - er it went.
right o - ver the place where Je - sus lay.

Text: English trad.
Music: Melody English trad. (17th cent.?), alt.; arr. John Stainer (1840–1901), alt.

Irregular with refrain
THE FIRST NOWELL

No - well, no - well, no - well, no - well,
born is the King of Is - ra - el.

5 Then entered in those wise men three,
full reverently upon their knee,
and offered there in his presence
their gold and myrrh and frankincense.
        *Refrain*

6 Then let us all with one accord
sing praises to our heavenly Lord,
who has made heaven and earth of nought,
and with his blood salvation bought.
        *Refrain*

*Descant to refrain*

No - well, no - well, no - well, no - well,
born is the King of Is - ra - el.

Ref. desc. and altern. harm.: Healey Willan (1880–1968). © *1926 Oxford University Press, Inc.*

# 141  It Came upon the Midnight Clear

1 It came up-on the mid-night clear, that glo-rious
2 Still through the clo-ven skies they come with peace-ful
3 Yet with the woes of sin and strife the world has
4 And you, be-neath life's crush-ing load, whose forms are
5 For lo, the days are hast-ening on, by proph-ets

song of old, from an-gels bend-ing near the earth to
wings un-furled, and still their heaven-ly mus-ic floats o'er
suf-fered long; be-neath the an-gel-strain have rolled two
bend-ing low, who toil a-long the climb-ing way with
seen of old, when with the ev-er-circ-ling years shall

touch their harps of gold: "Peace on the earth, to all good
all the wea-ry world; a-bove its sad and low-ly
thou-sand years of wrong; and we a-mid our wars hear
pain-ful steps and slow; look now, for glad and gold-en
come the time fore-told: when the new heaven and earth shall

Text: Edmund Hamilton Sears (1810–1876), alt.
Music: Melody English trad.; arr. Arthur Seymour Sullivan (1842–1900).

CMD
NOEL

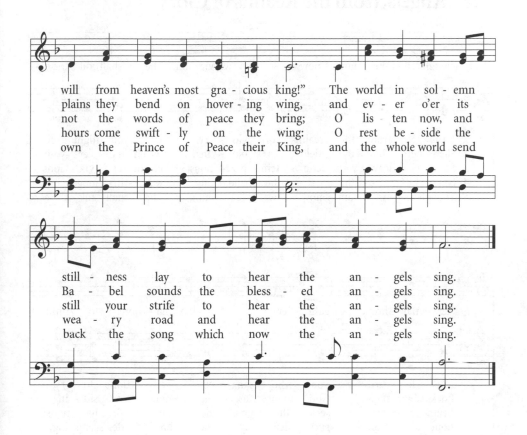

will from heaven's most gra - cious king!" The world in sol - emn
plains they bend on hover - ing wing, and ev - er o'er its
not the words of peace they bring; O lis - ten now, and
hours come swift - ly on the wing: O rest be - side the
own the Prince of Peace their King, and the whole world send

still - ness lay to hear the an - gels sing.
Ba - bel sounds the bless - ed an - gels sing.
still your strife to hear the an - gels sing.
wea - ry road and hear the an - gels sing.
back the song which now the an - gels sing.

Christmas/Epiphany CHRISTIAN YEAR

## Sleep, Sweet Child, Thy Mother Watches 142

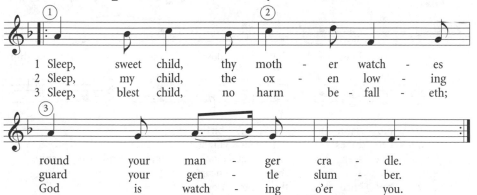

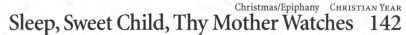

1 Sleep, sweet child, thy moth - er watch - es
2 Sleep, my child, the ox - en low - ing
3 Sleep, blest child, no harm be - fall - eth;

round your man - ger cra - dle.
guard your gen - tle slum - ber.
God is watch - ing o'er you.

*May be sung as a 3-part round or canon.*

Text: Margaret Fleming (1919– ) and Robert J. B. Fleming (1921–1976).
Music: Robert J. B. Fleming.
*Text and music © 1980 Waterloo Music Co. Ltd.*

# 143   Angels, from the Realms of Glory

*Descant*

5 Though an in-fant now   we view him, he   shall fill the e-
ter-nal throne,   gath-er   all   the na-tions to him;
ev-ery knee shall   then bow down:   come   and wor-ship,

1 An - gels, from   the   realms   of   glo - ry,   wing your flight o'er
2 Shep - herds in   the   field   a - bid - ing,   watch-ing o'er your
3 Sa - ges, leave your   con - tem - pla - tions;   bright-er   vis - ions
4 Saints be - fore   the   al - tar bend - ing,   watch-ing long in
5 Though an   in - fant   now   we view him,   he   shall fill the e-

all   the earth;   you   who   sang   cre - a - tion's sto - ry,
flocks by   night,   God   with   us   is   now   re - sid - ing;
beam a - far;   seek   the   great   de - sire   of   na - tions;
hope and   fear,   sud - den - ly   the   Lord,   de - scend - ing,
ter - nal   throne,   gath - er   all   the   na - tions to him;

now   pro - claim Mes - si - ah's birth:
yon - der shines the   in - fant Light:
you   have   seen his   na - tal   star:   come   and wor - ship,
in   his   tem - ple   shall ap - pear:
ev - ery   knee shall   then bow down:

Text: James Montgomery (1771–1854), alt.
Music: Henry Thomas Smart (1813–1879); desc. Craig Sellar Lang (1891–1971).
*Desc. © 1953 Novello & Co., Ltd. Reprinted by permission of Shawnee Press, Inc. (ASCAP).*

87 87 87
REGENT SQUARE

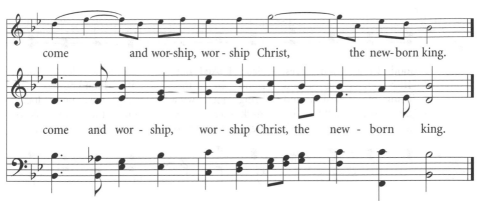

come and wor-ship, wor-ship Christ, the new-born king.

come and wor-ship, wor-ship Christ, the new-born king.

Christmas/Epiphany  CHRISTIAN YEAR

## Sleep, Holy Child, Now Hid Away 144

1 Sleep, ho - ly child, now hid a - way from hu - man
2 Rest, Lamb of God, for comes the day when earth will
3 Shine, fra - gile life, this star - ry night. In sleep, un -

heart - break, hate, and strife. What will you know of
judge you, strike you, scorn. Sleep sound - ly now as
know - ing, sigh and nod, for none on earth can

peace - ful days when e - ven now they stalk your life?
Ma - ry smiles and holds you in her arms, new - born.
ov - er - come the light in you that comes from God.

Text: Ruth Duck (1947– ). © 1992 G.I.A. Publications, Inc.
Music: John McIntosh (1932– ) ©.

LM
SELINA

# 146 'Twas in the Moon of Wintertime

Unison

1 'Twas in the moon of win-ter-time, when all the birds had fled, that might-y Git-chi Man-i-tou sent an-gel choirs in-stead; be-

2 With-in a lodge of bro-ken bark the ten-der babe was found; a rag-ged robe of rab-bit skin en-wrapped his beau-ty round. But

3 The ear-liest moon of win-ter-time is not so round and fair as was the ring of glo-ry on the help-less in-fant there. The

4 O chil-dren of the for-est free, be-loved of Man-i-tou, the ho-ly child of earth and heaven is born to-day for you. Come,

Text: Jean de Brébeuf (1593–1649); tr. Jesse Edgar Middleton (1872–1960), alt.
*Tr. © The Frederick Harris Music Co., Ltd.*
Music: Melody French trad. (16th cent.); harm. Frederick F. Jackisch (1922– ).
*Harm. © 1978 Lutheran Book of Worship. Reprinted by permission of Augsburg Fortress.*

86 86 88 with refrain
UNE JEUNE PUCELLE

fore their light the stars grew dim, and wan - dering hun - ters
as the hun - ter braves drew nigh, the an - gel song ran
chiefs from far be - fore him knelt with gifts of fox and
kneel be - fore the ra - diant boy, who brings you beau - ty,

heard the hymn:
loud and high: Je - sus your king is born,
bea - ver - pelt.
peace, and joy:

Je - sus is born, in ex - cel - sis glo - ri - a.

# 147 Break Forth, O Beauteous Heavenly Light

1 Break forth, O beau-teous heaven-ly light, and ush-er in the
2 This night of won-der, night of joy, was born the Christ, our
3 Come, dear-est child, in-to our hearts, and leave your crib be-

morn - ing; O shep-herds, shrink not with af-fright, but
broth - er; he comes, not might-y to de-stroy, to
hind you! Let this be where the new life starts for

hear the an-gel's warn - ing. This child, this lit-tle
bid us love each oth - er. How could he quit his
all who seek and find you. To you the hon-our,

Text: St. 1, Johann Rist (1607–1667); tr. John Troutbeck (1833–1889), alt.; st. 2–3, Fred Pratt Green (1903– ). St. 2–3 © 1989 Hope Publishing Co.
Music: Melody Johann Schop (1595?–1667?); harm. Johann Sebastian Bach (1685–1750).

87 87 88 77
ERMUNTRE DICH

help - less boy, shall    be    our    con - fi - dence and joy,    the    power of
king - ly state    for    such    a    world of    greed and hate? What deep hu -
thanks, and praise, for    all    your gifts    this    time    of    grace; come, con - quer

Sa - tan    break - ing,    our    peace e - ter - nal    mak -    ing.
mil - i - a    -    tion se - cured the world's sal - va    -    tion!
and de - liv    -    er    this world, and us,    for - ev    -    er.

## 148  See Amid the Winter's Snow

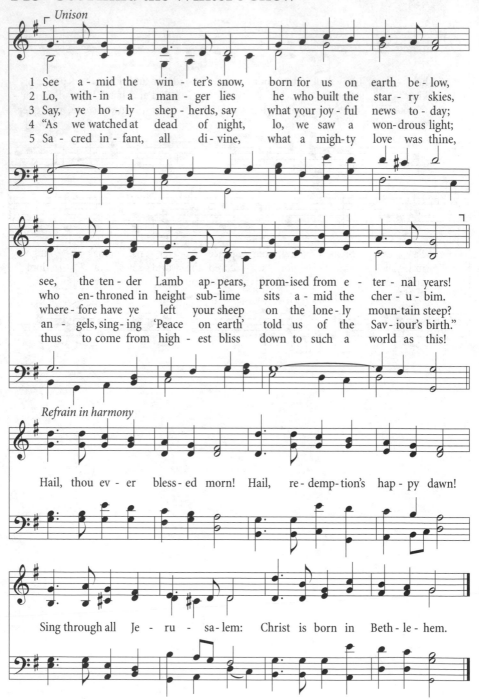

*Unison*

1 See a-mid the win-ter's snow, born for us on earth be-low,
2 Lo, with-in a man-ger lies he who built the star-ry skies,
3 Say, ye ho-ly shep-herds, say what your joy-ful news to-day;
4 "As we watched at dead of night, lo, we saw a won-drous light;
5 Sa-cred in-fant, all di-vine, what a might-y love was thine,

see, the ten-der Lamb ap-pears, prom-ised from e-ter-nal years!
who en-throned in height sub-lime sits a-mid the cher-u-bim.
where-fore have ye left your sheep on the lone-ly moun-tain steep?
an-gels, sing-ing 'Peace on earth' told us of the Sav-iour's birth."
thus to come from high-est bliss down to such a world as this!

*Refrain in harmony*

Hail, thou ev-er bless-ed morn! Hail, re-demp-tion's hap-py dawn!

Sing through all Je-ru-sa-lem: Christ is born in Beth-le-hem.

Text: Edward Caswall (1814–1878), alt.
Music: John Goss (1800–1880).

77 77 with refrain
SEE AMID THE WINTER'S SNOW

# All My Heart This Night Rejoices 149

1 All my heart this night re - joic - es as I hear,
2 Hark! A voice from yon - der man - ger, soft and sweet,
3 Come, then, let us has - ten yon - der! Here let all,
4 Thee, dear Lord, with heed I'll cher - ish, live to thee,

far and near, sweet - est an - gel voic - es; "Christ is
doth en - treat, "Flee from woe and dan - ger! Pil - grims,
great and small, kneel in awe and won - der! Love him
and with thee dy - ing, shall not per - ish; but shall

born," their choirs are sing - ing, till the air
come! From all that grieves you you are freed;
who with love is yearn - ing! Hail the star,
dwell with thee for - ev - er, far on high,

ev - ery - where now with joy is ring - ing.
all you need I will sure - ly give you."
that from far bright with hope is burn - ing!
in the joy that can al - ter nev - er.

Text: Paul Gerhardt (1607–1676); tr. Catherine Winkworth (1827–1878), alt.
Music: Johann George Ebeling (1637–1676).

8 33 6D
WARUM SOLLT ICH

# 150  On This Day Earth Shall Ring

1 On this day earth shall ring
2 His the doom, ours the mirth;
3 God's bright star, o'er his head,
4 On this day an - gels sing;

with the song chil - dren sing to the Lord, Christ our king,
when he came down to earth Beth - le - hem saw his birth;
wise men three to him led; kneel they low by his bed,
with their song earth shall ring, prais - ing Christ, heav - en's king,

born on earth to save us; him the Fa - ther gave us.
ox and ass be - side him from the cold would hide him.
lay their gifts be - fore him, praise him and a - dore him.
born on earth to save us; peace and love he gave us.

Text: *Piae Cantiones*, 1582; tr. Jane M. Joseph (1894–1929).
Music: Melody *Piae Cantiones*, 1582; harm. Gustav Theodore Holst (1874–1934).
*Text and harm. © 1924 (renewed) J. Curwen & Sons, Ltd. (London). Used by permission of G. Schirmer, Inc.*

666 66 with refrain
PERSONENT HODIE

* Translation: "Therefore, glory to God in the highest!" (Latin)

# 151 All Poor Folk and Humble

1 All poor folk and hum-ble, all lame folk who stum-ble,
2 The Christ child will lead us, the good Shep-herd feed us,

come haste ye, and be not a-fraid; for Je-sus, our trea-sure,
and with us a-bide till his day. Then ha-tred he'll ban-ish,

whose love pass-es mea-sure, in low-ly poor man-ger was laid.
then sor-row will van-ish, and death and des-pair flee a-way.

Though wise men who found him laid rich gifts a-round him,
And he shall reign ev-er, and noth-ing shall sev-er

Text: St. 1, Katharine E. Roberts (1877–1962), alt.; st. 2, William Thomas Pennar
Davies (1911–1996). St. 1 © 1928 Oxford University Press. St. 2 © Estate of William Thomas Pennar Davies.
Music: Melody Welsh trad.; arr. Erik Routley (1917–1982). Arr. © Oxford University Press.

668 668D with refrain
OLWEN

yet ox-en they gave him their hay; and Je-sus in beau-ty
from us the great love of our King. His peace and his pi-ty

ac-cept-ed their du-ty: con-ten-ted in man-ger he lay.
shall bless his fair cit-y; his prais-es we ev-er shall sing.

*Refrain*

Then haste we to show him the prais-es we owe him;

our ser-vice he ne'er can de-spise, whose love still is a-ble

to show us that sta-ble where soft-ly in man-ger he lies.

## 152 Let Folly Praise That Fancy Loves

1 Let folly praise that fancy loves; I
2 Love's sweetest mark, laud's highest theme, our
3 Though young, yet wise, though small, yet strong, though

praise and love that child whose heart no thought, whose
most desired light. To love him life, to
man, yet God he is; as wise he knows, as

tongue no word, whose hand no deed defiled. I
leave him death, to live in him delight. He
strong he can, as God he loves to bless. His

praise him most, I love him best; all
mine by gift, I his by debt, thus
knowledge rules, his strength defends, his

Text: Robert Southwell (1561–1595), alt.
Music: Melody David Wilson (1940– ); arr. Noel Tredinnick (1949– );
fl. desc. Melva Treffinger Graham (1947– ). *Melody © 1969, arr. © 1982, fl. desc. © 1998 Hope Publishing Co.*

CMD
A PURPLE ROBE

praise and love are his. While him I love, in
each to oth - er due: first friend he was, best
love doth cher - ish all; his birth our joy, his

him I live, and can - not live a - miss.
friend he is; all times will try him true.
life our light, his death our end of thrall.

*Flute descant*

# 153 Good Christians All, Rejoice

1 Good Chris-tians all, re-joice with heart and soul and
2 Good Chris-tians all, re-joice with heart and soul and
3 Good Chris-tians all, re-joice with heart and soul and

voice! Lis-ten now to what we say: Je-sus Christ is
voice! Hear the news of end-less bliss: Je-sus Christ was
voice! Now you need not fear the grave; Je-sus Christ was

born to-day; ox and ass be-fore him bow and he is in the
born for this; he has o-pened heav-en's door and we are blessed for
born to save: come at his most gra-cious call to find sal-va-tion,

man-ger now! Christ is born to-day; Christ is born to-day!
ev-er-more! Christ was born for this; Christ was born for this.
one and all! Christ was born to save; Christ was born to save!

Text: German-Latin carol (14th cent.); tr. John Mason Neale (1818–1866), alt.
Music: Melody *Geistliche Lieder*, Wittenberg, 1533;
   harm. Robert Lucas Pearsall (1795–1856); arr. John Stainer (1840–1901).

66 77 78 55
IN DULCI JUBILO

# Joy to the World  154

1 Joy to the world! The Lord is come: let earth re-
2 Joy to the earth! The Sav - iour reigns: let us glad
3 No more let wrongs and sor - rows grow, nor thorns in - the
4 He rules the world with truth and grace, and makes the

ceive the King; let ev - ery heart pre - pare him
songs em - ploy, while fields and floods, rocks, hills, and
fest the ground; he comes to make his bless - ings
na - tions prove the glo - ries of his right - eous -

room, and heaven and na - ture sing, and heaven and
plains re - peat the sound - ing joy, re - peat the
flow far as our sin is found, far as our
ness and won - ders of his love, and won - ders

and heaven and na - ture sing,

na - ture sing, and heaven and heaven and na - ture sing.
sound - ing joy, re - peat, re - peat the sound - ing joy.
sin is found, far as, far as our sin is found.
of his love, and won - ders, won - ders of his love.

and heaven and na - ture sing,

Text: Isaac Watts (1674–1748), alt.  CM with repeat
Music: Melody William Holford, *Voce de Melodia*, 1835; adapt. George Frideric Handel (1685–1759);  ANTIOCH
  harm. Lowell Mason (1792–1872).

# 155 From East to West, from Shore to Shore

1 From east to west, from shore to shore,
let ev - ery heart a - wake and sing
the ho - ly child whom Ma - ry bore,
the Christ, the ev - er - last - ing King.

2 Be - hold! The world's cre - a - tor wears
the form and fash - ion of a slave;
our ver - y flesh our Mak - er shares,
his fal - len crea - ture now to save.

3 For this how wond - rous - ly he wrought!
A maid - en, in her low - ly place,
be - came, in ways be - yond all thought,
the cho - sen ves - sel of his grace.

4 As - sent - ing to the an - gel's word,
she chose what God the Spir - it willed,
and sud - den - ly the prom - ised Lord
that pure and hal - lowed tem - ple filled.

Text: Caelius Sedulius (5th cent.?); tr. John Ellerton (1826–1893), alt.
Music: Melody Trier MS (15th cent.); adapt. Michael Praetorius (1571–1621);
   harm. George Ratcliffe Woodward (1848–1934). *Harm. © Mowbray (an imprint of Cassell plc, London).*

LM
PUER NOBIS NASCITUR

5 He shrank not from the oxen's stall,
  he lay within the manger bed,
  and he whose bounty feeds us all
  at Mary's breast himself was fed.

6 And while the angels in the sky
  sang praise above the silent field,
  to shepherds poor the Lord most high,
  the one great Shepherd, was revealed.

7 All glory for this blessèd morn
  to God, the source of all, is due;
  all praise to you, O Virgin-born;
  all praise, O Holy Ghost, to you.

Christmas/Epiphany  CHRISTIAN YEAR

## The People That in Darkness Sat  156

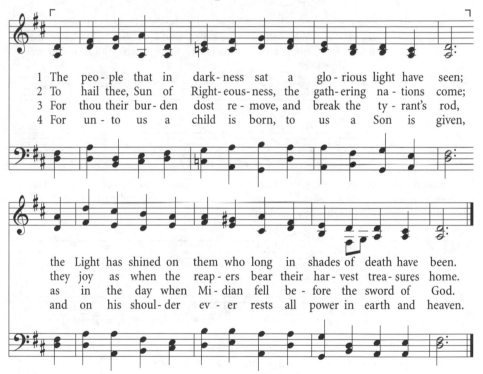

1 The peo-ple that in dark-ness sat a glo-rious light have seen;
2 To hail thee, Sun of Right-eous-ness, the gath-ering na-tions come;
3 For thou their bur-den dost re-move, and break the ty-rant's rod,
4 For un-to us a child is born, to us a Son is given,

the Light has shined on them who long in shades of death have been.
they joy as when the reap-ers bear their har-vest trea-sures home.
as in the day when Mi-dian fell be-fore the sword of God.
and on his shoul-der ev-er rests all power in earth and heaven.

5 His name shall be the Prince of Peace,
  the everlasting Lord,
  the Wonderful, the Counsellor,
  the God by all adored.

6 Lord Jesus, reign in us we pray,
  and make us thine alone,
  who with the Father ever art
  and Holy Spirit one.

Text: John Morison (1750–1798).
Music: Scottish Psalter, 1615.

CM
DUNDEE
*Higher key 282*
*Alt. tune DUNFERMLINE 197*

# 157  Rise Up and Shine

Unison

1 Rise up and shine! Your light has come; God's glory
2 Fling wide your gates, both day and night; no more keep
3 No more will you im - plore the sun to shed by

breaks like dawn. For though the earth be cloaked in night and
watch or guard. You will be called God's ho - ly hill, the
day its light, nor will you need the change - ful moon to

gloom shrouds ev - ery - one, yet ov - er you the
ci - ty of the Lord. No sound of strife will
glis - ten through the night. Your glo - ry then will

Lord will rise, with glo - ry gleam - ing clear, till na - tions
plague your land, nor harm be - siege your ways; "Sal - va - tion"
be your God, whose light will ne - ver cease. Rise up and

Text: *The New Jerusalem* (Is. 60.1–3, 11ab, 14cd, 18–19); para. Carl P. Daw Jr. (1944– ).
*Para. © 1990 Hope Publishing Co.*
Music: Alfred V. Fedak (1953– ). *© 1990 Selah Publishing Co., Inc.*

CMD
PETER'S BROOK

turn    to    seek   your   light  and    hum-bled  kings  draw   near.
will    you   name   your   walls, and    all    your   por-tals  "Praise."
shine! Your   light  has    come   to     give   you    joy    and    peace.

Christmas/Epiphany   CHRISTIAN YEAR

## Earth Has Many a Noble City   158

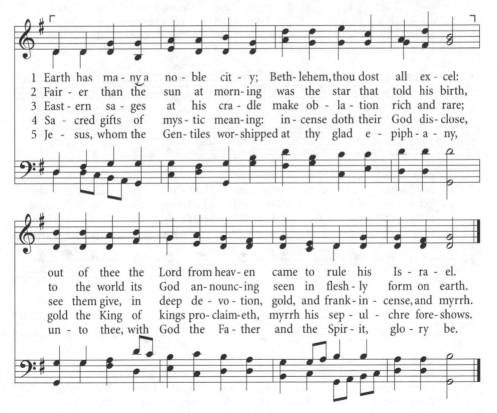

1 Earth has ma-ny a    no-ble cit-y; Beth-lehem, thou dost    all ex-cel:
2 Fair-er than the     sun at morn-ing  was the star that     told his birth,
3 East-ern sa-ges      at his cra-dle  make ob-la-tion       rich and rare;
4 Sa-cred gifts of     mys-tic mean-ing:  in-cense doth their  God dis-close,
5 Je-sus, whom the     Gen-tiles wor-shipped at thy glad e-    piph-a-ny,

out of thee the    Lord from heav-en  came to rule his    Is-ra-el.
to   the world its  God an-nounc-ing   seen in flesh-ly    form on earth.
see them give, in   deep de-vo-tion,   gold, and frank-in-cense, and myrrh.
gold the King of    kings pro-claim-eth,  myrrh his sep-ul-chre fore-shows.
un-to thee, with    God the Fa-ther    and the Spir-it,    glo-ry be.

Text: Aurelius Clemens Prudentius (348–413?); tr. Edward Caswall (1814–1878).   87 87
Music: Melody *Psalmodia Sacra*, Gotha, 1715; adapt. Henry John Gauntlett (1805–1876).   STUTTGART
*Alt. setting and lower key 88*

## 159 Brightest and Best

1 Bright-est and best of the stars of the morn - ing,
2 Cold on his cra - dle the dew-drops are shin - ing,
3 Say, shall we yield him, in cost-ly de - vo - tion,
4 Vain-ly we of - fer each am - ple o - bla - tion,
5 Bright-est and best of the stars of the morn - ing,

dawn on our dark - ness, and lend us thine aid:
low lies his head with the beasts of the stall;
o - dours of E - dom and off - erings di - vine,
vain - ly with gifts would his fav - our se - cure;
dawn on our dark - ness, and lend us thine aid:

gem of the East, the hor - i - zon a - dorn - ing,
an - gels a - dore him in slum - ber re - clin - ing,
gems of the moun - tain and pearls of the o - cean,
rich - er by far is the heart's a - dor - a - tion,
gem of the East, the hor - i - zon a - dorn - ing,

guide where our in - fant Re - deem - er is laid.
Ma - ker and Mon - arch and Sav - iour of all.
myrrh from the for - est and gold from the mine?
dear - er to God are the prayers of the poor.
guide where our in - fant Re - deem - er is laid.

Text: Reginald Heber (1783–1826), alt.
Music: Healey Willan (1880–1968). © 1994 Waterloo Music Co. Ltd.

11 10 11 10
STELLA ORIENTIS

# As with Gladness Men of Old   160

1 As with glad-ness men of old did the guid-ing
2 As with joy-ful steps they sped, Sa-viour, to thy
3 As they of-fered gifts most rare at that cra-dle
4 In the heaven-ly coun-try bright need they no cre-

star be-hold; as with joy they hailed its light,
low-ly bed, there to bend the knee be-fore
rude and bare, so may we with joy-ful song,
a-ted light: thou its light, its joy, its crown,

lead-ing on-ward, beam-ing bright; so, most gra-cious
thee, whom heaven and earth a-dore; so may we with
rais-ing voic-es pure and strong, all our cost-liest
thou its sun which goes not down; there for-ev-er

Lord, may we ev-er-more be led to thee.
will-ing feet ev-er seek thy mer-cy seat.
trea-sures bring, Christ, to thee our heaven-ly king.
may we sing al-le-lu-ias to our king.

Text: William Chatterton Dix (1837–1898), alt.
Music: Konrad Kocher (1786–1872).

77 77 77
DIX

# 161 Wise Men, They Came to Look for Wisdom

1 Wise men, they came to look for wis - dom,
2 Pil - grims they were, from un - known coun - tries,
3 Ma - gi, they stooped to see your splen - dour,
4 Guests of their God, they o - pened trea - sures—

find - ing one wi - ser than they knew;
search - ing for one who knows the world;
led by a star to light su - preme;
in - cense and gold and sol - emn myrrh;

rich men, they met with one yet rich - er—
lost are their names and strange their jour - neys,
pro - mised Mes - si - ah, Lord e - ter - nal,
wel - com - ing one too young to ques - tion

Text: Christopher Idle (1938– ). © 1982 Hope Publishing Co.
Music: Georg Neumark (1621–1681).

98 98 88
WER NUR DEN LIEBEN GOTT

King of the kings, they knelt to you:
famed is their zeal to find the child:
glo - ry and peace are in your name.
how came these gifts, and what they were.

Je - sus, our wis - dom from a - bove,
Je - sus, in you the lost are claimed,
Joy of each day, our song by night,
Gift be - yond price of gold or gem,

wealth and re - demp - tion, life and love.
a - liens are found and known and named.
shine on our path your ho - ly light.
make a - mong us your Beth - le - hem.

# 162 Sing of God Made Manifest

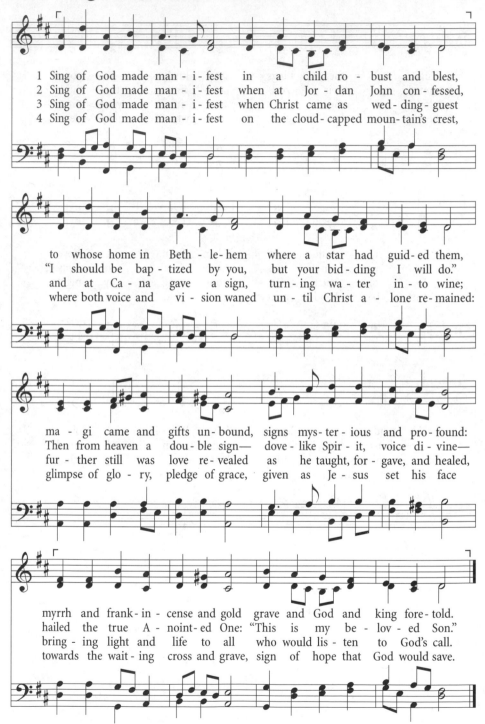

1 Sing of God made man-i-fest in a child ro-bust and blest,
2 Sing of God made man-i-fest when at Jor-dan John con-fessed,
3 Sing of God made man-i-fest when Christ came as wed-ding-guest
4 Sing of God made man-i-fest on the cloud-capped moun-tain's crest,

to whose home in Beth-le-hem where a star had guid-ed them,
"I should be bap-tized by you, but your bid-ding I will do."
and at Ca-na gave a sign, turn-ing wa-ter in-to wine;
where both voice and vi-sion waned un-til Christ a-lone re-mained:

ma-gi came and gifts un-bound, signs mys-ter-ious and pro-found:
Then from heaven a dou-ble sign— dove-like Spir-it, voice di-vine—
fur-ther still was love re-vealed as he taught, for-gave, and healed,
glimpse of glo-ry, pledge of grace, given as Je-sus set his face

myrrh and frank-in-cense and gold grave and God and king fore-told.
hailed the true A-noint-ed One: "This is my be-lov-ed Son."
bring-ing light and life to all who would lis-ten to God's call.
towards the wait-ing cross and grave, sign of hope that God would save.

Text: Carl P. Daw, Jr. (1944– ). © 1990 Hope Publishing Co.
Music: Melody Jakob Hintze (1622–1702); harm. Johann Sebastian Bach (1685–1750).

77 77D
SALZBURG
Alt. harm. 207

# When Christ's Appearing Was Made Known   163

1 When Christ's ap-pear-ing was made known, King Her-od
2 The east-ern sa-ges saw from far and fol-lowed
3 With-in the Jor-dan's sa-cred flood the heaven-ly
4 And O what mir-a-cle di-vine, when wa-ter
5 All glo-ry, Je-sus, be to thee for this, thy

trem-bled for his throne; but he who of-fers heaven-ly
on his gui-ding star; by light their way to Light they
Lamb in meek-ness stood, that he, to whom no sin was
red-dened in-to wine! He spake the word, and forth it
glad E-pi-pha-ny: whom with the Fa-ther we a-

birth sought not the king-doms of this earth.
trod, and by their gifts con-fessed their God.
known, might cleanse his peo-ple from their own.
flowed in streams that na-ture ne'er be-stowed.
dore and Ho-ly Ghost for ev-er-more.

Text: Caelius Sedulius (5th cent.?); st.1, tr. *The Hymn Book*, 1971;
st. 2–5, tr. John Mason Neale (1818–1866).
Music: Melody *Antiphoner*, Rouen, 1728; harm. Michael Fleming (1928– ). *Harm © Hope Publishing Co.*

LM
ST. VENANTIUS
*Alt. setting 12*

# 165 Mark How the Lamb of God's Self-Offering

1 Mark how the Lamb of God's self-of-fering our hu-man sin-ful-
2 From this as-sur-ance of God's fa-vour Je-sus goes to the
3 Grant us, O God, the strength and cour-age to live the faith our

ness takes on in the birth-wa-ters of the Jor-dan
wil-der-ness, there to en-dure a time of test-ing
lips de-clare; bless us in our bap-tis-mal call-ing;

as Je-sus is bap-tized by John. Hear how the voice from
that rea-died him to teach and bless. So we, by wa-ter
Christ's roy-al priest-hood help us share. Turn us from ev-ery

Text: Carl P. Daw, Jr. (1944– ). © 1990 Hope Publishing Co.
Music: Melody Strasbourg, 1545; Geneva, 1551; harm. Erik Routley (1917–1982).
  Harm. © 1977 Hope Publishing Co.

98 98D
RENDEZ À DIEU
Higher key 316
Alt. setting 15, 54

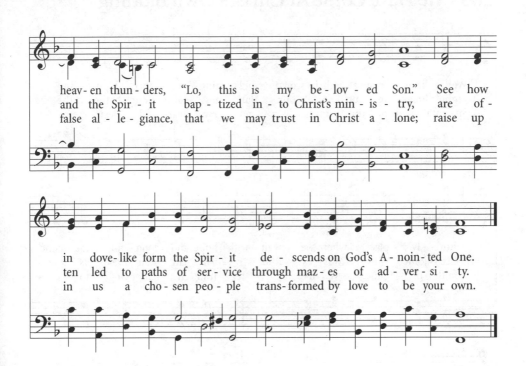

heav- en thun - ders, "Lo, this is my be - lov - ed Son." See how
and the Spir - it bap - tized in - to Christ's min - is - try, are of -
false al - le - giance, that we may trust in Christ a - lone; raise up

in dove- like form the Spir - it de - scends on God's A - noin - ted One.
ten led to paths of ser - vice through maz - es of ad - ver - si - ty.
in us a cho - sen peo - ple trans- formed by love to be your own.

# 166 We Have Come At Christ's Own Bidding

1 We have come at Christ's own bid-ding to this high and
2 Light breaks in up-on our dark-ness; splen-dour bathes the
3 Strength-ened by this glimpse of glo-ry, fear-ful lest our

ho - ly place, where we wait with hope and long-ing for some
flesh-joined Word. Mos-es and E-li-jah mar-vel as the
faith de - cline, we like Pe-ter find it tempt-ing to re -

to - ken of God's grace. Here we pray for new as -
heaven-ly voice is heard. Eyes and hearts be-hold with
main and build a shrine. But true wor-ship gives us

sur - ance that our faith is not in vain, search-ing
won - der how the law and proph-ets meet: Christ, with
cour - age to pro-claim what we pro-fess, that our

Text: Carl P. Daw, Jr. (1944– ). © 1988 Hope Publishing Co.
Music: Geistliche Volkslieder, 1858.

87 87D
O MEIN JESU, ICH MUSS STERBEN

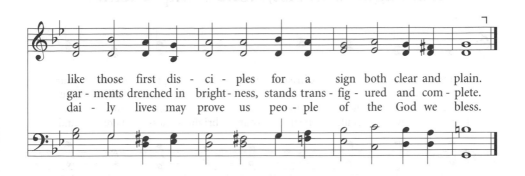

like those first dis - ci - ples for a sign both clear and plain.
gar - ments drenched in bright - ness, stands trans - fig - ured and com - plete.
dai - ly lives may prove us peo - ple of the God we bless.

## 'Tis Good, Lord, to Be Here  167

1 'Tis good, Lord, to be here! Thy glo - ry fills the night;
2 'Tis good, Lord, to be here, thy beau - ty to be - hold,
3 Ful - fil - ler of the past, prom - ise of things to be,
4 Be - fore we taste of death, we see thy king - dom come:
5 'Tis good, Lord, to be here! Yet we may not re - main;

thy face and gar - ments, like the sun, shine with un - bor - rowed light.
where Mo - ses and E - li - jah stand, thy mes - sen - gers of old.
we hail thy bo - dy glo - ri - fied, and our re - demp - tion see!
O might we hold the vi - sion bright and make this hill our home!
but, since thou bidst us leave the mount, come with us to the plain.

Text: Joseph Armitage Robinson (1858–1933).
Music: Charles Lockhart (1745?–1815).

SM
CARLISLE
*Lower key 454*

# 170 The Glory of These Forty Days

1 The glory of these forty days we
2 Alone and fasting, Moses saw the
3 So Daniel trained his mystic sight, de -
4 Then grant us, Lord, like them to be full
5 O Father, Son, and Spirit blest, to

cel - e - brate with songs of praise; for Christ, through whom all
lov - ing God who gave the law; and to E - li - jah,
liv - ered from the li - ons' might; and John, the bride- groom's
oft in fast and prayer with thee; our spir - its strength- en
thee be ev - ery prayer ad- dressed, who art in three - fold

things were made, him - self has fast - ed and has prayed.
fast - ing, came the steeds and char - i - ots of flame.
friend, be - came the her - ald of Mes - si - ah's name.
with thy grace, and give us joy to see thy face.
name a - dored, from age to age, the on - ly Lord.

Text: Latin (6th cent.); tr. Maurice F. Bell (1862–1947), alt. *Tr. © Oxford University Press.*
Music: Melody *Geistliche Lieder*, 1543; adapt. and harm. Johann Sebastian Bach (1685–1750).

LM
ERHALT UNS, HERR

# What Does the Lord Require   171

1 What does the Lord re - quire for praise and of - fer - ing?
2 Rul - ers of earth, give ear! Should you not jus - tice know?
3 All who gain wealth by trade, for whom the work - er toils,
4 How shall our life ful - fill God's law so hard and high?

What sac - ri - fice, de - sire, or trib - ute bid you bring?
Will God your plead - ing hear, while crime and cru el - ty grow?
think not to win God's aid, if greed your com - merce soils.
Let Christ en - due our will with grace to for - ti - fy.

1-3

Do just - ly; love mer - cy; walk hum - bly with your
Do just - ly; love mer - cy; walk hum - bly with your
Do just - ly; love mer - cy; walk hum - bly with your
Then just - ly, in mer - cy, we'll

4

God.
God.
God.

hum - bly walk with God.

Text: Albert Frederick Bayly (1901–1984), alt. © *Oxford University Press.*
Music: Erik Routley (1917–1982). © *1969 Hope Publishing Co.*

66 66 336
SHARPTHORNE

# 172 Now Let Us All with One Accord

1 Now let us all with one ac-cord, in com-pa-
2 The cov-e-nant, so long re-vealed to those of
3 Your love, O Lord, our sin-ful race has not re-
4 Re-mem-ber, Lord, though frail we be, in your own
5 There-fore, we pray you, Lord, for-give; so when our

ny with a-ges past, keep vi-gil with our
faith in for-mer time, Christ by his own ex-
turned, but fal-si-fied. Au-thor of mer-cy,
im-age were we made; help us, lest in anx-
wan-derings here shall cease, we may with you for-

heaven-ly Lord in his temp-ta-tion and his fast.
am-ple sealed, the Lord of love, in love sub-lime.
turn your face and grant re-pen-tance for our pride.
i-e-ty, we cause your name to be be-trayed.
ev-er live in love and u-ni-ty and peace.

Text: Attrib. Gregory the Great (540–604); tr. James Quinn, SJ (1919– ) ©.
*Used by permission of Selah Publishing Co., Inc., North American Agent.*
Music: Melody *Beauties of Harmony*, Pittsburgh, 1814; harm. John Leon Hooker (1944– ) ©.

LM
BOURBON

# Creator of the Earth and Skies  173

1 Cre - a - tor of the earth and skies, to whom the
2 We have not known you: to the skies our mon - u -
3 We have not loved you: far and wide the wreck - age
4 For this, our fool - ish con - fi - dence, our pride of
5 Teach us to know and love you, Lord, and hum - bly

words of life be - long, grant us your truth to
ments of fol - ly soar, and all our self - wrought
of our ha - tred spreads, and e - vils wrought by
knowl - edge, and our sin, we come to you in
fol - low in your way. Speak to our souls the

make us wise; grant us your power to make us strong.
mis - er - ies have made us trust our - selves the more.
hu - man pride re - coil on un - re - pen - tant heads.
pen - i - tence; in us the work of grace be - gin.
quick - ening Word, and turn our dark - ness in - to day.

Text: Donald W. Hughes (1911–1967), alt. © J. Donald P. Hughes.
Music: Jeremiah Clarke (1673?–1707).

LM
UFFINGHAM

# 175  Forty Days and Forty Nights

1 For - ty days and for - ty nights you were fas - ting
2 burn - ing heat through - out the day, bit - ter cold when
3 Shall not we your tri - als share, learn your dis - ci -
4 So if Sa - tan, press - ing hard, soul and bo - dy
5 Sav - iour, may we hear your voice— keep us con - stant

in the wild, for - ty days and for - ty nights
light had fled, prowl - ing beasts a - round your way,
pline of will, and with you by fast and prayer
would des - troy, Christ who con - quered, be our guard;
at your side; and with you we shall re - joice

tempt - ed, and yet un - de - filed:
stones your pil - low, earth your bed.
wres - tle with the powers of hell?
give to us the vic - tor's joy.
at the e - ter - nal Eas - ter - tide.

Text: George Hunt Smyttan (1822–1870), rev. *Hymns for Today's Church*.
© 1982 Hope Publishing Co.
Music: Melody attrib. Martin Herbst (1654–1681); harm. William Henry Monk (1823–1889).

77 77
HEINLEIN (AUS DER TIEFE)

# By the Holy Spirit Sent  176

1 By the Ho - ly Spir - it sent, Je - sus
2 With a word he could have made bread from
3 When the dev - il at his side tried to
4 Calm - ly he re - fused to win by a
5 Since our lov - ing Sav - iour thus kept a

to the des - ert went, that he might his
stones a - round him laid; yet till for - ty
make him sin through pride, he would give no
sin - gle act of sin of the whole wide
sa - cred Lent for us, we, through him, can

chil - dren show how sin's power to o - ver - throw.
days were past, still he kept a ho - ly fast.
out - ward sign that he was God's son di - vine.
world the throne; he would wor - ship God a - lone.
con - quer sin and a roy - al vic - tory win.

Text: Gertrude Hollis (1863–1943). © *Estate of Gertrude Hollis.*
Music: Melody English trad.

77 77
LEW TRENCHARD

# 179 Tree of Life and Awesome Mystery

1 Tree of Life and awe-some mys-tery, in your
2 Seed that dies to rise in glo-ry, may we
3 We re-mem-ber truth once spo-ken, love passed
4 Gen-tle Je-sus, might-y Spir-it, come in-
5 Christ, you lead and we shall fol-low, stum-bling

death we are re-born; though you die in all of
see our-selves in you; if we learn to live your
on through act and word; ev-ery per-son lost and
flame our hearts a-new. We may all your joy in-
though our steps may be; one with you in joy and

his-to-ry, still you rise with ev-ery morn, still you
sto-ry we may die to rise a-new, we may
bro-ken wears the bod-y of our Lord, wears the
her-it if we bear the cross with you, if we
sor-row, we the riv-er, you the sea, we the

Text and music: Marty Haugen (1950– ). © 1984 G.I.A. Publications, Inc.

87 87 with repeat
THOMAS

rise with ev - ery morn.
die to rise a - new.
bod - y of our Lord.
bear the cross with you.
riv - er, you the sea.

*Last time*

Bb    Am    Dm    Am7    Dm    Am7    Dm    Am7    Dm

*Last time*

*One of the following may be sung as a final stanza at the appropriate time:*

*General*

6a  Light of life beyond conceiving, mighty Spirit of our Lord;
    give new strength to our believing, give us faith to live your word,
    give us faith to live your word.

*1st Sunday*

6b  From the dawning of creation you have loved us as your own;
    stay with us through all temptation, make us turn to you alone,
    make us turn to you alone.

*2nd Sunday*

6c  In our call to be a blessing, may we be a blessing true;
    may we live and die confessing Christ as Lord of all we do,
    Christ as Lord of all we do.

*3rd Sunday*

6d  Living Water of salvation, be the fountain of each soul;
    springing up in new creation, flow in us and make us whole,
    flow in us and make us whole.

*4th Sunday*

6e  Give us eyes to see you clearly; make us children of your light.
    Give us hearts to live more nearly as your gospel shining bright,
    as your gospel shining bright.

*5th Sunday*

6f  God of all our fear and sorrow, God who lives beyond our death,
    hold us close through each tomorrow, love as near as every breath,
    love as near as every breath.

# 184 My Song Is Love Unknown

1 My song is love un-known, my Sav-iour's love to me;
2 He came from his blest throne sal-va-tion to be-stow;
3 Some-times they strew his way, and his sweet prais-es sing,
4 Why, what has my Lord done? What makes this rage and spite?

love to the love-less shown, that they might love-ly be.
but all made strange, and none the longed-for Christ would know:
re-sound-ing all the day ho-san-nas to their King;
He made the lame to run, he gave the blind their sight.

O who am I, that for my sake my Lord should
but O my friend, my friend in-deed, who at my
then "Cru-ci-fy!" is all their breath, and for his
Sweet in-ju-ries! Yet they at these them-selves dis-

take frail flesh, and die?
need his life did spend!
death they thirst and cry.
please, and 'gainst him rise.

5 They rise and needs will have
my dear Lord made away;
a murderer they save,
the Prince of life they slay.
Yet cheerful he to suffering goes,
that he his foes from thence might free.

6 Here might I stay and sing,
no story so divine;
never was love, dear King,
never was grief like thine!
This is my friend, in whose sweet praise
I all my days could gladly spend.

Text: Samuel Crossman (1624?–1683), alt.
Music: John N. Ireland (1879–1962). © *The John Ireland Trust.*

66 66 44 44
LOVE UNKNOWN

# Sing, My Tongue, the Glorious Battle 185

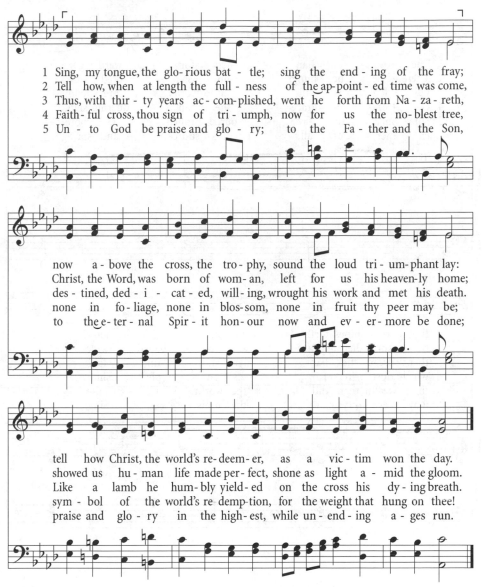

1 Sing, my tongue, the glo-rious bat-tle; sing the end-ing of the fray;
2 Tell how, when at length the full-ness of the ap-point-ed time was come,
3 Thus, with thir-ty years ac-com-plished, went he forth from Na-za-reth,
4 Faith-ful cross, thou sign of tri-umph, now for us the no-blest tree,
5 Un-to God be praise and glo-ry; to the Fa-ther and the Son,

now a-bove the cross, the tro-phy, sound the loud tri-um-phant lay:
Christ, the Word, was born of wom-an, left for us his heaven-ly home;
des-tined, ded-i-cat-ed, will-ing, wrought his work and met his death.
none in fo-liage, none in blos-som, none in fruit thy peer may be;
to the e-ter-nal Spir-it hon-our now and ev-er-more be done;

tell how Christ, the world's re-deem-er, as a vic-tim won the day.
showed us hu-man life made per-fect, shone as light a-mid the gloom.
Like a lamb he hum-bly yield-ed on the cross his dy-ing breath.
sym-bol of the world's re-demp-tion, for the weight that hung on thee!
praise and glo-ry in the high-est, while un-end-ing a-ges run.

Text: Venantius Fortunatus (540?–600?); tr. Percy Dearmer (1867–1936), alt. *Tr. © Oxford University Press.*   87 87 87
Music: Kaspar Ett (1788–1847), *Cantica Sacra*, Munich, 1840.   ORIEL
*Lower key 299; Alt. tune* PANGE LINGUA *50*

# 186  The Royal Banners Forward Go

1 The roy - al ban - ners for - ward go;
2 There while he hung, his sa - cred side
3 Ful - filled is all his words fore - told;
4 O tree of grace, the con - quering sign,
5 For once thy fav - oured branch - es bore
6 Fa - ther of all, life's source and spring,

the cross shines forth in mys - tic glow,
by sol - dier's spear was o - pened wide
then spread the ban - ners, and un - fold
which dost in roy - al pur - ple shine,
the wealth that did the world re - store,
may ev - ery soul thy prais - es sing;

Text: Venantius Fortunatus (540?–600?); tr. John Mason Neale (1818–1866)
and Percy Dearmer (1867–1936), alt. *Tr. © Oxford University Press.*
Music: Plainsong, Mode 1 (12th cent.); harm. Healey Willan (1880–1968). *Harm. © Estate of Healey Willan.*

LM
VEXILLA REGIS

where he, the Life, did death en - dure,
to cleanse us in the pre - cious flood
love's crown - ing power, that all may see
gone is thy shame; for, lo, each bough
the price - less trea - sure, free - ly spent
may those o - bey the rule of heaven,

and by that death did life pro - cure.
of wa - ter min - gled with his blood.
he reigns and tri - umphs from the tree.
pro - claims the prince of glo - ry now.
to pay for our en - fran - chise - ment.
for whom the per - fect life was given.

# 187  As Royal Banners Are Unfurled

┌ *Unison*

1 As roy-al ban-ners are un-furled, the cross dis-
2 Al-read-y deep-ly wound-ed: see his side now
3 See ev-ery-thing the pro-phets wrote ful-filled in
4 This tree, a-blaze with roy-al light and with the

plays its mys-ter-y: the Mak-er of our
riv-en by a spear, and all our sins are
its to-tal-i-ty, and tell the na-tions
blood-red robe it wears, is hal-lowed and em-

flesh, in flesh, im-paled and hang-ing help-less-ly.
swept a-way by blood and wa-ter flow-ing here.
of the world our God is reign-ing from the tree.
bel-lished by the weight of ho-li-ness it bears.

5 Stretched like a balance here, his arms
have gauged the price of wickedness;
but, hanging here, his love outweighs
hell's unforgiving bitterness.

6 The Saviour, victim, sacrifice,
is, through his dying, glorified;
his life is overcome by death
and leaps up, sweeping death aside.

7 We hail the cross, faith's one true hope:
God's passion set in time and space,
by which our guilt is blotted out,
engulfed in such stupendous grace. Amen.

A - men.

Text: Venantius Fortunatus (540?–600?), tr. Alan Gaunt (1935– ).
Tr. © 1991 Stainer & Bell Ltd. All rights reserved. Used by permission of Hope Publishing Co.
Music: Percy Carter Buck (1871–1947). © Oxford University Press.

LM
GONFALON ROYAL

# Sunset to Sunrise Changes Now   188

1 Sun - set   to   sun - rise   chang - es   now,   for
2 Even   though the   sun   with - holds   its   light,   lo!
3 Here   in   o'er - whelm - ing   fi - nal   strife   the

God doth make   the   world a - new;   on   the Re - deem - er's
a   more heaven-ly   lamp shines here,   and   from the cross   on
Lord   of   life   hath   vic - to - ry,   and   sin   is   slain,   and

thorn- crowned brow   the   won- ders of   that   dawn we   view.
Cal - vary's height gleams   of   e - ter - ni - ty   ap - pear.
death brings   life,   and   earth in - her - its   heav- en's   key.

Text: Clement of Alexandria (170?–220?); para. Howard Chandler Robbins (1876–1952), alt.
Music: Attrib. Elkanah Kelsay Dare (1782–1826).

LM
KEDRON

# 189 Alone Thou Goest Forth, O Lord

1 A - lone thou go - est forth, O Lord, in
2 Our sins, not thine, thou bear - est, Lord; make
3 This is earth's dark - est hour, but thou dost
4 Give us com - pas - sion with thee, Lord, that,

sac - ri - fice to die: is this thy sor - row
us thy sor - row feel, till through our pi - ty
light and life re - store; then let all praise be
as we share this hour, thy cross may bring us

naught to us who pass un - heed - ing by?
and our shame, love an - swers love's ap - peal.
giv - en thee who liv - est ev - er - more.
to thy joy and res - ur - rec - tion power.

Text: Peter Abelard (1079–1142); tr. F. Bland Tucker (1895–1984). *Tr.* © *The Church Pension Fund.*
Music: William Tans'ur (1706–1783), *Compleat Melody*, 1734.

CM
BANGOR

# Go to Dark Gethsemane   190

1 Go to dark Gethsemane, ye that feel the tempter's power. Your Redeemer's conflict see; watch with him one bitter hour; turn not from his griefs away; learn of Jesus Christ to pray.

2 Follow to the judgement-hall; view the Lord of life arraigned. O the wormwood and the gall! O the grief his soul sustained! Shun not suffering, shame, or loss; learn of him to bear the cross.

3 Calvary's mournful mountain climb; there, adoring at his feet, mark that miracle of time— God's own sacrifice complete. "It is finished," hear him cry; learn of Jesus Christ to die.

Text: James Montgomery (1771–1854), alt.
Music: Johann Sebastian Bach (1685–1750).

77 77 77
NICHT SO TRAURIG
*Alt. tune* REDHEAD *No. 76 (*PETRA*)* 522

# 191 To Mock Your Reign

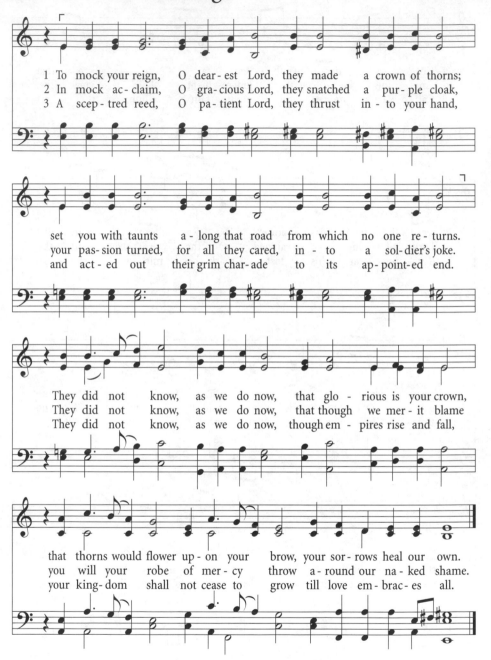

1 To mock your reign, O dear-est Lord, they made a crown of thorns;
2 In mock ac-claim, O gra-cious Lord, they snatched a pur-ple cloak,
3 A scep-tred reed, O pa-tient Lord, they thrust in-to your hand,

set you with taunts a-long that road from which no one re-turns.
your pas-sion turned, for all they cared, in-to a sol-dier's joke.
and act-ed out their grim char-ade to its ap-point-ed end.

They did not know, as we do now, that glo-rious is your crown,
They did not know, as we do now, that though we mer-it blame
They did not know, as we do now, though em-pires rise and fall,

that thorns would flower up-on your brow, your sor-rows heal our own.
you will your robe of mer-cy throw a-round our na-ked shame.
your king-dom shall not cease to grow till love em-brac-es all.

Text: Fred Pratt Green (1903– ). © 1973 Hope Publishing Co.
Music: Thomas Tallis (1505?–1585).

CMD
THE THIRD TUNE

# Were You There 192

1 Were you there when they cru-ci-fied my Lord? Were you
2 Were you there when they nailed him to the tree? Were you
3 Were you there when they pierced him in the side? Were you
4 Were you there when the sun re-fused to shine? Were you

there when they cru-ci-fied my Lord? Oh!
there when they nailed him to the tree? Oh!
there when they pierced him in the side? Oh!
there when the sun re-fused to shine? Oh!

Some-times it caus-es me to trem-ble, trem-ble,

trem-ble:

were you there when they cru-ci-fied my Lord?
were you there when they nailed him to the tree?
were you there when they pierced him in the side?
were you there when the sun re-fused to shine?

5 Were you there when they laid him in the tomb?
6 Were you there when he burst the bonds of death?

Text: African-American spiritual.
Music: Melody African-American spiritual; harm. C. Winfred Douglas (1867–1944).

Irregular
WERE YOU THERE

# 193 Calvary, Calvary

*Refrain*

Cal - va - ry, Cal - va - ry,

Cal - va - ry, Cal - va - ry, Cal - va -

ry, Cal - va - ry, sure - ly he

*Last time*

died on Cal - va - ry.

1 Ev - ery time I think a - bout Je - sus, ev - ery time I
2 Don't you hear the ham - mer ring - ing? Don't you hear the
3 Don't you hear him call - ing his Fa - ther? Don't you hear him
4 Don't you hear him say "It is fin - ished"? Don't you hear him

Text and music: African-American spiritual.

Irregular with refrain
CALVARY

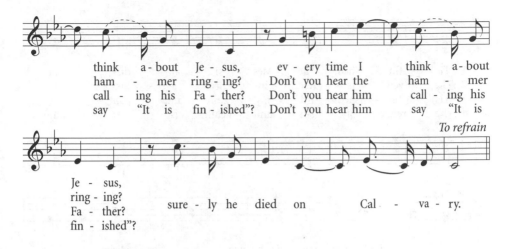

think a- bout Je - sus, ev - ery time I think a- bout
ham - mer ring - ing? Don't you hear the ham - mer
call - ing his Fa - ther? Don't you hear him call - ing his
say "It is fin - ished"? Don't you hear him say "It is

*To refrain*

Je - sus,
ring - ing?
Fa - ther?          sure - ly he died on Cal - va - ry.
fin - ished"?

5 Jesus furnished my salvation…

6 Sinner, do you love my Jesus?…

# Stay with Us 194

Stay with us, O Lord Je - sus Christ, night will soon fall. Then
*Bleib mit dei - ner Gna - de bei uns, Herr Je - su Christ. Ach,*

stay with us, O Lord Je - sus Christ, light in our dark - ness.
*bleib mit dei - ner Gna - de bei uns, du treu - er Gott.*

Text: Taizé Community (France).
Music: Jacques Berthier (1923–1994).                              STAY WITH US
*Text and music © 1991 Les Presses de Taizé. Used by permission of G.I.A. Publications, Inc., exclusive agent.*

# 195 'Tis Finished! The Messiah Dies

1 'Tis fin - ished! The Mes - si - ah dies, cut
2 The veil is rent; in Christ a - lone the
3 'Tis fin - ished! All my guilt and pain, I
4 The reign of sin and death is o'er, and

off for sins, but not his own. Ac - com - plished is the
liv - ing way to heaven is seen. The mid - dle wall is
want no sac - ri - fice be - side; for me, for me the
all may live from sin set free; Sa - tan hath lost his

sac - ri - fice; the great re - deem - ing work is done.
bro - ken down, and all the world may en - ter in.
Lamb is slain; 'tis fin - ished! I am jus - ti - fied.
mor - tal power; 'tis swal - lowed up in vic - to - ry.

Text: Charles Wesley (1707–1788).
Music: Melody Thomas Campion (1570–1619);
    adapt. and arr. Edmund Horace Fellowes (1870–1951).

LM
BABYLON'S STREAMS

# Ah, Holy Jesus, How Hast Thou Offended  196

1 Ah, ho-ly Je-sus, how hast thou of-fend-ed, that we to
2 Who was the guilt-y? Who brought this up-on thee? A-las, my
3 Lo, the good Shep-herd for the sheep is of-fered; the slave hath
4 For me, kind Je-sus, was thy in-car-na-tion, thy mor-tal
5 There-fore, kind Je-sus, since I can-not pay thee, I do a-

judge thee have in hate pre-tend-ed? By foes de-rid-ed,
trea-son, Je-sus, hath un-done thee. 'Twas I, Lord Je-sus,
sor-row, and thy life's ob-la-tion, thy death of an-guish
sin-ned, and the Son hath suf-fered; for our a-tone-ment,
dore thee, and will ev-er pray thee, think on thy pit-y

by thine own re-ject-ed, O most af-flict-ed.
I it was de-nied thee: I cru-ci-fied thee.
while we noth-ing heed-ed, God in-ter-ced-ed.
and thy bit-ter pas-sion, for my sal-va-tion.
and thy love un-swerv-ing, not my de-serv-ing.

Text: Johann H. Heermann (1585–1647); tr. Robert Seymour Bridges (1844–1930), alt.
Tr. © Oxford University Press. Alt. with permission.
Music: Melody Johann Crüger (1598–1662); adapt. Johann Sebastian Bach (1685–1750).

11 11 11 5
HERZLIEBSTER JESU

# 197   O Dearest Lord, Thy Sacred Head

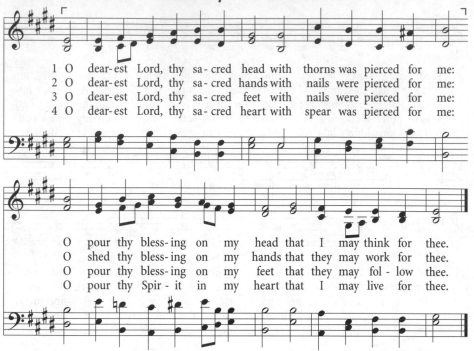

1 O dear-est Lord, thy sa-cred head with thorns was pierced for me:
2 O dear-est Lord, thy sa-cred hands with nails were pierced for me:
3 O dear-est Lord, thy sa-cred feet with nails were pierced for me:
4 O dear-est Lord, thy sa-cred heart with spear was pierced for me:

O pour thy bless-ing on my head that I may think for thee.
O shed thy bless-ing on my hands that they may work for thee.
O pour thy bless-ing on my feet that they may fol-low thee.
O pour thy Spir-it in my heart that I may live for thee.

*Alternate setting*

Text: Henry Ernest Hardy (1869–1946). © *Mowbray (an imprint of Cassell plc, London).*
Music: Melody Scottish Psalter, 1615; harm. *The English Hymnal,* 1906;
   altern. setting Thomas Tomkins (1573–1656).

CM
DUNFERMLINE
*Alt. tune DETROIT 47, 614*

# O Sacred Head, Surrounded  198

1 O sa-cred head, sur-round-ed by crown of pierc-ing thorn;
2 Your youth-ful-ness and vig-our are spent, your strength is gone,
3 Your sin-less soul's op-press-ion was all for sin-ners' gain;
4 What lan-guage shall I bor-row to thank you, dear-est friend,

O roy-al head so wound-ed, re-viled, and put to scorn,
and in your tor-tured fig-ure I see death draw-ing on:
mine, mine was the trans-gres-sion, but yours the dead-ly pain:
for this your dy-ing sor-row, your mer-cy with-out end?

death's shad-ows rise be-fore you, the glow of life de-cays,
what ag-o-ny of dy-ing, what love, to sin-ners free!
I bow my head, my Sav-iour, for I de-serve your place;
Lord, make me yours for-ev-er: your ser-vant let me be,

yet an-gel hosts a-dore you and trem-ble as they gaze!
My Lord, all grace sup-ply-ing, O turn your face on me!
O grant to me your fa-vour, and heal me by your grace.
and may I nev-er, nev-er be-tray your love for me.

Text: Latin (*Salve caput*, 13th cent.); attrib. Arnulf of Louvain (1200?–1250?);
German tr. Paul Gerhardt (1607–1676); Eng. tr. James Waddell Alexander (1804–1853)
and Henry Williams Baker (1821–1877); rev. *Hymns for Today's Church*. Rev. © 1982 Hope Publishing Co.
Music: Melody Hans Leo Hassler (1564–1612); harm. Johann Sebastian Bach (1685–1750).

76 76D
PASSION CHORALE

# 199 Who Would Ever Have Believed It

1 Who would ev-er have be-lieved it? Who could
2 Like a sap-ling in dry soil, he was
3 We de-spised him; we dis-owned him, though he
4 Yet it was the pain and tor-ment we de-

ev-er have con-ceived it? Who dared trace God's
root-ed in our pres-ence; lack-ing beau-ty,
clear-ly hurt and suf-fered: we, be-liev-ing
served which he ac-cept-ed, while we rec-koned

hand be-hind it when a ser-vant came a-mong us?
grace, and splen-dour, no one felt at-tract-ed to him.
he was worth-less, nev-er turned our eyes to-wards him.
his af-flic-tions must have come by heaven's in-struc-tion.

5 Though our sins let him be wounded,
   though our cruelty left him beaten,
   yet, through how and why he suffered,
   God revealed our hope of healing.

6 We, like sheep despite our wisdom,
   all had wandered from God's purpose;
   and our due in pain and anger
   God let fall on one among us.

7 Who would ever have believed it?
   Who could ever have conceived it?
   Who dared trace God's hand behind it
   when a servant came among us?

Text: *The Lord's Servant* (Is. 53.3–6); para. Graham Maule (1958– ).
Music: Melody Scottish trad.; arr. The Iona Community (Scotland).
*Text and arr. © 1988 WGRG The Iona Community (Scotland). Used by permission of G.I.A. Publications, Inc., exclusive agent.*

LM
AE FOND KISS

# We Sing the Praise of Him Who Died  200

1 We sing the praise of him who died, of him who
2 In - scribed up - on the cross we see in shin - ing
3 The cross— it takes our guilt a - way; it holds the
4 it makes the cow - ard spir - it brave, and nerves the
5 the balm of life, the cure of woe, the mea - sure

died up - on the cross. The sin - ner's hope let flesh de -
let - ters, "God is love." He bears our sins up - on the
faint - ing spir - it up; it cheers with hope the gloom - y
fee - ble arm for fight; it takes the ter - ror from the
and the pledge of love, the sin - ner's ref - uge here be -

ride; for this we count the world but loss.
tree; he brings us mer - cy from a - bove.
day, and sweet - ens ev - ery bit - ter cup;
grave, and gilds the bed of death with light:
low, the an - gel's theme in heaven a - bove.

Text: Thomas Kelly (1769–1855), alt.
Music: Sydney Hugo Nicholson (1875–1947).
Music © 1939 Hope Publishing Co.

LM
BOW BRICKHILL
Alt. tune DEUS TUORUM MILITUM 351, 580

# 201 People Draw Near to God in Their Distress

1 Peo - ple draw near to God in their dis - tress,
2 Peo - ple draw near when they see God's dis - tress:
3 And God draws near to peo - ple in dis - tress,

plead - ing for help and beg - ging peace and bread,
find God re - ject - ed, home - less, with - out bread,
feed - ing their souls and bod - ies with his bread;

res - cue from guilt and sick - ness, near - ly dead.
bur - dened with sin and weak - ness, near - ly dead.
Chris - tian or not, for both he's hang - ing dead,

Chris - tian or not, all come in help - less - ness.
Chris - tians reach out to meet God's wretch - ed - ness.
for - giv - ing, from the cross, their wick - ed - ness.

Text: Dietrich Bonhöffer (1906–1945); vers. Alan Gaunt (1935– ).
*Vers. © 1991 Stainer & Bell, Ltd. All rights reserved. Used by permission of Hope Publishing Co.*
Music: Alfred Morton Smith (1879–1971). © The Estate of Doris Wright Smith.

10 10 10 10
SURSUM CORDA

# There Is a Green Hill Far Away  202

1 There is a green hill far a - way, out -
2 We may not know, we can - not tell what
3 He died that we might be for - given, he
4 There was no oth - er good e - nough to
5 O dear - ly, dear - ly has he loved, and

side a ci - ty wall, where the dear Lord was
pains he had to bear; but we be - lieve it
died to make us good, that we might go at
pay the price of sin; he on - ly could un -
we must love him too, and trust in his re -

cru - ci - fied who died to save us all.
was for us he hung and suf - fered there.
last to heaven, saved by his pre - cious blood.
lock the gate of heaven, and let us in.
deem - ing blood, and try his works to do.

Text: Cecil Frances Alexander (1818–1895).
Music: William Horsley (1774–1858).

CM
HORSLEY

## 203 Jesus Christ Is Risen Today

*Descant*

3 But the pains which he en-dured, al - le-lu - ia!

1 Je - sus Christ is risen to-day, al - le-lu - ia!
2 Hymns of praise then let us sing, al - le-lu - ia!
3 But the pains which he en-dured, al - le-lu - ia!

our sal - va - tion have pro - cured; al - le-lu - ia!

our tri - um-phant ho - ly day, al - le-lu - ia!
un - to Christ our heaven-ly King, al - le-lu - ia!
our sal - va - tion have pro - cured; al - le-lu - ia!

now a - bove the sky he's king, al - le-lu - ia!

who did once, up - on the cross, al - le-lu - ia!
who en - dured the cross and grave, al - le-lu - ia!
now a - bove the sky he's king, al - le-lu - ia!

Text: *Lyra Davidica*, 1708, alt.
Music: *Lyra Davidica*, 1708; desc. Derek Holman (1931– ) ©.

77 77 with Alleluias
EASTER HYMN

where the an - gels ev - er sing. Al - le - lu - ia!

suf - fer to re - deem our loss. Al - le - lu - ia!
sin - ners to re - deem and save. Al - le - lu - ia!
where the an - gels ev - er sing. Al - le - lu - ia!

*Nisga'a text*

gi´nitkwt miinim ahl sa guun
hlits´m wat gahl miinim
gan hisgwis gitw sim sa-loom
hlits´m wat gahl miinim
hlihax gwit lax ga Jaak
hlits´m wat gahl miinim
hax gwit dimwila ksi git giigum
hlits´m wat gahl miinim.

aamhl dim limum ahl limim amaadalk´askw
hlits´m wat gahl miinim
ha nii t´aam an hlg´omskw tsim lax hagi
hlits´m wat gahl miinim
galksi´ak hlkw ahl wo k´eskw
hlits´m wat gahl miinim
dim wila ksi git haditax gwit
hlits´m wat gahl miinim.

ganum k´askw gal ksi akhl gwit
hlits´m wat gahl miinim
ksi di akhlgwit dim gan lit moot gum
hlits´m wat gahl miinim
hlaa wii t´ishl sim´oogit ts´m laxha
hlits´m wat gahl miinim
wil gani li mx hligadihl lax´ha
hlits´m wat gahl miinim.

Tr.: George Nelson, Sr. (1940– ) ©.

## 204 Truly, He Comes to Us

1 Tru - ly, he comes to us: dark - ness is end - ed; now night is
2 Night has made way for the great pro - cla - ma - tion; morn - ing has
3 Stripped of the grave- clothes, the bo - dy now glor - ious ris - es im -
4 Weep - ing is ov - er, and death is de - feat - ed; life is re -

ov - er, his light is as - cend - ed: ul - ti - mate sun - rise, that
bro - ken, with songs of e - la - tion. Christ comes in light from the
mor - tal, for - ev - er vic - to - rious; comes to ful - fill all the
cov - ered and joy is com - plet - ed. Guards, at the sep - ul - chre,

floods all cre - a - tion, bring - ing his se - cret from death's des - o - la - tion.
depths of his pris - on, death is a - ban - doned, and Je - sus is ris - en.
pro - phets have spo - ken; pro - mise of life that will nev - er be bro - ken.
scat - ter be - fore him; Je - sus is ris - en, and an - gels a - dore him.

5 Highest, most holy, once lost and forsaken:
   now, from the sleep of the dead you awaken;
   angels appear at the tomb with the story:
   "He is not here, but is risen in glory."

6 Give God the glory and glad adoration,
   from whom and through whom and in whom, creation
   looks for the joy which, in Christ, we inherit:
   praising the Father, the Son, and the Spirit!

Text: Peter Abelard (1079–1142); tr. Alan Gaunt (1935– ).
*Tr. © 1991 Stainer & Bell Ltd. All rights reserved. Used by permission of Hope Publishing Co.*
Music: Melody *Antiphoner*, Paris, 1681; adapt. *Hymnal Noted*, London, 1854.

11 11 11 11
O QUANTA QUALIA
*Lower key 274*

# The Day of Resurrection 205

1 The day of res-ur-rec-tion! Earth, tell it out a-broad,
2 Our hearts be pure from e-vil, that we may see a-right
3 Now let the heavens be joy-ful; let earth her song be-gin;

the pass-o-ver of glad-ness, the pass-o-ver of God!
the Lord in rays e-ter-nal of res-ur-rec-tion light,
the round world keep high tri-umph, and all that is there-in.

From death to life e-ter-nal, from earth un-to the sky,
and, lis-tening to his ac-cents, may hear so calm and plain
Let all things seen and un-seen their notes of glad-ness blend,

our Christ hath brought us o-ver with hymns of vic-to-ry.
his own "All hail!" and, hear-ing, may raise the vic-tor strain.
for Christ the Lord is ris-en, our joy that hath no end.

Text: John of Damascus (696?–754?); tr. John Mason Neale (1818–1866).
Music: Melody *Gesangbuch*, Württemburg, 1784.

76 76D
ELLACOMBE

# 207 At the Lamb's High Feast We Sing

1 At the Lamb's high feast we sing praise to our vic-
to-rious King, who hath washed us in the tide flow-ing
from his pierc-ed side; praise we him, whose love di-vine
gives his sa-cred blood for wine, gives his bod-y

2 Where the pas-chal blood is poured, death's dark an-gel
sheathes his sword; Is-rael's hosts tri-um-phant go through the
wave that drowns the foe. Praise we Christ, whose blood was shed,
pas-chal vic-tim, pas-chal bread; with sin-cer-i-

3 Might-y vic-tim from on high, hell's fierce powers be-
neath thee lie; death is bro-ken in the fight, thou hast
brought us life and light. Now no more can death ap-pal,
now no more the grave en-thral! Thou hast o-pened

4 This, our gift of Eas-ter joy, sin a-lone can
now de-stroy; from sin's power do thou set free souls new-
born, O Lord, in thee. Hymns of glo-ry and of praise,
Fa-ther, un-to thee we raise; ris-en Lord, all

Text: Latin (*Ad cenam Agni,* 1632); tr. Robert Campbell (1814–1868), alt.                77 77D
Music: Melody Jakob Hintze (1622–1702); harm. Johann Sebastian Bach (1685–1750);        SALZBURG
altern. harm. Derek Holman (1931– ) ©.

for the feast, Christ the vic - tim, Christ the priest.
ty and love, eat we man - na from a - bove.
par - a - dise, and in thee thy saints shall rise.
praise to thee, with the Spir - it, ev - er be.

*Alternate harmonization*
Unison

## 208 Thou Hallowed Chosen Morn of Praise

1 Thou hal-lowed cho-sen morn of praise, that best and great-est
2 Come, let us taste the vine's new fruit, for heaven-ly joy pre-

shin-est: fair Eas-ter, queen of all the days, of
par-ing; to-day the branch-es with the root in

sea-sons, best, di-vin-est! Christ rose from death, and
res-ur-rec-tion shar-ing: whom as true God our

we a-dore for-ev-er and for ev-er-more.
hymns a-dore for-ev-er and for ev-er-more.

Text: John of Damascus (675?–749?); tr. John Mason Neale (1818–1866), alt.
Music: Melody *Das ander Theil*, 1605;
    attrib., adapt., and harm. Johann Hermann Schein (1586–1630).

87 87 88
MACH'S MIT MIR, GOTT

# Walk Softly in Springtime 209

1 Walk soft-ly in spring-time, to hear the grass sing
2 Sing gent-ly in spring-time, and join with the birds,
3 Praise glad-ly in spring-time when earth seems to glow

its whis-per-ing car-ols to Je-sus our king;
who war-ble their mu-sic, a song with-out words,
with new life and col-our in all things that grow;

to see the new flow-ers bright col-ours dis-play;
that floats through the air and that reach-es the sky,
for all na-ture's chil-dren are hap-py to say,

to tell all the chil-dren of glad Eas-ter day.
a mes-sage of love to the Fa-ther on high.
"Re-joice, for the Sav-iour is ris-en to-day."

Text: Edna Fay Grant (1905–1981). © 1965, renewal 1993 The Hymn Society in the United States and Canada. All rights reserved. Used by permission of Hope Publishing Co.
Music: F. Alan E. Reesor (1935– ) ©.

11 11 11 11
MARCHE DOUCEMENT

## 211 Good Christians All, Rejoice and Sing

1 Good Chris-tians all, re-joice and sing! Now is the tri-umph
2 The Lord of life is risen to-day! Sing songs of praise a-
3 Praise we in songs of vic-to-ry that love, that life which
4 Your name we bless, O ris-en Lord, and sing to-day with

of our King! To all the world glad news we bring:
long his way; let all the earth re-joice and say:
can-not die, and sing with hearts up-lift-ed high:
one ac-cord the life laid down, the life re-stored:

al-le-lu-ia, al-le-lu-ia, al-le-lu-ia!

Text: Cyril Argentine Alington (1872–1955), alt. © 1958, renewal 1986 Hope Publishing Co.       888 with Alleluias
Music: Melody Melchior Vulpius (1570?–1615); harm. Ernest Campbell MacMillan       VULPIUS (GELOBT SEI GOTT)
(1893–1973). Harm © Estate of Sir Ernest Campbell MacMillan, Ross A. MacMillan, executor.

Al - le - lu - ia! Al - le - lu - ia! Al - le - lu - ia!

*Beginning only*

1 The strife is o'er, the bat - tle done;
2 Death's might - iest powers have done their worst,
3 He closed the yawn - ing gates of hell;
4 On the third morn he rose a - gain,
5 Lord, by the stripes which wound - ed thee,

now is the vic - tor's tri - umph won;
and Je - sus hath his foes dis - persed;
the bars from heaven's high por - tals fell.
glo - rious in maj - es - ty to reign.
from death's dread sting thy ser - vants free,

O let the song of praise be sung:
let shouts of praise and joy out - burst:
Let songs of praise his tri - umph tell:   al - le - lu - ia!
O let us swell the joy - ful strain:
that we may live, and sing to thee:

*Alleluias serve only as the introduction to stanza 1.*

Text: Latin (*Finita jam*, 17th cent.); tr. Francis Pott (1832–1909).
Music: Giovanni Pierluigi da Palestrina (1525–1594); adapt. William Henry Monk (1823–1889).

888 with Alleluias
VICTORY
*Alt. tune* VULPIUS 211, 298

## 213 His Battle Ended There

*Unison*

1 His bat - tle end - ed there, death was o - ver - come.
2 Dread powers of death and sin had him in their hold.
3 Dead in the grave he lay, mourned by ev - ery friend.
4 He burst the chains of sin, o - pened death's dark jail.
5 Lord, by the pains you bore in your dark - est hour,

Je - sus, a - live a - gain, wore the vic - tor's crown.
When Je - sus rose a - gain all their plans were foiled.
Those dark and fear - ful days then did reach their end.
God filled him with new life, life that could not fail.
free us from fear of death, and from all sin's power.

Clear - ly sin had failed, good - ness had pre - vailed,
Je - sus lived a - gain, tri - umphed o - ver sin,
God raised him to life, vic - tor in the strife,
Right be - fore their eyes Je - sus did a - rise,
May we with you live, to you our - selves give,

al - le - lu - ia, al - le - lu - ia; al - le - lu - ia, al - le - lu - ia.

*Best when sung unaccompanied.*

Text: African Chewa hymn; para. Tom Colvin (1925– ).
Music: Melody trad. Angoni war song; adapt. and harm. Tom Colvin (1925– ).
  *Para. and adapt. © 1976 Hope Publishing Co.*

11 11 10 8 8
NCHEU

# The Lamb's High Banquet Called to Share   214

1 The Lamb's high ban - quet called to share, ar - rayed in
2 Up - on the al - tar of the cross, his bod - y
3 Pro - tect - ed in the pas - chal night from the de -
4 Now Christ our pass - o - ver is slain, the Lamb of

gar - ments white and fair, the Red Sea past, we
hath re - deemed our loss; and, tast - ing of his
stroy - ing an - gel's might, in tri - umph went the
God with - out a stain; his flesh, the true un -

long to sing to Je - sus our tri - um - phant king.
pre - cious blood, our life is hid with him in God.
ran - somed free from Phar - aoh's cru - el tyr - an - ny.
leav - ened bread, is free - ly of - fered in our stead.

5  O all-sufficient sacrifice,
   beneath thee hell defeated lies;
   thy captive people are set free,
   and endless life restored in thee.

6  We hymn thee rising from the grave,
   from death returning, strong to save;
   thine own right hand the tyrant chains,
   and paradise for us regains.

7  All praise be thine, O risen Lord,
   from death to endless life restored;
   all praise to God the Father be
   and Holy Ghost eternally.

Text: Latin (*Ad cenam Agni*, 6th cent.); tr. John Mason Neale (1818–1866), alt.
Music: Melody *Antiphoner*, Rouen, 1728; harm. Michael Fleming (1928– ).
*Harm. © Hope Publishing Co.*

LM
ST. VENANTIUS
*Alt. setting 12*
*Alt. tune* CHURCH TRIUMPHANT 599

# 217  Christ the Lord Is Risen Again

*Descant*

6 Christ, our pas - chal lamb in - deed, all your ran - somed

1 Christ the Lord is risen a - gain; Christ has bro - ken
2 He who gave for us his life, who for us en -
3 He who bore all pain and loss com - fort - less up -
4 He who slum - bered in the grave is ex - alt - ed

peo - ple feed! Take our sins and guilt a - way;

ev - ery chain. Hear the an - gel voi - ces cry,
dured the strife, is our pas - chal lamb to - day;
on the cross lives in glo - ry now on high,
now to save; through the u - ni - verse it rings

let us sing by night and day: al - le - lu - ia, al - le - lu - ia!

sing - ing ev - er - more on high:
we too sing for joy and say:
pleads for us, and hears our cry:      al - le - lu - ia!
that the lamb is King of kings:

5 Now he bids us tell abroad
  how the lost may be restored,
  how the penitent forgiven,
  how we too may enter heaven: alleluia!

6 Christ, our paschal lamb indeed,
  all your ransomed people feed!
  Take our sins and guilt away;
  let us sing by night and day: alleluia!

Text: Michael Weisse (1488?–1534); tr. Catherine Winkworth (1827–1878), alt.          77 77 with Alleluia
Music: Melody *Hundert Arien,* appendix to *Haus-Buch,* Dresden, 1694;          WÜRTEMBURG (STRAF MICH NICHT)
adapt. and harm. William Henry Monk (1823–1889); desc. Stephen A. Crisp (1939– ) ©.

# Rejoice, Angelic Choirs, Rejoice 218

1 Re - joice, an - gel - ic choirs, re - joice! Re - joice now, all cre - a - tion! Let trum - pets loud - ly raise their voice to hail the Lord's sal - va - tion; let all Christ's ho - ly peo - ple sing the tri - umph of their might - y King in fes - tive cel - e - bra - tion!

2 O earth, ex - ult in ra - diance bright, il - lu - mined by Christ's splen - dour! Your dark - ness now is put to flight; to him due prais - es ren - der! Be glad, O church! Sing out your songs! Your tem - ples fill with shout - ing throngs to hail the glo - rious vic - tor!

3 Let all who gath - er round this flame, the sign of Christ's a - ris - ing, the death - less light of Christ ac - claim, his sav - ing mer - cy priz - ing; that all may live by faith in him who con - quered death, des - pair, and sin to make us his for - ev - er.

Text: *Rejoice, heavenly powers* (*Exsultet*, Latin, 7th cent.?); para. Joel W. Lundeen (1918–1990).
*Para.* © *1978* Lutheran Book of Worship. *Reprinted by permission of Augsburg Fortress.*
Music: Melody *Kirchengesänge*, Berlin, 1566; harm. *The English Hymnal*, 1906, alt.

87 87 887
MIT FREUDEN ZART
*Higher key 310*

# 221   Alleluia, Alleluia! Let the Holy Anthem Rise

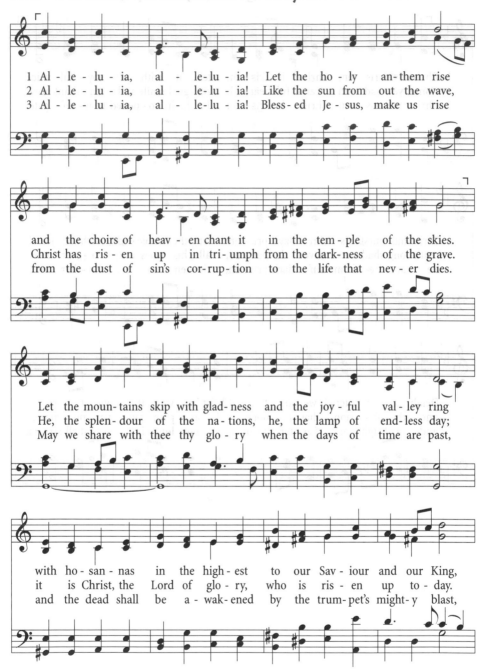

1 Al - le - lu - ia, al - le - lu - ia! Let the ho - ly an - them rise
2 Al - le - lu - ia, al - le - lu - ia! Like the sun from out the wave,
3 Al - le - lu - ia, al - le - lu - ia! Bless - ed Je - sus, make us rise

and the choirs of heav - en chant it in the tem - ple of the skies.
Christ has ris - en up in tri - umph from the dark - ness of the grave.
from the dust of sin's cor - rup - tion to the life that nev - er dies.

Let the moun - tains skip with glad - ness and the joy - ful val - ley ring
He, the splen - dour of the na - tions, he, the lamp of end - less day;
May we share with thee thy glo - ry when the days of time are past,

with ho - san - nas in the high - est to our Sav - iour and our King,
it is Christ, the Lord of glo - ry, who is ris - en up to - day.
and the dead shall be a - wak - ened by the trum - pet's might - y blast,

Text: Edward Caswall (1841–1878), alt.
Music: Richard Runciman Terry (1865–1938). © *Burns & Oates Ltd.*

87 87D with repeat
ECCLESIA

with ho - san - nas in the high - est to our Sav - iour and our King.
It is Christ, the Lord of glo - ry, who is ris - en up to - day.
and the dead shall be a - wak - ened by the trum - pet's might - y blast.

## All Shall Be Well  222

1 All shall be well! For on our Eas - ter skies
2 All shall be well! The sac - ri - fice is made,
3 All shall be well! The cross and pas - sion past,
4 All shall be well! Lift ev - ery voice on high;
5 Je - sus a - live! Re - joice and sing a - gain;

see Christ the sun of right - eous - ness a - rise.
the sin - ner freed, the price of par - don paid.
dark night is done, bright morn - ing come at last.
"Death has no more do - min - ion, but shall die."
all shall be well for ev - er - more, A - men!

Text: Timothy Dudley-Smith (1926– ). © 1984 Hope Publishing Co.
Music: First strain of SONG 46, Orlando Gibbons (1583–1625).

46 46
SONG 46

# 223 Christ Is Risen

1 Christ is ris - en! Shout ho - san - na! Cel - e - brate this
2 Christ is ris - en! Raise your spir - its from the cav - erns
3 Christ is ris - en! Earth and heav - en nev - er more shall

day of days. Christ is ris - en! Hush in won - der; all cre -
of de - spair. Walk with glad - ness in the morn - ing, see what
be the same. Break the bread of new cre - a - tion where the

a - tion is a - mazed. In the des - ert all sur - round - ing,
love can do and dare. Drink the wine of res - ur - rec - tion,
world is still in pain. Tell its grim, de - mon - ic chor - us:

see, a spread - ing tree has grown. Heal-ing leaves of grace a -
not a ser - vant, but a friend. Je - sus is our strong com -
"Christ is ris - en! Get you gone!" God the First and Last is

Text: Brian Wren (1936– ). © 1986 Hope Publishing Co.
Music: Melody Polish trad.; harm. David Hugh Jones (1900–1983).
Harm. © 1955, 1983 John Ribble. Used by permission of Westminister/John Knox Press.

87 87D
POLISH CAROL (W ZLOBIE LEZY)
*Lower key 125*

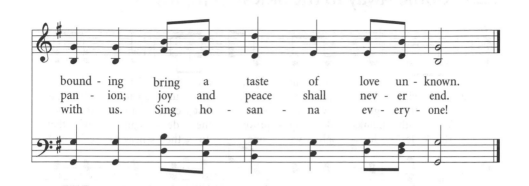

bound - ing    bring    a    taste    of    love    un - known.
pan - ion;    joy    and    peace    shall    nev - er    end.
with    us.    Sing    ho - san - na    ev - ery - one!

Easter  CHRISTIAN YEAR

## Awake, Arise, Lift Up Your Voice 224

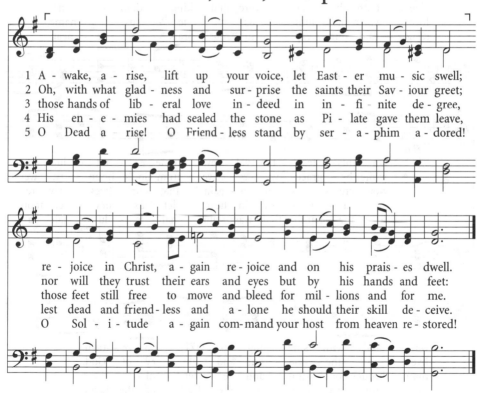

1 A - wake, a - rise,    lift    up    your voice,    let East - er    mu - sic    swell;
2 Oh, with what    glad - ness    and    sur - prise    the saints their    Sav - iour greet;
3 those hands of    lib - eral    love    in - deed    in    in - fi - nite    de - gree,
4 His    en - e - mies    had sealed    the    stone    as    Pi - late gave them leave,
5 O    Dead a - rise!    O    Friend - less stand    by    ser - a - phim    a - dored!

re - joice    in Christ,    a - gain    re - joice and    on    his    prais - es    dwell.
nor    will    they trust    their ears    and eyes    but    by    his hands and feet:
those feet    still    free    to move    and bleed    for    mil - lions and    for me.
lest    dead    and friend - less    and    a - lone    he should their    skill    de - ceive.
O    Sol - i - tude    a - gain    com - mand your host    from heaven re - stored!

Text: Christopher Smart (1722–1771), alt.
Music: Thomas Haweis (1734–1820); adapt. Samuel Webbe the younger (1770?–1843).

CM
RICHMOND
*Lower key 306*

# 227 Israel Went Out from Egypt

*Unison*

1 Is - ra - el went out from E - gypt, trem - ble at the pres - ence of God; sanc - tu - ar - y found in Ju - dah, trem - ble at the pres - ence of God. Great seas saw them come and ran a - way in fright,

2 Moun - tains skipped just like scared rams, so trem - ble at the pres - ence of God. Hills were bound - ing like young lambs, yes, trem - ble at the pres - ence of God. Tell us, great roar - ing sea, why do you run a - way?

3 Trem - ble, O you earth and sky, yes, trem - ble at the pres - ence of God. God is strong, how great and high, so trem - ble at the pres - ence of God, who has brought cool - ing rains when days grew hot - ter,

✖ =*stomp and clap*

*The last 2 measures may serve as an interlude between stanzas.*

Text: Ps. 114; para. Paul W. Quinlan (1938– ), alt. ©.
Music: Melody Paul W. Quinlan (1938– ) ©; acc. Patrick Wedd (1948– ) ©.

Irregular
ISRAEL WENT OUT FROM EGYPT

## 228  Alleluia! O Sons and Daughters

*Unison*

Al - le - lu - ia!   Al - le - lu - ia!   Al - le - lu - ia!

*Beginning only*

1 O   sons   and   daugh - ters,   let   us   sing!   The
2 That   Eas - ter   morn,   at   break   of   day,   the
3 An   an - gel   clad   in   white   they   see,   who
4 That   night   the a - pos - tles   met   in   fear;   a -

King   of   heaven,   the   glo - rious   King,   o'er
faith - ful   wom - en   went   their   way   to
sat,   and   spoke   un - to   the   three,   "Your
midst   them   came   their   Lord   most   dear,   and

death   to - day   rose   tri - umph - ing.
seek   the   tomb   where   Je - sus   lay.   Al - le - lu - ia!
Lord   goes   on   to   Gal - i - lee."
said,   "My   peace   be   on   all   here."

*Alleluias serve only as the introduction to stanza 1.*

Text: Latin; attrib. Jean Tisserand (15th cent.); tr. John Mason Neale (1818–1866).
Music: Melody *Airs sur les hymnes sacrez, odes et noëls*, Paris, 1623;
   harm. Edmund W. Goldsmith (1860–1934). Harm. © Estate of Edmund W. Goldsmith.

888 with Alleluias
O FILII ET FILIAE
*Alt. setting 457*

5 When Thomas first the tidings heard,
  how they had seen the risen Lord,
  he doubted the disciples' word.
  Alleluia!

6 "My piercèd side, O Thomas, see;
  behold my hands, my feet," said he;
  "not faithless, but believing be."
  Alleluia!

7 No longer Thomas then denied;
  he saw the feet, the hands, the side;
  "Thou art my Lord and God," he cried.
  Alleluia!

8 How blest are they who have not seen,
  and yet whose faith has constant been,
  for they eternal life shall win.
  Alleluia!

9 On this most holy day of days,
  to God your hearts and voices raise
  in laud and jubilee and praise.
  Alleluia!

*May be sung as stanzas 1, 2, 3, 4, 9 or stanzas 1, 4, 5, 6, 7, 8, 9.*

# 231 That Eastertide with Joy Was Bright

*Unison*

1 That Eas-ter-tide with joy was bright; the sun shone out
2 He bade them see his hands, his side, where yet the glo-
3 From ev-ery weap-on death can wield thine own re-deemed
4 Je-sus, the king of gen-tle-ness, do thou thy-self

*Harmony*

with fair-er light,
rious wounds a-bide;   al-le-lu-ia, al-le-lu-ia!
for-ev-er shield:
our hearts pos-sess,

*Unison*

when, to their long-ing eyes re-stored, the a-pos-tles saw
the to-kens true which made it plain their Lord in-deed
O Lord of all, with us a-bide in this our joy-
that we may give thee all our days the tri-bute of

*Harmony*

their ris-en Lord.
was risen a-gain.   Al-le-lu-ia, al-le-lu-ia,
ful Eas-ter-tide.
our grate-ful praise.

Text: Latin (*Aurora lucis rutilat*, part 3, 5th cent.?); tr. John Mason Neale (1818–1866), alt.
Music: Melody *Geistliche Kirchengesänge*, Köln, 1623; adapt. Ralph Vaughan
Williams (1872–1958), © Oxford University Press; harm. Derek Holman (1931– ) ©.

LM with Alleluias
LASST UNS ERFREUEN
*Higher key 320, 344; alt. setting 355*

al - le - lu - ia, al - le - lu - ia, al - le - lu - ia!

## Jesus Is Risen from the Grave  232

*Unison*

1 Je - sus is ris - en from the grave, Je - sus is ris - en
2 Je - sus was seen by Ma - ry, Je - sus was seen by
3 Pe - ter will soon be smil - ing, Pe - ter will soon be
4 Thom - as will stop his doubt - ing, Thom - as will stop his

from the grave, Je - sus is ris - en from the grave,
Ma - ry, Je - sus was seen by Ma - ry,
smil - ing, Pe - ter will soon be smil - ing,
doubt - ing, Thom - as will stop his doubt - ing,

al - le - lu - ia.

5 Jesus will meet his people…

6 Jesus is here in bread and wine…

7 Jesus will live forever…

Irregular with Alleluia
CHILDER

## 233 He Rose

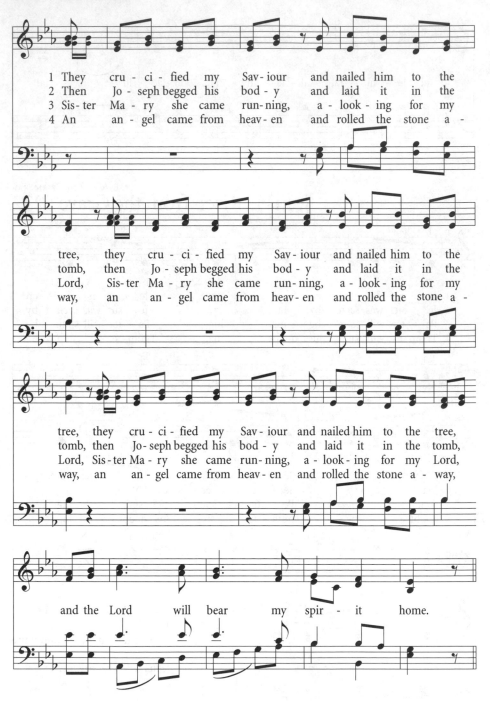

1 They cru-ci-fied my Sav-iour and nailed him to the
2 Then Jo-seph begged his bod-y and laid it in the
3 Sis-ter Ma-ry she came run-ning, a-look-ing for my
4 An an-gel came from heav-en and rolled the stone a-

tree, they cru-ci-fied my Sav-iour and nailed him to the
tomb, then Jo-seph begged his bod-y and laid it in the
Lord, Sis-ter Ma-ry she came run-ning, a-look-ing for my
way, an an-gel came from heav-en and rolled the stone a-

tree, they cru-ci-fied my Sav-iour and nailed him to the tree,
tomb, then Jo-seph begged his bod-y and laid it in the tomb,
Lord, Sis-ter Ma-ry she came run-ning, a-look-ing for my Lord,
way, an an-gel came from heav-en and rolled the stone a-way,

and the Lord will bear my spir-it home.

Text: African-American spiritual.
Music: African-American spiritual; adapt. and arr. William Farley Smith (1941–1997).
*Adapt. and arr. © 1989 The United Methodist Publishing House. (Administered by The Copyright Company, Nashville, TN). All rights reserved. International copyright secured. Used by permission.*

76 76 76 9 with refrain
ASCENSIUS

*Refrain*

He rose, (he rose) he rose, (he rose) he rose from the dead! He

rose, (he rose) he rose, (he rose) he rose from the dead! He

rose, (he rose) he rose, (he rose) he rose from the dead, and the

Lord will bear my spir - it home.

## 236 Apostle of the Word

1 A - pos - tle of the Word of res - ur -
rec - tion grace, her ears that voice had heard;
her eyes had seen his face, whose ris - en power with -
in her heart bade grief de - part one shin - ing hour.

2 Now in her life was born a new and
glo - rious faith, when on that Eas - ter morn
the van - quish - er of death but spoke her name and
found in her a mes - sen - ger with heart a - flame.

3 For doubt of wom - an's tale, they all but
failed to hear. O God, in us pre - vail
to make your Gos - pel clear, that nev - er may our
hearts re - fuse, but ev - er choose your liv - ing way.

Text: Rosemary Anne Benwell, SSJD (1915– ). © *The Sisterhood of St. John the Divine.*
Music: George Frideric Handel (1685–1759).

66 66 88
GOPSAL

# Now the Green Blade Rises   237

1 Now the green blade ris-es from the bur-ied grain,
2 In the grave they laid him, Love by ha-tred slain,
3 Forth he came at Eas-ter, like the ris-en grain,
4 When our hearts are win-try, griev-ing, or in pain,

wheat that in dark earth ma-ny days has lain;
think-ing that he would nev-er wake a-gain,
he that for three days in the grave had lain;
your touch can call us back to life a-gain,

love lives a-gain, that with the dead has been;
laid in the earth like grain that sleeps un-seen;
raised from the dead, my liv-ing Lord is seen;
fields of our hearts that dead and bare have been;

*Refrain*

love is come a-gain like wheat a-ris-ing green.

Text: John M. C. Crum (1872–1958), alt.
Music: Melody French (15th cent.); harm. Martin Shaw (1875–1958).
*Text and harm. © 1928 Oxford University Press.*

11 10 10 11
NOËL NOUVELET

## 238 God's Love Bursts into Bloom

1 God's love bursts in - to bloom deep in the dark's la - ment,
2 Three loy - al wom - en bring spice to a - noint their friend—
3 Christ kicks down death's grim door and lets us pris - oners out—

and fills a star - tled tomb with live - ly, gra - cious scent;
they hear a Glo - ry sing, come see, no corpse to tend!
the sick, the blind, the poor— we hear the pas - chal shout:

the stone gives way, hell's head is bruised
What fear - ful joy! Their wild sweet cry
be - cause I live, you all shall be

and dawn re - veals a grave un - used.
of hope sa - lutes the sun - rise sky.
God's guests at heaven's high feast with me.

Text: Ian Sowton (1929– ) ©.
Music: Charles Steggall (1826–1905).

66 66 88
CHRISTCHURCH
*Alt. setting 99*

# Jesus Lives! Thy Terrors Now  239

1 Je - sus lives! Thy ter - rors now can no more, O
2 Je - sus lives! Hence-forth is death but the gate of
3 Je - sus lives! For us he died; then, a - lone to
4 Je - sus lives! Our hearts know well nought from us his

death, ap - pal us. Je - sus lives! By this we know
life im - mor - tal; this shall calm our trem - bling breath
Je - sus liv - ing, pure in heart may we a - bide,
love shall sev - er; life, nor death, nor powers of hell

thou, O grave, canst not en - thral us.
when we pass its gloom - y por - tal.
glo - ry to our Sav - iour giv - ing. Al - le - lu - ia!
tear us from his keep - ing ev - er.

Text: Christian Furchtegott Gellert (1715–1769); tr. Frances Elizabeth Cox (1812–1897), alt.    78 78 with Alleluia
Music: Henry John Gauntlett (1805–1876).    ST. ALBINUS

# 240 Retell What Christ's Great Love Has Done

1 Re - tell what Christ's great love has done, how crib and
2 Re - call the cov - e - nant of grace in which you
3 Re - view the tap - es - try of saints, that can - vas
4 Re - hearse the cho - rus of the heart; let all earth's
5 Re - joice at what Christ yet will do, in - tent on

cross the vic - tory won: God's call o - beyed, temp -
free - ly find your place: with wa - ter washed, at
which the Spir - it paints: a pro - phet scorned, a
hopes and fears take part: the shouts of youth, the
mak - ing all things new: the hun - gry filled, the

ta - tions faced, the good news preached, then death em -
ta - ble fed, in Christ a - live, to self now
teach - er famed, a host un - known and un - ac -
cries of age, the pris - oners' groans, the vic - tims'
peace - ful blessed, the wound - ed healed, each heart at

Text: Jeffery Rowthorn (1934– ). © 1987 The Shadyside Presbyterian Church.
Music: Walter L. Pelz (1926– ); adapt. W. Thomas Jones (1956– ) ©.
  Melody © 1977 Hinshaw Music, Inc. Used with permission.

88 88 88
MEADVILLE

braced.      Let us who share his Eas - ter light
dead.      Then with your lives, by day and night,
claimed,      yet one and all who fought the fight
rage.      And may each voice which seeks the right
rest.      Then sing, till faith gives way to sight,

sing praise to God,    our chief de - light.
sing praise to God,    your chief de - light.
sing praise to God,    their chief de - light.
sing praise to God,    its chief de - light.
in praise of God,    our chief de - light.

# 241  Christians, to the Paschal Victim

Chris-tians, to the Pas-chal vic-tim of-fer your thank-ful prais-es!

A lamb, the sheep re-deem-ing: Christ, who on-ly is sin-
Death and life have con-tend-ed in that com-bat stu-pend-

less, rec-on-ciles a lost world to the Fath-er.
ous: the Prince of life, who died, reigns im-mor-tal.

Text: Wigbert (Wipo of Burgundy) (?–1050?); tr. *The Antiphoner and Grail*, 1880, alt.
Music: Plainsong, Mode 1; melody attrib. Wigbert (Wipo of Burgundy) (?–1050?);
  harm. Patrick Wedd (1948– ) ©.

Irregular
VICTIMAE PASCHALI LAUDES

Tell, Ma - ry, we will hear-ken, what you saw in the gar - den:
bright an - gels at - test - ing, the shroud and nap - kin rest - ing.

"The tomb of Christ, who is liv - ing; the
For Christ my hope is a - ris - en; to

glo - ry of Je - sus' res - ur - rec - tion;
Gal - i - lee he will go be - fore you."

# This Is the Feast of Victory for Our God  242

**Unison**  **Refrain**

This is the feast of vic-to-ry for our God, Al-le-

lu - ia, al-le-lu - ia, al-e-lu - ia! *Last time* lu - ia!

1 Wor - thy is Christ, the lamb who was slain, whose
2 Pow - er, rich - es, wis - dom, and strength and
3 Sing with all the peo - ple of God, and
4 Bless - ing, hon - our, glo - ry, and might be to
5 For the Lamb who was slain has be -

*To refrain*

blood set us free to be peo - ple of God.
hon - our, bless - ing and glo - ry are his.
join in the hymn of all cre - a - tion.
God and the Lamb for - ev - er. A - men.
gun his reign. Al - le - lu - ia!

Text: *Song to the Lamb* (Rev. 4.11; 5.9–10, 13); para. John W. Arthur (1922–1980).
Music: Richard Hillert (1923– ).
*Para. and music © 1978 Lutheran Book of Worship. Reprinted by permission of Augsburg Fortress.*

Irregular with refrain
FESTIVAL CANTICLE

# 243  Christ Is Atonement, the Paschal Victim

*Introduction and interlude between stanzas*

1 Christ is a - tone - ment, the Pas - chal vic - tim;
2 Christ is the great priest who sets a ta - ble,
3 Christ is com - pas - sion, with us in sor - row;
4 Christ is our free - dom, true lib - er - a - tion;

he gave his life that we might live for - ev - er.
mak - ing of bread and wine a sac - red ban - quet.
he bears our bur - dens, shares our in - most dark - ness.
in free - ing us he bids us live for oth - ers.

Text and music: Patrick Wedd (1948– ) ©.

10 11 11 10
CHRIST IS ATONEMENT

We for re - demp - tion
We for this man - na      sing in ex - al - ta - tion
We for such car - ing
We for this chal - lenge

*Refrain*

"Glo - ry to God, glo - ry to God on high." high."

*Refrain descant and alternative accompaniment*

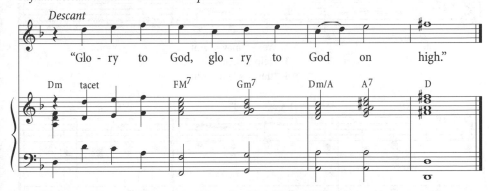

*Descant*

"Glo - ry to God, glo - ry to God on high."

# 244 We Walk by Faith, and Not by Sight

1 We walk by faith, and not by sight;
no gra-cious words we
(2 We may not) touch his hands and side, nor fol-low where he
(3 Help then, O) Lord, our un-be-lief; and may our faith a-
(4 that, when our) life of faith is done, in realms of clear-er

hear from him who spoke as none e'er spoke; but we be-lieve him
trod; but in his prom-ise we re-joice and cry, "My Lord and
bound, to call on you when you are near, and seek where you are
light we may be-hold you as you are, with full and end-less

near. 2 We may not
God!" 3 Help then, O
found: 4 that, when our
sight.

Text: Henry Alford (1810–1871), alt.
Music: Marty Haugen (1950– ). © 1984 G.I.A. Publications, Inc.

CM
SHANTI
*Alt. tune* ST. BOTOLPH 617

# O Lord Most High, Eternal King 245

1 O Lord most high, eternal king, by thee redeemed thy praise we sing. The bonds of death are burst by thee, and grace has won the victory.

2 Ascending to the sapphire throne, thou claim'st the kingdom as thine own; and angels wonder when they see how changed is our humanity.

3 Be thou our joy, O mighty Lord, as thou wilt be our great reward; let all our glory be in thee both now and through eternity.

4 O risen Christ, ascended Lord, all praise to thee let earth accord, who art, while endless ages run, with Father and with Spirit, one.

*St. 4 to Alleluia*

Alleluia!

Text: Latin (*Aeterne Rex altissime*, 10th cent.?); st. 1–3, tr. John Mason Neale (1818–1866), and others; rev. F. Bland Tucker (1895–1984), alt.; st. 4, tr. attrib. Laurence Housman (1865–1959).
*St. 1–3 rev. © 1982 The Church Pension Fund.*
Music: Percy Carter Buck (1871–1947). © Oxford University Press.

LM
GONFALON ROYAL

# 246  Hail, Thou Once Despised Jesus

*Descant*

1 Hail, thou once de - spis - ed Je - sus! Hail, thou Gal - i -
2 Pas - chal Lamb, by God ap - point - ed, all our sins on
3 Je - sus, hail! En - throned in glo - ry, there for - ev - er

All the heaven - ly host seat -

le - an King! Thou didst suf - fer to re - lease us;
thee were laid; by al - might - y love a - noint - ed,
to a - bide, all the heaven - ly host a - dore thee,

- ed at thy Fa - ther's side. Wor - ship, hon - our,

thou didst free sal - va - tion bring. Hail, thou u - ni -
thou hast full a - tone - ment made. All thy peo - ple
seat - ed at thy Fa - ther's side. Wor - ship, hon - our,

Text: John Bakewell (1721–1819), alt.
Music: Melody Dutch trad.; arr. Julius Röntgen (1855–1932); desc. Kenneth Hull (1952– ) ©.

87 87D
IN BABILONE
*Alt. tune* EBENEZER *369, 587*

power,  and  bless - ing  thou  art  wor - thy

ver - sal  Sav - iour!  Thou  hast  borne  our
are  for - giv - en  through  the  vir - tue
power,  and  bless - ing  thou  art  wor - thy

to  re - ceive;  loud - est  prais - es, with - out ceas - ing,

sin  and  shame;  by  thy  mer - its  we  find  fa - vour;
of  thy  blood;  o - pened  is  the  gate  of  heav - en;
to  re - ceive;  loud - est  prais - es,  with - out  ceas - ing,

meet  it  is  for  us  to  give.

life  is  giv - en  through  thy  name.
peace  is  made  'twixt  us  and  God.
meet  it  is  for  us  to  give.

# 247 Hail the Day That Sees Him Rise

1 Hail the day that sees him rise,
2 There for him high tri-umph waits;
3 High-est heaven its Lord re-ceives,
4 See! He lifts his hands a-bove,

al - le - lu - ia!

to his throne a-bove the skies;
lift your heads, e-ter-nal gates;
yet he loves the earth he leaves;
See! He shows the prints of love;

al - le - lu - ia!

Christ, the Lamb for sin-ners given,
he hath con-quered death and sin;
though re-turn-ing to his throne,
Hark! His gra-cious lips be-stow

al - le - lu - ia!

en-ters now the high-est heaven!
take the King of glo-ry in.
still he calls the world his own.
bless-ings on his church be-low.

Al - le - lu - ia!

Text: Charles Wesley (1707–1788), alt.
Music: William Henry Monk (1823–1889).

77 77 with Alleluias
ASCENSION

5 Still for us he intercedes; alleluia!
  his prevailing death he pleads, alleluia!
  near himself prepares our place, alleluia!
  he the first-fruits of our race. Alleluia!

6 Lord, though parted from our sight, alleluia!
  far above the starry height, alleluia!
  grant our hearts may thither rise, alleluia!
  seeking thee above the skies. Alleluia!

Ascension  CHRISTIAN YEAR

## And Have the Bright Immensities 248

1 And have the bright im - men - si - ties re - ceived our ris - en Lord,
2 The heaven that hides Christ from our sight knows nei - ther near nor far;

where light-years frame the Ple - ia - des and point O - ri - on's sword?
an al - tar can - dle sheds its light as sure - ly as a star.

Do flam-ing suns his foot-steps trace through cor - ri - dors sub - lime,
And where his lov-ing peo - ple meet to share the gift di - vine,

the Lord of in - ter - stel - lar space and con - quer - or of time?
there stands he with un - hur - rying feet; there heaven - ly splen - dours shine.

Text: Howard Chandler Robbins (1876–1952), alt. © *Morehouse Publishing.*
Music: John Day (1522–1584), *Psalmes*, 1562.

CMD
OLD 137TH
*Alt. tune* HURRLE 335

# 249 Wind Who Makes All Winds That Blow

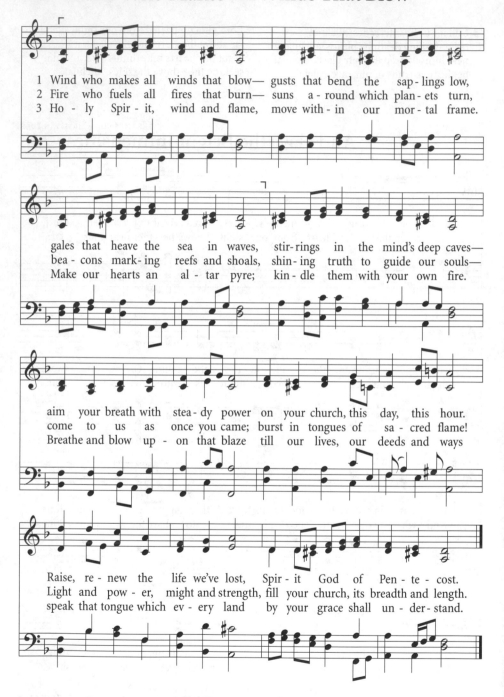

1 Wind who makes all winds that blow— gusts that bend the sap-lings low,
2 Fire who fuels all fires that burn— suns a-round which plan-ets turn,
3 Ho - ly Spir - it, wind and flame, move with-in our mor-tal frame.

gales that heave the sea in waves, stir-rings in the mind's deep caves—
bea - cons mark-ing reefs and shoals, shin-ing truth to guide our souls—
Make our hearts an al - tar pyre; kin - dle them with your own fire.

aim your breath with stea-dy power on your church, this day, this hour.
come to us as once you came; burst in tongues of sa - cred flame!
Breathe and blow up - on that blaze till our lives, our deeds and ways

Raise, re - new the life we've lost, Spir - it God of Pen - te - cost.
Light and pow - er, might and strength, fill your church, its breadth and length.
speak that tongue which ev - ery land by your grace shall un - der-stand.

Text: Thomas H. Troeger (1945– ). © 1983 Oxford University Press, Inc.
Music: Joseph Parry (1841–1903).

77 77D
ABERYSTWYTH
*Higher key 250*

# Soaring Spirit, Set Us Free  250

1 Soar-ing Spir - it,   set us free   from the tyr - an - ny of fear;
2 Un - seen mem - ber   of the dance   that u - nites the Trin - i - ty,

life of glo - rious lib - er - ty,   let your prom - ised power ap - pear:
let the grace your pres - ence grants   twine us   in like mys - ter - y.

drown the noise of   Ba - bel's tongues   in   the mur - mur   of the dove;
Breath of God, our   lives in - spire   till   our hope and   faith in - crease;

burn a - way our   wast-ing wrongs   with the heal - ing   fire of love.
speak through us with tongues of fire;   send us forth to spread God's peace.

Text: Carl P. Daw, Jr. (1944– ). © 1990 Hope Publishing Co.
Music: Joseph Parry (1841–1903).

77 77D
ABERYSTWYTH
*Lower key 249, 533*

# 251 Come, Ever Blessed Spirit, Come

1 Come, ev - er bless - ed Spir - it, come, and make thy
2 En - rich that tem - ple's ho - ly shrine with seven - fold
3 O Trin - i - ty in Un - i - ty, one on - ly
4 O grant us so to use thy grace, that we may

ser - vants' hearts thy home; may each a liv - ing tem - ple
gifts of grace di - vine: with wis - dom, light, and knowl - edge
God and per - sons three, in whom, through whom, by whom we
see thy glo - rious face, and ev - er with the heaven - ly

be, hal - lowed for - ev - er, Lord, to thee.
bless, strength, coun - sel, fear, and god - li - ness.
live, to thee we praise and glo - ry give.
host praise Fa - ther, Son, and Ho - ly Ghost.

Text: Christopher Wordsworth (1807–1885).
Music: *The Sacred Harp*, Mason, 1844; arr. Jonathan McNair (1959– ). *Arr. © 1993 The Pilgrim Press.*

LM
DISTRESS
*Alt. tune WAREHAM 40, 353*

# Spirit, Come, Dispel Our Sadness  252

1 Spir - it, come, dis - pel our sad - ness; pierce the clouds of na - ture's night.
2 Au - thor of the new cre - a - tion, come, a - noint us with your power.

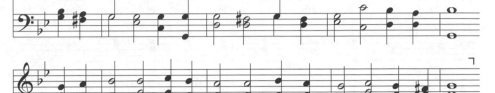

Come, O Source of joy and glad - ness, breathe your life, and spread your light.
Make our hearts your hab - i - ta - tion; with your grace our spir - its shower.

From the height which knows no mea - sure, as a gra - cious shower de - scend,
Hear, O hear our sup - pli - ca - tion, bless - ed Spir - it, God of peace!

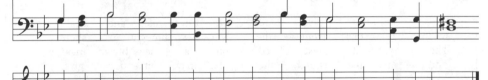

bring - ing down the rich - est trea - sure we can wish, or God can send.
Rest up - on this con - gre - ga - tion with the full - ness of your grace.

Text: Paul Gerhardt (1607–1676); tr. John C. Jacobi (1670–1750), alt.
Music: *Geistliche Volkslieder*, 1858.

87 87D
O MEIN JESU, ICH MUSS STERBEN

# 253  O Glorious Day

1 O glo-rious day when God's love o-ver-flowed
2 More glo-rious still that day of storm and flame
3 Most won-der-ful of all that ho-ly dawn
4 Christ rose from death, vic-to-rious o-ver sin;

and all its beau-ty on the earth be-stowed;
when God on Si-nai's mount to Mo-ses came;
in which the Sav-iour of the world was born!
the as-cend-ed Lord now reigns, the world to win;

the Spir-it gave all crea-tures life and health
when Is-rael, from the wa-ters brought a-shore,
The Spir-it rest-ed on a He-brew maid
and on the church that it may wit-ness give,

Text: J. R. Peacey (1896–1971). © 1991 Hope Publishing Co.
Music: John Wainwright (1723–1768).

10 10 10 10 10 10
YORKSHIRE

and on them breathed the life of God's own self.
re - ceived its call - ing and God's ho - ly law.
and God in hu - man form came to our aid.
God's love was poured, that through it all might live.

In all cre - a - tion, in each tin - y flower,
For on that day of God, the great I AM,
Then, Ho - ly Spir - it, your great love ex - celled
On this fresh Pen - te - cost, life - giv - ing Lord,

in ev - ery life we see God's liv - ing power.
the Spir - it on the chos - en peo - ple came.
when we our God in flesh and blood be - held.
come, spread through us your sav - ing love a - broad.

# 256  Yours the Hand That Made Creation

1 Yours the hand that made cre - a - tion, womb of
2 Je - sus, from the first de - scend - ing, by your
3 Ho - ly Wis - dom, ev - er near us, tongue of

ev - ery con - stel - la - tion, ev - ery spe - cies,
birth the bro - ken mend - ing, Word of God the
fire to teach all hear - ers, sanc - ti - fy and

ev - ery na - tion:
nev - er - end - ing: glo - ry to the Three - in - One.
guard and cheer us:

Text: Elliot Rose (1928–1994), alt. © *Estate of Elliot Rose.*
Music: Melody German (14th cent.); harm. Ralph Vaughan Williams (1872–1958).
  *Harm.* © Oxford University Press.

88 87
QUEM PASTORES

# Have Mercy on Us, God Most High  257

1 Have mer - cy on us, God most high,
2 When heaven and earth were yet un - made,
3 How won - der - ful cre - a - tion is,
4 Most an - cient of all mys - ter - ies!

who lift our hearts to thee; have mer - cy
when time was yet un - known, thou, in thy
the work that thou didst bless; and O what
Low at thy throne we lie; have mer - cy

now, most mer - ci - ful, most ho - ly Trin - i - ty.
bliss and maj - es - ty, didst live and love a - lone.
then must thou be like, e - ter - nal Love - li - ness!
now, most mer - ci - ful, most ho - ly Trin - i - ty.

Text: Frederick William Faber (1814–1863).
Music: Thomas Ravenscroft (1590?–1634?), *Psalmes*, 1621.

CM
LINCOLN

## 259  For the Fruit of All Creation

1 For the fruit of all cre-a-tion, thanks be to God;
2 In the just re-ward of la-bour, God's will is done.
3 For the har-vests of the Spir-it, thanks be to God.

gifts be-stowed on ev-ery na-tion, thanks be to God.
In the help we give our neigh-bour, God's will is done.
For the good we all in-her-it, thanks be to God.

For the plough-ing, sow-ing, reap-ing, si-lent growth while we are
In our world-wide task of car-ing for the hun-gry and de-
For the won-ders that as-tound us, for the truths that still con-

sleep-ing, fu-ture needs in earth's safe-keep-ing, thanks be to God.
spair-ing, in the har-vests we are shar-ing, God's will is done.
found us, most of all, that love has found us, thanks be to God.

Text: Fred Pratt Green (1903– ). © 1970 Hope Publishing Co.
Music: Melody Welsh trad.; harm. *The English Hymnal*, 1906, alt.

84 84 88 84
AR HYD Y NOS
*Higher key 20*

# As Saints of Old  260

1 As saints of old their first fruits brought of or-chard, flock, and field
2 A world in need now sum-mons us to lab-our, love, and give;
3 In gra-ti-tude and hum-ble trust we bring our best to-day,

to God the giv-er of all good, the source of boun-teous yield;
to make our life an of-fer-ing that oth-ers too may live.
to serve your cause and share your love with all hu-man-i-ty.

so we to-day first fruits would bring: the wealth of this good land,
The church of Christ is call-ing us to make the dream come true:
O God, who gave your-self to us in Je-sus Christ your Son,

of farm and mar-ket, shop and home, of mind, and heart, and hand.
a world re-deemed, your king-dom come, all life in Christ made new.
teach us to give our-selves each day un-til life's work is done.

Text: Frank von Christierson (1900–1996), alt. © *1961, renewal 1989 The Hymn Society*
*in the United States and Canada. All rights reserved. Used by permission of Hope Publishing Co.*
Music: Melody Tyrolean trad.

CMD
TYROL
*Alt. tune FOREST GREEN 121, 427*

# 261 God, Whose Farm Is All Creation

1 God, whose farm is all cre - a - tion, take the
2 Take our plough - ing, seed - ing, reap - ing, hopes and
3 All our la - bour, all our watch - ing, all our

grat - i - tude we give; take the fin - est
fears of sun and rain, all our think - ing,
cal - en - dar of care, in these crops of

of our har - vest, crops we grow that all may live.
plan - ning, wait - ing, rip - ening in - to fruit and grain.
your cre - a - tion, take, O God: they are our prayer.

Text: John Arlott (1914–1991), alt. © *Estate of John Arlott. Reprinted by permission of the Trustees.*
Music: Melody English trad.; adapt. and harm. Ralph Vaughan Williams (1872–1958).
    *Harm. © Oxford University Press.*

87 87
SHIPSTON

# Come, Ye Thankful People, Come   262

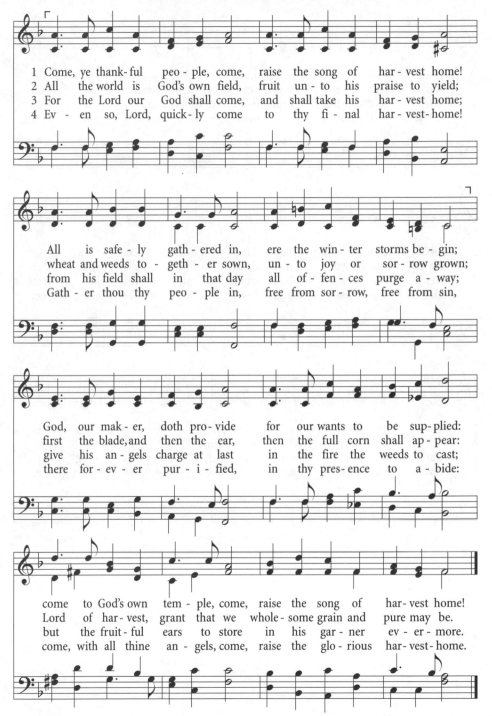

1 Come, ye thank-ful  peo - ple, come,  raise the song of  har - vest home!
2 All  the world is  God's own field,  fruit un - to his  praise to yield;
3 For  the Lord our  God shall come,  and shall take his  har - vest home;
4 Ev - en so, Lord, quick - ly come  to  thy fi - nal  har - vest - home!

All  is safe - ly  gath - ered in,  ere the win - ter  storms be - gin;
wheat and weeds to - geth - er sown,  un - to joy or  sor - row grown;
from his field shall  in that day  all of - fen - ces  purge a - way;
Gath - er thou thy  peo - ple in,  free from sor - row,  free from sin,

God,  our mak - er,  doth pro - vide  for  our wants to  be sup - plied:
first  the blade, and  then the ear,  then  the full corn  shall ap - pear:
give  his an - gels  charge at last  in  the fire the  weeds to cast;
there  for - ev - er  pur - i - fied,  in  thy pres - ence  to a - bide:

come  to God's own  tem - ple, come,  raise the song of  har - vest home!
Lord  of har - vest,  grant that we  whole - some grain and  pure may be.
but  the fruit - ful  ears to store  in  his gar - ner  ev - er - more.
come, with all thine  an - gels, come,  raise the glo - rious  har - vest - home.

Text: Henry Alford (1810–1871), alt.
Music: George Job Elvey (1816–1893).

77 77D
ST. GEORGE'S, WINDSOR

## 263  Praise to God, Immortal Praise

1 Praise to God, immortal praise, for the
2 for the blessings of the fields, for the
3 all that spring with bounteous hand scatters
4 These to thee, O God, we owe, Source whence

love that crowns our days; bounteous Source of
stores the garden yields, flocks that whiten
o'er the smiling land, all that liberal
all our blessings flow; and for these our

every joy, let thy praise our tongues employ:
all the plain, yellow sheaves of ripened grain,
autumn pours from her rich o'er-flowing stores.
souls shall raise grateful vows and solemn praise.

Text: Anna Laetita Barbauld (1743–1825).
Music: Melody French (13th cent.); attrib. Pierre de Corbeil (?–1222);
     adapt. Richard Redhead (1820–1901); harm. Derek Holman (1931– ) ©.

77 77
ORIENTIS PARTIBUS

# Now Greet the Swiftly Changing Year   264

*Unison*

1 Now greet the swift - ly chang - ing year with
2 This Je - sus came to wage sin's war; the
3 His love a - bun - dant far ex - ceeds the
4 With such a Lord to lead our way in
5 "All glo - ry be to God on high and

joy and pen - i - tence sin - cere; re - joice, re - joice, with
name of names for us he bore; re - joice, re - joice, with
vol - ume of a whole year's needs; re - joice, re - joice, with
want and in pros - per - i - ty, what need we fear in
peace on earth," the an - gels cry; re - joice, re - joice, with

thanks em - brace an - oth - er year of grace.
thanks em - brace an - oth - er year of grace.
thanks em - brace an - oth - er year of grace.
earth or space in this new year of grace?
thanks em - brace an - oth - er year of grace.

Text: Slovak (17th cent.); tr. Jaroslav J. Vajda (1919– ), alt. © *1996 Concordia Publishing House.*
Music: Alfred V. Fedak (1953– ). © *1989 Selah Publishing Co., Inc.*

88 86
SIXTH NIGHT

# 265  As Powers of Good

*Unison*

1 As powers of good so won-der-ful-ly hide us,
2 Yet still old tor-ments cause us con-ster-na-tion;
3 Then of-fer us the cup of des-o-la-tion,
4 Yet should you bring us back to share the glad-ness

we face the fu-ture bold-ly, come what may;
through days of fear and grief we have de-spaired.
brim-full of bit-ter-ness, and we will stand
of this bright world, your sun-shine break-ing through,

at dawn or dusk our God is still be-side us,
O, give our tor-tured souls, Lord, your sal-va-tion:
and drink with thanks, in spite of tre-pi-da-tion,
we would re-mem-ber times of pain and sad-ness

to whom we trust, com-plete-ly, each new day.
the heal-ing you have prom-ised and pre-pared.
from such a dear-ly loved and gra-cious hand.
and of-fer up the whole of life to you.

Text: Alan Gaunt (1935– ). © 1991 Stainer & Bell Ltd. All rights reserved.
*Used by permission of Hope Publishing Co.*
Music: Melody Herbert G. Hobbs (1934– ) ©; harm. Jan Helmut Wubbena (1947– ) ©.

11 10 11 10
BONHOEFFER
*Alt. tune* DONNE SECOURS 411

5 As evening falls, the candles we have lighted
will point us through the darkness to your light;
we long to be with loved ones, reunited;
we know your love outshines the darkest night.

6 As silence deepens, let us hear the chorus
that harmonizes earth's discordant days,
poured out from the unseen that lies before us:
your children's soaring song of endless praise.

7 By powers of good so faithfully surrounded,
secure and comforted in spite of fear,
we live each day with you Lord, unconfounded,
and go with you to meet the coming year.

## Lord, Let Your Servant Go in Peace   266

1 Lord, let your ser - vant go in peace: your prom - is - es have
2 My eyes have seen sal - va - tion's dawn: the Sun of life as -

been ful - filled; your sav - ing power has been dis -
cend - ing bright; your peo - ple's glo - ry ev - er -

played be - fore the face of all the world.
more, the na - tions' ev - er - last - ing light.

Text: *Song of Simeon* (Luke 2.29–32); para. Paul Gibson (1932– ) ©.
Music: Melody and bass Orlando Gibbons (1583–1625), alt.; harm. *The English Hymnal*, 1906, alt.

LM
SONG 34

# 267 The God Whom Earth and Sea and Sky

*Unison*

1 The God whom earth and sea and sky adore and
2 The Lord whom sun and moon obey, whom all things
3 How blest that mother, in whose shrine the world's Cre-
4 blest in the message Gabriel brought, blest by the
5 O Lord, the virgin-born, to thee eternal

laud and magnify, whose might they own, whose
serve from day to day, was borne upon a
a-tor, Lord divine, whose hand contains the
work the Spir-it wrought; from whom the great De-
praise and glory be, whom in the Godhead

praise they swell, in Mary's womb vouchsafed to dwell.
maiden's breast who fullest heavenly grace possessed.
earth and sky, vouchsafed, as in his ark, to lie;
sire of earth took human flesh and human birth.
we adore forever and for evermore.

Text: Attrib. Venantius Fortunatus (540?–600?); tr. John Mason Neale (1818–1866), alt.          LM
Music: Melody French; harm. Basil Harwood (1859–1949).          O AMOR QUAM ECSTATICUS
*Harm. published by permission of the executors of the late Dr. Basil Harwood.*          *Alt. tune EISENACH 79, 644*

# Gabriel's Message Does Away 268

1 Ga - briel's mes - sage does a - way   Sa - tan's curse and
2 He that comes de - spised shall reign;   he that can - not
3 Weak - ness shall the strong con - found;   by the hands, in

Sa - tan's sway, out of dark - ness brings our Day:
die, be slain; death by death its death shall gain:
grave - clothes wound, Ad - am's chains shall be un - bound:

*Refrain*

so, be - hold, all the gates of heaven un - fold.

Text: *Piae Cantiones*, 1582; tr. John Mason Neale (1818–1866).
Music: Melody *Piae Cantiones*, 1582;
   harm. Melva Treffinger Graham (1947– ) ©.

777 with refrain
ANGELUS EMITTITUR (GABRIEL'S MESSAGE)

# 269  Heavenly Message

1 Heav-en - ly mes - sage, brought by an an - gel, com - ing to
2 Ma - ry re - plied to Ga - bri - el's mess - age, "I am the
3 In the be - gin - ning, when God had spo - ken, through God's own

Capo 1 E        A      E      C♯m        F♯m        C♯m
      ⌐ F       B♭     F      Dm         Gm         Dm

lift  the  hopes  of  the  earth;  bring-ing  to  Ma - ry
ser - vant,  maid  of  the  Lord.  Let  it  be  done  just
Word  all  things came to  be;  now  by  that  Word,  em -

        E          B          E          A      E
        F          C      ⌐   F          B♭     F

hum - ble  and  low - ly,  God's in - vi - ta - tion  to  give the Christ
as  you  have  spo - ken.  My soul re - joic - es  in  God's sav - ing
bod - ied through Ma - ry,  God's glo - ry blaz - es, that our eyes may

C♯m        F♯m              E          F♯m        B
Dm         Gm               F          Gm         C

Text: Paul Gibson (1932– ) ©.
Music: Melody Basque trad.; harm. Patrick Wedd (1948– ) ©.

10 9 10 10 with refrain
PIED-DE-PORT

*Refrain*

birth.
word."
see.

Ma - ry we hail you, full of God's fav - our,
bless-ed are you, and bless-ed your son; he will be called the
child of the high - est, Sav-iour of all, the ho - ly one.

## 270  Lamb of God, to Thee We Raise

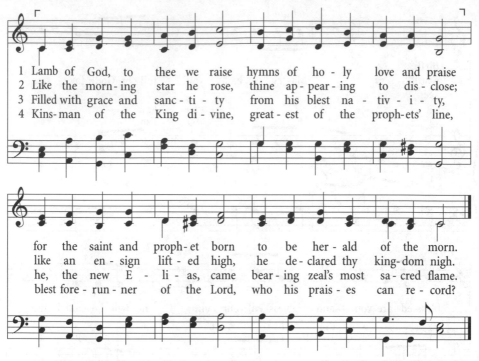

1 Lamb of God, to thee we raise hymns of ho-ly love and praise
2 Like the morn-ing star he rose, thine ap-pear-ing to dis-close;
3 Filled with grace and sanc-ti-ty from his blest na-tiv-i-ty,
4 Kins-man of the King di-vine, great-est of the proph-ets' line,

for the saint and proph-et born to be her-ald of the morn.
like an en-sign lift-ed high, he de-clared thy king-dom nigh.
he, the new E-li-as, came bear-ing zeal's most sa-cred flame.
blest fore-run-ner of the Lord, who his prais-es can re-cord?

5 Mighty preacher, by whose word
souls to penitence were stirred
those who long in sin had strayed
then the call divine obeyed.

6 Make us, Lord, like him to be
fearless witnesses for thee;
faithful unto death be found,
and at last by thee be crowned.

Text: William Edgar Enman (1869–1950).
Music: Melody *Geistreiches Gesangbuch*, 1704;
   adapt. and harm. William Henry Havergal (1793–1870), alt.

77 77
LÜBECK

## 271  You Are the Christ, O Lord

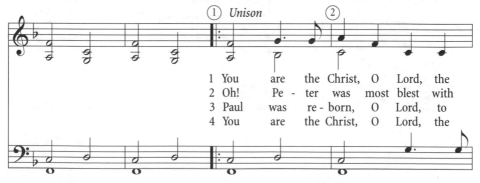

*Unison*

1 You    are the Christ, O Lord, the
2 Oh!    Pe-ter was most blest with
3 Paul   was re-born, O Lord, to
4 You    are the Christ, O Lord, the

Text: St. 1, 2, and 4, William Walsham How (1823–1897); st. 3, Richard Wayne Dirksen (1921– ) ©.
Music: Richard Wayne Dirksen (1921– ) ©.

66 66 88
WYNGATE CANON

Son of God most high! For-ev-er be a-dored that
bless-ed-ness un-priced, who, taught of God, con-fessed the
preach your ho-ly word; he made your gos-pel shine through-
Son of God most high! For-ev-er be a-dored that

name in earth and sky, in which, though mor-tal
God-head in the Christ! For of your church, Lord,
out the whole wide world. His right-eous teach-ing
name in earth and sky, in which, though mor-tal

strength may fail, the saints of God at last pre-vail!
you made known this saint a true foun-da-tion stone.
lights our way, pre-par-ing us for judge-ment day.
strength may fail, the saints of God at last pre-vail!

for canon only

*This hymn may be sung as a 2- or 4-part round or canon
with entrances alternating between treble and male voices.*

# 272 Christ, the Fair Glory of the Holy Angels

*Unison*

1 Christ, the fair glo - ry of the ho - ly an - gels, mak - er of
2 Send thine arch - an - gel Mi - chael to our suc - cour; peace - mak - er
3 Send thine arch - an - gel Ga - bri - el, the might - y; her - ald of
4 Send from the heav - ens Ra - phael thine arch - an - gel, health - bring - er

all things, rul - er of all na - tions, grant of thy mer - cy
bless - ed, may he ban - ish from us striv - ing and ha - tred,
heav - en, may he, from us mor - tals, drive ev - ery e - vil,
bless - ed, aid - ing ev - ery suf - ferer, that, in thy ser - vice,

un - to us thy ser - vants steps up to heav - en.
so that for the peace - ful all things may pros - per.
watch - ing o'er the tem - ples where thou art wor - shipped.
he may wise - ly guide us, heal - ing and bless - ing.

5 May the blest mother of our God and Saviour,
   may the celestial company of angels,
   may the assembly of the saints in heaven,
   help us to praise thee.

6 Father almighty, Son, and Holy Spirit,
   God ever blessèd, hear our thankful praises;
   thine is the glory which from all creation
   ever ascendeth.

Text: Attrib. Rabanus Maurus (776?–856); tr. J. Athelstan L. Riley (1858–1945), alt.
Music: Melody *Antiphoner*, Rouen, 1728; harm. Ralph Vaughan Williams (1872–1958).
   *Tr. and harm.* © Oxford University Press.

11 11 11 5
COELITES PLAUDANT

# Sing of Andrew, John's Disciple 273

1 Sing of An - drew, John's dis - ci - ple, led by faith through
2 Sing of An - drew, called by Je - sus from the shores of
3 Sing of An - drew, bold a - pos - tle, sent to make the

ways un - trod, till the Bap - tist cried at Jor - dan,
Gal - i - lee, leav - ing boats and nets and kin - dred,
gos - pel known, faith - ful to his Lord's ex - am - ple,

"There be - hold the Lamb of God!" Stirred by hear - ing this new
trust - ing in that "Fol - low me." When a lad's small meal fed
called to make a cross his own. So may we who prize his

teach - er, An - drew, freed from doubt and fear, ran to
thou - sands, when in - quir - ing Greeks found care, when the
mem - ory hon - our Christ in our own day, bear - ing

tell his broth - er Si - mon, "God's A - noint - ed One is here!"
Spir - it came in bless - ing, An - drew faith - ful - ly was there.
wit - ness to our neigh - bours, liv - ing what we sing and pray.

Text: Carl P. Daw, Jr. (1944– ).
Music: Cyril Vincent Taylor (1907–1991).
*Text © 1987, music © 1942, renewal 1970 Hope Publishing Co.*

87 87D
ABBOT'S LEIGH
*Higher key 433*

## 274 Here from All Nations, All Tongues

1 Here from all nations, all tongues, and all peoples,
2 These have come out of the hardest oppression;
3 Gone is their thirst, and no more shall they hunger;
4 He will go with them to clear living water
5 Blessing and glory and wisdom and power

countless the crowd, but their voices are one;
now may they stand in the presence of God,
God is their shelter, his power at their side;
flowing from springs which his mercy supplies.
be to the Saviour again and again;

vast is the sight and majestic their singing:
serving their Lord day and night in his temple,
sun shall not pain them, no burning will torture;
Gone is their grief, and their trials are over;
might and thanksgiving and honour forever

"God has the victory and reigns from the throne!"
ransomed and cleansed by the Lamb's precious blood.
Jesus the Lamb is their shepherd and guide.
God wipes away every tear from their eyes.
be to our God: alleluia! Amen.

Text: Christopher Idle (1938– ). © 1973 Hope Publishing Co.
Music: Melody *Antiphoner*, Paris, 1681.

11 10 11 10
O QUANTA QUALIA
*Higher key 204, 275*

# O What Their Joy and Their Glory Must Be 275

1 O what their joy and their glo-ry must be, those end-less
2 What are the mon-arch, the court, and the throne? What are the
3 Tru-ly Je-ru-sa-lem name we that shore, vi-sion of
4 There, where no trou-bles dis-trac-tion can bring, we the sweet

sab-baths the bless-ed ones see: crowns for the val-iant, to
peace and the joy that they own? O that the blest ones, who
peace, that brings joy ev-er-more; wish and ful-fil-ment can
an-thems of Si-on shall sing, while for thy grace, Lord, their

wea-ry ones, rest; God shall be all and in all ev-er blest.
in it have share, all that they feel could as ful-ly de-clare!
sev-ered be ne'er, nor the thing prayed for come short of the prayer.
voic-es of praise thy bless-ed peo-ple e-ter-nal-ly raise.

5 Now in the meantime, with hearts raised on high,
we for that country must yearn and must sigh,
seeking Jerusalem, dear native land,
through our long exile on Babylon's strand.

6 Low before God with our praises we fall,
of whom, and in whom, and through whom are all:
praise to the Father, and praise to the Son,
praise to the Spirit, with them ever one.

Text: Peter Abelard (1079–1142); tr. John Mason Neale (1818–1866), alt.
Music: Melody *Antiphoner*, Paris, 1681.

10 10 10 10
O QUANTA QUALIA
*Lower key 274*

# 276  For All the Saints

*Unison*

1 For all the saints who from their la - bours rest, who
2 Thou wast their rock, their for - tress, and their might;
3 O may thy sol - diers, faith - ful, true, and bold,
7 But lo, there breaks a yet more glo - rious day— the
8 From earth's wide bounds, from o - cean's far - thest coast, through

thee by faith be - fore the world con - fessed, thy
thou, Lord, their cap - tain in the well - fought fight;
fight as the saints who no - bly fought of old, and
saints tri - um - phant rise in bright ar - ray: the
gates of pearl, streams in the count - less host,

name, O Je - sus, be for - ev - er blest.
thou, in the dark - ness drear, their one true light.
win with them the vic - tor's crown of gold.
King of glo - ry pass - es on his way.
sing - ing to Fa - ther, Son, and Ho - ly Ghost.

Al - le - lu - ia! Al - le - lu - ia!

*St. 4–6 follow*

Text: William Walsham How (1823–1897).
Music: Ralph Vaughan Williams (1872–1958). © *Oxford University Press.*

10 10 10 with Alleluias
SINE NOMINE
*Lower key 387*

4 O blest com - mu - nion, fel - low-ship di - vine! We feeb - ly
5 And when the strife is fierce, the war - fare long, steals on the
6 The gol - den eve - ning bright-ens in the west; soon, soon to

strug - gle, they in glo - ry shine; yet all are one in
ear the dis - tant tri - umph-song, and hearts are brave a -
faith - ful war - riors comes their rest; sweet is the calm of

thee, for all are thine.
gain, and arms are strong. Al - le - lu - ia! Al - le - lu - ia!
Pa - ra - dise the blest.

*To beginning for st. 7*

# 279  Lo! Round the Throne, a Glorious Band

1 Lo! Round the throne, a glo-rious band, the saints in count-less
2 Through trib-u-la-tion great, they came, they bore the cross, de-
3 They see their Sav-iour face to face, and sing the tri-umphs
4 "Wor-thy the Lamb, for sin-ners slain, through end-less years to

myr-iads stand, of ev-ery tongue re-deemed to God,
spised the shame; from all their la-bours now they rest,
of God's grace; and day and night with cease-less praise,
live and reign; thou hast re-deemed us by thy blood

ar-rayed in gar-ments washed in blood. Al-le-lu-ia!
in God's e-ter-nal glo-ry blest. Al-le-lu-ia!
to Christ their loud thanks-giv-ing raise: al-le-lu-ia!
and made us roy-al priests to God." Al-le-lu-ia!

Text: Rowland Hill (1744–1833), alt.
Music: Melody Nikolaus Herman (1480?–1561).

LM with Alleluia
ERSCHIENEN IST DER HERRLICH TAG

# How Bright These Glorious Spirits Shine 280

1 How bright these glo - rious spir - its shine!
2 Lo, these are they from suf - ferings great
3 Now, with tri - um - phal palms, they stand
4 His pres - ence fills each heart with joy,

Whence all their white ar - ray? How came they to the
who came to realms of light, and in the blood of
be - fore the throne on high, and serve the God they
tunes ev - ery mouth to sing; by day, by night, the

bliss - ful seats of ev - er - last - ing day?
Christ have washed those robes which shine so bright.
love, a - midst the glo - ries of the sky.
sa - cred courts with glad ho - san - nas ring.

5 Hunger and thirst are felt no more,
 nor sun with scorching ray:
 God is their sun, whose cheering beams
 diffuse eternal day.

6 The Lamb who dwells amidst the throne
 shall o'er them still preside,
 feed them with nourishment divine,
 and all their footsteps guide.

7 To pastures green he'll lead his flock
 where living streams appear;
 and God the Lord from every eye
 shall wipe off every tear.

Text: Isaac Watts (1674–1748).
Music: John Bacchus Dykes (1823–1876).

CM
BEATITUDO

## 283 By All Your Saints Still Striving

*Unison*

1 By all your saints still striv - ing, for all your saints at rest,
2 *(One of the following dated stanzas may be inserted here.)*
3 Then let us praise the Fa - ther and wor - ship God the Son

your ho - ly name, O Je - sus, for ev - er - more be blessed.
and sing to God the Spi - rit, e - ter - nal Three - in - One,

You rose, our King vic - to - rious, that they might wear the crown
till all the ran - somed num - ber who stand be - fore the throne,

and ev - er shine in splen - dour re - flect - ed from your throne.
a - scribe all power and glo - ry and praise to God a - lone.

Text: Horatio Bolton Nelson (1823–1913), rev. *The Hymnal 1982. Rev. © 1982 The Church Pension Fund.*
Music: Melody English trad.; coll. and arr. Ralph Vaughan Williams (1872–1958).
    *Arr. © Oxford University Press.*

76 76D
KING'S LYNN
*Alt. setting 389*

*January 11 or December 28: The Holy Innocents*
2a  Praise for your infant martyrs,
    victims of human fear,
    and for the weeping mothers
    who live, their pain to bear.
    Lord, form our will to struggle,
    to stand firm in the hour
    when others come for victims
    to feed their love of power.
        Text: Walter W.G. Deller (1954– ) ©.

*January 18: Confession of Peter*
2b  We praise you, Lord, for Peter,
    so eager and so bold:
    thrice falling, yet repentant,
    thrice charged to feed your fold.
    Lord, make your pastors faithful
    to guard your flock from harm
    and hold them when they waver
    with your almighty arm.

*January 25: Conversion of Paul*
2c  Praise for the light from heaven
    and for the voice of awe:
    praise for the glorious vision
    the persecutor saw.
    O Lord, for Paul's conversion,
    we bless your name today.
    Come shine within our darkness
    and guide us in the way.

*March 19: Joseph of Nazareth*
2d  All praise, O God, for Joseph,
    the guardian of your Son,
    who saved him from King Herod,
    when safety there was none.
    He taught the trade of builder,
    when they to Nazareth came,
    and Joseph's love made "Father"
    to be, for Christ, God's name.

*March 25: Annunciation of the Lord*
2e  We sing with joy of Mary
    whose heart with awe was stirred
    when, youthful and unready,
    she heard the angel's word;
    yet she her voice upraises
    God's glory to proclaim,
    as once for our salvation
    your mother she became.

*April 25: Mark, Evangelist*
2f  For Mark, O Lord, we praise you,
    the weak by grace made strong;
    his witness in his Gospel
    becomes victorious song.
    May we, in all our weakness,
    receive your power divine,
    and all, as faithful branches,
    grow strong in you, the Vine.

*May 1: Philip and James, Apostles*
2g  We praise you, Lord, for Philip,
    blest guide to Greek and Jew,
    and for young James the faithful,
    who heard and followed you.
    O grant us grace to know you,
    the victor in the strife,
    that we, with all your servants
    may wear the crown of life.

*May 6 or December 27:*
    *John, Apostle and Evangelist*
2h  For John, your loved disciple,
    exiled to Patmos' shore,
    and for his faithful record,
    we praise you evermore:
    praise for the mystic vision
    his words to us unfold.
    Instill in us his longing,
    your glory to behold.

*May 14: Matthias, Apostle*

2i   For one in place of Judas,
the apostles sought God's choice:
the lot fell to Matthias
for whom we now rejoice.
May we like true apostles
your holy church defend,
and not betray our calling,
but serve you to the end.

*June 11: Barnabas, Apostle*

2j   For Barnabas we praise you,
who kept your law of love
and, leaving earthly treasures,
sought riches from above.
O Christ, our Lord and Saviour,
let gifts of grace descend,
that your true consolation
may through the world extend.

*June 24: Birth of John the Baptist*

2k   All praise for John the Baptist,
forerunner of the Word,
our true Elijah, making
a highway for the Lord.
The last and greatest prophet,
he saw the dawning ray
of light that grows in splendour
until the perfect day.

*June 29: Peter and Paul, Apostles*

2m   We praise you for Saint Peter;
we praise you for Saint Paul.
They taught both Jew and Gentile
that Christ is all in all.
To cross and sword they yielded
and saw the kingdom come:
O God, your two apostles
won life through martyrdom.
> Text: F. Bland Tucker (1895–1984).

*July 3: Thomas, Apostle*

2n   All praise, O Lord, for Thomas
whose short-lived doubtings prove
your perfect twofold nature,
the depth of your true love.
To all who live with questions,
a steadfast faith afford;
and grant us grace to know you,
made flesh, yet God and Lord.

*July 22: Mary Magdalene*

2o   All praise for Mary Magdalene
whose wholeness was restored
by you, her faithful Master,
her Saviour and her Lord.
On Easter morning early,
a word from you sufficed;
her faith was first to see you,
her Lord, the risen Christ.
> Text: Jerry D. Godwin (1944– ).

*July 25: James, Apostle*
2p  O Lord, for James, we praise you,
    who fell to Herod's sword.
    He drank the cup of suffering
    and thus fulfilled your word.
    Lord, curb our vain impatience
    for glory and for fame,
    equip us for such sufferings
    as glorify your name.

*August 3 or December 26:*
   *Stephen, Deacon and Martyr*
2q  All praise, O Lord, for Stephen
    who, martyred, saw you stand
    to help in time of torment,
    to plead at God's right hand.
    Like you, our suffering Saviour,
    his enemies he blessed,
    with "Lord, receive my spirit,"
    his faith, in death, confessed.

*August 24: Bartholomew, Apostle*
2r  Praise for your blest apostle
    surnamed Bartholomew;
    we know not his achievements
    but know that he was true,
    for he at the Ascension
    was an apostle still.
    May we discern your presence
    and seek, like him, your will.

*September 21: Matthew, Apostle and Evangelist*
2s  We praise you, Lord, for Matthew,
    whose gospel words declare
    that, worldly gain forsaking,
    your path of life we share.
    From all unrighteous mammon,
    O raise our eyes anew,
    that we, whate'er our station,
    may rise and follow you.

*October 18: Luke, Evangelist*
2t  For Luke, beloved physician,
    all praise; whose gospel shows
    the healer of the nations,
    the one who shares our woes.
    Your wine and oil, O Saviour,
    upon our spirits pour,
    and with true balm of Gilead
    anoint us evermore.

*October 28: Simon and Jude, Apostles*
2u  Praise, Lord, for your apostles,
    Saint Simon and Saint Jude.
    One love, one hope impelled them
    to tread the way, renewed.
    May we with zeal as earnest
    the faith of Christ maintain,
    be bound in love together,
    and life eternal gain.

*November 1: All Saints*
   *(This stanza may be sung before or instead*
   *of the final doxology on any occasion.)*
2v  Apostles, prophets, martyrs,
    and all the noble throng
    who wear the spotless raiment
    and raise the ceaseless song:
    for them and those whose witness
    is only known to you,
    by walking in their footsteps
    we give you praise anew.

*November 30: Andrew, Apostle*
2w  All praise, O Lord, for Andrew,
    the first to follow you;
    he witnessed to his brother,
    "This is Messiah true."
    You called him from his fishing
    upon Lake Galilee;
    he rose to meet your challenge,
    "Leave all and follow me."

3    Then let us praise the Father
    and worship God the Son
    and sing to God the Spirit,
    eternal Three-in-One,
    till all the ransomed number
    who stand before the throne,
    ascribe all power and glory
    and praise to God alone.

## 286  Give Me the Wings of Faith

*Descant*

5 Our glo - rious Lead - er claims our praise, for

1 Give me the wings of faith, to rise with -
2 Once they were mourn - ing here be - low, and
3 I ask them whence their vic - tory came; they
4 They marked the foot - steps that he trod; his
5 Our glo - rious Lead - er claims our praise, for

his own pat - tern given; while the long cloud of

in the veil, and see the saints a - bove, how
wet their couch with tears; they wrest - led hard, as
with u - ni - ted breath as - cribe their con - quest
zeal in - spired their breast; and, fol - lowing their in -
his own pat - tern given; while the long cloud of

wit - ness - es show the same path to heaven.

great their joys, how bright their glo - ries be.
we do now, with sins and doubts and fears.
to the Lamb, their tri - umph to his death.
car - nate God, pos - sess the prom - ised rest.
wit - ness - es show the same path to heaven.

Text: Isaac Watts (1674–1748).
Music: James Turle (1802–1882); desc. Norman Warren (1934– ). *Desc. © 1982 Hope Publishing Co.*

CM
WESTMINSTER

# Come to a Wedding, Come to a Blessing 287

*Descant*

Ah...    Ah...

*Unison*

1 Come to a wed - ding, come to a bless - ing, come on a
2 Thanks for the love that holds us to - geth - er— par - ent and
3 Love is the gift, and love is the giv - er, love is the
4 Come to this wed - ding, ask - ing a bless - ing for all the

Ah...

day when hap - pi - ness sings! Come rain or sun, come win - ter or
child, and lov - er and friend; thanks to the God whose love is our
gold that makes the day shine; love for - gets self to care for the
years that liv - ing will prove: health of the bo - dy, health of the

Ah...

sum - mer, cel - e - brate love and all that it brings.
cen - tre, source of com - pass - ion, know - ing no end.
oth - er, love chang - es life from wa - ter to wine.
spir - it— *(name) and (name), we of - fer our love.

*or, "now to you both"*

Text: Shirley Erena Murray (1931– ).
Music: Melody Gaelic trad.; arr. and desc. John W. Wilson (1905–1992).
*Text © 1992, arr. and desc. © 1983 Hope Publishing Co.*

55 54D
BUNESSAN
*Higher key and alt. settings 3, 445*

# 288 Lord and Lover of Creation

1 Lord and lov-er of cre-a-tion, bless the mar-riage
2 Praise and grat-i-tude we of-fer for the past which
3 On your chil-dren, wed and wel-come, here a-mong us,
4 Take them hence that, in each oth-er, love ful-fill-ing

wit-nessed now: sign of lives no lon-ger sep-arate,
shaped to-day: words which stirred and deep-ened con-science,
we re-quest health in home and hearts, and hu-mour
love shall find much to share and more to trea-sure,

sealed by sym-bol, bound by vow, cel-e-brat-ing
fam-i-ly life, good com-pa-ny, friends who touched and
through which heaven and earth are blessed; o-pen doors and
such that none dare break or bind those your name has

love's com-mit-ment made to live and last and grow.
sum-moned tal-ent, nour-ished all words can't con-vey.
hu-man plea-sure, time for touch and trust and rest.
joined to-geth-er, one in bo-dy, heart, and mind.

Text: Graham Maule (1958– ). © 1989 WGRG The Iona Community (Scotland).
Used by permission of G.I.A. Publications, Inc., exclusive agent.
Music: Henry Purcell (1659–1695), O God, thou art my God; adapt. The Psalmist, 1842.

87 87 87
WESTMINSTER ABBEY
Higher key 300

# Great God, We Praise Your Mighty Love  289

1 Great God, we praise your might-y love which urg-es
2 We praise you for the love we see in hus-band,
3 We praise you most for love su-preme which breaks through
4 For by your per-fect love re-fined, our own will

us to rise a-bove con-strict-ing doubts and fears;
wife, and fam-i-ly, in friends and neigh-bours too;
pain and death to stream in un-re-strict-ed light;
not be un-der-mined by fu-tile guilt and shame;

your pur-pose is to set us free to live our
the love which nur-tured us from birth, the love which
which from Christ's re-sur-rec-tion dawn has shone, and
but through dis-as-ter, grief, and strife we'll re-af-

lives cre-a-tive-ly through-out the com-ing years.
teach-es hu-man worth, and lifts our minds to you.
nev-er been with-drawn, to make our fu-ture bright.
firm the joy of life and glo-ri-fy your name.

88 6D
WILLOUGHBY NEW

# 290 O Thou Whose Power

1 O thou whose power o'er mov - ing worlds pre - sides,
2 'Tis thine a - lone to calm the trou - bled breast

whose voice cre - a - ted, and whose wis - dom guides,
with si - lent con - fi - dence and ho - ly rest.

on dark - ened souls in pure ef - ful - gence shine,
From thee, great God, we spring, to thee we tend—

and cheer the cloud - ed mind with light di - vine.
path, mo - tive, guide, o - rig - i - nal, and end.

Text: Anicius Manlius Severinus Boethius (475?–525); tr. Samuel Johnson (1709–1784).
Music: Orlando Gibbons (1583–1625).

10 10 10 10
SONG 4

1 O Christ, the heal - er, we have come to pray for
2 From ev - ery ail - ment flesh en - dures our bod - ies
3 How strong, O Lord, are our des - ires, how weak our
4 In con - flicts that de - stroy our health, we di - ag -
5 Grant that we all, made one in faith, in your com -

health, to plead for friends. How can we fail to be re -
clam - our to be freed; yet in our hearts we would con -
know - ledge of our - selves! Re - lease in us those heal - ing
nose the world's dis - ease; our com - mon life de - clares our
mun - i - ty may find the whole - ness that, en - rich - ing

stored, when reached by love that nev - er ends?
fess that whole - ness is our deep - est need.
truths un - con - scious pride re - sists or shelves.
ills: is there no cure, O Christ, for these?
us, shall reach the whole of hu - man - kind.

Text: Fred Pratt Green (1903– ). © 1969 Hope Publishing Co.
Music: Melody *Heilige Seelenlust*, 1657; alt. *Cantica Spiritualia*, 1847
    and *Hymns Ancient and Modern*, 1875.

LM
ANGELUS

# 292 We Cannot Measure How You Heal

1 We can - not mea - sure how you heal or an - swer
2 The pain that will not go a - way, the guilt that
3 So some have come who need your help and some have

ev - ery suf - ferer's prayer, yet we be - lieve your
clings from things long past, the fear of what the
come to make a - mends, as hands which shaped and

grace re - sponds where faith and doubt u - nite to care.
fu - ture holds, are pres - ent as if meant to last.
saved the world are pres - ent in the touch of friends.

Text: John L. Bell (1949– ).
Music: Melody Scottish trad., alt.; arr. The Iona Community (Scotland).
*Text and arr. © 1989 WGRG The Iona Community (Scotland).*
*Used by permission of G.I.A. Publications, Inc., exclusive agent.*

LMD
YE BANKS AND BRAES (CANDLER)
*Alt. setting 304*

Your hands, though blood - ied on the cross, sur - vive to
But pres - ent too is love which tends the hurt we
Lord, let your Spir - it meet us here to mend the

hold and heal and warn, to car - ry all through
nev - er hope to find, the pri - vate ag - o -
bod - y, mind, and soul, to dis - en - tan - gle

death to life and cra - dle chil - dren yet un - born.
nies in - side, the mem - o - ries that haunt the mind.
peace from pain and make your bro - ken peo - ple whole.

# 293 Your Hands, O Lord, in Days of Old

1 Your hands, O Lord, in days of old were strong to heal and save; they triumphed over pain and death, o'er darkness and the grave. To you they went, the blind, the mute, the palsied and the lame, the leper

2 And then your touch brought life and health, gave speech and strength and sight; and youth renewed, with health restored, claimed you, the Lord of light. And so, O Lord, be near to bless, almighty now as then, in every

3 O be our mighty healer still, O Lord of life and death; restore and strengthen, soothe and bless with your almighty breath. On hands that work and eyes that see, your healing wisdom pour, that whole and

Text: Edward Hayes Plumptre (1821–1891), alt.
Music: Attrib. Franz Josef Haydn (1732–1809).

CMD
ST. MICHAEL'S

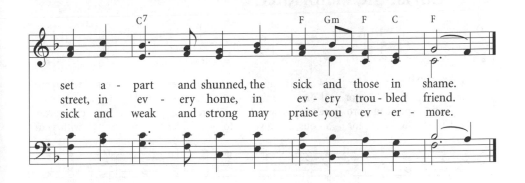

set a - part and shunned, the sick and those in shame.
street, in ev - ery home, in ev - ery trou - bled friend.
sick and weak and strong may praise you ev - er - more.

## By the Waters, the Waters of Babylon 294

By the wa - ters, the wa - ters of Ba - by - lon,

we sat down and wept, and wept for thee, Zi - on.

We re-mem- ber thee, re-mem- ber thee, re-mem- ber thee, Zi - on.

*May be sung as 3-part round or canon.*

Text: Ps. 137.1
Music: American trad.

Irregular
BY THE WATERS

## 295 Christ the Victorious

1 Christ the vic-tor-i-ous, give to your ser-vants rest with your
2 On-ly im-mor-tal one, might-y Cre-a-tor! We are your
3 God-spo-ken pro-phe-cy, word at cre-a-tion: "You came from
4 Christ the vic-tor-i-ous, give to your ser-vants rest with your

saints in the re-gions of light. Grief and pain end-ed, and
crea-tures and child-ren of earth. From earth you formed us, both
dust and to dust shall re-turn." Yet at the grave shall we
saints in the re-gions of light. Grief and pain end-ed, and

sigh-ing no long-er, there may they find ev-er-last-ing life.
glor-i-ous and mor-tal, and to the earth shall we all re-turn.
raise up our glad song, "Al - le-lu - ia, al-le-lu - ia!"
sigh-ing no long-er, there may they find ev-er-last-ing life.

Text: *Give rest, O Christ*; para. Carl P. Daw, Jr. (1944– ). *Para. © 1982 Hope Publishing Co.*
Music: Alexis Feodorovich Lvov (1799–1870).

11 10 11 9
RUSSIAN ANTHEM

# O Christ, You Wept When Grief Was Raw  296

1 O Christ, you wept when grief was raw and felt for
those who mourned their friend; come close to where we
would not be and hold us, numbed by this life's end.

2 The well - loved voice is si - lent now and we have
much we meant to say; col - lect our lost and
wan - dering words and keep them till the end - less day.

3 We try to hold what is not here and fear for
what we do not know; O take our hands in
yours, good Lord, and free us to let our friend go.

4 In all our lone - li - ness and doubt, through what we
can - not re - al - ize, ad - dress us from your
emp - ty tomb and tell us that life nev - er dies.

Text: The Iona Community (Scotland). © 1989 WGRG The Iona Community (Scotland).
Used by permission of G.I.A. Publications, Inc., exclusive agent.
Music: Melody *Heilige Seelenlust*, 1657; alt. *Cantica Spiritualia*, 1847, and *Hymns Ancient and Modern*, 1875.

LM
ANGELUS

# 297 God Give Us Life

1 God give us life when all a - round spells
2 God give us love in heart and hand to
3 God give us skill, in - sight, and will to
4 God give us faith, should all else fail and
5 Then, in the end, make death a friend, and

death and some have died; and none are clear that
hold the hurt - ing one, to free the an - ger,
find, where none are sure, new threads to mend the
death un - sheath its sting. O help us hear, through
give us strength to stand and walk to where no

hope is near or fate can be de - fied.
meet the need, and wait till wait - ing's done.
web of life, new means to heal and cure.
pain and fear, the songs that an - gels sing.
eye can stare, but Christ can clasp our hand.

Text and music: John L. Bell (1949– ).

446D
CAMPBELL

# O Lord of Life, Where'er They Be  298

1 O Lord of life, wher-e'er they be, safe in thy own e-
2 All souls are thine, and here or there they rest with-in thy
3 Thy word is true, thy ways are just; a - bove the re - quiem,
4 O hap-py they in God who rest, no more by fear and

ter - ni - ty, our dead are liv - ing un - to thee.
shel - tering care; one prov - i - dence a - like they share.
"Dust to dust," shall rise our psalm of grate-ful trust.
doubt op - pressed; liv - ing or dy - ing, they are blest.

Al - le - lu - ia, al - le - lu - ia, al - le - lu - ia!

Text: Frederick Lucian Hosmer (1840–1929).  
Music: Melody Melchior Vulpius (1570?–1615);  
harm. Ernest Campbell MacMillan (1893–1973). *Harm. © Estate of Sir Ernest MacMillan, Ross A. MacMillan, executor.*

888 with Alleluias  
VULPIUS (GELOBT SEI GOTT)

# 299 In the Name of Christ We Gather

*Descant*

Word of joy, en - liven - ing Spir - it, more than lov - er,

1 In the name of Christ we gath - er, in the name of
2 Sons and daugh - ters of the Spir - it— these are called to
3 In the min - is - try of preach - ing may the word spring
4 Now with - in this sol - emn mo - ment we in - voke the
5 Word of joy, en - liven - ing Spir - it, more than lov - er,

par - ent, friend, born in Je - sus, born in Ma - ry,

Christ we sing, cel - e - brate new vows, new prom - ise
teach and care, called as were the first dis - ci - ples,
in - to life; in the time of doubt and chal - lenge,
power of God— by the hands laid on in bless - ing
par - ent, friend, born in Je - sus, born in Ma - ry,

Text: Shirley Erena Murray (1931– ). © 1992 Hope Publishing Co.
Music: Kaspar Ett (1788–1847), *Cantica Sacra*, Munich, 1840; desc. Gerald Manning (1943– ) ©.

87 87 87
ORIEL
*Higher key 185, 377*

born in us, that love ex - tend, grow with - in your

of      a  life's whole  of - fer - ing,     here   or - dained  to
com - mon - wealth  of  Christ   to  share,   by   the  bread  and
may   its   truth  af - firm   be - lief;    in   the   day   of
be    there strength to   take  the  load,   be   there faith - ful -
born   in   us,    that  love  ex - tend,   grow  with - in  your

chos - en  *ser - vant,  life  of  God  that  has  no  end!

lead  God's  peo - ple   at   the  Gos - pel's  beck - on - ing.
wine   and   wa - ter   sac - ra - ments  of   grace  de - clare.
pain   and   dark - ness,  heal  the  hurt   of   guilt  and  grief.
ness   in   lov - ing,    be  there cour - age  for  this  road.
chos - en  *ser - vant,  life   of   God  that  has  no  end!

* originally was "daughter"

# 300 Christ Is Made the Sure Foundation

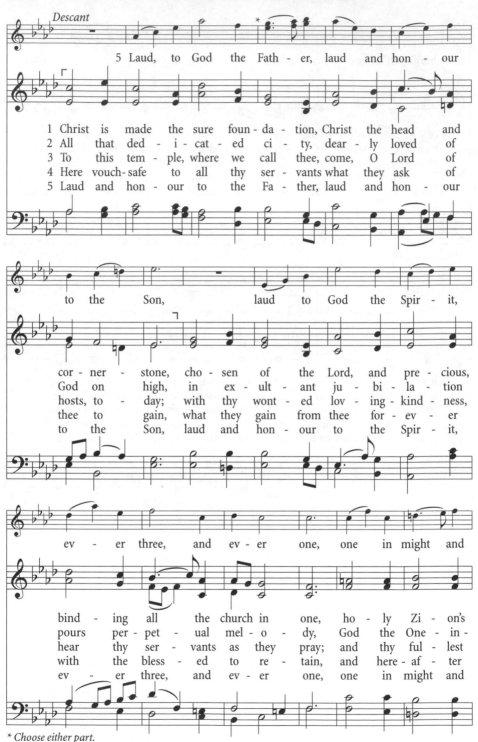

*Descant*

5 Laud, to God the Fath-er, laud and hon-our

1 Christ is made the sure foun-da-tion, Christ the head and
2 All that ded-i-cat-ed ci-ty, dear-ly loved of
3 To this tem-ple, where we call thee, come, O Lord of
4 Here vouch-safe to all thy ser-vants what they ask of
5 Laud and hon-our to the Fa-ther, laud and hon-our

to the Son, laud to God the Spir-it,

cor-ner-stone, cho-sen of the Lord, and pre-cious,
God on high, in ex-ult-ant ju-bi-la-tion
hosts, to-day; with thy wont-ed lov-ing-kind-ness,
thee to gain, what they gain from thee for-ev-er
to the Son, laud and hon-our to the Spir-it,

ev-er three, and ev-er one, one in might and

bind-ing all the church in one, ho-ly Zi-on's
pours per-pet-ual mel-o-dy, God the One-in-
hear thy ser-vants as they pray; and thy ful-lest
with the bless-ed to re-tain, and here-af-ter
ev-er three, and ev-er one, one in might and

* Choose either part.

Text: Latin (*Angularis fundamentum*, 7th cent.); tr. John Mason Neale (1818–1866), alt.
Music: Henry Purcell (1659–1695), *O God, thou art my God*; adapt. *The Psalmist*, 1842;
  desc. Barry Rose (1934– ) ©.

LMD
WESTMINSTER ABBEY
*Lower key 288, 576*

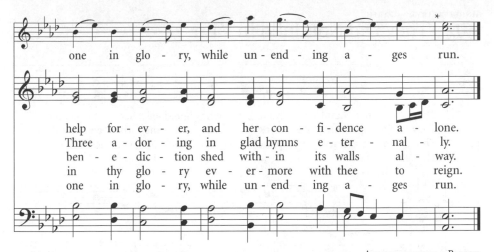

one in glo-ry, while un-end-ing a-ges run.

help for-ev-er, and her con-fi-dence a-lone.
Three a-dor-ing in glad hymns e-ter-nal-ly.
ben-e-dic-tion shed with-in its walls al-way.
in thy glo-ry ev-er-more with thee to reign.
one in glo-ry, while un-end-ing a-ges run.

## How Blessed Is This Place   301

1 How bless-ed is this place, O Lord, where you are
2 Here let your sa-cred fire of old de-scend to
3 Here let the wea-ry one find rest; the trou-bled
4 Here your an-gel-ic spir-its send their sol-emn

wor-shipped and a-dored; in faith we here an
kin-dle spir-its cold; and may our prayers, when
heart, your com-fort blest; the guilt-y one, a
praise with ours to blend, and grant the vi-sion,

al-tar raise to your great glo-ry, God of praise.
here we bend, like in-cense sweet to you as-cend.
sure re-treat; the sin-ner, par-don at your feet.
in-ly given, of this your house, the gate of heaven.

Text: Ernest E. Ryden (1886–1981), alt. *St. 1–3 © Board of Publication, Lutheran Church in America;*
*st. 4 © 1958 Service Book and Hymnal. Reprinted by permission of Augsburg Fortress.*
Music: John Beaver (1942– ) ©.

LM
ANNESLEY

# 302 They Did Not Build in Vain

*Unison*

1 They did not build in vain who found-ed here a church
2 They built up-on the rock that is the ris-en Lord,
3 Those who have loved this place, a cloud of wit-ness-es,
4 Though the ho-ri-zon's bend con-ceals the way a-head,

as wit-ness to God's love a-mid a world of
the one foun-da-tion laid which stands each earth-ly
sur-round and urge us on as we now run our
the foot-prints on the road show Christ waits at the

pain; for still to those who wish to
shock; that, Spir-it-filled, we here might
race; and so we lay a-side each
end. In him a-lone, our faith shall

see, this place pro-claims God's mys-ter-y.
raise, as liv-ing tem-ples, prayer and praise.
sin in our re-solve to strive and win.
stand, who waits for us at God's right hand.

Text: Alan Luff (1928– ). © 1990 Hope Publishing Co.
Music: Martin Shaw (1875–1958). © 1915 (renewed) J. Curwen & Sons, Ltd. (London).
    Used by permission of G. Schirmer, Inc.

66 66 88
LITTLE CORNARD
Alt. tune DARWALL 323, 365, 379

5 In every place our world
  is storm and tempest tossed;
  the flames of fear and hate
  are evil's flags unfurled;
  yet still the Spirit's wind and fire
  pour gifts for service in this hour.

6 Here is our meeting place
  where doubt finds grounds of faith;
  where hurt finds healing love,
  our penitence finds grace;
  where bridging time to eternity
  is God the holy Trinity.

## Unto Thy Temple, Lord, We Come  303

1 Un - to thy tem - ple, Lord, we come with thank - ful
2 the com - mon home of rich and poor, of bond and
3 And dwell thou with us in this place, thou and thy
4 May thy whole truth be spo - ken here, thy gos - pel

hearts to wor - ship thee, and pray that this may
free, and great and small; large as thy love for
Christ, to guide and bless. Here make the well - springs
light for - ev - er shine, thy per - fect love cast

be our home un - til we touch e - ter - ni - ty;
ev - er - more, and warm and bright and good to all.
of thy grace like foun - tains in the wil - der - ness.
out all fear, and hu - man life be - come di - vine.

Text: Robert Collyer (1823–1912).
Music: Melody *Psalmody in Miniature*, Second Supplement, 1780;
    adapt. Edward Miller (1731–1807); harm. Samuel Webbe the elder (1740–1816),
    *Collection of Psalm-Tunes*, 1820, alt.

LM
ROCKINGHAM
*Alt. setting and higher key 386*

# 304 All Things Are Thine

1 All things are thine; no gift have we, Lord of all
gifts, to of-fer thee; and so with grate-ful hearts to-
day, thine own be-fore thy feet we lay. Thy

2 No lack thy per-fect full-ness knew; for hu-man
needs and long-ings grew this house of prayer, this home of
rest, where grace is shared and truth ad-dressed. In

3 All things are thine; no gift have we, Lord of all
gifts, to of-fer thee; and so, with grate-ful hearts to-
day, thine own be-fore thy feet we lay. Come

Text: John Greenleaf Whittier (1807–1892).
Music: Scottish trad., alt.

LMD
YE BANKS AND BRAES (CANDLER)
*Alt. setting 292*

will in - formed the build - ers' thought; thy hand un -
weak - ness and in want, we call on thee for
now and deign these walls to bless; fill with thy

seen a - midst us wrought; through mor - tal mo - tive,
whom the heavens are small; thy glo - ry is thy
love their emp - ti - ness, and let their door a

scheme, and plan thy wise e - ter - nal pur - pose ran.
chil - dren's good, thy joy ful - filled in ser - vant-hood.
gate - way be to lead us from our - selves to thee.

# 305 God Is Our Song

1 God is our song, and every singer blest
2 God is our song, for Jesus comes to save;
3 This is the song no conflict ever drowns;
4 God is our silence when no songs are sung,

who, giving praise, finds energy and rest.
while praising him, we offer all we have.
who praises God all human wrath disowns.
when ecstasy or sorrow still the tongue.

All who praise God with unaffected joy
New songs we sing, in ventures new unite,
Love knows what rich complexities of sound
Glorious the faith which silently obeys

give back to us the blessing we destroy.
when Jesus leads us upward into light.
God builds upon a simple, common ground.
until we find again the voice of praise.

Text: Fred Pratt Green (1903– ), alt. © 1976 Hope Publishing Co.
Music: Henry Lawes (1596–1662).

10 10 10 10
FARLEY CASTLE

*Descant*

5 My gra - cious Mas - ter and my God, as -

1 O for a thou - sand tongues to sing my
2 Je - sus! the name that charms our fears, that
3 He speaks, and, lis - tening to his voice, new
4 Hear him, ye deaf, ye voice - less ones, your
5 My gra - cious Mas - ter and my God, as -

sist me to pro - claim, to spread through all the

dear Re - deem - er's praise, the glo - ries of my
bids our sor - rows cease; 'tis mu - sic in the
life the dead re - ceive, the mourn - ful bro - ken
loos - ened tongues em - ploy; ye blind, be - hold your
sist me to pro - claim, to spread through all the

earth a - broad the hon - ours of thy name.

God and King, the tri - umphs of his grace.
sin - ner's ears, 'tis life, and health, and peace.
hearts re - joice, the hum - ble poor be - lieve.
Sav - iour come, and leap, ye lame, for joy!
earth a - broad the hon - ours of thy name.

Text: Charles Wesley (1707–1788), alt.
Music: Thomas Haweis (1734–1820); adapt. Samuel Webbe the younger (1770?–1843);
desc. Craig Sellar Lang (1891–1971). *Desc. © Novello & Co., Ltd. Reprinted by permission of
Shawnee Press, Inc. (ASCAP).*

CM
RICHMOND
*Higher key 224*
*Alt. tune* AZMON *230*

# 307 When Long Before Time

1 When long be-fore time and the worlds were be-gun,
2 ...the si-lence was bro-ken when God sang the Song,
3 The sounds of the crea-tures were one with their Lord's,
4 Though, down through the a-ges, the Song dis-ap-peared—

when there was no earth and no sky and no sun,
and light pierced the dark-ness and rhy-thm be-gan,
their harm-o-nies sweet and be-fit-ting the Word;
its harm-o-nies bro-ken and al-most un-heard—

and all was deep si-lence and night reigned su-preme,
and with its first birth-cries cre-a-tion was born,
the Sing-er was pleased as the earth sang the Song,
the Sing-er comes to us to sing it a-gain:

Text and melody: Peter Davison (1936– ) ©; harm. George Black (1931– ) ©.

11 11 11 11
THE SINGER AND THE SONG

and     e - ven our   Mak - er    had    on - ly    a    dream...
and   crea - ture - ly   voi - ces   sang   praise   to    the    morn.
the   choir of   the   crea - tures   re - echo - ed    it    long.
our   God - is - with - us   in    the   world   now   as   then.

5 The Light has returned as it came once before,
   the Song of the Lord is our own song once more;
   so let us all sing with one heart and one voice
   the Song of the Singer in whom we rejoice.

6 To you, God, the Singer, our voices we raise;
   to you, Song incarnate, we give all our praise;
   to you, Holy Spirit, our life and our breath,
   be glory, forever, through life and through death.

## Jubilate Deo **308**

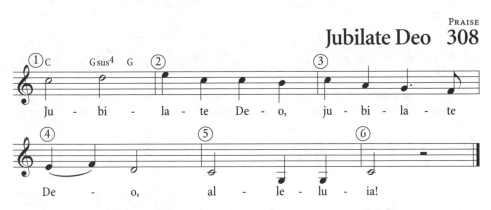

Ju - bi - la - te De - o,   ju - bi - la - te
De - o,    al - le - lu - ia!

*May be sung as a 6-part round or canon.*
*Guitar chords continue in same pattern as in measure 1.*

*Translation: "Be joyful in God" (Latin)*

Text: Ps. 100.1.
Music: Michael Praetorius (1571–1621).

JUBILATE DEO

# 309 Praise the Lord with the Sound of Trumpet

F Unison    Dm    Gm    C    F    Dm

1 Praise the Lord with the sound of trum - pet, praise the Lord with the
2 Praise the Lord with the crash - ing cym - bal, praise the Lord with the

Gm    C    Am    Dm⁷    Gm    C⁷

harp and lute,    praise the Lord with the gen - tle - sound - ing
pipe and string,    praise the Lord with the joy - ful songs you

F    Am    B♭    C    F    Dm    Gm    C

flute.    Praise the Lord in the field and for - est,
sing.    Praise the Lord on a week - day morn - ing,

F    Dm    Gm    C    Am    Dm⁷    Gm    C⁷

praise the Lord in the ci - ty square, praise the Lord an - y - time and an - y -
praise the Lord on a Sun - day noon, praise the Lord by the light of sun or

F    F⁷    B♭    Gm    Am    Dm

where.    Praise the Lord in the wind and sun - shine,
moon.    Praise the Lord in the time of sor - row,

Text and music: Natalie Sleeth (1930–1992). © 1976 Hinshaw Music, Inc. Used with permission.

98 10D 98 14 98 10
PRAISE THE LORD

praise the Lord in the dark of night, praise the Lord in the rain or
praise the Lord in the time of joy, praise the Lord ev-ery mo-ment;

snow or in the morn-ing light. Praise the Lord in the
noth-ing let your praise de-stroy. Praise the Lord in the

deep-est val-ley, praise the Lord on the high-est hill,
peace and qui-et, praise the Lord in your work or play,

praise the Lord; nev-er let your voice be still.
praise the Lord ev-ery-where in ev-ery way.

*Stanza 2 may be sung as a 2-part round or canon,*
*using both endings to conclude.*

# 310 Sing Praise to God Who Reigns Above

1 Sing praise to God who reigns a-bove, the God of all
cre - a - tion, the God of power, the God of love, the
God of our sal - va - tion. With heal-ing balm my
soul is filled and ev-ery faith - less mur-mur stilled:

2 The Lord is nev - er far a-way, but, through all grief
dis - tress-ing, an ev - er pres-ent help and stay, our
peace and joy and bless - ing. As with a moth-er's
ten - der hand, God gent-ly leads the chos-en band:

3 Thus, all my glad-some way a-long, I sing a-loud
your prais - es, that all may hear the grate-ful song my
voice un-wear - ied rais - es. Be joy-ful in the
Lord, my heart; both soul and bo - dy bear your part:

4 Let all who name Christ's ho - ly name give God all praise
and glo - ry; let all who own his power pro-claim a -
loud the won - drous sto - ry! Cast each false i - dol
from its throne, for Christ is Lord and Christ a - lone:

Text: Johan Jakob Schütz (1640–1690); tr. Frances Elizabeth Cox (1812–1897).
Music: Melody *Kirchengesänge*, Berlin, 1566; arr. *The English Hymnal*, 1906, alt.

87 87 887
MIT FREUDEN ZART
*Lower key 218, 419*

to God all praise and glo - ry.

## Awake, Arise: O Sing a New Song

A - wake, a - rise: O sing a new song of joy and cel - e - bra - tion. A new day has come; bring praise to the Son of God, of God.

*May be sung as a 3-part round or canon.*

Text and music: Marna Leasure. ©1975 Choristers Guild.

97 57 with repeat
AWAKE, ARISE

## 312 Sing a New Song unto the Lord

Text and music: Daniel L. Schutte (1947– ). © 1972, 1974, 1979 Daniel L. Schutte and New Dawn Music.
    *Administered by Oregon Catholic Press.*
    Arr. Theophane Hytrek, OSF (1915–1992).

76 96 with refrain
SING A NEW SONG

1 Yah - weh's peo - ple dance for joy. O come be -
2 Rise, O chil - dren, from your sleep; your Sav - iour
3 Glad my soul, for I have seen the glo - ry

fore the Lord and play for him on glad tam - bou -
now has come. He has turned your sor - row to
of the Lord. The trum - pet sounds; the dead shall be

rines, and let your trum - pet sound.
joy, and filled your soul with song.
raised. I know my Sav - iour lives.

# 313 Laudate Dominum

Lau - da - te Do - mi - num, lau - da - te Do - mi - num,
*Sing, praise, and bless the Lord, sing, praise and bless the Lord,*

om - nes gen - tes, al - le - lu - ia! al - le - lu - ia!
*peo - ples, na - tions! Al - le - lu - ia! Al - le - lu - ia!*

Text: Ps. 117.1. Eng. para. Taizé Community (France).
Music: Jacques Berthier (1923–1994).

SING, PRAISE

*Eng. para. and music © 1991 Les Presses de Taizé. Used by permission of G.I.A. Publications, Inc., exclusive agent.*

# 314 Laudate Omnes Gentes

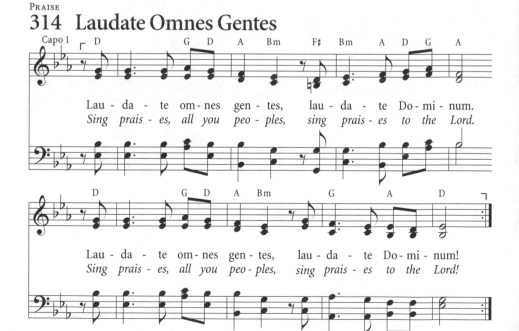

Lau - da - te om - nes gen - tes, lau - da - te Do - mi - num.
*Sing prais - es, all you peo - ples, sing prais - es to the Lord.*

Lau - da - te om - nes gen - tes, lau - da - te Do - mi - num!
*Sing prais - es, all you peo - ples, sing prais - es to the Lord!*

Text: Ps. 117.1. Eng. para. Taizé Community (France).
Music: Jacques Berthier (1923–1994).

LAUDATE OMNES GENTES

*Eng. para. and music © 1991 Les Presses de Taizé. Used by permission of G.I.A. Publications, Inc., exclusive agent.*

# When the Morning Stars Together 315

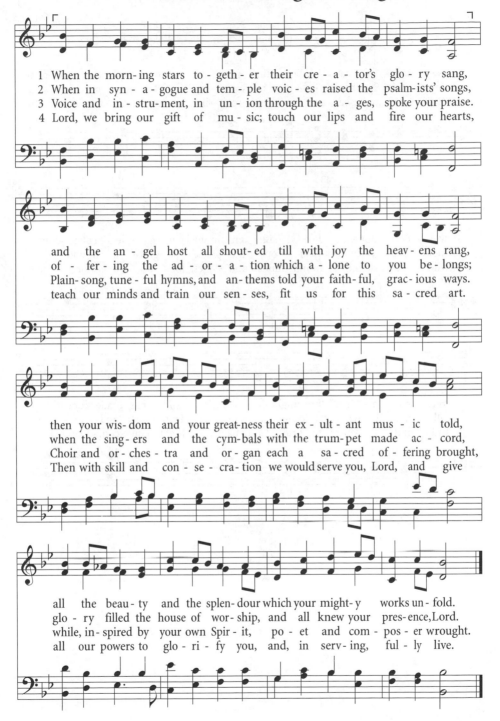

1 When the morn-ing stars to-geth-er their cre-a-tor's glo-ry sang,
2 When in syn-a-gogue and tem-ple voic-es raised the psalm-ists' songs,
3 Voice and in-stru-ment, in un-ion through the a-ges, spoke your praise.
4 Lord, we bring our gift of mu-sic; touch our lips and fire our hearts,

and the an-gel host all shout-ed till with joy the heav-ens rang,
of-fer-ing the ad-o-ra-tion which a-lone to you be-longs;
Plain-song, tune-ful hymns, and an-thems told your faith-ful, grac-ious ways.
teach our minds and train our sen-ses, fit us for this sa-cred art.

then your wis-dom and your great-ness their ex-ult-ant mus-ic told,
when the sing-ers and the cym-bals with the trum-pet made ac-cord,
Choir and or-ches-tra and or-gan each a sa-cred of-fering brought,
Then with skill and con-se-cra-tion we would serve you, Lord, and give

all the beau-ty and the splen-dour which your might-y works un-fold.
glo-ry filled the house of wor-ship, and all knew your pres-ence, Lord.
while, in-spired by your own Spir-it, po-et and com-pos-er wrought.
all our powers to glo-ri-fy you, and, in serv-ing, ful-ly live.

Text: Albert F. Bayly (1901–1984). © 1969 Oxford University Press.
Music: Melody *Tochter Sion*, Köln, 1741.

87 87D
WEISSE FLAGGEN

# 316 New Songs of Celebration Render

1 New songs of cel - e - bra - tion ren - der to God who has great
2 Joy - ful - ly, heart - i - ly re - sound - ing, let ev - ery in - stru -
3 Riv - ers and seas and tor - rents roar - ing, hon - our the Lord with

won - ders done; love sits en - throned in age - less splen - dour;
ment and voice peal out the praise of grace a - bound - ing,
wild ac - claim; moun - tains and stones, look up a - dor - ing,

come and a - dore the might - y one. God has made known the
call - ing the whole world to re - joice. Trum - pets and or - gans,
and find a voice to praise God's name. Right - eous, com - mand - ing,

Text: Ps. 98; Eng. para. Erik Routley (1917–1982), alt. *Eng. para.* © 1974 Hope Publishing Co.
Fr. para. Roger Chapal (1912– ). *Fr. para.* © 1995 Réveil Publications.
Music: Melody Strasbourg, 1545; Geneva, 1551; harm. Erik Routley (1917–1982).
*Harm.* © 1977 Hope Publishing Co.

98 98D
RENDEZ À DIEU
*Lower key 165*
*Alt. setting 15, 54*

great sal - va - tion   which all  the saints with joy con - fess.   God  has re-
set  in mo - tion   such sounds as make the hea - vens ring;   all things that
ev - er glo - rious,  prais - es  be sung that nev - er cease:   just  is  our

vealed  to   ev - ery na - tion   truth and un - end - ing right- eous - ness.
live   in  earth and o - cean,  sound forth the song, your prais - es   bring.
God, whose truth vic - to - rious   es - tab - lish - es   the world  in   peace.

*Texte français*

1 Entonnons un nouveau cantique
  pour célébrer le Dieu sauveur:
  ce qu'il a fait est magnifique,
  levant pour nous un bras vainqueur.
  Le salut de Dieu se révèle
  et tous les yeux l'ont reconnu;
  de proche en proche la nouvelle
  jusqu'au bout du monde a couru.

2 Chantez pour lui vos chants de fête.
  Psalmodiez! Criez de joie!
  Au son du cor et des trompettes,
  acclamez tous le Roi des rois!
  Le Seigneur vient juger la terre,
  sa vérité va s'imposer.
  Que tous les peuples qui espèrent
  en l'apprenant soient apaisés.

3 Que tous les océans mugissent;
  fleuves aussi, battez des mains;
  et que les montagnes bondissent
  pour acclamer le Roi qui vient!
  Le Seigneur va juger le monde
  avec droiture et vérité,
  et partout sa justice fonde
  son éternelle royauté.

# 317 Praise the Lord, Sing Hallelujah

1 Praise the Lord, sing hal - le - lu - jah, from the heav - ens
2 Let them praise the Lord their ma - ker: they were made at
3 All you fruit - ful trees and ce - dars, ev - ery hill and

praise God's name; praise the Lord, our great Cre - a - tor;
God's com - mand, who es - tab - lished them for - ev - er,
moun - tain high, creep - ing things and beasts and cat - tle,

all you an - gels, praise pro - claim. All you hosts, to - geth - er
whose de - cree shall ev - er stand. Let the earth sing hal - le -
birds that in the heav - ens fly, kings of earth and all you

prais - ing, sun and moon and stars on high; praise the
lu - jah, rag - ing seas, you mon - sters all, fire and
peo - ple, prin - ces great, earth's jud - ges all: praise God's

*Refrain may be sung only after stanza 3*

Text: Ps. 148; para. *Bible Songs Hymnal*, 1927, alt.
Music: William James Kirkpatrick (1838–1921).

87 87D with refrain
PRAISE JEHOVAH

Lord, O heavens of heav - ens, and the floods a - bove the sky.
hail and snow and va - pours, storm - y winds that hear God's call.
name, young men and maid - ens, ag - ed men, and chil - dren small.

*Refrain*

Praise the Lord, sing ha - le - lu - jah, for God's
Praise the Lord,

name a - lone is high, and God's glo - ry is ex-
and God's glo - ry

alt - ed, and God's glo - ry is ex - alt - ed, and God's
and God's glo - ry

glo - ry is ex - alt - ed, far a - bove the earth and sky.
and God's glo - ry

## 318 Rejoice Today with One Accord

1 Re - joice to-day with one ac - cord, sing out with ex - ul -
  ta - tion; re - joice and praise our might - y Lord, whose
  arm hath brought sal - va - tion. His works of love pro -
  claim the great - ness of his name, for he is God a -

2 When in dis - tress to him we cried, he heard our sad com -
  plain - ing. O trust in him, what - e'er be - tide; his
  love is all - sus - tain - ing. Tri - um - phant songs of
  praise to him our hearts shall raise; now ev - ery voice shall

Text: Henry William Baker (1821–1877).
Music: Melody Martin Luther (1483–1546), alt.; harm. composite of settings by
   Johann Sebastian Bach (1685–1750), *Hymns Ancient and Modern*, 1904.

87 87 66 66 7
EIN' FESTE BURG
*Alt. setting and lower key 526*

lone    who    hath    his    mer - cy    shown;
say,    "O    praise    our    God    al - way";

let    all    his    saints    a - dore    him!
let    all    his    saints    a - dore    him!

## Come, Let Us Join Our Cheerful Songs    319

PRAISE

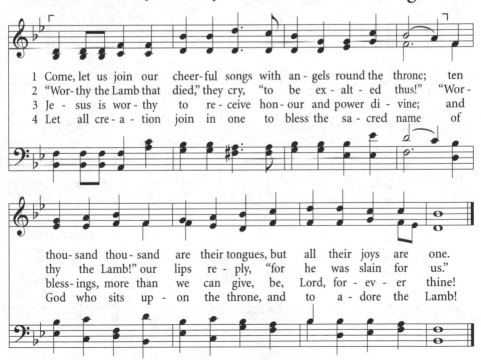

1 Come, let us join our   cheer-ful songs with an - gels round the throne;   ten
2 "Wor-thy the Lamb that   died," they cry, "to be ex - alt - ed thus!"   "Wor -
3 Je - sus is wor - thy   to re - ceive hon - our and power di - vine;   and
4 Let all cre - a - tion   join in one to bless the sa - cred name   of

thou- sand thou- sand   are their tongues, but all their joys are one.
thy the Lamb!" our   lips re - ply, "for he was slain for us."
bless- ings, more than   we can give, be, Lord, for - ev - er thine!
God who sits up - on   the throne, and to a - dore the Lamb!

Text: Isaac Watts (1674–1748), alt.
Music: Henry Lahee (1826–1912).

CM
NATIVITY

# 320 Ye Watchers and Ye Holy Ones

**Descant**

4 O friends, in glad-ness let us sing su - per-nal

*Unison*

1 Ye watch-ers and ye ho - ly ones, bright ser - aphs,
2 O high - er than the cher - u - bim, more glo - rious
3 Re - spond, ye souls in end - less rest, fore - bears in
4 O friends, in glad - ness let us sing su - per - nal

an - thems: al - le - lu - ia,

*Harmony*

cher - u - bim, and thrones, raise the glad strain:
than the ser - a - phim, lead their prais - es:
faith and proph - ets blest: al - le - lu - ia,
an - thems ech - o - ing: al - le - lu - ia,

al - le - lu - ia! Fa - ther, God the

*Unison*

al - le - lu - ia!

Cry out, do - min - ions, prince - doms,
Thou bear - er of the e - ter - nal
Ye ho - ly twelve, ye mar - tyrs
To God the Fa - ther, God the

Text: J. Athelstan L. Riley (1858–1945), alt. © Oxford University Press.
Music: Melody *Geistliche Kirchengesänge*, Köln, 1623;
  harm. Ralph Vaughan Williams (1872–1958); desc. Christopher Gower (1939– ).
  *Harm. © Oxford Univeristy Press. Desc. © Kevin Mayhew Ltd. Used by permission.*

LM with Alleluias
Lasst uns erfreuen
*Lower key 355*
*Alt. setting and lower key 231*

# 321 All Hail the Power of Jesus' Name

*Descant*

6 O that, with heav-en's sac-red throng, we at his feet may fall,

1 All hail the power of Je-sus' name! Let an-gels pros-trate fall;
2 Hail him, the heir of Dav-id's line, whom Dav-id Lord did call;
3 Crown him, you mar-tyrs of your God, who from his al-tar call;
4 Sin-ners, whose love can ne'er for-get the worm-wood and the gall,

lift high the song, and crown him Lord of all;

bring forth the roy-al di-a-dem
the God in-car-nate, life di-vine,
praise him whose burn-ing path you trod, and crown him Lord of all;
go, spread your troph-ies at his feet,

lift high the song, and crown him Lord of all!

bring forth the roy-al di-a-dem
the God in-car-nate, life di-vine,
praise him whose burn-ing path you trod, and crown him Lord of all.
go, spread your troph-ies at his feet,

5 Let every tongue and every tribe,
  delivered from the fall,
  to Christ all majesty ascribe,
  and crown him Lord of all;
  to Christ all majesty ascribe,
  and crown him Lord of all.

6 O that, with heaven's sacred throng,
  we at his feet may fall,
  lift high the universal song,
  and crown him Lord of all;
  lift high the universal song,
  and crown him Lord of all!

Text: Edward Perronet (1726–1792), alt.
Music: Oliver Holden (1765–1844); desc. Michael E. Young (1939– ). *Desc. © 1979 G.I.A. Publications, Inc.*

CM with repeat
CORONATION

# All Hail the Power of Jesus' Name

1 All hail the power of Je - sus' name! Let an - gels pros - trate
2 Hail him, the heir of Dav - id's line, whom Dav - id Lord did
3 Crown him, you mar - tyrs of your God, who from his al - tar
4 Sin - ners, whose love can ne'er for - get the worm - wood and the

fall; bring forth the roy - al di - a - dem and crown him,
call, the God in - car - nate, life di - vine, and crown him,
call; praise him whose burn - ing path you trod, and crown him,
gall, go, spread your troph - ies at his feet, and crown him,

crown him, crown him, crown him Lord of all.

5 Let every tongue and every tribe,
   delivered from the fall,
   to Christ all majesty ascribe,
   and crown him, crown him,
   crown him, crown him Lord of all.

6 O that, with heaven's sacred throng,
   we at his feet may fall,
   lift high the universal song,
   and crown him, crown him,
   crown him, crown him Lord of all!

Text: Edward Perronet (1726–1792), alt.
Music: William Shrubsole (1759?–1806).

868 with refrain
MILES LANE

# 323 Ye Holy Angels Bright

*Descant*

4 My soul, bear thou thy part, tri - umph in God a - bove,

1 Ye ho - ly an - gels bright, who wait at God's right hand,
2 Ye bless - ed souls at rest, who ran this earth - ly race,
3 Ye saints, who toil be - low, a - dore your heaven - ly King,
4 My soul, bear thou thy part, tri - umph in God a - bove,

and with a well - tuned heart sing thou the

or through the realms of light fly at your Lord's
and now, from sin re - leased, be - hold the Sav -
and on - ward as ye go some joy - ful an -
and with a well - tuned heart sing thou the songs

songs of love! Let all thy days till life shall

com - mand, as - sist our song, or else the
iour's face, your prais - es sound as in God's
them sing; in God re - joice, and thus pro -
of love! Let all thy days till life shall

Text: Richard Baxter (1615–1691), alt.
Music: John Darwall (1731–1789); desc. Sydney Hugo Nicholson (1875–1947).
*Desc. © Hope Publishing Co.*

66 66 88
DARWALL
*Alt. tune CROFT'S 136TH, 356*
*Lower key 365, 379*

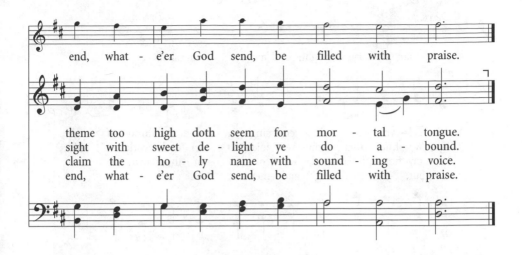

end, what - e'er God send, be filled with praise.

theme too high doth seem for mor - tal tongue.
sight with sweet de - light ye do a - bound.
claim the ho - ly name with sound - ing voice.
end, what - e'er God send, be filled with praise.

# Hallelujah 324

Hal - le - lu - jah, hal - le - lu - jah,
Hal - le - lu - jah, hal - le - lu,
Hal - le - lu - jah, hal - le - lu - jah,

hal - le - lu - jah, hal - le - lu - jah!
hal - le - lu - jah, hal - le - lu - jah!
hal - le - lu - jah, hal - le - lu - jah!

Text: Trad. liturgical.
Music: Dumisani Abraham Maraire (1943– ) ©.

HALLELUJAH

# 325 Angel-Voices, Ever Singing

*Descant*

4 Hon - our, glo - ry, might, and mer - it, thine shall ev - er be,

1 An - gel - voic - es, ev - er sing - ing, round thy throne of light,
2 Yea, we know that thou re - joic - est o'er each work of thine;
3 In thy house, great God, we of - fer of thine own to thee;
4 Hon - our, glo - ry, might, and mer - it, thine shall ev - er be,

Fa - ther, Son, and Spir - it, bless - ed Trin - i - ty!

an - gel - harps, for - ev - er ring - ing, rest not day nor night;
thou didst ears and hands and voic - es for thy praise de - sign;
and for thine ac - cep - tance prof - fer, in hu - mil - i - ty,
Fa - ther, Son, and Ho - ly Spir - it, bless - ed Trin - i - ty!

Of the best that thou hast giv - en, earth and heav - en ren - der thee.

thou - sands on - ly live to bless thee, and con - fess thee, Lord of might!
art - ist's craft and mu - sic's mea - sure for thy pleas - ure all com - bine.
hearts and minds and hands and voic - es, in our choic - est psalm - o - dy.
Of the best that thou hast giv - en, earth and heav - en ren - der thee.

Text: Francis Pott (1832–1909), alt.
Music: Edwin George Monk (1819–1900); desc. John Barnard (1948– ). *Desc. © 1982 Hope Publishing Co.*

85 85 843
ANGEL-VOICES

# Bright the Vision That Delighted

*Descant*

6 "Lord, thy glo-ry fills the heav-en; earth is with its full-ness stored;

1 Bright the vi-sion that de-light-ed once the sight of Ju-dah's seer;
2 Round the Lord, in glo-ry seat-ed, cher-u-bim and ser-a-phim
3 "Lord, thy glo-ry fills the heav-en; earth is with its full-ness stored;
4 Heaven is still with glo-ry ring-ing; earth takes up the an-gels' cry,

un-to thee be glo-ry giv-en, ho-ly, ho-ly, ho-ly Lord."

sweet the count-less tongues u-nit-ed to en-trance the proph-et's ear.
filled the tem-ple, and re-peat-ed each to each the al-ter-nate hymn:
un-to thee be glo-ry giv-en, ho-ly, ho-ly, ho-ly Lord."
"Ho-ly, ho-ly, ho-ly," sing-ing, "Lord of hosts, the Lord most high."

5 With his seraph train before him,
with his holy church below,
thus unite we to adore him;
bid we thus our anthem flow:

6 "Lord, thy glory fills the heaven;
earth is with its fullness stored;
unto thee be glory given,
holy, holy, holy Lord."

Text: Richard Mant (1776–1848).
Music: Richard Redhead (1820–1901); desc. Percy W. Whitlock (1930–1946).
*Desc. © Oxford University Press.*

87 87
REDHEAD No. 46 (LAUS DEO)

# 327 Lo, God Is Here! Let Us Adore

1 Lo, God is here! Let us a-dore and own how awe-some
is this place; let all with-in us feel God's power and
bow be-fore the hid-den face. Re-deem-ing Lord, your
grace we prove, serve you with awe, with rev-er-ence love.

2 Lo, God is here! Both day and night u-nit-ed choirs of
an-gels sing; to God, en-throned a-bove all height, heaven's
host their no-blest prais-es bring; dis-dain not, Lord, our
mean-er song, who praise you with a stam-mering tongue.

3 Be-ing of be-ings, may our praise your courts with grate-ful
fra-grance fill; still may we stand be-fore your face, still
hear and do your sov-ereign will; to you may all our
thoughts a-rise, cease-less, ac-cept-ed sac-ri-fice.

Text: Gerhard Tersteegen (1697–1769); tr. John Wesley (1703–1791), alt.
Music: Melody *Geistliche Lieder*, Leipzig, 1539.

88 88 88
VATER UNSER (OLD 112TH)

# Lo, God Is Here! Let Us Adore 328

1 Lo, God is here! Let us a-dore and own how awe-some
2 Lo, God is here! Both day and night u-nit-ed choirs of
3 Be-ing of be-ings, may our praise your courts with grate-ful

is this place; let all with-in us feel God's power
an-gels sing; to God, en-throned a-bove all height,
fra-grance fill; still may we stand be-fore your face,

and bow be-fore the hid-den face. Re-deem-ing Lord, your
heaven's host their no-blest prais-es bring; dis-dain not, Lord, our
still hear and do your sov-ereign will; to you may all our

grace we prove, serve you with awe, with rev-erence love.
mean-er song, who praise you with a stam-mering tongue.
thoughts a-rise, cease-less, ac-cept-ed sac-ri-fice.

Text: Gerhard Tersteegen (1697–1769); tr. John Wesley (1703–1791), alt.  88 88 88
Music: Henri F. Hemy (1818–1888); adapt. James G. Walton (1821–1905).  ST. CATHERINE (ST. FINBAR)

# 329 Maker, in Whom We Live

1 Ma - ker, in whom we live, in whom we are and move, the glo-ry,
2 In - car-nate De - i - ty, let all the ran - somed race ren - der in
3 Spir - it of ho - li - ness, let all thy saints a - dore thy sa - cred
4 E - ter - nal, tri - une God, let all the hosts a - bove, let all on

power, and praise re - ceive for thy cre - a - ting love. Let all the
thanks their lives to thee for thy re - deem-ing grace. The grace to
en - er - gy, and bless thine heart-re - new-ing power. Not an - gel
earth be - low re - cord and dwell up - on thy love. When heaven and

an - gel throng give thanks to God on high, while earth re -
sin - ners showed, ye heaven-ly choirs pro - claim, and cry, "Sal -
tongues can tell thy love's ec - stat - ic height, the glo - rious
earth are fled be - fore thy glo - rious face, sing all the

peats the joy - ful song and ech - oes to the sky.
va - tion to our God, sal - va - tion to the Lamb!"
joy un - speak - a - ble, the be - a - ti - fic sight.
saints thy love hath made thine ev - er - last - ing praise.

Text: Charles Wesley (1707–1788).
Music: Edward W. Naylor (1867–1934). © *Estate of Edward W. Naylor.*

SMD
FROM STRENGTH TO STRENGTH

1 O praise ye the Lord! Give praise in the height;
re - joice in God's Word, ye an - gels of light;
ye hea - vens, a - dore him by whom ye were made,
and wor - ship be - fore him in bright - ness ar - rayed.

2 O praise ye the Lord! Give praise up - on earth;
in tune - ful ac - cord, give thanks for new birth;
praise God who hath brought you all grace from a - bove,
praise God who hath taught you the path - ways of love.

3 O praise ye the Lord, all things that give sound;
each ju - bi - lant chord re - ec - ho a - round;
loud or - gans, God's glo - ry pro - claim in deep tone,
and sweet harp, the sto - ry of what God hath done.

4 O praise ye the Lord! Thanks - giv - ing and song
be ev - er out - poured all a - ges a - long;
for love in cre - a - tion, for hea - ven re - stored,
for grace of sal - va - tion, O praise ye the Lord!

Text: Ps. 150; para. Henry Williams Baker (1821–1877), alt.
Music: Charles Hubert Hastings Parry (1848–1918).

10 10 11 11
LAUDATE DOMINUM

## 331 God, We Praise You

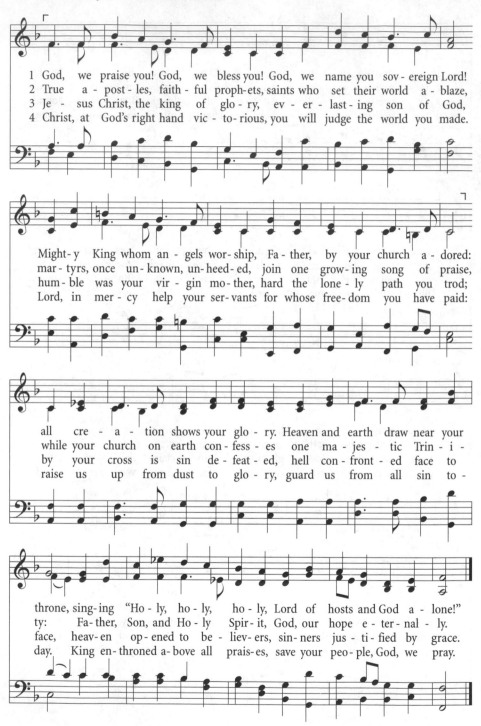

1 God, we praise you! God, we bless you! God, we name you sov-ereign Lord!
2 True a-pos-tles, faith-ful proph-ets, saints who set their world a-blaze,
3 Je-sus Christ, the king of glo-ry, ev-er-last-ing son of God,
4 Christ, at God's right hand vic-to-rious, you will judge the world you made.

Might-y King whom an-gels wor-ship, Fa-ther, by your church a-dored:
mar-tyrs, once un-known, un-heed-ed, join one grow-ing song of praise,
hum-ble was your vir-gin mo-ther, hard the lone-ly path you trod;
Lord, in mer-cy help your ser-vants for whose free-dom you have paid:

all cre-a-tion shows your glo-ry. Heaven and earth draw near your
while your church on earth con-fess-es one ma-jes-tic Trin-i-
by your cross is sin de-feat-ed, hell con-front-ed face to
raise us up from dust to glo-ry, guard us from all sin to-

throne, sing-ing "Ho-ly, ho-ly, ho-ly, Lord of hosts and God a-lone!"
ty: Fa-ther, Son, and Ho-ly Spir-it, God, our hope e-ter-nal-ly.
face, heav-en op-ened to be-liev-ers, sin-ners jus-ti-fied by grace.
day. King en-throned a-bove all prais-es, save your peo-ple, God, we pray.

Text: *You are God (Te Deum,* Latin hymn 400?); para. Christopher Idle (1938– ).
   *Para.* © 1982 Hope Publishing Co.
Music: Charles Hubert Hastings Parry (1848–1918).

87 87D
RUSTINGTON

# Thee We Adore, Eternal Lord 332

1 Thee we a - dore, e - ter - nal Lord! We praise thy
2 To thee a - loud all an - gels cry, the heavens and
3 The a - pos - tles join the glo - rious throng, the pro - phets
4 From day to day, O Lord, do we high - ly ex -
*5 Vouch- safe, O Lord, we hum - bly pray, to keep us

name with one ac - cord; thy saints, who here thy
all the powers on high; thee, ho - ly, ho - ly,
swell the im - mor - tal song, the mar - tyrs' no - ble
alt and hon - our thee; thy name we wor - ship
safe from sin this day; have mer - cy, Lord, we

good - ness see, through all the world do wor - ship thee.
ho - ly King, Lord God of hosts, they ev - er sing.
ar - my raise e - ter - nal an - thems to thy praise.
and a - dore, world with - out end, for ev - er - more!
trust in thee; Oh, let us ne'er con - found - ed be!

*Stanza 5 is optional.

Text: *You are God (Te Deum,* Latin hymn, 400?); tr. Thomas Cotterill (1779–1823), alt.
Music: Melody *Methodist Harmonist,* 1821; adapt. and harm. Lowell Mason (1792–1872).

LM
MENDON

# 333 Grand Dieu, nous te bénissons

1 Grand Dieu, nous te bé - nis - sons, nous cé - lé - brons
2 L'il - lu - stre choeur des té - moins, des dis - ci - ples,
3 Puis - se ton rè - gne de paix s'é - ten - dre par
4 Gloi - re soit au Saint - Es - prit! Gloi - re soit au

tes lou - an - ges! É - ter - nel, nous t'ex - al - tons
des pro - phè - tes, cé - lè - bre le Dieu sau - veur
tout le mon - de! Dès main - te - nant, à ja - mais,
Dieu de vi - e! Gloi - re soit à Jé - sus Christ,

de con - cert a - vec les an - ges, et pro - ster - nés
dont ils sont les in - ter - prè - tes; et ton é - glise
que sur la terre et sur l'on - de tous ge - noux soient
no - tre sau - veur, no - tre a - mi! Son im - men - se

de - vant toi, nous t'a - do - rons: louange à toi.
en tous lieux bé - nit ton nom glo - ri - eux.
a - bat - tus au nom du Sei - gneur Jé - sus.
cha - ri - té dure à per - pé - tu - i - té.

Text: *You Are God* (*Te Deum*, Latin hymn, 400?); para. Ignaz Franz (1719–1790);
    tr. Henri-Louis Empaytaz (1790–1853).
Music: Melody *Katholisches Gesangbuch*, Vienna, 1774, alt.

78 78 77
GROSSER GOTT
*Lower key 334*

1 Ho - ly God, we praise your name; Lord of all, we
2 Hark, the glad cel - es - tial hymn an - gel choirs a -
3 Lo, the a - pos - tol - ic train join the sa - cred
4 Glo - ry through e - ter - ni - ty: Spir - it, Word, and

bow be - fore you. All on earth your scep - tre claim;
bove are rais - ing; cher - u - bim and ser - a - phim,
name to hal - low; proph - ets swell the glad re - frain,
blest Cre - a - tor. God of gra - cious ten - der - ness,

all in heaven a - bove a - dore you. In - fin - ite your
in un - ceas - ing chor - us prais - ing, fill the heavens with
and the white robed mar - tyrs fol - low; and from morn to
at your feet we sin - ners gath - er; light and mer - cy,

vast do - main; ev - er - last - ing is your reign.
sweet ac - cord: "Ho - ly, ho - ly, ho - ly Lord."
set of sun through the church the song goes on.
now, we pray, give your peo - ple for this day.

Text: *You Are God* (*Te Deum*, Latin hymn, 400?); para. Ignaz Franz (1719–1790);
  tr. Clarence Alphonsus Walworth (1820–1900), alt.
Music: Melody *Katholisches Gesangbuch*, Vienna, 1774, alt.

78 78 77
GROSSER GOTT
*Higher key 333*

## 335 How Shall I Sing That Majesty

1 How shall I sing that maj-es-ty which an-gels do ad-mire? Let dust in dust and si-lence lie; sing, ye heaven-ly choir! Thou-sands of thou-sands stand a-round thy throne, O God most high; ten thou-sand

2 Thy bright-ness un-to them ap-pears, whilst I thy foot-steps trace; a sound of God comes to my ears, but they be-hold thy face. They sing be-cause thou art their sun; Lord, send a beam on me; for where

3 En-light-en with faith's light my heart, in-flame it with love's fire; then shall I sing and bear a part with that ce-les-tial choir. I shall, I fear, be dark and cold, with all my fire and light; yet when thou

4 How great a be-ing, Lord, is thine, which doth all be-ings keep! Thy knowl-edge is the on-ly line to sound so vast a deep: thou art a sea with-out a shore, a sun with-out a sphere; thy time is

Text: John Mason (1645?–1694)
Music: Walter MacNutt (1910–1996). © 1973 Waterloo Music Co. Ltd.

CMD
Hurrle

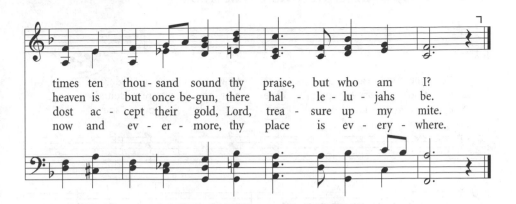

times ten thou-sand sound thy praise, but who am I?
heaven is but once be-gun, there hal - le - lu - jahs be.
dost ac - cept their gold, Lord, trea - sure up my mite.
now and ev - er - more, thy place is ev - ery - where.

# Masithi: Amen 336

Leader All Leader

Ma - si - thi: A - men, si - ya - ku - du - mi - sa. Ma - si - thi:
*Sing a - men:* *A - men,* *we praise your name, O Lord. Sing a - men:*

All Leader All

A - men, si - ya - ku - du - mi - sa. Ma - si - thi: A - men, Ba - wo,
*A - men,* *we praise your name, O Lord. Sing a - men: A - men, a - men,*

a - men, Ba - wo, a - men, si - ya - ku - du - mi - sa.
*a - men, a - men, a - men, we praise your name, O Lord.*

*Translation: "Let us say" (Xhosa)*

Text: Stephen Cuthbert Molefe (1921–1983).
Music: Stephen Cuthbert Molefe (1921–1983); arr. Dave Dargie (1938– ).
*Text, music, and arr. © 1991 Lumko Institute.*

Irregular
Masithi: Amen

# 337 God, Your Glorious Presence

1 God, your glo - rious pres - ence draws us to a - dore you,
2 In God's glo - rious pres - ence hear the harps re - sound - ing!
3 Fount of end - less bless - ing, pu - ri - fy my spir - it,

and with awe ap - pear be - fore you. In your ho - ly
See the hosts the throne sur - round - ing! "Ho - ly, ho - ly,
trust - ing on - ly in your mer - it. Like the ho - ly

tem - ple all keep mys - tic si - lence, pros - trate lie with
ho - ly," hear the hymn as - cend - ing, an - gels, saints, their
an - gels who be - hold your splen - dour, may I cease - less

deep - est rev - erence. You a - lone God we own,
voic - es blend - ing! Bow your ear to us here:
wor - ship ren - der. Let your will ev - er still

Text: Gerhard Tersteegen (1697–1769); tr. Frederick William Foster (1760–1835),
    John Miller (1756–1810), and William Mercer (1811–1873), alt.
Music: Joachim Neander (1650–1680).

668D 33 66
ARNSBERG

you our God and Sav - iour: praise your name for - ev - er.
hear, O Christ, the prais - es that your church now rais - es.
rule your church ter - res - trial, as the hosts ce - les - tial.

## Adoremus Te Jesu Christe

A - do - re - mus te Je - su Chri - ste, al - le -
*Let us praise your name, God our Sav - iour, al - le -*

lu - ia, al - le - lu - ia! Et lau - de - mus te Je - su
*lu - ia, al - le - lu - ia! Praise and bless your name, God our*

Chri - ste, et lau - de - mus te, al - le - lu - ia!
*Sav - iour, praise and bless your name, al - le - lu - ia!*

Text: Taizé Community (France).
Music: Jacques Berthier (1923–1994).
Text and music © 1991 Les Presses de Taizé. Used by permission of G.I.A. Publications, Inc., exclusive agent.

ADOREMUS TE

# 339 From Glory to Glory

1 From glo-ry to glo-ry ad-vanc-ing, we praise thee, O Lord;
2 Thanks-giv-ing and glo-ry and wor-ship and bless-ing and love,

thy name with the Fa-ther and Spir-it be ev-er a-dored.
one heart and one song have the saints up-on earth and a-bove.

From strength un-to strength we go for-ward on Zi-on's high-way,
O Lord, ev-er-more to thy ser-vants thy pres-ence be nigh;

to ap-pear be-fore God in the ci-ty of in-fi-nite day.
ev-er fit us by ser-vice on earth for thy ser-vice on high.

Text: The Liturgy of St. James; tr. Charles W. Humphreys (1840–1921).
Music: Gustav Theodore Holst (1874–1934). © *Oxford University Press.*

14 14 14 15
SHEEN

# Je louerai l'Éternel

1 Je loue-rai l'É-ter-nel de tout mon coeur, je
2 J'ai - me-rai l'É-ter-nel de tout mon coeur, je
3 Je ser-vi-rai mon Dieu de tout mon coeur, je
1 Praise, I will praise you, Lord, with all my heart. O

ra - con-te-rai tou-tes tes mer-veilles, je chan-te-rai ton
ra - con-te-rai tou-tes tes mer-veilles, je chan-te-rai ton
ra - con-te-rai tou-tes tes mer-veilles, je chan-te-rai ton
God, I will tell the won-ders of your ways, and glo-ri-fy your

nom. Je loue-rai l'É-ter-nel de tout mon coeur, je
nom. J'ai - me-rai l'É-ter-nel de tout mon coeur, je
nom. Je ser-vi-rai mon Dieu de tout mon coeur, je
name. Praise, I will praise you, Lord, with all my heart. In

fe - rai de toi le su-jet de ma joie. Al-lé-lu-ia!
fe - rai de toi le su-jet de ma joie. Al-lé-lu-ia!
fe - rai de toi le su-jet de ma joie. Al-lé-lu-ia!
you I will find the source of all my joy. Al-le-lu-ia!

*For more English stanzas, substitute (2) "love" and (3) "serve" for "praise."*

Text: Claude Fraysse (1941– ); Eng. tr. st. 1, Kenneth I. Morse (1913– ).
*Eng tr. st. 1 © 1989 The Hymnal Project.*
Music: Claude Fraysse (1941– ); vocal arr. Alain Bergèse (19??– ). *Text and music © 1997 Claude Fraysse.*

10 10 6 10 11 4
JE LOUERAI L'ÉTERNEL

# 341 God of Mercy, God of Grace

1 God of mercy, God of grace,
show the bright-ness of your face;
shine up-on us, Sav-iour, shine,
fill your church with light di-vine;
and your sav-ing health ex-tend
un-to earth's re-mot-est end.

2 Let the peo-ple praise you, Lord;
be by all that live a-dored;
let the na-tions shout and sing
glo-ry to their Sav-iour King;
at your feet their trib-ute pay,
and your ho-ly will o-bey.

3 Let the peo-ple praise you, Lord;
earth shall then its fruits af-ford,
God to us all bless-ings give,
we to God de-vot-ed live:
all be-low and all a-bove
one in joy and light and love.

Text: Henry Francis Lyte (1793–1847), alt.
Music: Henry Thomas Smart (1813–1879).

77 77 77
HEATHLANDS

# We Praise You, O God 342

1 We praise you, O God, our re-deem-er, cre-a-tor; in
2 We wor-ship you, God of our moth-ers and fa-thers, through
3 With voic-es u-nit-ed, our prais-es we of-fer and

grate-ful de-vo-tion our trib-ute we bring. We
tri-al and tem-pest com-pan-ion and guide. When
glad-ly our songs of thanks-giv-ing we raise. Our

lay it be-fore you; we kneel and a-dore you; we
per-ils o'er-take us, you will not for-sake us, but
sins now con-fess-ing, we pray for your bless-ing. To

bless your ho-ly name; glad prais-es we sing.
faith-ful to your prom-ise, you walk by our side.
you, our great re-deem-er, for-ev-er be praise!

Text: Julia Cory (1822–1963).
Music: Melody *Nederlandtsch Gedenckclank*, 1626; arr. Edward Kremser (1838–1914).

12 11 12 11
KREMSER

# 343 When All Thy Mercies, O My God

1 When all thy mer - cies, O my God, my
2 Un - num - bered com - forts to my soul thy
3 Ten thou - sand thou - sand pre - cious gifts my
4 Through ev - ery per - iod of my life thy
5 Through all e - ter - ni - ty to thee a

ris - ing soul sur - veys, trans - port - ed with the
ten - der care be - stowed, be - fore my in - fant
dai - ly thanks em - ploy; nor is the least a
good - ness I'll pur - sue; and af - ter death, in
joy - ful song I'll raise; for O, e - ter - ni -

view, I'm lost in wond - er, love, and praise.
heart con - ceived from whom those com - forts flowed.
cheer - ful heart, that tastes those gifts with joy.
dis - tant worlds, the glo - rious theme re - new.
ty's too short to ut - ter all thy praise!

Text: Joseph Addison (1672–1719).
Music: William Jones (1726–1800).

CM
St. Stephen

# From All That Dwell Below the Skies  344

*Unison*

1 From all that dwell be-low the skies let the Cre - a - tor's praise a-
2 E - ter - nal are thy mer-cies, Lord: e - ter - nal truth at - tends thy

*Harmony*      *Unison*

rise: al - le - lu - ia, al - le - lu - ia! Let the Re - deem - er's
Word; al - le - lu - ia, al - le - lu - ia! Thy praise shall sound from

name be sung through ev - ery land, in ev - ery tongue:
shore to shore till suns shall rise and set no more:

*Harmony*

al - le - lu - ia, al - le - lu - ia, al - le - lu - ia,

*Unison*

al - le - lu - ia, al - le - lu - ia!

Text: Ps. 117; para. Isaac Watts (1674–1748).
Music: Melody *Geistliche Kirchengesänge*, Köln, 1623;
  harm. Ralph Vaughan Williams (1872–1958). *Harm. © Oxford University Press.*

LM with Alleluias
LASST UNS ERFREUEN
*Lower key 355*
*Alt. setting and lower key 231*

# 345 King of Glory, King of Peace

1 King of glo - ry, King of peace, I will love thee;
and that love may nev - er cease, I will move thee.
Thou hast grant - ed my re - quest, thou hast heard me;
thou didst note my work - ing breast, thou has spared me.

2 Where - fore with my ut - most art I will sing thee,
and the cream of all my heart I will bring thee.
Though my sins a - gainst me cried, thou didst clear me;
and a - lone, when they re - plied, thou didst hear me.

3 Seven whole days, not one in seven, I will praise thee;
in my heart, though not in heaven, I can raise thee.
Small it is, in this poor sort to en - rol thee:
even e - ter - ni - ty's too short to ex - tol thee.

Text: George Herbert (1593–1633).
Music: Joseph David Jones (1827–1870).

74 74D
GWALCHMAI

# I'll Praise My Maker While I've Breath 346

1 I'll praise my Ma - ker while I've breath, and when my voice is
2 Hap - py are they whose hopes re - ly on Is - rael's God; who
3 The Lord pours eye - sight on the blind; the Lord sup - ports the
4 I'll praise God while I'm grant - ed breath; and when my voice is

lost in death, praise shall em - ploy my no - bler powers;
made the sky and earth and seas, with all their train;
faint - ing mind; and sends the la - bouring con - science peace.
lost in death, praise shall em - ploy my no - bler powers;

my days of praise shall ne'er be past, while life and thought
whose truth for - ev - er stands se - cure, who saves the op - pressed,
God helps the strang - er in dis - tress, the wid - ow and
my days of praise shall ne'er be past, while life and thought

and be - ing last, or im - mor - tal - i - ty en - dures.
who feeds the poor, whose prom - ise none shall trust in vain.
the fa - ther - less, and grants the pris - oner sweet re - lease.
and be - ing last, or im - mor - tal - i - ty en - dures.

Text: Ps. 146; para. Isaac Watts (1674–1748); adapt. John Wesley (1703–1791), alt.
Music: Lowell Mason (1792–1872).

888 888
NASHVILLE

# 347 The God of Abraham Praise

1 The God of A-braham praise who reigns en-throned a-bove;
2 The great I AM has sworn; I on this oath de-pend.
3 The good-ly land I see with peace and plen-ty blest;
4 Tri-umph-ant hosts on high give thanks e-ter-nal-ly

An-cient of ev-er-last-ing Days, and God of love;
I shall, on eag-le wings up-borne, to heaven a-scend.
a land of sac-red li-ber-ty, and end-less rest.
and "Ho-ly, ho-ly, ho-ly" cry, "great Trin-i-ty!"

Je-hov-ah, great I AM! by earth and heaven con-fessed;
I shall be-hold God's face; I shall God's power a-dore,
There milk and hon-ey flow, and oil and wine a-bound,
Hail A-braham's God and ours! One might-y hymn we raise:

I bow and bless the sac-red name for-ev-er blest.
and sing the won-ders of God's grace for-ev-er-more.
and trees of life for-ev-er grow with mer-cy crowned.
all power and maj-es-ty be yours and end-less praise!

Text: The Yigdal of Daniel ben Judah (1400?); st. 1–3, para. Thomas Olivers (1725–1799), alt.; st. 4, rev. *Hymns for Today's Church*. St. 4 © 1982 Hope Publishing Co.
Music: Melody Yigdal trad.; trsc. Meier Leon (1751–1797) and Thomas Olivers (1725–1799); harm. *Hymns Ancient and Modern*, 1875, alt.

66 84D
LEONI
*Lower key 348*

# The Living God Be Praised 348

1 The liv-ing God be praised! Give hon-our to God's name,
2 With-out a form is God, nor can we com-pre-hend
3 God's Spir-it flow-eth free, high surg-ing where it will;
4 E-ter-nal life hath God im-plant-ed in the soul;

who was, and is, and is to be, for aye the same;
the meas-ure of God's love for us with-out an end.
in proph-et's word God spoke of old and speak-eth still.
God's love shall be our strength and stay while a-ges roll.

the one e-ter-nal God ere all that now ap-pears,
For God is Lord of all, cre-a-tion speaks God's praise;
Es-tab-lished is God's law and change-less it shall stand,
The liv-ing one be praised! Give hon-our to God's name,

the First, the Last, be-yond all thought God's time-less years!
the hu-man race and all that lives God's will o-beys.
in-scribed up-on the hu-man heart in ev-ery land.
who was, and is, and is to be, for aye the same.

Text: The Yigdal of Daniel ben Judah (1400?); tr. Max Landsberg (1845–1928)
and Newton Mann (1836–1926), alt.
Music: Melody Yigdal trad.; trsc. Meier Leon (1751–1797) and Thomas Olivers (1725–1799);
harm. *Hymns Ancient and Modern*, 1875, alt.

66 84D
LEONI
*Higher key 347*

# 349 All People That on Earth Do Dwell

1 All peo-ple that on earth do dwell, sing
2 Know that the Lord is God in-deed; with-
3 O en-ter then his gates with praise, ap-
4 For why, the Lord our God is good; his

to the Lord with cheer-ful voice, him serve with mirth, his
out our aid he did us make; we are his folk, he
proach with joy his courts un-to; praise, laud, and bless his
mer-cy is for-ev-er sure; his truth at all times

praise forth tell; come ye be-fore him and re-joice.
doth us feed, and for his sheep he doth us take.
name al-ways, for it is seem-ly so to do.
firm-ly stood, and shall from age to age en-dure.

*Texte français*

1 Vous qui sur la terre habitez,
chantez à pleine voix, chantez!
Réjouissez-vous au Seigneur,
égayez-vous à son honneur.

2 Lui seul est notre souverain.
c'est lui qui nous fit de sa main:
nous, le peuple qu'il mènera,
le troupeau qu'il rassemblera.

3 Présentez-vous tous devant lui
dans sa maison dès aujourd'hui;
célébrez son nom glorieux,
exaltez-le jusques aux cieux.

4 Pour toi, Seigneur, que notre amour
se renouvelle chaque jour;
ta bonté, ta fidélité
demeurent pour l'éternité.

Text: Ps. 100; Eng. para. attrib. William Kethe (1530?–1594?). Fr. para. Roger Chapal (1912– ).
*Fr. para. © 1995 Réveil Publications.*
Music: Melody Geneva, 1551.

LM
OLD 100TH

| Moose Cree text | Inuktitut text |
|---|---|

*Moose Cree text*

1 ᐃᓂᓂᑐᒃ ᐅᑕ ᐊᔅᑭᒃ.
ᓂᑯᒧᔅᑖᒃ ·ᐁᐧᔅᐃ·ᐁᐧᑦ,
ᔑᒃ ᓄᔅᑕ ᐊᑐᔅᑲᔅᑖᒃ
ᓇᔅᐱᒃ ᐁ ᓯᑭᓚᓯᔭᒃ.

2 ·ᐁᓚ ᑭᑭᒪᓄᑐ·ᐃᐧᐅ
ᐊᓄ ᑲ ᑭᐅᔑᐃᑕᒃᒃ,
ᑭᑦ ᐃᓂᓂᒥᒥᑯᓇᐅ
ᒧᔕᒃ ᑲᓄ·ᐁᐧᓕᒥᑐᒃᒃ.

3 ᐱᑐᖃᒃ ᐅᑦ ᐃᔅᐧᑯ ᑎᒪᒃ
ᓇᔅᐱᒃ ᑭᒋ ᒪᒥᒋᒪᒃ:
ᓄᓇᑐᒥᒃ, ᓄᓇᔅᑯᒥᒃ
ᖃ ᐃᔑ ᑐᑐᒪᑭᐳᐊ.

4 ᒋᐦᐅᐸ ᑭᔖ·ᐊ ᑎᔦᐅ
ᒧᔕᒃ ·ᐃᐧᐁᔅ·ᐁᐧᓕᒋᖄᐅ
ᐅ ᑖ·ᐁᐧ·ᐃᐧᐊ ᔅᑯᓂᓂᐅ
ᑲᑭᖄ ᑲᑕ ᐋᔦᐄᐊ.

*Inuktitut text*

1 ᑮᓚᐱᒌ ᐃᔫᓱᔅ
ᐊᑕᓄᐳᑦ ᓂᖅᒍᖅᓚᐳᑦ,
ᖐᓚᓂᖢᑦ ᑭᔪᖅᔪᖅᓚᐳᑦ
ᖁᕐᕆᒃᓯᓚᓐᒍᖢ.

2 ᑖᓇ ᒍᓂᕆᓯᓐᒍ
ᓴᓇᐅᖅᔪᖅ ᐅᐸᑎᓂᓯᒃ
ᐃᓄᖅᓄᕆᓪᕿᓐᒍᑦ
ᑲᒪᕆᓗᐊᖅᓅᑕ.

3 ᐃᓪᔪᖅᓗᓂᒃ ᐃᓐᓕᖅᓴᑕ
ᐊᓐᖢᓪ ᓇᑎᓐᓚᐳᑦ,
ᖁᓕᐊᕐᔪᓗᖢᑦ ᑦᖢᐳᖅ
ᒍᓐᑦᑦ ᖀᖢᕿᒌ ᓚᑕ.

4 ᒍᓐᓚᐳᑦ ᓇᖅᑯᓲᕐᖢᖅ
ᐱᓕᕐᖃᖅᔪᖅᖏᓕᓐᖅᒌᓗ
ᑦᓕᕐᓚ ᒌᕐᔪᖅᖏᓂᖅᖢᓪ
ᐃᓂ ᓯᖅᔭᕝᐃᓯᐄᑦᐳᖅ.

5 ᒍᓐ ᐊᑦᑦ ᖀᓐᒌ
ᐃᖅᓴᓂᖢᓗ, ᐊᓯᖅᓴᖅᓗᖢ
ᓂᖅᑐᖅᑕᑕᓐ ᔪᕐᕿᓂ
ᖁᕐᕆᒃᑦᕿᖃᓐᖅᓂᓚᐳᓪᓗ.

Tr. Benjamin T. Arreak (1947– ) ©.

1 Ililitok otu uskik
Nikumostak washihiwat,
Soka nasta utoskastak
Naspich a sikilasiyak.

2 Welu kichimunitoweo
Ahnu ka ki oshiituk,
Kit ililimimikonao
Moshuk kanuwalimituk.

3 Petokak ot iskwotamik
Naspich kichimamichimak:
Nunatomik, nunaskomik
Kay ishi totumakipun.

4 Chihova kishawatiseo
Moshuk we shawalichikao,
Otapwaywin sokunileo
Kakikay kutuayaleo.

Tr. *A Collection of Hymns and Psalms in the Language of the Cree Indians of North-West America*, 1887, rev. 1946.

# 350 Stand Up and Bless the Lord

1 Stand up and bless the Lord, you peo - ple
2 Though high a - bove all praise, a - bove all
3 O for the liv - ing flame from God's own
4 God is our strength and song, who makes sal -
5 Stand up and bless the Lord; the Lord your

of God's choice; stand up and bless the
bless - ing high, who would not fear God's
al - tar brought, to touch our lips, our
va - tion ours; then be God's love in
God a - dore; stand up and bless the

Lord of hosts with heart and soul and voice.
ho - ly name, and laud and mag - ni - fy?
minds in - spire, and wing to heaven our thought!
Christ pro - claimed with all our ran - somed powers.
glo - rious name hence - forth for ev - er - more.

Text: James Montgomery (1771–1854), alt.
Music: Aaron Williams (1731–1776).

SM
ST. THOMAS

# Rejoice in God, All Earthly Lands

1 Re - joice in God, all earth - ly lands, and lift your
2 Know this: we serve the Ho - ly One, to whom our
3 Like sheep, we wan - der with - out aim un - less our
4 On God, our Ma - ker, we de - pend for love that's

hands in song and prayer. De - light to live by
rest - less souls be - long. We have our breath through
shep - herd's voice is heard. In trust we call up -
gra - cious, strong, and sure. God's faith - ful - ness shall

God's com - mands; sing joy - ful prais - es ev - ery - where.
God a - lone, to whom we raise our grate - ful song.
on God's name for dai - ly bread and gra - cious word.
nev - er end; from age to age it shall en - dure.

Text: Ps. 100; para. Ruth Duck (1947– ). © 1992 G.I.A. Publications, Inc.
Music: Melody *Antiphoner*, Grenoble, 1753; harm. Basil Harwood (1859–1949).
*Harm. published by permission of the executors of the late Dr. Basil Harwood.*

LM
DEUS TUORUM MILITUM
*Lower key 580*

# 352 Amazing Grace

1 A - maz - ing grace! How sweet the sound that
2 'Twas grace that taught my heart to fear, and
3 The Lord has prom - ised good to me, his
4 Through man - y dan - gers, toils, and snares I
5 When we've been there ten thou - sand years, bright

saved a wretch like me! I once was lost, but
grace my fears re - lieved; how pre - cious did that
word my hope se - cures; he will my shield and
have al - read - y come; 'tis grace that brought me
shin - ing as the sun, we've no less days to

now am found: was blind, but now I see.
grace ap - pear the hour I first be - lieved!
por - tion be as long as life en - dures.
safe thus far, and grace will lead me home.
sing God's praise than when we'd first be - gun.

Text: St. 1–4, John Newton (1725–1807). St. 5, *A Collection of Sacred Ballads*, Richmond, 1790.
Music: Melody *Columbian Harmony*, Cincinnati, 1829; adapt. Edwin Othello Excell (1851–1921);
   harm. John Campbell (1950– ) ©.

CM
NEW BRITAIN

*Plains Cree text*

1 ᑭᐦᒋ ᑭᓵᐚᑎᓯᐎᐣ
ᐁ ᑭ ᐱᒫᒋᐦᐃᐟ
ᑭᓴᒧᐣᑐ ᓂᑭ ᒥᐢᑲᐠ
ᒣᑳᐧᐨ ᐊᐧᓂᐦᐅᔮᐣ

2 ᓂ ᑭ ᑯᐢᑌᐣ ᑖᓂᐱᔮᐣ
ᐁᑲᐧ ᓂ ᒫᒥᓯᐣ
ᑭᓵᐚᐟᓯᐎᓂᕽ ᒋᓴᐣ
ᓂ ᑭ ᓂᐳᐢᑖᒫᐠ

3 ᑭᐦᒋ ᐊᔨᒥᓯᐎᓇ
ᐁ ᐅᑎᐦᑎᑯᔭᐣ
ᒋᓴᐣ ᒫᑲ ᓂ ᐃᐧᒋᐦᐃᐠ
ᐁ ᓂᓱᐦᑲᒫᐃᐧᐟ

4 ᑳᑭᑫ ᑭᐦᒋ ᑭᓯᑯᕽ
ᓂᑲ ᒫᒥᐦᒋᒪᐤ
ᒋᓴᐣ ᓄᐱᒪᒋᐦᐃᐁᐧᐨ
ᑳ ᓂᐳᐢᑕᒪᐃᐧᐟ

1 Ḵiche kisāwatisewin
Ā ke pimachihit
Kisāmunto ne ke miskak
Mākwach wuneyoyan.

2 Ne ke kostān ta nipayun
Makwach ne mumiseen
Kisāwat´sewinik Jesus
Ne ke nipoostumak.

3 Ḵiche Ayimisewin
Ā ot titikoyun
Jesus maka ne wechāhik
A nesokumuwit.

4 Kakekā kiche kesikok
Ne ku mumichimaw
Jesus noopimachiwām
Ka nipoostumawit.

Tr. James Settee (1910– ) ©.

*Inuktitut text*

1 ᐊᑕᓂᐅᑉ ᓲᒻᒦᓂᖕᖓᓄᑦ
ᐱᐅᓕᔭᐅᕗᖕᖓ,
ᐊᔪᐅᒪᓪᓗᖕᖓ ᓇᒡᕚᖅᐹᖕᖓ
ᑕᐅᑐᒃᑎᑉᐹᖕᖓᓗ.

2 ᑖᑦᓱᒪ ᖁᐊᖅᓵᖅᑎᑉᐹᖕᖓ
ᖃᕿᐊᓕᖁᓪᓗᖕᖓ,
ᐅᒃᐱᖅᑎᓪᓗᖕᖓᓕ ᓴᐳᑎᕚᖕᖓ,
ᐃᖅᓯᔪᓐ2ᖅᓗᖕᖓ.

3 ᑕᓯᐅᖅᐹᖕᖓ ᒫᓐᓇᒎᑦ
ᓲᒻᒦᓂᖅᔭᐊᒥᓄᑦ,
ᐃᓱᖅᑲᖕᒋᑦᑐᒧᑦ ᓱᓕ 1ᒫᒃ
ᑕᓯᐅᖅᖕᓂᐊᖅᐹᖕᖓ.

4 ᐃᓐᖏᖅᑲᐱᕆᔩᒫᖅᐸᕗᑦ
ᐋᖅᑭᒃᑕᐅᓂᑦᑎᓐᓂ,
ᐃᓱᖅᑲᖕᒋᑦᑐᒧᑦ ᓂᖅᑐᖅᓗᒍ
ᐊᑕᓂᕗᑦ ᔩᓱᓯ.

Tr. Benjamin T. Arreak (1947– ) ©.

*Mohawk text*

1 Ioh ne ra a kwat ra o ten raht
Ne se wa ah tsia tah kwen
Wa ka a tsia a tah ton ha tie es kwe
Ses ha tsia a tah tsen rion.

2 Ra o ten en raht ne wa kro ri
Iah te se e wak te rons
Ne se a ka at ka toh ra o ten en raht
Oni son tah keh tah kwe.

3 Eso te e wa ka to hets ton
Tsi non ni i iot te ron,
Ra oh o ten en raht se wak ne ren en shon
Ra on ten raht wa ka wi.

4 No nen tho o non ien te wa we
Tsi non te e tsios we te,
Ten tsi i te e wa ri wa a kwa a se
En tsi te wa sen na ien.

Tr. Josephine S. (Konwenne) Day (1905– ).

*Ojibway text*

1 Kihcishawencikewin
Kaapimaaci´ ikoyaan
Ninkakippiinkwenaapan hsa
Nookom itahsh niwaap

2 Ninkiihsekis imaa nte ´ink
Oshawencikewin tahsh
Ninkii ´oncipisaa´ nentam
Ehtepweyentamaan.

Tr. *Voices United*, 1996.

# 353 My God, How Endless Is Your Love

*Descant*

3 I yield my powers to your com - mand; to you I

1 My God, how end - less is your love! Your gifts are
2 You spread the cur - tains of the night, great Guard - ian
3 I yield my powers to your com - mand; to you I

con - se - crate my days: per - pe - tual bless - ings

ev - ery eve - ning new, and morn - ing mer - cies
of my sleep - ing hours; your sov - ereign Word re -
con - se - crate my days: per - pe - tual bless - ings

from your hand de - mand per - pe - tual songs of praise.

from a - bove gent - ly dis - til, like ear - ly dew.
stores the light, and quick - ens all my drows - y powers.
from your hand de - mand per - pe - tual songs of praise.

Text: Isaac Watts (1674–1748), alt.
Music: William Knapp (1698–1768); desc. Sydney Hugo Nicholson (1875–1947).
*Desc. © Royal School of Church Music.*

LM
WAREHAM
*Lower key 40*

# Come, Thou Fount of Every Blessing 354

1 Come, thou Fount of ev-ery bless-ing, tune my heart to sing thy grace;
2 Here I make faith's af-firm-a-tion: thus far by thy help I've come,
3 O to grace how great a debt-or dai-ly I'm con-strained to be!

streams of mer-cy, nev-er ceas-ing, call for songs of loud-est praise.
and I hope, by thy com-pas-sion, safe-ly to ar-rive at home.
Let thy good-ness, like a fet-ter, bind my wan-dering heart to thee.

Teach me some me-lo-dious mea-sure, sung by flam-ing tongues a-bove;
Je-sus sought me when a stran-ger, wan-dering from the fold of God;
Prone to wan-der, Lord, I feel it, prone to leave the God I love;

O the vast, the bound-less trea-sure of my God's un-chang-ing love.
he, to res-cue me from dan-ger, in-ter-posed his pre-cious blood.
take my heart, O take and seal it, seal it for thy courts a-bove.

Text: Robert Robinson (1735–1790), alt.
Music: *A Repository of Sacred Music: Part Second*, Harrisburg, 1813.

87 87D
NETTLETON

# 355 All Creatures of Our God and King

*Unison*

1 All crea-tures of our God and King, lift up your
2 Great rush-ing winds and breez-es soft, you clouds that
3 Swift flow-ing wa-ter, pure and clear, make mu-sic
4 Earth ev-er fer-tile, day by day un-fold your

*Harmony*

voic-es, let us sing: al-le-lu-ia, al-le-lu-ia!
ride the heavens a-loft, O sing now, al-le-lu-ia!
for your Lord to hear, al-le-lu-ia, al-le-lu-ia!
bless-ings on our way, O sing now, al-le-lu-ia!

*Unison*

Bright burn-ing sun and gold-en beams, pale
Fair ris-ing morn, with praise re-joice; stars
Fire, so in-tense and fierce-ly bright, you
All flowers and fruit that in you grow, God's

*Harmony*

sil-ver moon that gent-ly gleams, al-le-
night-ly shin-ing, find a voice, al-le-
give to us both warmth and light, al-le-
glo-ry let them al-so show: al-le-

Text: Francis of Assisi (1182–1226); tr. William Henry Draper (1855–1933), alt.
© 1923 (renewed) by J. Curwen & Sons, Ltd. Reprinted by permission of G. Schirmer, Inc. (ASCAP)
Music: Melody *Geistliche Kirchengesänge*, Köln, 1623;
    harm. Ralph Vaughan Williams (1872–1958). *Harm. © Oxford University Press.*

LM with Alleluias
LASST UNS ERFREUEN
*Higher key 344*
*Alt. setting 231*

lu - ia, al - le - lu - ia, al - le - lu - ia,

*Unison*

al - le - lu - ia, al - le - lu - ia!

5 All you with mercy in your heart,
   forgiving others, take your part,
   alleluia, alleluia!
   All you that pain and sorrow bear,
   sing praise and cast on God your care:
   alleluia, alleluia, alleluia, alleluia, alleluia!

6 And even you, most gentle death,
   waiting to hush our final breath,
   O sing now, alleluia!
   You lead back home the child of God,
   for Christ our Lord that way has trod:
   alleluia, alleluia, alleluia, alleluia, alleluia!

7 Let all things their creator bless,
   and worship God in humbleness,
   alleluia, alleluia!
   Praise God the Father, praise the Son,
   and praise the Spirit, Three-in-One:
   alleluia, alleluia, alleluia, alleluia, alleluia!

# 356 Ye Boundless Realms of Joy

1 Ye bound-less realms of joy, ex-alt your Mak-er's fame, his praise your song em-ploy a-bove the star-ry frame; your voi-ces raise, ye cher-u-bim and ser-a-phim, to sing his praise.

2 Thou moon, that rulest the night, and sun, that guidest the day, ye glit-tering stars of light, to him your hom-age pay. His praise de-clare, ye heavens a-bove, and clouds that move in liq-uid air.

3 Let them a-dore the Lord, and praise his ho-ly name, by whose al-might-y Word they all from noth-ing came; and all shall last from chang-es free; his firm de-cree stands ev-er fast.

4 U-nit-ed zeal be shown his wond-rous fame to raise, whose glo-rious name a-lone de-serves our end-less praise; earth's ut-most ends his power o-bey: his glo-rious sway the sky tran-scends.

Text: Ps. 148; para. Nahum Tate (1652–1715) and Nicholas Brady (1659–1726).
Music: William Croft (1678–1727).

66 66 44 44
CROFT'S 136TH
*Alt. tune* DARWALL 323, 365, 379

# Let All the World in Every Corner Sing  357

1 Let all the world in ev-ery cor-ner sing: my God and King!
2 Let all the world in ev-ery cor-ner sing: my God and King!

The heavens are not too high, his praise may thith-er fly;
The church with psalms must shout, no door can keep them out;

the earth is not too low, his prais-es there may grow.
but a-bove all, the heart must bear the long-est part.

Let all the world in ev-ery cor-ner sing: my God and King!
Let all the world in ev-ery cor-ner sing: my God and King!

Text: George Herbert (1593–1633).
Music: Basil Harwood (1859–1949).
*Music published by permission of the executors of the late Dr. Basil Harwood.*

10 4 66 66 with refrain
LUCKINGTON

# 358 Earth and All Stars

1 Earth and all stars, loud rush-ing plan-ets,
2 Hail, wind, and rain, loud blow-ing snow storm, sing to the
3 Trum-pet and pipes, loud clash-ing cym-bals,
4 En-gines and steel, loud pound-ing ham-mers,

Lord a new song!
Oh vic-to-ry,
Flow-ers and trees,
Harp, lute, and lyre,
Lime-stone and beams,

loud shout-ing ar-my,
loud rust-ling dry leaves,
loud hum-ming cel-los, sing to the Lord a new song!
loud build-ing work-ers,

Text: Herbert F. Brokering (1926– ).
Music: David N. Johnson (1922–1987); ref. desc. Melva Treffinger Graham (1947– ) ©.
*Text and music © 1968 Augsburg Publishing House. Reprinted by permission of Augsburg Fortress.*

457D with refrain
EARTH AND ALL STARS

*Descant*

God has done mar - - - vel - lous things. I sing

*Refrain*

God has done mar - vel - lous things.

prais - - es with a new song!

I too will praise him with a new song!

5 Classrooms and labs,
   loud boiling test tubes,
   sing to the Lord a new song!
   Athlete and band,
   loud cheering people,
   sing to the Lord a new song!
     *Refrain*

6 Knowledge and truth,
   loud sounding wisdom,
   sing to the Lord a new song!
   Daughter and son,
   loud praying members,
   sing to the Lord a new song!
     *Refrain*

# 359 This Is the Day

Text and music: Marty Haugen (1950– ). © 1980 G.I.A. Publications, Inc.

Irregular with refrain
THIS IS THE DAY

lu - ia, al - le - lu - ia.

*Last time*

F♯m7    A    B7    A/E    E    *Last time*

E    *Unison*    F♯m7

1 Let    us    sing    un - to    the    Lord,
2 Let    the    heav    –    ens    be    glad,
3 Bring your    gifts    be - fore    the    Lord,

B7    E    A    E

praise God's    name    with our    joy - ful    shouts,
let    the    earth    now re - joice and    sing,
bring your    of - ferings in - to God's    court;

G♯7    C♯m    C♯m7/B

en - ter    in    with our    joy - ful    hearts,    to    the
let    the    fields    and the    trees    cry    out    and the
tell God's    glo - ry    to    all    the    earth,    might - y

Rock of our sal - va - tion.
o - ceans thun - der God's praise.
won - ders for all time.

## 360 Bless the Lord, My Soul

Bless the Lord, my soul, and bless God's ho - ly name.

Bless the Lord, my soul, who leads me in - to life.

Text: Ps. 103.1–2; para. Taizé Community (France).
Music: Jacques Berthier (1923–1994).
*Para. and music © 1991 Les Presses de Taizé. Used by permission of G.I.A. Publications, Inc., exclusive agent.*

BLESS THE LORD

# Surely It Is God Who Saves Me

1 Sure - ly it is God who saves me; I shall trust and
2 Make God's deeds known to the peo - ples: tell out his ex -

have no fear. For the Lord de - fends and shields me
alt - ed name. Praise the Lord, who has done great things;

and his sav - ing help is near. So re - joice as you draw
all his works God's might pro - claim. Zi - on, lift your voice in

wa - ter from sal - va - tion's heal - ing spring; in the day of
sing - ing; for with you has come to dwell, in your ve - ry

your de - liv - erance thank the Lord, his mer - cies sing.
midst, the great and Ho - ly One of Is - ra - el.

Text: *Song of Thanksgiving* (Is. 12.2–6); para. Carl P. Daw, Jr. (1944– ). *Para. © 1982 Hope Publishing Co.*
Music: Alfred V. Fedak (1953– ). *© 1990 Selah Publishing Co., Inc.*

87 87D
ECCE, DEUS

# 362 Tell Out, My Soul

**Descant**

4 Tell out, my soul, the glo-ries of his word!

**Unison**

1 Tell out, my soul, the great-ness of the Lord!
2 Tell out, my soul, the great-ness of his name!
3 Tell out, my soul, the great-ness of his might!
4 Tell out, my soul, the glo-ries of his word!

Firm is his prom-ise, and his mer-cy sure.

Un-num-bered bless-ings, give my spir-it voice;
Make known his might, the deeds his arm has done;
Powers and do-min-ions lay their glo-ry by;
Firm is his prom-ise, and his mer-cy sure.

Tell out, my soul, the great-ness of the Lord

ten-der to me the prom-ise of his word;
his mer-cy sure, from age to age the same;
proud hearts and stub-born wills are put to flight,
Tell out, my soul, the great-ness of the Lord

Text: *Song of Mary* (Luke 1.46–56); para. Timothy Dudley-Smith (1926– ).
*Para. © 1962, renewal 1990 Hope Publishing Co.*
Music: Walter Greatorex (1877–1949); desc. David Iliff (1939– ); altern. harm. Derek Homan (1931– ) ©.
*Melody and harm. © Oxford University Press. Desc. © 1982 Hope Publishing Co.*

10 10 10 10
WOODLANDS

to chil - dren's chil - dren and for ev - er - more!

in God my Sav - iour shall my heart re - joice.
his ho - ly name—the Lord, the might - y one.
the hun - gry fed, the hum - ble lift - ed high.
to chil - dren's chil - dren and for ev - er - more!

*Alternative harmonization*

# 363 My Soul Proclaims Your Glory, Lord

1 My soul pro-claims your glo-ry, Lord,
2 Na-tions un-born will bless your name,
3 You have made bare your might-y arm
4 You fill the hun-gry mouths with food,
5 Glo-ry to God, all be-ing's Spring,

my spir-it sings with thank-ful voice,
giv-er of bound-less grace to me,
to break the yoke of self-ish power,
and show the pov-er-ty of wealth.
to God the Word, sal-va-tion's voice,

for you my low-ly prayer have heard:
in ev-ery age you are the same,
and lift your bro-ken ones from harm,
Your an-cient vow you have made good,
to God the Spir-it, praise we sing:

in you, my Sav-iour, I re-joice.
you make the hum-ble whole and free.
burst-ing the gates of greed's proud tower.
and raised your chil-dren to new health.
with all the a-ges we re-joice.

Text: *Song of Mary* (Luke 1.46–56); para. Paul Gibson (1932– ) ©.
Music: John Hatton (?–1793).

LM
DUKE STREET

# Splendour and Honour

*Unison*

1. Splen-dour and hon-our, maj-es-ty and pow-er,
2. Praised be the true Lamb, slain for our re-demp-tion,
3. To the Al-might-y, throned in heaven-ly splen-dour,

are yours, O Lord God, fount of ev-ery
by whose self-of-fering we are made God's
and to the Sav-iour, Christ our Lamb and

bless-ing, for by your bid-ding was the whole cre-
peo-ple: a priest-ly king-dom, from all tongues and
Shep-herd, be ad-o-ra-tion, praise, and glo-ry

a-tion called in-to be-ing.
na-tions, called to God's ser-vice.
giv-en, now and for-ev-er.

Text: *Song to the Lamb* (Rev. 4.11; 5.9–10, 13); para. Carl P. Daw, Jr. (1944– ).
*Para. © 1990 Hope Publishing Co.*
Music: Melody Poitiers, 1746; harm. Healey Willan (1880–1968). *Harm. © Estate of Healey Willan.*

11 11 11 5
ISTE CONFESSOR

# 365 Glory to God on High

1 Glo - ry to God on high, and peace to all on earth.
2 Our Sav - iour, Je - sus Christ, the Fa - ther's on - ly Son,
3 You on - ly are the Lord. You on - ly are most high.

We wor - ship you, we give you thanks, our heaven - ly King.
the sac - ri - fi - cial Lamb, who saves the world from sin,
You on - ly are the ho - ly one, Lord Je - sus Christ.

We give you praise, al - might - y God and
have mer - cy Lord. Be - side the Fa - ther's
And now you reign with Fa - ther and with

Fa - ther blessed in glo - ry bright.
hand en - throned, now hear our prayer.
Spir - it one in glo - rious light.

Text: *Glory to God* (*Gloria in excelsis*, Greek hymn, 200?); para. Paul Gibson (1932– ) ©.
Music: John Darwall (1731–1789).

66 66 88
DARWALL
*Higher key 323*

# Glory, in the Highest Glory

1 Glo - ry, in the high - est glo - ry, peace to all, in all their days.
2 Je - sus Christ, the world's Re - deem - er, Lamb of God, for sin - ners given,

Wor - ship, thanks, and praise un - ceas - ing to the Source of all we raise:
Word e - ter - nal, born of Ma - ry, Word made flesh, the face of heaven:

reign - ing in the sap - phire height, hid - den from our mor - tal sight,
ho - ly one, to you we pray, hear us in the realms of day,

now re - ceive our a - dor - a - tion, as we make our sup - pli - ca - tion.
with the Spir - it there u - nit - ed, and the God - head high ex - alt - ed.

Text: *Glory to God (Gloria in excelsis,* Greek hymn, 200?); para. Paul Gibson (1932– ) ©.
Music: Melody Geneva, 1551; harm. based on Claude Goudimel (1505–1572); rev. Alain Mabit (19??– ).
*Rev. © 1995 Réveil Publications.*

87 87 77 88
PSALM 42

# 367 Hosanna

Ho- san - na, ho- san - na, ho- san - na in ex - cel - sis. Ho-

*May be sung as a 4-part round or canon.*

Keyboard

Guitar

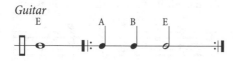

Choir

(hum)

Soprano or Instrument (at the end of the canon)

In ex - cel - sis, in ex - cel - sis. A - men, a - men,

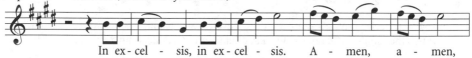

a - men, a - men, a - men, a - men, a - men,

a - men, a - men, a - men, a - men, a - men.

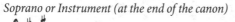

Text: Mark 11.10b.
Music: Jacques Berthier (1923–1994).
© 1978, 1980, 1981, Les Presses de Taizé. Used by permission of G.I.A. Publications, Inc., exclusive agent.

HOSANNA

1 He came down that we may have love;  he
2 He came down that we may have peace;  he
3 He came down that we may have joy;  he

came down that we may have love;  he came down that we may
came down that we may have peace;  he came down that we may
came down that we may have joy;  he came down that we may

*Leader St. 1–2*

Why did he come?

*Last time*

have love, hal - le - lu - jah for ev - er - more.
have peace, hal - le - lu - jah for ev - er - more.
have joy, hal - le - lu - jah for ev - er - more.

Text: African trad.
Music: Melody African; arr. John L. Bell (1949– ).
*Arr. © 1990 WGRG The Iona Community (Scotland). Used by permission of G.I.A. Publications, Inc., exclusive agent.*

888 8
HE CAME DOWN

# 369 Thy Strong Word Did Cleave the Darkness

1 Thy strong Word did cleave the dark-ness; at thy speak-ing
it was done; for cre - a - ted light we thank thee
while thine or - dered sea - sons run: al - le - lu - ia,
al - le - lu - ia! Praise to thee who light dost send!

2 Lo, on those who dwelt in dark-ness, dark as night and
deep as death, broke the light of thy sal - va - tion,
breathed thine own life - giv - ing breath: al - le - lu - ia,
al - le - lu - ia! Praise to thee who light dost send!

3 Thy strong Word be - speaks us right - eous; bright with thine own
ho - li - ness, glo - rious now, we press toward glo - ry,
and our lives our hopes con - fess: al - le - lu - ia,
al - le - lu - ia! Praise to thee who light dost send!

4 God the Fa - ther, Light-Cre - a - tor, to thee laud and
hon - our be; to thee, Light of Light be - got - ten,
praise be sung e - ter - nal - ly; Ho - ly Spir - it,
Light-Re - veal - er, glo - ry, glo - ry be to thee:

Text: Martin H. Franzmann (1907–1976), alt. © *1969 Concordia Publishing House.*
Music: Thomas John Williams (1869–1944). © *Estate of Gwenlyn Evans.*

87 87D
EBENEZER
*Lower key 587*

Al - le - lu - ia! al - le - lu - ia! al - le - lu - ia with- out end!
Al - le - lu - ia! al - le - lu - ia! al - le - lu - ia with- out end!
Al - le - lu - ia! al - le - lu - ia! al - le - lu - ia with- out end!
mor- tals, an- gels, now and ev - er praise the ho - ly Tri - ni - ty!

## Songs of Praise the Angels Sang 370

1 Songs of praise the    an- gels sang, heaven with al - le - lu - ias rang
2 Songs of praise a - woke the morn when the Prince of    Peace was born;
3 Heaven and earth must    pass a - way; songs of praise shall crown that day.
4 And    shall Chris- tians    fail to sing    till    on earth Christ come as King?

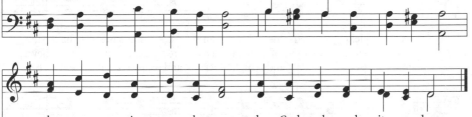

when cre - a - tion    was    be- gun, when God spoke and    it    was done.
songs of praise a - rose when he    cap - tive led cap - ti - vi - ty.
God    will make new heavens and earth; songs    of    praise shall    hail their birth.
No,    the church de - lights to    raise psalms and hymns and    songs of praise.

5 Saints below, with heart and voice,
   still in songs of praise rejoice,
   learning here, by faith and love,
   songs of praise to sing above.

6 Hymns of glory, songs of praise,
   Father, unto you we raise.
   Jesus, Saviour, living Word,
   with the Spirit be adored.

Text: James Montgomery (1771–1854), alt.                                                 77 77
Music: Melody *Heilige Seelenlust*, Breslau, 1657; adapt. and harm. William Henry Havergal (1793–1870). CULBACH

# 371 To God Be the Glory

1 To God be the glory, who great things has done!
2 O perfect redemption, the purchase of blood,
3 Great things God has taught us, great things God has done,

God so loved the world, freely sending the Son,
to every believer the promise of God:
and great our rejoicing through Jesus the Son;

who yielded his life an atonement for sin,
that when the offender, repenting, believes,
but purer and higher and greater will be

and opened the life-gate that all may go in.
through Jesus' atonement, God's pardon receives.
our wonder, our gladness when Jesus we see!

Text: Fanny Crosby (1820–1915), alt.; rev. *The Book of Praise*, 1997.
  *Rev. © 1996 The Presbyterian Church in Canada.*
Music: William Howard Doane (1832–1915).

11 11 11 11 with refrain
TO GOD BE THE GLORY

Praise the Lord! Praise the Lord! Let the earth hear God's voice.

Praise the Lord! Praise the Lord! Let the peo - ple re - joice!

O come to the Fa - ther through Je - sus the Son,

and give God the glo - ry, who great things has done!

# 372 Praise to the Holiest in the Height

1 Praise to the Holiest in the height,
and in the depth be praise,
in all his words most wonderful,
most sure in all his ways.

2 O loving wisdom of our God!
When all was sin and shame,
a second Adam to the fight
and to the rescue came.

3 O generous love! that flesh and blood,
which did in Adam fail,
should strive afresh against the foe,
should strive and should prevail;

4 and that the highest gift of grace
should flesh and blood refine,
God's presence, and his very self,
and essence all divine;

5 who in the garden secretly,
and on the cross on high,
should teach his followers, and inspire
to suffer and to die.

6 Praise to the Holiest in the height,
and in the depth be praise,
in all his words most wonderful,
most sure in all his ways.

Text: John Henry Newman (1801–1890), alt.
Music: John Bacchus Dykes (1823–1876).

CM
GERONTIUS
*Alt. tune* RICHMOND *224, 306*

# This Is the Day the Lord Hath Made

1 This is the day the Lord hath made, its
2 To - day Christ rose and left the dead, and
3 Ho - san - na to the a - noint - ed King, to
4 Ho - san - na in the high - est strains the

hours to God are known; let heaven re - joice, let
Sa - tan's em - pire fell; to - day the saints his
Da - vid's ho - ly Son! Help us, O Lord; de -
church on earth can raise; the high - est heavens in

earth be glad, and praise sur - round the throne.
tri - umph spread, and all his won - ders tell.
scend and bring sal - va - tion from thy throne.
which he reigns shall give him no - bler praise.

Text: Isaac Watts (1647–1748), alt.
Music: *Hymns and Sacred Poems*, Dublin, 1749.

CM
IRISH
*Alt. tune NATIVITY 319*

# 374 Alleluia! Sing to Jesus

1 Al - le - lu - ia! Sing to Je - sus! His the
2 Al - le - lu - ia! Not as or - phans are we
3 Al - le - lu - ia! Bread of heav - en, thou on
4 Al - le - lu - ia! King e - ter - nal, thee the
5 Al - le - lu - ia! Sing to Je - sus! His the

scep - tre, his the throne; al - le - lu - ia!
left in sor - row now; al - le - lu - ia!
earth our food, our stay; al - le - lu - ia!
Lord of lords we own; al - le - lu - ia!
scep - tre, his the throne; al - le - lu - ia!

his the tri - umph, his the vic - tor - y a - lone.
he is near us, faith be - lieves, nor ques - tions how.
here the sin - ful flee to thee from day to day;
born of Ma - ry, earth thy foot - stool, heaven thy throne.
his the tri - umph, his the vic - tor - y a - lone.

Text: William Chatterton Dix (1837–1898).
Music: Rowland Huw Prichard (1811–1887).

87 87D
HYFRYDOL

Hark! The songs of peace - ful Zi - on thun - der
Though the cloud from sight re - ceived him, when the
In - ter - ces - sor, Friend of sin - ners, earth's Re -
Thou with - in the veil hast en - tered, robed in
Hark! The songs of peace - ful Zi - on thun - der

like a might - y flood; Je - sus, out of ev - ery
for - ty days were o'er, shall our hearts for - get his
deem - er, plead for me, where the songs of all the
flesh, our great high priest; thou on earth both priest and
like a might - y flood; Je - sus, out of ev - ery

na - tion, hath re - deemed us by his blood.
prom - ise, "I am with you ev - er - more"?
sin - less sweep a - cross the crys - tal sea.
vic - tim in the eu - cha - ris - tic feast.
na - tion hath re - deemed us by his blood.

# 375 At the Name of Jesus

*Unison*

1 At the name of Je - sus ev - ery knee shall bow,
2 Hum - bled for a sea - son to re - ceive a name
3 Name him, Chris - tians, name him, with love as strong as death,
4 In your hearts en - throne him; there let him sub - due
5 Chris - tians, this Lord Je - sus shall re - turn a - gain,

ev - ery tongue con - fess him King of glo - ry now;
from the lips of sin - ners un - to whom he came,
but with awe and won - der, and with ba - ted breath;
all that is not ho - ly, all that is not true;
with his Fa - ther's glo - ry, with his an - gel train;

'tis his Fa - ther's plea - sure we should call him Lord,
faith - ful - ly he bore it, spot - less to the last,
he is God the Sav - iour, he is Christ the Lord,
crown him as your Sav - iour in temp - ta - tion's hour;
for all wreaths of em - pire meet up - on his brow,

Text: Caroline Maria Noel (1817–1877), alt.
Music: Ralph Vaughan Williams (1872–1958). © *Oxford University Press.*

11 11 11 11
KING'S WESTON

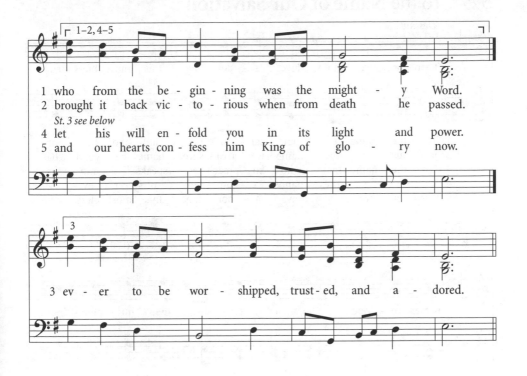

1 who from the be-gin-ning was the might-y Word.
2 brought it back vic-to-rious when from death he passed.
St. 3 see below
4 let his will en-fold you in its light and power.
5 and our hearts con-fess him King of glo-ry now.

3 ev-er to be wor-shipped, trust-ed, and a-dored.

## Gloria, Gloria, in Excelsis Deo  376

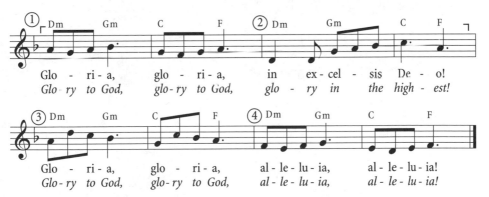

① Dm  Gm  C  F  ② Dm  Gm  C  F
Glo-ri-a,  glo-ri-a,  in ex-cel-sis De-o!
*Glo-ry to God,  glo-ry to God,  glo-ry in the high-est!*

③ Dm  Gm  C  F  ④ Dm  Gm  C  F
Glo-ri-a,  glo-ri-a,  al-le-lu-ia,  al-le-lu-ia!
*Glo-ry to God,  glo-ry to God,  al-le-lu-ia,  al-le-lu-ia!*

*May be sung as a 4-part round or canon.*

Text: Luke 2.14a; Eng. para. Taizé Community (France).
Music: Jacques Berthier (1923–1994).
  Para. and music © 1991 Les Presses de Taizé. Used by permission of GIA Publications, Inc, exclusive agent.

# 377 To the Name of Our Salvation

*Descant*

5 There-fore we in love a - dor - ing, this most bless - ed

1 To the name of our sal - va - tion, laud and hon - our
2 Je - sus is the name we trea - sure, name be - yond what
3 'Tis the name that who - so preach - es speaks like mu - sic
4 Je - sus is the name ex - alt - ed o - ver ev - ery
5 There-fore we in love a - dor - ing, this most bless - ed

name re - vere, ho - ly Je - sus, thee im - plor - ing

let us pay, which for ma - ny a gen - er - a - tion
words can tell; name of glad - ness, name of plea - sure,
to the ear; who in prayer this name be - seech - es
oth - er name; in this name, when - e'er as - sault - ed,
name re - vere, ho - ly Je - sus, thee im - plor - ing

Text: Latin (*Gloriosi salvatoris*, 15th cent.); tr. John Mason Neale (1818–1866), alt.
Music: Kaspar Ett (1788–1847), *Cantica Sacra*, Munich, 1840; desc. Gerald Manning (1943– ) ©.

87 87 87
ORIEL
*Lower key 299*
*Alt. tune* PANGE LINGUA *50*

so to write it in us here that, here-af-ter

hid in God's fore-knowl-edge lay, but with ho-ly
ear and heart de-light-ing well; name of sweet-ness
finds its com-fort ev-er near; who its per-fect
we can put our foes to shame: strength to them who
so to write it in us here that, here-af-ter

heaven-ward soar-ing, we may sing with an-gels there.

ex-ul-ta-tion we may sing a-loud to-day.
pass-ing mea-sure, sav-ing us from sin and hell.
wis-dom reach-es, heaven-ly joy pos-sess-es here.
else had halt-ed, eyes to blind and feet to lame.
heaven-ward soar-ing, we may sing with an-gels there.

# 378 Crown Him with Many Crowns

1 Crown him with man-y crowns, the Lamb up-on his throne:
2 Crown him the Lord of life, who tri-umphed o'er the grave,
3 Crown him the Lord of peace, whose power a scep-tre sways
4 Crown him the Lord of love; be-hold his hands and side,

hark, how the heaven-ly an-them drowns all mu-sic but its own!
and rose vic-to-rious in the strife for those he came to save.
from pole to pole, that wars may cease, ab-sorbed in prayer and praise.
rich wounds yet vis-i-ble a-bove, in beau-ty glo-ri-fied.

A-wake, my soul, and sing of him who died for thee,
His glo-ries now we sing who died and rose on high,
His reign shall know no end; and round his pierc-ed feet
All hail, Re-deem-er, hail! for thou hast died for me;

and hail him as thy match-less King through all e-ter-ni-ty.
who died e-ter-nal life to bring, and lives that death may die.
fair flowers of par-a-dise ex-tend their fra-grance ev-er sweet.
thy praise shall nev-er, nev-er fail through-out e-ter-ni-ty.

Text: Matthew Bridges (1800–1894) and Godfrey Thring (1823–1903), alt.
Music: George Job Elvey (1816–1893).

SMD
DIADEMATA

# Rejoice, the Lord Is King

1 Re - joice, the Lord is King! Your Lord and King a - dore!
2 Je - sus the Sav - iour reigns, the God of truth and love;
3 His king - dom can - not fail; he rules o'er earth and heaven;
4 He sits at God's right hand till all his foes sub - mit,
5 Re - joice in glo - rious hope; Je - sus, the judge, shall come

Re - joice, give thanks and sing and tri - umph ev - er -
when he had purged our stains, he took his seat a -
the keys of death and hell are to our Je - sus
and bow to his com - mand, and fall be - neath his
and take his ser - vants up to their e - ter - nal

more. Lift up your heart, lift up your voice:
bove. Lift up your heart, lift up your voice:
given. Lift up your heart, lift up your voice:
feet. Lift up your heart, lift up your voice:
home. We soon shall hear the arch - an - gel's voice;

re - joice; a - gain I say, re - joice!
re - joice; a - gain I say, re - joice!
re - joice; a - gain I say, re - joice!
re - joice; a - gain I say, re - joice!
the trump of God shall sound, re - joice!

Text: Charles Wesley (1707–1788).
Music: John Darwall (1731–1789).

66 66 88
DARWALL
*Higher key 323; Alt. tune* GOPSAL *236*

# 380 O Worship the King

*Descant*

6 O mea-sure-less Might, in-ef-fa-ble Love,

1 O wor-ship the King, all glo-rious a - bove;
2 O tell of his might, O sing of his grace,
3 The earth with its store of won-ders un - told,
4 Thy boun-ti-ful care what tongue can re - cite?

while an-gels de-light to hymn thee a - bove,

O grate-ful-ly sing his power and his love;
whose robe is the light, whose can-o-py space;
Al-might-y, thy power hath found-ed of old,
It breathes in the air, it shines in the light;

the hum-bler cre-a-tion, though fee-ble their lays,

our shield and de-fend-er, the An-cient of Days,
his char-iots of wrath the deep thun-der-clouds form,
hath stab-lished it fast by a change-less de - cree,
it streams from the hills, it de-scends to the plain,

Text: Robert Grant (1779–1838).
Music: Melody and bass William Croft (1678–1727); desc. Alan Gray (1855–1935);
   fauxbourdon Harvey Grace (1874–1944). *Desc. © Cambridge University Press. Fauxb. © Faith Press.*

10 10 11 11
HANOVER

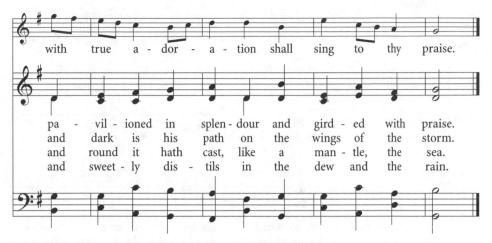

with true a - dor - a - tion shall sing to thy praise.

pa - vil - ioned in splen - dour and gird - ed with praise.
and dark is his path on the wings of the storm.
and round it hath cast, like a man - tle, the sea.
and sweet - ly dis - tils in the dew and the rain.

5 Frail children of dust, and feeble as frail,
   in thee do we trust, nor find thee to fail;
   thy mercies how tender, how firm to the end,
   our maker, defender, redeemer, and friend.

6 O measureless Might, ineffable Love,
   while angels delight to hymn thee above,
   the humbler creation, though feeble their lays,
   with true adoration shall sing to thy praise.

*Fauxbourdon*

# 381 Praise, My Soul

*Unison*

1 Praise, my soul, the King of heav - en; to his feet your tri - bute
*1 Praise, my soul, the God of heav - en; glad of heart your car - ols*

bring; ran - somed, healed, re - stored, for - giv - en, ev - er - more his prais - es
*raise; ran - somed, healed, re - stored, for - giv - en, who, like me, should sing God's*

sing. Al - le - lu - ia, al - le - lu - ia, praise the ev - er - last - ing King.
*praise? Al - le - lu - ia, al - le - lu - ia, praise the Ma - ker all your days.*

*Harmony*

2 Praise him for his grace and fa - vour to our fore - bears in dis -
*2 Praise God for the grace and fa - vour shown our fore - bears in dis -*

*The accompaniment for stanza 2 may be used for all stanzas.*

Text: Ps. 103; para. Henry Francis Lyte (1793–1847), alt.
Music: John Goss (1800–1880); desc. Gerald Manning (1943– ) ©.

87 87 87
PRAISE, MY SOUL

tress; praise him, still the same for - ev - er, slow to chide and swift to
*tress. God is still the same for - ev - er, slow to chide and swift to*

bless; al - le - lu - ia, al - le - lu - ia, glo - rious in his faith-ful - ness.
*bless; al - le - lu - ia, al - le - lu - ia, sing our Mak-er's faith-ful - ness.*

*Unison*

3 Fa - ther - like he tends and spares us; well our fee - ble frame he
*3 Like a lov - ing par - ent car - ing, God knows well our fee - ble*

knows; in his hands he gent - ly bears us, res - cues us from all our
*frame; glad - ly all our bur - dens bear - ing, still to count - less years the*

foes: al - le - lu - ia, al - le - lu - ia, wide - ly as his mer - cy flows.
*same. Al - le - lu - ia, al - le - lu - ia, all with - in me, praise God's name.*

4 Frail as sum-mer's flower we flour-ish; blows the wind and it is
*4 Frail as sum-mer's flower we flour-ish; blows the wind and it is*

gone; but, while mor-tals rise and per-ish, God en-dures un-chang-ing
*gone; but, while mor-tals rise and per-ish, God en-dures un-chang-ing*

on: al-le-lu-ia, al-le-lu-ia, praise the high e-ter-nal one.
*on: al-le-lu-ia, al-le-lu-ia, praise the high e-ter-nal one.*

**Descant**

5 An-gels, help us to a-dore him; you be-hold him face to
*5 An-gels, teach us a-dor-a - tion; you be-hold God face to*

5 An-gels, help us to a-dore him; you be-hold him face to
*5 An-gels, teach us a-dor-a - tion; you be-hold God face to*

face; sun and moon bow down be - fore him, dwell - ers all in time and
*face; sun and moon and all cre - a - tion, dwell - ers all in time and*

face; sun and moon bow down be - fore him, dwell-ers all in time and
*face; sun and moon and all cre - a - tion, dwell- ers all in time and*

space. Al - le - lu- ia, al - le - lu- ia, praise with us the God of grace.
*space. Al - le - lu- ia, al - le - lu- ia, praise with us the God of grace.*

space. Al - le - lu- ia, al - le - lu- ia, praise with us the God of grace.
*space. Al - le - lu- ia, al - le - lu- ia, praise with us the God of grace.*

# 382 Praise to the Lord

1 Praise to the Lord, all of you, God's ser-vants.
2 There is none like our God in the heav'ns or on earth, who

Bless- ed be the name of our God now and
lifts the weak out of dust, plac - ing them with the

ev - er. From the ris - ing up of the sun
might- y, who stoops to raise the weak and low:

may the Lord be praised, praise to the name of the Lord!

Text: Ps. 113; para. Ron Klusmeier (1946– ) ©.
Music: Ron Klusmeier (1946– ) ©.

Irregular
RICHARDSON-BURTON

# Jesus Shall Reign Where'er the Sun

1 Je - sus shall reign wher - e'er the sun
2 Peo - ple and realms of ev - ery tongue
3 Bless - ings a - bound wher - e'er he reigns;
4 Let ev - ery crea - ture rise and bring

doth its suc - ces - sive jour - neys run;
dwell on his love with sweet - est song,
the pris - oners leap to lose their chains;
pe - cu - liar hon - ours to our King,

his king - dom stretch from shore to shore,
and in - fant voic - es shall pro - claim
the wear - y find e - ter - nal rest,
an - gels de - scend with songs a - gain,

till moons shall wax and wane no more.
their ear - ly bless - ings on his name.
and all who suf - fer want are blest.
and earth re - peat the loud A - men.

Text: Isaac Watts (1674–1748), alt.
Music: John Hatton (?–1793).

LM
DUKE STREET

# 384 Praise to the Lord, the Almighty

*Descant*

6 Praise to the Lord! O let all that is in me a -

1 Praise to the Lord, the Al - might - y, the King of cre -
2 Praise to the Lord, who o'er all things so wond - rous - ly
3 Praise to the Lord, who doth pros - per thy work and de -
4 Praise to the Lord, who, when tem - pests their war - fare are

dore him! All that hath life and breath

a - tion; O my soul, praise him, for
reign - eth, shel - ters thee un - der his
fend thee; sure - ly his good - ness and
wag - ing, who, when the el - e - ments

come now with prais - es be - fore him! Let the A -

he is thy health and sal - va - tion: all ye who
wings, yea, so gent - ly sus - tain - eth: hast thou not
mer - cy here dai - ly at - tend thee: pon - der a -
mad - ly a - round thee are rag - ing, bid - deth them

Text: Joachim Neander (1650–1680); tr. Catherine Winkworth (1827–1878), alt.
Music: *Ernewerten Gesangbuch*, Stralsund, 1665, alt.; desc. Craig Sellar Lang (1891–1971).
*Desc. © 1953 Novello & Co., Ltd. Reprinted by permission of Shawnee Press, Inc. (ASCAP)*

14 14 4 7 8
LOBE DEN HERREN

men sound from his peo - ple a - gain:

hear, bro - thers and sis - ters draw near,
seen how thy en - treat - ies have been
new what the Al - might - y can do,
cease, turn - eth their fu - ry to peace,

glad - ly for aye we a - dore him.

praise him in glad ad - o - ra - tion.
grant - ed in what he or - dain - eth?
if with his love he be - friend thee.
whirl - winds and wa - ters as - suag - ing.

5 Praise to the Lord, who when darkness of sin is abounding,
who when the godless do triumph, all virtue confounding,
sheddeth his light,
chaseth the horrors of night,
saints with his mercy surrounding.

6 Praise to the Lord! O let all that is in me adore him!
All that hath life and breath come now with praises before him!
Let the Amen
sound from his people again:
gladly for aye we adore him.

# 385 Worship the Lord in the Beauty of Holiness

1 Wor- ship the Lord in the beau- ty of ho- li- ness;
2 Low at his feet lay thy bur- den of care- ful- ness;
3 Fear not to en- ter his courts in the slen- der- ness
4 These though we bring them in trem- bling and fear- ful- ness,
5 Wor- ship the Lord in the beau- ty of ho- li- ness;

bow down be- fore him, his glo- ry pro- claim;
high on his heart he will bear it for thee,
of the poor wealth thou canst reck- on as thine;
he will ac- cept for the name that is dear,
bow down be- fore him, his glo- ry pro- claim;

gold of o- be- dience and in- cense of low- li- ness
com- fort thy sor- rows, and ans- wer thy prayer- ful- ness,
truth in its beau- ty and love in its ten- der- ness,
morn- ings of joy give for eve- nings of tear- ful- ness,
gold of o- be- dience and in- cense of low- li- ness

bring, and a- dore him: the Lord is his name!
guid- ing thy steps as may best for thee be.
these are the of- ferings to lay on his shrine.
trust for our trem- bling, and hope for our fear.
bring, and a- dore him: the Lord is his name!

Text: John Samuel Bewley Monsell (1811–1875).
Music: Melody *Choral-buch vor Johann Heinrich Rheinhardt*, Üttingen, 1754;
harm. *The English Hymnal*, 1906.

12 10 12 10
ÜTTINGEN (WAS LEBET)

*Descant*

4 Were the whole realm of na - ture mine, that were an

1 When I sur - vey the won - drous cross on which the
2 For - bid it, Lord, that I should boast, save in the
3 See, from his head, his hands, his feet, sor - row and
4 Were the whole realm of na - ture mine, that were an

of - fering far too small; love so a - maz - ing,

Prince of glo - ry died, my rich - est gain I
cross of Christ, my God; all the vain things that
love flow min - gled down; did e'er such love and
of - fering far too small; love so a - maz - ing,

so di - vine, de - mands my soul, my life, my all.

count but loss, and pour con - tempt on all my pride.
charm me most, I sac - ri - fice them to his blood.
sor - row meet, or thorns com - pose so rich a crown?
so di - vine, de - mands my soul, my life, my all.

Text: Isaac Watts (1674–1748).
Music: Melody *Psalmody in Miniature*, Second Supplement, 1780?;
harm. Edward Miller (1731–1807); desc. David R. Riley (1947– ) ©.

LM
ROCKINGHAM
*Alt. setting and lower key 303*

# 387 All Praise to Thee

*Unison*

1 All praise to thee, for thou, O King di-vine, didst
2 Thou camest to us in low-li-ness of thought; by
5 Let ev-ery tongue con-fess with one ac-cord in

yield the glo-ry that of right was thine, that
thee the out-cast and the poor were sought, and
heaven and earth that Je-sus Christ is Lord; and

in our dark-ened hearts thy grace might shine:
by thy death was God's sal-va-tion wrought:
God the Fa-ther be by all a-dored:

al-le-lu-ia, al-le-lu-ia!

*St. 3 & 4 follow*

Text: *Jesus Christ is Lord* (Phil. 2.5–11); para. F. Bland Tucker (1895–1984).
*Para. © 1985 The Church Pension Fund.*
Music: Ralph Vaughan Williams (1872–1958). © *Oxford University Press.*

10 10 10 with Alleluias
SINE NOMINE
*Higher key 276*

*Harmony*

3 Let this mind be in us which was in thee, who wast a
4 Where-fore, by God's e - ter - nal pur- pose, thou art high ex -

ser - vant that we might be free, hum - bling thy - self to death on
alt - ed o'er all crea - tures now, and given the name to which all

Cal - va - ry: al - le - lu - ia, al - le - lu - ia!
knees shall bow: al - le - lu - ia, al - le - lu - ia!

*To beginning for st. 5*

# 388 Glorious Things of Thee Are Spoken

1 Glo - rious things of thee are spo-ken, Zi - on, ci - ty of our God;
2 See! The streams of liv - ing wa - ters, spring-ing from e - ter - nal love,
3 Round each hab - i - ta - tion hov-ering, see the cloud and fire ap - pear
4 Sav - iour, if of Zi - on's ci - ty I through grace a mem-ber am,

he whose word can - not be bro - ken formed thee for his own a - bode.
well sup - ply thy sons and daugh-ters and all fear of want re - move.
for a glo - ry and a cov-ering—show-ing that the Lord is near.
let the world de - ride or pi - ty, I will glo - ry in thy name.

On the rock of a - ges found-ed, what can shake thy sure re - pose?
Who can faint, when such a riv - er ev - er flows their thirst to as-suage?
Thus they march, the pil - lar lead-ing, light by night and shade by day;
Fad - ing is the world's best plea-sure, all its boast - ed pomp and show:

With sal - va-tion's walls sur-round-ed, thou mayest smile at all thy foes.
Grace, which like the Lord, the giv - er, nev - er fails from age to age.
dai - ly on the man - na feed-ing which God gives them when they pray.
sol - id joys and last - ing trea-sure none but Zi - on's chil - dren know.

Text: John Newton (1725–1807), alt.
Music: Franz Josef Haydn (1732–1809).

87 87D
AUSTRIA
*Alt. tune RUSTINGTON 331*

# O God of Font and Altar

1 O God of font and al - tar, of mu - sic, gran - deur, light;
2 O life - be - stow - ing Spir - it, in - spire this hal - lowed space;
3 O Christ, who cleansed the tem - ple, bap - tize us with your zeal,

toward whom the soar - ing arch - es as - pire be - yond their height:
breathe through us with new fer - vour and fill us with your grace.
and teach us your com - pas - sion to love, for - give, and heal.

as beau - ty draws us to you with - in this house of prayer,
A - rouse our lag - ging spir - its, en - flame our hearts with joy;
Be in our midst to claim us and mark us as your own;

let wor - ship form and feed us to help us show your care.
here let a love be kin - dled that death can - not de - stroy.
then send us forth in wit - ness to make your mer - cy known.

Text: Carl P. Daw, Jr. (1944– ). © 1990 Hope Publishing Co.
Music: Melody English trad.; coll. and arr. Ralph Vaughan Williams (1872–1958);
    harm. adapt. Patrick Wedd (1948– ) ©. Arr. © Oxford University Press.

76 76D
KING'S LYNN
*Alt. setting 283*

# 390 Womb of Life and Source of Being

1 Womb of life and source of be - ing, home of ev -
2 Word in flesh, our broth - er Je - sus, born to bring
3 Brood - ing Spir - it, move a - mong us; be our part -
4 Moth - er, Broth - er, ho - ly Part - ner; Fath - er, Spir -

ery rest - less heart, in your arms the worlds a -
us sec - ond birth, you have come to stand be -
ner, be our friend. When our mem - ory fails, re -
it, on - ly Son: we would praise your name for -

wak - ened; you have loved us from the start.
side us, know - ing weak - ness, know - ing earth.
mind us whose we are, what we in - tend.
ev - er, One - in - Three, and Three - in - One.

Text: Ruth Duck (1947– ). © 1992 G.I.A. Publications, Inc.
Music: Ronald Arnatt (1930– ). © 1971 Walton Music Corp.

87 87D
LADUE CHAPEL

We, your chil - dren, gath - er 'round you at the ta -
Priest who shares our hu - man strug - gles, Life of Life,
La - bour with us, aid the birth - ing of the new
We would share your life, your pas - sion, share your word

ble you pre - pare. Shar - ing stor - ies, tears, and
and Death of Death, ris - en Christ, come stand a -
world yet to be, free of serv - ant, lord, and
of world made new, ev - er sing - ing, ev - er

laugh - ter, we are nur - tured by your care.
mong us, send the Spir - it by your breath.
mas - ter, free for love and u - ni - ty.
prais - ing, one with all, and one with you.

# 391 Sing Ye Praises to the Father

1 Sing ye prais-es to the Fa-ther, sing ye prais-es to the Son,
2 Join the praise of ev-ery crea-ture, sing with sing-ing birds at dawn;
3 prais-ing on our days of glad-ness for the sum-mons to re-joice,

sing ye prais-es to the Spir-it, liv-ing and e-ter-nal One.
when the stars shine forth at night-fall, hear their heaven-ly an-ti-phon.
prais-ing in our times of sad-ness for the com-fort of God's voice.

God has made us, and has blessed us, and has called us to be true;
Praise our God for light of sum-mer, aut-umn glo-ries, win-ter snows,
Hail, Cre-a-tor, strong and lov-ing, Christ our Sav-iour, Lead-er, Lord,

God is Lord of all cre-a-tion, dai-ly mak-ing all things new.
for the com-ing of the spring-time and the life of all that grows,
liv-ing God, sus-tain-ing Spir-it— be thy ho-ly name a-dored!

Text: R.B.Y. Scott (1899–1987), alt. © 1988 Emmanuel College, Toronto.
Music: Melody Welsh trad.; coll. Edward Jones (1752–1824), *Musical & Poetical Relicks of the Welsh Bards*, 1784, alt., harm. George Black (1931– ) ©.

87 87D
ARFON MAJOR

*Unison*

1 Who comes from God, as Word and Breath? Ho- ly
2 Who lifts her voice for all to hear? Joy- ful
3 Whom should we seek with all our heart? Lov- ing

Wis- dom. Who holds the keys of life and death? Might- y
Wis- dom. Who shapes a thought and makes it clear? Truth- ful
Wis- dom. Who once re- vealed will not de- part? Faith- ful

Wis- dom: Craft- er and Cre- a- tor too, eld- est, she makes
Wis- dom: Teach- er, draw- ing out our best, mag- ni- fies what
Wis- dom: Part- ner, Coun- sellor, Com- fort er, love has found none

all things new; she com- pletes what God would do.
we in- vest, names our truth, di- rects our quest. Wis- est one,
love- li- er; life is glad- ness lived with her.

rad- iant one, wel- come, ho- ly Wis- dom!*

*\* or "welcome, great Sophia!"*

Text: Patrick Michaels (1954– ), alt. © *1989 Hope Publishing Co.*
Music: Melody *Choralemelodien zum heiligen Gesänge*, 1808;
arr. Hal H. Hopson (1933– ). *Arr.* © *1991 Hope Publishing Co.*

84 84 777 66
SALVE REGINA COELITUM

# 393 Immortal, Invisible, God Only Wise

1 Im - mor - tal, in - vis - i - ble, God on - ly wise,
2 Un - rest - ing, un - hast - ing, and si - lent as light,
3 To all life thou giv - est, to both great and small;
4 Great Source of all glo - ry and wis - dom and light,

in light in - ac - ces - si - ble hid from our eyes;
nor want - ing, nor wast - ing, thou rul - est in might;
in all life thou liv - est, the true life of all;
thine an - gels a - dore thee, all veil - ing their sight;

most bless - ed, most glo - rious, the An - cient of Days,
thy jus - tice like moun - tains high soar - ing a - bove
we blos - som and flour - ish as leaves on the tree,
all laud we would ren - der: O help us to see

al - might - y, vic - tor - ious, thy great name we praise.
thy clouds which are foun - tains of good - ness and love.
and with - er and per - ish, but nought chang - eth thee.
'tis on - ly the splen - dour of light hid - eth thee.

Text: Walter Chalmers Smith (1824–1908), alt.
Music: Melody Welsh trad.; adapt. John Roberts of Henllan (1808–1876), *Caniadau y Cyssegr*, 1839;
    harm. *The English Hymnal*, 1906.

11 11 11 11
St. Denio

# Eternal, Unchanging

1 E - ter - nal, Un - chang - ing, we sing to your praise;
2 A - gain we re - joice in the world you have made,
3 We praise you for Je - sus, our Mas - ter and Lord,

your mer - cies are end - less, and right - eous your ways;
your might - y cre - a - tion in beau - ty ar - rayed;
the might of his Spir - it, the truth of his word,

your ser - vants pro - claim the re - nown of your name.
we thank you for life and we praise you for joy,
his com - fort in sor - row, his pa - tience in pain,

You rule in om - ni - po - tence, ev - er the same.
for love and for hope that no power can des - troy.
the faith sure and stead - fast that Je - sus shall reign.

Text: R.B.Y. Scott (1899–1987), alt. © 1988 Emmanuel College, Toronto.
Music: Healey Willan (1880–1968). © 1994 Waterloo Music Co. Ltd.

11 11 11 11
ST. BASIL
*Alt. tune* ST. DENIO 393

## 395 Bring Many Names

*Unison*

1 Bring    ma - ny   names,    beau - ti - ful and  good,
2 Strong  moth - er  God,     work - ing  night and  day,
3 Warm    fa - ther  God,     hug - ging ev - ery  child,
4 Old,     ach - ing  God,     grey with  end - less  care,

cel - e - brate, in    par - a - ble and    sto - ry,
plan - ning  all   the   won - ders  of   cre - a - tion,
feel - ing  all   the   strains of  hu - man  liv - ing,
calm - ly  pierc - ing  e - vil's  new  dis - guis - es,

ho - li - ness in   glo - ry,   liv - ing, lov - ing God.
set - ting each e - qua - tion,  gen - ius at   play:
car - ing and for - giv - ing   till we're rec - on - ciled:
glad  of good sur - pris - es,   wis - er than des - pair:

Hail   and ho - san - na!  Bring  ma - ny  names!
Hail   and ho - san - na,  strong  moth - er  God!
Hail   and ho - san - na,  warm   fa - ther  God!
Hail   and ho - san - na,  old    ach - ing  God!

Text: Brian Wren (1936– ). © 1989, 1994 Hope Publishing Co.
Music: Patrick Wedd (1948– ) ©.

9 10 11 9
WATERDOWN

5 Young, growing God, eager, on the move,
saying no to falsehood and unkindness,
crying out for justice, giving all you have:
Hail and hosanna, young, growing God!

6 Great, living God, never fully known,
joyful darkness far beyond our seeing,
closer yet than breathing, everlasting home:
Hail and hosanna, great, living God!

PRAISE

## O Praise the Gracious Power 396

1 O praise the gra-cious power that tum-bles walls of fear and
2 O praise per-sis-tent truth that o-pens fist-ed minds and
3 O praise in-clu-sive love, en-cir-cling ev-ery race, ob-
4 O praise the tide of grace that laps at ev-ery shore with

gath-ers in one house of faith all stran-gers far and near:
eas-es from their anx-ious clutch the pre-ju-dice that blinds:
liv-i-ous to gen-der, wealth, to so-cial rank or place:
vi-sions of a world at peace, no lon-ger bled by war:

*Refrain*

we praise you, Christ! Your cross has made us one!

5 O praise the word of faith
that claims us as God's own,
a living temple built on Christ,
our rock and cornerstone.
*Refrain*

6 O praise the living Christ
with faith's bright songful voice!
Announce the gospel to the world
and with these words rejoice:
*Refrain*

Text: Thomas H. Troeger (1945– ), alt.
Music: Carol Doran (1936– ). *Text © 1985 and music © 1984 Oxford University Press, Inc.*

SM with refrain
CHRISTPRAISE RAY

# 397 Praise the One Who Breaks the Darkness

1 Praise the one who breaks the dark-ness with a lib-er-
2 Praise the one who blessed the chil-dren with a strong yet
3 Praise the one true love in-car-nate: Christ who suf-fered

a-ting light. Praise the one who frees the pris-oners, turn-ing
gen-tle word. Praise the one who drove out de-mons with a
in our place. Je-sus died and rose for ma-ny that we

blind-ness in-to sight. Praise the one who preached the
pier-cing two-edged sword. Praise the one who brings cool
may know God by grace. Let us sing for joy and

gos-pel, heal-ing ev-ery dread dis-ease, calm-ing
wa-ter to the des-ert's burn-ing sand. From this
glad-ness, see-ing what our God has done. Praise the

Text: Rusty Edwards (1955– ). © 1987 Hope Publishing Co.
Music: *A Repository of Sacred Music: Part Second*, Harrisburg, 1813.

87 87D
NETTLETON

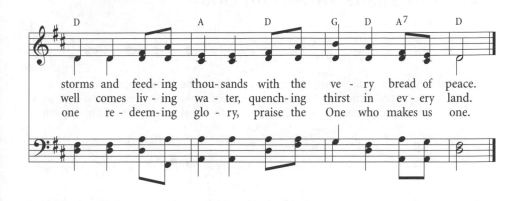

storms and feed-ing thou-sands with the ve - ry bread of peace.
well comes liv - ing wa - ter, quench-ing thirst in ev - ery land.
one re - deem-ing glo - ry, praise the One who makes us one.

## Let Us with a Gladsome Mind 398

1 Let us with a glad - some mind praise the Lord, for - ev - er kind:
2 Who with all - com - mand-ing might filled the new-made world with light:
3 Who the gol - den - tress - ed sun caused all day its course to run:
4 All things liv - ing God doth feed, with full hand sup - plies their need:
5 Let us then with glad - some mind, praise the Lord, for - ev - er kind:

for his mer - cies aye en - dure, ev - er faith - ful, ev - er sure.

Text: Ps. 136, abbrev.; para. John Milton (1608–1674), alt.
Music: Melody John Antes (1740–1811); harm. John B. Wilkes (1785–1869).

77 77
MONKLAND

# 399 Now Thank We All Our God

1 Now thank we all our God, with heart and hands and voic - es,
2 O may this boun-teous God through all our life be near us,
3 All praise and thanks to God e - ter - nal now be giv - en,

who won-drous things hath done, in whom this world re - joic - es;
with ev - er joy - ful hearts and bless-ed peace to cheer us,
to Spir - it and to Word, who reign in high-est heav - en:

who from our moth-er's arms hath blessed us on our way
and nour-ish us with grace, and guide us when per - plexed,
our ev - er faith-ful God, whom heaven and earth a - dore;

with count-less gifts of love, and still is ours to - day.
and free us from all ills in this world and the next.
for thus it was, is now, and shall be ev - er - more.

Text: Martin Rinckart (1596–1649); tr. Catherine Winkworth (1827–1878), alt.
Music: Melody Johann Crüger (1598–1662); harm. Felix Mendelssohn (1809–1847), *Lobgesang*, alt.

67 67 66 66
NUN DANKET

# What Wondrous Love Is This 400

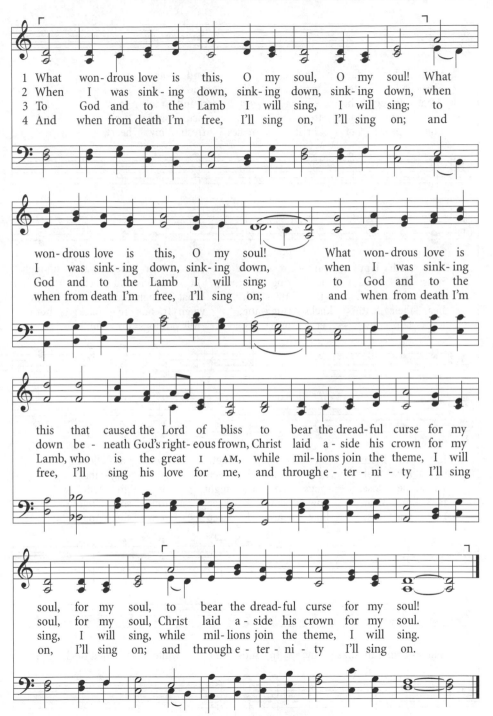

1 What won-drous love is this, O my soul, O my soul! What
2 When I was sink-ing down, sink-ing down, sink-ing down, when
3 To God and to the Lamb I will sing, I will sing; to
4 And when from death I'm free, I'll sing on, I'll sing on; and

won-drous love is this, O my soul! What won-drous love is
I was sink-ing down, sink-ing down, when I was sink-ing
God and to the Lamb I will sing; to God and to the
when from death I'm free, I'll sing on; and when from death I'm

this that caused the Lord of bliss to bear the dread-ful curse for my
down be - neath God's right-eous frown, Christ laid a - side his crown for my
Lamb, who is the great I AM, while mil-lions join the theme, I will
free, I'll sing his love for me, and through e - ter - ni - ty I'll sing

soul, for my soul, to bear the dread-ful curse for my soul!
soul, for my soul, Christ laid a - side his crown for my soul.
sing, I will sing, while mil-lions join the theme, I will sing.
on, I'll sing on; and through e - ter - ni - ty I'll sing on.

Text: *General Selection of the Newest and Most Admired Hymns and Spiritual Songs Now in Use,* 1811, alt.
Music: Melody William Walker (1809–1875), appendix to *The Southern Harmony,* New Haven, 1840 ed.; harm. *The New Century Hymnal,* 1995. Harm. © 1993 The Pilgrim Press.

12 9 12 12 9
WONDROUS LOVE

# 401 My Life Flows On in Endless Song

1 My life flows on in endless song a-
2 Through all the tumult and the strife, I
3 What though the tempest 'round me roar, I
4 When tyrants tremble, sick with fear, and
5 The peace of Christ makes fresh my heart, a

bove earth's lamentation. I hear the real though
hear that music ringing; it sounds and echoes
hear the truth it liveth. What though the darkness
hear their death knells ringing; when friends rejoice both
fountain ever springing. All things are mine since

far-off hymn that hails a new creation.
in my soul; how can I keep from singing?
'round me close, songs in the night it giveth.
far and near, how can I keep from singing?
I am his; how can I keep from singing?

*Refrain*

No storm can shake my in-most calm, while to that Rock I'm

Text: St. 1–2, Robert Lowry (1826–1899); st. 3, Doris Plenn.
*St. 3 © 1957 (renewed) Sanga Music, Inc. All rights reserved. Used by permission.*
Music: Attrib. Robert Lowry (1826–1899), alt.

87 87 with refrain
HOW CAN I KEEP FROM SINGING

cling - ing. Since Love is lord of

heaven and earth, how can I keep from sing - ing?

## Confitemini Domino 402

Con - fi - te - mi - ni Do - mi - no quo - ni - am bo - nus.
*Come and fill our hearts with your peace. You a - lone, O Lord, are ho - ly.*

Con - fi - te - mi - ni Do - mi - no, al - le - lu - ia!
*Come and fill our hearts with your peace, al - le - lu - ia!*

Text: Latin: Ps. 118.1; Eng. para. Taizé Community (France).
Music: Jacques Berthier (1923–1994). CONFITEMINI
*Eng. para. and music © 1991 Les Presses de Taizé. Used by permission of G.I.A. Publications, Inc. exclusive agent.*

# 403 Let All Things Now Living

*Unison*

1 Let all things now liv-ing a song of thanks-giv-ing
2 God's law still en-forc-es the stars in their cours-es

to God the cre-a-tor tri-um-phant-ly raise,
and caus-es the sun in its splen-dour to shine;

who fash-ioned and made us, pro-tect-ed and stayed us,
the hills and the moun-tains, the riv-ers and foun-tains,

who still guides us on to the end of our days.
the deeps of the o-cean in prais-es com-bine.

Text: Katherine K. Davis (1892–1980), alt. © *1939 E.C. Schirmer Music Co.*
Music: Melody Welsh trad. *Harm.* © *1978 Lutheran Book of Worship.*
*Reprinted by permission of Augsburg Fortress.*

12 11 12 11D
THE ASH GROVE

Love's ban - ners are o'er us; God's light goes be - fore us,
We too should be voic - ing our love and re - joic - ing;

a pil - lar of fire shin - ing forth in the night,
with glad ad - o - ra - tion a song let us raise

till shad - ows have van - ished and dark - ness is ban - ished,
till all things now liv - ing u - nite in thanks - giv - ing:

as for - ward we trav - el from light in - to Light.
"To God in the high - est, ho - san - na and praise!"

# 404 The Trumpets Sound, the Angels Sing

1 The trum-pets sound, the an-gels sing, the feast is
2 Ta-bles are la-den with good things; O taste the
3 The hun-gry heart he sat - is-fies, of - fers the

rea-dy to be-gin; the gates of heaven are o-pen wide
peace and joy he brings; he'll fill you up with love di-vine,
poor his par - a-dise; now hear all heaven and earth ap-plaud

and Je - sus wel-comes you in - side.
he'll turn your wa - ter in - to wine. Sing with
the a - maz - ing good - ness of the Lord.

*Repeat 1st stanza only*  *Refrain*

thank-ful-ness songs of pure de-light, come and re-vel in

*May be sung in unison or S.S.A.*

Text and music: Graham Kendrick (1950– ). © 1989 Make Way Music.
*Administered in North and South America by Integrity's Hosanna! Music (ASCAP).*
*All rights reserved. International copyright secured. Used by permission.*

LM with refrain
THE TRUMPETS SOUND

heav - en's love   and light;   take your place at the   ta - ble of
the King,   the   feast is   rea - dy to   be-gin,   the   feast is
rea - dy to   be - gin.

*Repeat st. 1–2 only*

*Last time*

# 405 Alleluia No. 1

*Descant*

Al - le - lu - ia, al - le - lu - ia, al - le - lu - ia! Give thanks to the

lu - ia, al - le - lu - ia! ris - en Lord. Al - le - lu - ia, al - le - lu - ia! Give

*To st. 1-4* | *Final Ending*

Praise to his name. name. praise to his name. name.

Text: Donald Fishel (1950– ).
Music: Melody Donald Fishel (1950– ); arr. Betty Carr Pulkingham (1928– ),
  Charles Mallory (1950– ), and George Mims (1938– ). *Text and music © 1973 Word of God Music. (Administered by The Copyright Company, Nashville, TN). All rights reserved. International copyright secured. Used by permission.*

88 with refrain
ALLELUIA No. 1

1 Je - sus is Lord of all the earth;
2 Spread the good news o'er all the earth:
3 We have been cru - ci - fied with Christ:
4 Come, let us praise the liv - ing God,

he is the king of cre - a - tion.
Je - sus has died and is ri - sen.
now we shall live for ev - er.
joy - ful - ly sing to our Sav - iour.          Al - le -

# 406 When the Lord Brought Back

1 When the Lord brought back from cap-tiv-i-ty his flock,
2 Then they said a-mong the na-tions, "God for them has done great things;
3 Re - store, O Lord, our for-tunes as of old,

we were all like peo-ple in a dream.
might-y mar - vels God has done in - deed."
like the tor-rents of the des-erts in the south.

Then our throats with laugh-ter rang and our tongues burst out in song;
Yes, the Lord has won-ders done, sav - ing won-ders from a - bove,
Those who weep-ing sow the seed shall in joy the har - vest reap.

Text and music: Ps. 126; para., alt., and music Henry Bryan Hays, OSB (1920– ).
*Para. and music © 1979, 1991, Order of St. Benedict Inc.*

Irregular with refrain
LOOKOUT MOUNTAIN

we a - woke like peo - ple from a dream.
and we are glad in - deed.
Life shall be re - stored as tor - rents of the south.

*Refrain* Unison

Though with tears we set out sad - ly in the ear - ly morn, bear - ing

forth the seed to be sown, we shall come back re - joic - ing at the

set - ting of the sun, we shall come back car - ry - ing the sheaves.

We shall come back re-joic - ing, car - ry-ing the sheaves, we shall
come back re-joic - ing all the way. Though we left in the
morn - ing with a bit - ter seed to sow, we shall

*Last time to Coda*

come back re - joic - ing all the way.

*Coda (to be sung after last refrain)*

We shall come back re-joic - ing all the way.

# Many and Great, O God, Are Your Works 407

1 Ma-ny and great, O God, are your works,
2 Grant un-to us com-mun-ion with you,
1 Ka-ti-pe-yi-ci-ket ki-si-pas-
2 O-pe-wii ce-wi-naan Ma-ni-to

mak-er of earth and sky. Your hands have
O star-a-bid-ing one. Come un-to
ka-mi-kaahk kii-me-kiw. O-si-taw
is-pi-mihk oh-ci. E-ko-si wii-

set the heavens with stars; your fin-gers spread the
us and dwell with us; with you are found the
mi-na a-ca-ko-sak Ma-ni-to o-to-
ci-tas-ke-mi-naan. Kih-ci-me-ki-wi-na

moun-tains and plains. Lo, at your Word the wa-ters were
gifts of life. Bless us with life that has no
te-naw wii-ya. Ciist wii-ya ka-pi-maa-cii-ko-
maa-ka mii-yi-naan kaa-ki-ke pi-maa-ti-si-

formed; deep seas o-bey your voice.
end, e-ter-nal life in you.
yahk e-pe-mi-ci-wa-ki.
win e-ko-te is-pi-mik.

*Optional drums*

Small frame drum ostinato    Tom tom ostinato

Text: Dakota hymn. English text: Joseph R. Renville (1779–1846); para. Philip F. Frazier (1892–1964), Irregular
alt. Oji-cree text: Stan McKay (1941– ) ©. *Para. © South Dakota Conference, United Church of Christ.* LACQUIPARLE
Music: Melody Dakota hymn; adapt. Joseph R. Renville (1779–1846); perc. arr. Brian Barlow (1952– ) ©.

# 408 Wind upon the Waters

1 Wind up-on the wa - ters, voice up-on the
2 Show - ers from the heav - ens, wa - ter from the
3 Rock and hill and gar - den, wood and des - ert
4 Blaz - ing light of won - der, flame that pierc - es
5 Wind up-on the wa - ters, rains up - on the

deep, rouse your sons and daugh - ters,
earth, gift so whol - ly giv - en,
sand, prai - rie, field, and mead - ow
night, burst the dark a - sun - der,
sand, grace your sons and daugh - ters,

Text and music: Marty Haugen (1950– ). © *1986 G.I.A. Publications, Inc.*

65 65 77 11
WIND UPON THE WATERS

wake us from our sleep, breath-ing life in-to all
source of ev-ery birth, joy of ev-ery liv-ing
shaped by Love's own hand, Love that fills the world a -
fill our souls with light. Lord of glo - ry, fill the
new-born by your hand. Come, O Spir - it, and re -

flesh, breath-ing love in - to all hearts, liv - ing
thing, mak-ing all cre - a - tion sing, show - er
round, spring-ing up from bar - ren ground, grow your
skies, make an end to ha - tred's cries, be the
new all the life that comes from you, send your

wind up - on the wa - ters of my soul.
down up - on the dry earth of my soul.
love with - in the gar - den of my soul.
blaz - ing sun of jus - tice in our lives.
winds up - on the wa - ters of my soul.

# 409 Before the Earth Had Yet Begun

1 Be - fore the earth had yet be - gun her jour - ney
2 In that bright dawn - ing of the world, ere o - cean
3 Thus when cre - a - tion's Lord did take the clay of
4 For us who would this God at - tend, no earth - ly

round the burn - ing sun, be - fore a seed of life had
surged or wind un - furled, the vaults of heaven with prais - es
earth our form to make, God willed that to our race be -
mind can com - pre - hend e - ter - nal glo - ry; praise a -

stirred, there sound - ed God's cre - a - ting Word.
rang; the morn - ing stars to - geth - er sang.
long the gifts of mu - sic, word, and song.
lone is our com - pan - ion by that throne.

Text: Herbert O'Driscoll (1928– ) ©.
Music: David M. Young (1928–1997). © *Estate of David M. Young.*

LM
CRAIGLEITH

# Creating God, Your Fingers Trace 410

1 Cre - at - ing God, your fin - gers trace the
2 Sus - tain - ing God, your hands up - hold earth's
3 Re - deem - ing God, your arms em - brace all
4 In - dwell - ing God, your gos - pel claims one

bold de - signs of far - thest space; let sun and moon and
mys - teries known or yet un - told; let wa - ter's fra - gile
now de - spised for creed or race; let peace, de - scend - ing
fam - ily with a bil - lion names; let ev - ery life be

stars and light and what lies hid - den praise your might.
blend with air, en - a - bling life, pro - claim your care.
like a dove, make known on earth your heal - ing love.
touched by grace un - til we praise you face to face.

Text: Jeffery Rowthorn (1934– ). © 1979 The Hymn Society in the United States and Canada.
All rights reserved. Used by permission of Hope Publishing Co.
Music: Attrib. Elkanah Kelsay Dare (1782–1826).

LM
KEDRON

# 411 O Lord of Every Shining Constellation

1 O Lord of ev - ery shin - ing con - stel - la - tion
2 You, Lord, have made the a - tom's hid - den forc - es;
3 You, Lord, have stamped your im - age on your crea - tures,

that wheels in splen - dour through the mid - night sky,
your laws its might - y en - er - gies ful - fil.
and though they mar that im - age, love them still;

grant us your Spir - it's true il - lu - mi - na - tion
Teach us, to whom you give such rich re - sourc - es,
lift up our eyes to Christ, that in his fea - tures

to read the se - crets of your work on high.
in all we use, to serve your ho - ly will.
we may dis - cern the beau - ty of your will.

Text: Albert Frederick Bayly (1901–1984). © Oxford University Press.
Music: Melody Geneva, 1551; harm. based on Claude Goudimel (1514–1572); rev. Jacques Feuillie (19??– ). Harm. and rev. © 1995 Réveil Publications.

11 10 11 10
DONNE SECOURS
Alt. tune HIGHWOOD 67, 255

# O God, Beyond All Face and Form 412

1 O God, be-yond all face and form, you willed it that cre-
2 The glo-ry of the gal-ax-ies, the beau-ty of a
3 You gave our race both form and name, and love for us was
4 Of this great love all loves are born, of self, of neigh-bour,

a -tion's night should blaze, and cha-os still its storm, and
ba -by's hand, the thun-dering of the rest-less seas, the
your in -tent; then to a wo-man's womb love came, and
and of earth. By love shall night be turned to morn, and

birth a u -ni -verse of light. All things be-low, all
glo -ry of the for-est's stand— all things be-low, all
on a cross was whol-ly spent. All things be-low, all
death shall nev-er con-quer birth. All things be-low, all

things a -bove are formed of your e -ter -nal love.
things a -bove are formed of your e -ter -nal love.
things a -bove are formed of this in -car -nate love.
things a -bove are formed of God's e -ter -nal love.

Text: Herbert O'Driscoll (1928– ) ©.
Music: John Bacchus Dykes (1823–1876).

88 88 88
MELITA

# 413 The Stars Declare His Glory

1 The stars de-clare his glo - ry; the vault of heav-en springs,
2 The dawn re-turns in splen - dour, the heav-ens burn and blaze,
3 So shine the Lord's com-mand - ments to make the sim-ple wise;
4 So or-der too this life of mine, di - rect it all my days;

mute wit-ness of the Mas-ter's hand in all cre-at-ed things,
the ris-ing sun re-news the race that mea-sures all our days,
more sweet than hon-ey to the taste, more rich than an - y prize,
the med-i-ta-tions of my heart be in-no-cence and praise,

and through the si - lenc-es of space their sound-less mu - sic sings.
and writes in fire a - cross the skies God's maj-es - ty and praise.
a law of love with-in our hearts, a light be-fore our eyes.
my rock, and my re-deem-ing Lord, in all my words and ways.

Text: Ps. 19; para. Timothy Dudley-Smith (1926– ). *Para. © 1981 Hope Publishing Co.*
Music: Patrick Wedd (1948– ) ©.

76 86 86
GIBSON

# God of the Sparrow  414

**Unison**

1 God of the spar - row God of the whale God of the
2 God of the earth - quake God of the storm God of the
3 God of the rain - bow God of the cross God of the
4 God of the hun - gry God of the sick God of the

swirl - ing stars How does the crea - ture say Awe
trum - pet blast How does the crea - ture cry Woe
emp - ty grave How does the crea - ture say Grace
pro - di - gal How does the crea - ture say Care

How does the crea - ture say Praise
How does the crea - ture cry Save
How does the crea - ture say Thanks
How does the crea - ture say Life

Home

5 God of the neighbour
God of the foe
God of the pruning hook
How does the creature say Love
How does the creature say Peace

6 God of the ages
God near at hand
God of the loving heart
How do your children say Joy
How do your children say Home

Text: Jaroslav J. Vajda (1919– ) ©.
Music: Carl F. Schalk (1929– ). © 1983 G.I.A. Publications, Inc.

546 77
ROEDER

# 415 All Things Bright and Beautiful

*Refrain*

All things bright and beau-ti-ful, all crea-tures great and small,

*Last time*

all things wise and won-der-ful, the Lord God made them all.

1 Each ra-diant flower that o - pens, each vi-brant bird that sings,
2 The cold wind in the win - ter, the pleas-ant sum-mer sun,
3 The rock-y moun-tain splen - dour, the loon's wild, haunt-ing call,
4 God gave us eyes to see them, and lips that we might tell

*To refrain*

God made their glow-ing col - ours, God made their live-ly wings.
the ripe fruit in the gar - den, God made them ev-ery one.
the great lakes and the prai - ries, the for-est in the fall.
how great is the Cre - a - tor, who has made all things well.

Text: Cecil Frances Alexander (1818–1895), alt.
Music: William Henry Monk (1823–1889).

76 76 with refrain
ALL THINGS BRIGHT

# All Things Bright and Beautiful

*Refrain* Unison

All things bright and beau - ti - ful, all crea - tures great and small,

all things wise and won - der - ful, the Lord God made them all.

*Last time*

1 Each ra - diant flower that o - pens, each vi - brant bird that sings,
2 The cold wind in the win - ter, the pleas - ant sum - mer sun,
3 The rock - y moun - tain splen- dour, the loon's wild, haunt - ing call,
4 God gave us eyes to see them, and lips that we might tell

*To refrain*

God made their glow - ing col - ours, God made their live - ly wings.
the ripe fruit in the gar - den, God made them ev - ery one.
the great lakes and the prair - ies, the for - est in the fall.
how great is the Cre - a - tor, who has made all things well.

*The refrain may be sung at the beginning and end only.*

Text: Cecil Frances Alexander (1818–1895), alt.
Music: Melody English trad.; adapt. and arr. Martin Shaw (1875–1958).
Arr. © 1921 (renewed) J. Curwen & Sons Ltd. (London). Used by permission of G. Schirmer, Inc.

76 76 with refrain
ROYAL OAK

# 417 Let's Sing unto the Lord

1 Let's sing un-to the Lord a hymn of glad re-joic-ing.
2 Let's sing un-to the Lord a hymn of ad-o-ra-tion,

Let's sing a hymn of love, join-ing hearts and hap-py voic-es.
ex-press un-to the Lord our songs of faith and hope.

God made the sky a-bove, the stars, the sun, the o-ceans.
Cre-a-tion's broad dis-play pro-claims the work of gran-deur,

Their good-ness does pro-claim the glo-ry of God's name.
the bound-less love of one who bless-es us with beau-ty.

*Refrain*

Al - le - lu - ia, al - le - lu - ia!

Text: Carlos Rosas (1939– ); Eng. tr. Roberto Escamilla (1931– ), Elise Eslinger (1942– ), and George Lockwood (1946– ). Tr. © 1983 The United Methodist Publishing House (Administered by The Copyright Company, Nashville, TN). All rights reserved. International copyright secured. Used by permission.
Music: Melody Carlos Rosas (1939– ); acc. Melva Treffinger Graham (1947– ) ©. Melody © 1976 Resource Publications, Inc.

67 68D with refrain
ROSAS

Let's sing un-to the Lord. Al-le-lu - ia!

*Coda after final refrain*

Let's sing un-to the Lord. Al-le-lu - ia!

Creation

# Draw the Circle Wide  418

*Refrain*

Draw the cir-cle wide.  Draw it wid-er still.

Let this be our song, no one stands a-lone, stand-ing side by

side, draw the cir-cle wide.  *Last time*

1 God the still-point of the cir-cle, 'round whom all cre - a-tion turns;
2 Let our hearts touch far hor-i-zons, so en-com-pass great and small;
3 Let the dreams we dream be lar-ger, than we've ev - er dreamed be-fore;

*To refrain*

no-thing lost, but held for-ev - er, in God's gra-cious arms.
let our lov - ing know no bor-ders, faith-ful to God's call.
let the dream of Christ be in us, o - pen ev-ery door.

Text and music: Gordon Light (1944– ). © 1994 Common Cup Company.

87 85 with refrain
BROWNING

# 419 Let All Creation Bless the Lord

1 Let all cre-a-tion bless the Lord, till heaven with praise
2 All liv-ing things up-on this earth, green fer-tile hills
3 O men and wom-en ev-ery-where, lift up a hymn

is ring-ing. Sun, moon, and stars, peal out a chord, stir
and moun-tains, sing to the God who gave you birth; be
of glo-ry; all you who know God's stead-fast care, tell

up the an-gels' sing-ing. Sing, wind and rain! Sing,
joy-ful, springs and foun-tains. Lithe wa-ter-life, bright
out sal-va-tion's sto-ry. No tongue be si-lent;

snow and sleet! Make mu-sic, day, night, cold, and heat:
air-borne birds, wild rov-ing beasts, tame flocks and herds:
sing your part, you hum-ble souls and meek of heart;

Text: *Song of Creation* (Song of the Three 35–51); para. Carl. P. Daw, Jr. (1944– ).
*Para.* © 1989 Hope Publishing Co.
Music: Melody *Kirchengesänge*, Berlin,1566; arr. *The English Hymnal*, 1906, alt.

87 87 887
MIT FREUDEN ZART
*Higher key 310*

ex - alt the God who made you.

## Praise the Lord, Ye Heavens Adore Him  **420**

1 Praise the Lord, ye heavens a-dore him; praise him, an-gels in the height;
2 Praise the Lord, for he is glo-rious; nev-er shall his prom-ise fail;

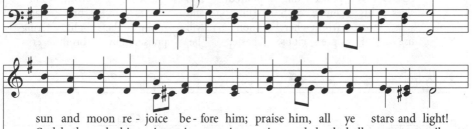

sun and moon re-joice be-fore him; praise him, all ye stars and light!
God hath made his saints vic-to-rious; sin and death shall not pre-vail.

Praise the Lord for he hath spo-ken; worlds his might-y voice o-beyed;
Praise the God of our sal-va-tion! Hosts on high, his power pro-claim;

laws which nev-er shall be bro-ken for their guid-ance hath he made.
heaven and earth and all cre-a-tion, laud and mag-ni-fy his name.

Text: Ps. 148; para. unknown author; *Foundling Hospital Collection*, 1796.
Music: Henry Thomas Smart (1813–1879).

87 87D
REX GLORIAE
*Alt. tune AUSTRIA 388*

# 421 Most High, Omnipotent, Good Lord

*Unison*

1 Most high, om - ni - po - tent, good Lord, to thee be
2 My Lord, be praised by broth - er sun who through the
3 My Lord, be praised by sis - ter moon and all the
4 By sis - ter wa - ter be thou blessed, most hum - ble,

cease - less praise out - poured and bless - ing with - out
skies his course doth run and shines in bril - liant
stars, that with her soon will point the glit - tering
use - ful, pre - cious, chaste; be praised by broth - er

mea - sure. From thee a - lone all crea - tures
splen - dour; with bright - ness he doth fill the
heav - ens. Let wind and air and cloud and
fire; joc - und is he, ro - bust and

came; no one is wor - thy thee to name.
day; and sig - ni - fies thy bound - less sway.
calm and weath - ers all, re - peat the psalm.
bright, and strong to light - en all the night.

Text: Francis of Assisi (1182–1226); tr. Howard Chandler Robbins, (1876–1952), alt.
Music: Alfred Morton Smith (1879–1971). © *Estate of Doris Wright Smith.*

887 88
ASSISI

5 By mother earth my Lord be praised;
  governed by thee she hath upraised
  what for our life is needful.
  Sustained by thee, through every hour,
  she bringeth forth fruit, herb, and flower.

6 My Lord, be praised by those who prove
  in free forgivingness their love,
  nor shrink from tribulation.
  Happy, who peaceably endure;
  with thee, Lord, their reward is sure.

7 For death our sister, praisèd be,
  from whom no one alive can flee.
  Woe to the unpreparèd!
  But blest be they who do thy will
  and follow thy commandments still.

8 Most high, omnipotent, good Lord,
  to thee be ceaseless praise outpoured
  and blessing without measure.
  Let creatures all give thanks to thee
  and serve in great humility.

CREATION

# God, Who Touchest Earth with Beauty 422

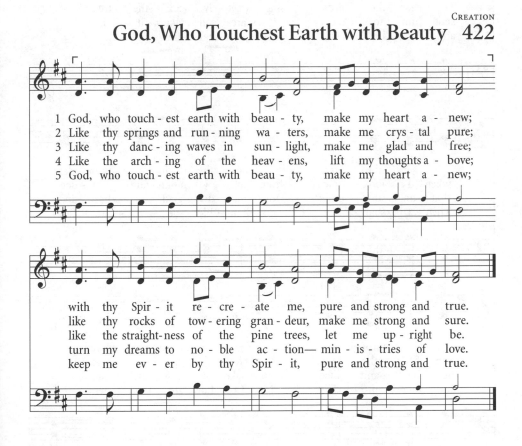

1 God, who touch-est earth with beau-ty, make my heart a-new;
2 Like thy springs and run-ning wa-ters, make me crys-tal pure;
3 Like thy danc-ing waves in sun-light, make me glad and free;
4 Like the arch-ing of the heav-ens, lift my thoughts a-bove;
5 God, who touch-est earth with beau-ty, make my heart a-new;

with thy Spir-it re-cre-ate me, pure and strong and true.
like thy rocks of tow-ering gran-deur, make me strong and sure.
like the straight-ness of the pine trees, let me up-right be.
turn my dreams to no-ble ac-tion— min-is-tries of love.
keep me ev-er by thy Spir-it, pure and strong and true.

Text: Mary Susannah Edgar (1889–1973). © *Estate of Mary Susannah Edgar.*
Music: Henry Walford Davies (1869–1941).
  © *Estate of Henry Walford Davies. Used by permission of Oxford University Press.*

85 85
SPIRITUS CHRISTI

# 423 How Great Thou Art

1 O Lord my God, when I in awe-some won-der
2 When through the woods and for-est glades I wan-der,
3 But when I think that God, his Son not spar-ing,
4 When Christ shall come, with shout of ac-cla-ma-tion

con-sid-er all the works thy hand hath made,
I hear the birds sing sweet-ly in the trees;
sent him to die, I scarce can take it in,
and claim his own, what joy shall fill my heart!

I see the stars, I hear the might-y thun-der,
when I look down from loft-y moun-tain gran-deur
that on the cross, my bur-den glad-ly bear-ing,
Then I shall bow in hum-ble ad-o-ra-tion

thy power through-out the u-ni-verse dis-played.
and hear the brook and feel the gen-tle breeze;
he bled and died to take a-way my sin;
and there pro-claim, "My God, how great thou art!"

Text: Stuart K. Hine (1899–1989), inspired by Swedish text
   by Carl Gustav Boberg (1859–1940).
Music: Melody Swedish trad.; harm. Stuart K. Hine (1899–1989).
*Text and harm. © 1953, 1981 Manna Music, Inc. All rights reserved. Used by permission.*

11 10 11 10 with refrain
HOW GREAT THOU ART

Then sings my soul, my Sav-iour God, to thee: how great thou art, how great thou art! Then sings my soul, my Sav-iour God, to thee: how great thou art, how great thou art!

## 424 Sing Praise to God

1 Sing praise to God on moun-tain tops and in earth's low-est pla-ces,
2 Sing praise to God where grass-es grow and flowers dis-play their beau-ty,
3 Sing praise to God where fish-es swim and birds fly in for-ma-tion,
4 Sing praise to God where hu-man-kind its maj-es-ty em-bra-ces,

from blue la-goon to po-lar waste, from o-cean to o-a-sis. No
where na-ture weaves her myr-iad web through love as much as du-ty. The
where an-i-mals of ev-ery kind di-ver-si-fy cre-a-tion. All
where dif-ferent rac-es, creeds, and tongues dis-tin-guish dif-ferent fa-ces.God's

ran-dom rock pro-duced this world, but God's own will and won-der. Thus
sea-sons in their cy-cle speak of earth's com-plete pro-vi-sion. Let
life that finds its home on earth is meant to be re-spec-ted. Let
im-age in each child of earth shall nev-er pale or per-ish. So

hills re-joice and val-leys sing and clouds con-cur with thun-der.
noth-ing mock in-her-ent good, nor treat it with de-ri-sion.
noth-ing threat-en, for base ends, what God through grace per-fect-ed.
treat with love each hu-man soul, and thus God's good-ness cher-ish.

Text: John L. Bell (1949– ) and Graham Maule (1958– ).
Music: Melody English trad.; arr. John L. Bell (1949– ).

87 87D
THE VICAR OF BRAY

# Joyful, Joyful We Adore Thee  425

1 Joy-ful, joy-ful we a-dore thee, God of glo-ry, Lord of love;
2 All thy works with joy sur-round thee, earth and heaven re-flect thy rays;
3 Thou art giv-ing and for-giv-ing, ev-er bless-ing, ev-er blest,

hearts un-fold like flowers be-fore thee, o-pening to the sun a-bove.
stars and an-gels sing a-round thee, cen-tre of un-bro-ken praise.
well-spring of the joy of liv-ing, o-cean depth of hap-py rest!

Melt the clouds of sin and sad-ness, drive the dark of doubt a-way;
Field and for-est, vale and moun-tain, flow-ery mead-ow, flash-ing sea,
Thou our Fa-ther and our Moth-er, all who live in love are thine;

giv-er of im-mor-tal glad-ness, fill us with the light of day.
chant-ing bird and flow-ing foun-tain call us to re-joice in thee.
teach us how to love each oth-er, lift us to the joy di-vine.

Text: Henry van Dyke (1852–1933), alt.
Music: Ludwig van Beethoven (1770–1827); arr. Edward Hodges (1796–1867).

87 87D
HYMN TO JOY

# 426 The Spacious Firmament on High

1 The spa - cious fir - ma - ment on high, with all the
2 Soon as the eve - ning shades pre - vail, the moon takes
3 What though in sol - emn si - lence all move round the

blue e - the - real sky, and span - gled heavens, a
up the won - drous tale, and night - ly to the
dark ter - res - trial ball, what though no re - al

shin - ing frame, their great O - rig - i - nal pro - claim.
lis - tening earth re - peats the sto - ry of her birth;
voice, nor sound, a - midst their ra - diant orbs be found;

The un-wea - ried sun from day to day does his Cre -
while all the stars that round her burn, and all the
in rea - son's ear they all re - joice and ut - ter

Text: Joseph Addison (1672–1719).
Music: Franz Josef Haydn (1732–1809); adapt. *Dulcimer, or New York Collection of Sacred Music*, 1850, alt.; trb. arr. Melva Treffinger Graham (1947– ) ©.

LMD
CREATION

a - tor's power dis - play, and pub - lish - es to
plan - ets in their turn con - firm the tid - ings,
forth a glo - rious voice, for - ev - er sing - ing

ev - ery land the work of an al - might - y hand.
as they roll, and spread the truth from pole to pole.
as they shine, "The hand that made us is di - vine."

*For 2 trombones or 1 trombone on part 1*

# 427 All Beautiful the March of Days

1 All beau-ti-ful the march of days as sea-sons come and go;
2 O'er white ex-pans-es, spark-ling pure, the ra-diant morns un-fold;
3 O thou, from whose un-fath-omed law the year in beau-ty flows,

the hand that shaped the rose hath wrought the crys-tal of the snow,
the sol-emn splen-dours of the night burn bright-er through the cold;
thy-self the vi-sion pass-ing by in crys-tal and in rose;

hath sent the hoar-y frost of heaven, the flow-ing wa-ters sealed,
life mounts in ev-ery throb-bing vein, love deep-ens round the hearth,
day un-to day doth ut-ter speech, and night to night pro-claim

and laid a si-lent love-li-ness on hill and wood and field.
and clear-er sounds the an-gel hymn, "Good will and peace on earth."
in ev-er-chang-ing words of light the won-der of thy name.

Text: Frances Whitmarsh Wile (1878–1939), alt.
Music: Melody English trad.; coll. and harm. Ralph Vaughan Williams (1872–1958).
*Harm. © Oxford University Press.*

CMD
FOREST GREEN
*Lower key 121*

# God Who Gives to Life Its Goodness  428

1 God who gives to life its good-ness, God cre-a-tor
2 God who fills the earth with beau-ty, God who binds each

of all joy, giv-er of all hu-man free-dom,
friend to friend, giv-er of all hu-man tal-ent,

God who bless-es tool and toy: teach us now to
God who wills that cha-os end: grant us now cre-

laugh and praise you, deep with-in your prais-es sing, till the
a-tive spir-its, minds re-spon-sive to your mind, hearts and

whole cre-a-tion dan-ces for the good-ness of its King.
wills your rule ex-tend-ing, all our acts by love re-fined.

Text: Walter Henry Farquharson (1936– ), alt. ©.
Music: Cyril Vincent Taylor (1907–1991). © 1942, renewal 1970 Hope Publishing Co.

87 87D
ABBOT'S LEIGH
*Higher key 433*

# 429 For the Beauty of the Earth

1 For the beau-ty of the earth, for the glo-ry of the skies,
2 For the beau-ty of each hour of the day and of the night,
3 For the joy of ear and eye, for the heart and mind's de - light,
4 For the joy of hu-man love, broth-er, sis - ter, par - ent, child,
5 For each per-fect gift of thine to our race so free-ly given,

for the love which from our birth o - ver and a - round us lies,
hill and vale and tree and flower, sun and moon and stars of light,
for the mys - tic har - mo - ny link-ing sense to sound and sight,
friends on earth and friends a - bove, for all gen - tle thoughts and mild,
grac - es hu - man and di - vine, flowers of earth and buds of heaven,

Christ our God, to thee we raise this our sac - ri - fice of praise.

Text: Folliott Sandford Pierpoint (1835–1917), alt.
Music: Melody English trad.; adapt. and harm. Geoffrey Turton Shaw (1879–1943).
    *Harm. © Oxford University Press.*

77 77 77
ENGLAND'S LANE
*Alt. tune DIX 160*

# Will You Come and Follow Me 430

*Unison*

1 Will you come and fol-low me if I but call your name?
2 Will you leave your-self be-hind if I but call your name?
3 Will you let the blind-ed see if I but call your name?
4 Will you love the "you" you hide if I but call your name?
5 Lord, your sum-mons ech-oes true when you but call my name.

Will you go where you don't know and nev-er be the same?
Will you care for cruel and kind and nev-er be the same?
Will you set the pris-oners free and nev-er be the same?
Will you quell the fear in-side and nev-er be the same?
Let me turn and fol-low you and nev-er be the same.

Will you let my love be shown, will you let my name be known,
Will you risk the hos-tile stare should your life at-tract or scare?
Will you kiss the lep-er clean and do such as this un-seen,
Will you use the faith you've found to re-shape the world a-round,
In your com-pa-ny I'll go where your love and foot-steps show.

will you let my life be grown in you and you in me?
Will you let me an-swer prayer in you and you in me?
and ad-mit to what I mean in you and you in me?
through my sight and touch and sound in you and you in me?
Thus I'll move and live and grow in you and you in me.

Text: John L. Bell (1949– ).
Music: Melody Scottish trad.; arr. John L. Bell (1949– ).

76 76 77 76
KELVINGROVE

# 431 Take Up Your Cross, the Saviour Said

*Descant*

5 Take up your cross and fol - low Christ, nor think till

1 Take up your cross, the Sav - iour said, if you would
2 Take up your cross; let not its weight fill your weak
3 Take up your cross, nor heed the shame, and let your
4 Take up your cross, then, in his strength, and calm - ly
5 Take up your cross and fol - low Christ, nor think till

death to lay it down; for on - ly those who

my dis - ci - ple be; de - ny your - self, the
soul with vain a - larm; his strength shall bear your
fool - ish pride be still; your Lord for you en -
ev - ery dan - ger brave: 'twill guide you to a
death to lay it down; for on - ly those who

bear the cross may hope to wear the glo - rious crown.

world for - sake, and hum - bly fol - low af - ter me.
spir - it up, and brace your heart, and nerve your arm.
dured to die up - on a cross, on Cal - vary's hill.
bet - ter home and lead to vic - tory o'er the grave.
bear the cross may hope to wear the glo - rious crown.

Text: Charles William Everest (1814–1877).
Music: Melody *Lochamer Liederbuch*, 1450?, alt.; harm. Felix Mendelssohn-Bartholdy (1809–1847), alt.;
desc. Alan Gray (1855–1935). *Desc.* © *Cambridge University Press.*

LM
BRESLAU

# Jesus Calls Us! O'er the Tumult 432

1 Je - sus calls us! O'er the tu - mult of our
2 As of old Saint An - drew heard it by the
3 Je - sus calls us from the wor - ship of the
4 In our joys and in our sor - rows, days of
5 Je - sus calls us! By thy mer - cies, Sav - iour,

life's wild rest - less sea, day by day his
Gal - i - le - an lake, turned from home and
vain world's gold - en store, from each i - dol
toil and hours of ease, still he calls, in
may we hear thy call, give our hearts to

sweet voice sound - eth, say - ing, "Chris - tian, fol - low me!"
toil and kin - dred, leav - ing all for his dear sake.
that would keep us, say - ing, "Chris - tian, love me more."
cares and plea - sures, "Chris - tian, love me more than these."
thine o - be - dience, serve and love thee best of all.

Text: Cecil Frances Alexander (1818–1895).
Music: John Bacchus Dykes (1823–1876).

87 87
ST. OSWALD

# 433 Lord, You Give the Great Commission

1 Lord, you give the great com-mis-sion: "Heal the sick and
2 Lord, you call us to your ser-vice: "In my name bap-
3 Lord, you make the com-mon ho-ly: "This my bod - y,
4 Lord, you show us love's true meas-ure: "Fa - ther, what they
5 Lord, you bless with words as-sur-ing: "I am with you

preach the word." Lest the church ne-glect its mis-sion
tize and teach." That the world may trust your prom-ise,
this my blood." Let your priests, for earth's true glo - ry,
do, for-give." Yet we hoard as pri - vate trea-sure
to the end." Faith and hope and love re - stor-ing,

and the gos - pel go un-heard, help us wit - ness
life a - bun - dant meant for each, give us all new
dai - ly lift life hea - ven-ward, ask - ing that the
all that you so free - ly give. May your care and
may we serve as you in-tend, and, a - mid the

*A selection of stanzas may be chosen.*

Text: Jeffery Rowthorn (1934– ). © 1978 Hope Publishing Co.
Music: Cyril Vincent Taylor (1907–1991). © 1942, renewal 1970 Hope Publishing Co.

87 87D
ABBOT'S LEIGH
*Lower key 273, 428*

to       your pur-pose   with re-newed in - teg - ri - ty;
fer - vour, draw us      clo - ser in   com-mu - ni - ty;
world  a - round us      share your chil - dren's lib - er - ty;   with the
mer - cy lead us        to   a   just   so - ci - e - ty;
cares  that claim us,    hold in mind  e - ter - ni - ty;

Spir - it's gifts em - power us      for   the work of min - is - try.

# 434 The Love of Jesus Calls Us

1 The love of Je-sus calls us our joy-ous praise to sing;
2 The love of Je-sus calls us, that we may al-ways be
3 The love of Je-sus calls us to go where he would go,
4 The love of Je-sus calls us in swift-ly chang-ing days,

our deep-ly felt thanks-giv-ings we now to-geth-er bring,
com-pan-ions on a jour-ney, where all the world may see
to chal-lenge all that lim-its, to change, to learn, to grow,
to be God's co-cre-a-tors in new and won-drous ways;

for all God's man-y bless-ings, un-asked yet still re-ceived,
that serv-ing Christ is free-dom which time does not des-troy;
to know that Christ has freed us, that pris-ons are no more;
that God with men and wom-en may so trans-form the earth,

and for the gen-er-a-tions who faith-ful-ly be-lieved.
where Christ's com-mand is du-ty, and ev-ery du-ty joy.
for those who seek his king-dom, Christ o-pens ev-ery door.
that love and peace and jus-tice may give God's king-dom birth.

Text: Herbert O'Driscoll (1928– ) ©.
Music: Samuel Sebastian Wesley (1810–1876).

76 76D
AURELIA
Lower key 524

# Take My Life, and Let It Be  435

1 Take my life, and let it be con - se -
2 Take my hands, and let them move at the
3 Take my lips, and let them be filled with
4 Take my will, and make it thine; it shall
5 Take my love: my Lord, I pour at thy

cra - ted, Lord, to thee; take my mo - ments
im - pulse of thy love; take my feet, and
mes - sa - ges from thee; take my in - tel -
be no long - er mine; take my heart, it
feet its trea - sure store; take my - self, and

and my days, let them flow in cease - less praise.
let them be swift and pur - pose - ful for thee.
lect, and use ev - ery power as thou shalt choose.
is thine own; it shall be thy roy - al throne.
I will be ev - er, on - ly, all for thee.

Text: Frances Ridley Havergal (1836–1879).
Music: composer unknown.

77 77
MOZART

# 436  I Bind unto Myself Today

*Unison*

1 I bind un-to my-self to-day the strong name

of the Trin - i - ty, by in - vo - ca - tion

of the same, the Three - in - One, and One - in - Three.

2 I bind this day to me for - ev - er, by power of
3 I bind un - to my - self to - day the vir - tues
4 I bind un - to my - self to - day the power of
6 I bind un - to my - self the name, the strong name

Text: Attrib. Patrick of Ireland (389?–461?); tr. Cecil Frances Alexander (1818–1895).
Music: Melody Irish hymn; arr. Charles Villiers Stanford (1852–1924).

Irregular
ST. PATRICK'S BREASTPLATE

faith, Christ's in - car - na - tion, his bap - tism in the
of the star - lit heav - en, the glo - rious sun's life -
God to hold and lead, his eye to watch, his
of the Trin - i - ty, by in - vo - ca - tion

Jor - dan riv - er, his death on cross for my sal -
giv - ing ray, the white - ness of the moon at
might to stay, his ear to heark - en to my
of the same, the Three - in - One, and One - in -

va - tion. His burst - ing from the spic - ed tomb, his
e - ven, the flash - ing of the light - ning free, the
need, the wis - dom of my God to teach, his
Three, of whom all na - ture hath cre - a - tion, e -

rid - ing up the heaven - ly way, his com - ing at the
whirl - ing wind's tem - pes - tuous shocks, the sta - ble earth, the
hand to guide, his shield to ward, the word of God to
ter - nal Fa - ther, Spir - it, Word. Praise to the Lord of

*Last time*

day of doom, I bind un - to my - self to - day.
deep salt sea a - round the old e - ter - nal rocks.
give me speech, his heaven - ly host to be my guard.
my sal - va - tion; sal - va - tion is of Christ the Lord.

*Harmony*

5 Christ be with me, Christ with - in me, Christ be -
Christ be - neath me, Christ a - bove me, Christ in

hind me, Christ be - fore me, Christ be - side me, Christ to
qui - et, Christ in dan - ger, Christ in hearts of all that

*Second time to the sign 𝄋 on p. 1*

win me, Christ to com - fort and re - store me.
love me, Christ in mouth of friend and strang - er.

Music of st. 5: Melody Irish hymn; arr. Charles Villiers Stanford (1852–1924).

LM
DEIRDRE

# Jesus, Come, for We Invite You 437

1 Je - sus, come, for we in - vite you, guest and mas - ter,
2 Je - sus, come! Trans - form our pleas - ures, guide us in - to
3 Je - sus, come in new cre - a - tion, heaven brought near in
4 Je - sus, come! Sur - prise our dull - ness; make us will - ing

friend and Lord; now, as once at Ca - na's wed - ding,
paths un - known; bring your gifts, com - mand your ser - vants;
power di - vine; give your un - ex - pect - ed glo - ry,
to re - ceive more than we can yet im - ag - ine,

speak, and let us hear your word: lead us through our
let us trust in you a - lone: though your hand may
chang - ing wa - ter in - to wine: rouse the faith of
all the best you have to give: let us find your

need or doubt - ing, hope be born and joy re - stored.
work in se - cret, all shall see what you have done.
your dis - ci - ples— come, our first and great - est sign!
hid - den rich - es, taste your love, be - lieve and live!

Text: Christopher Idle (1938– ). © 1982 Hope Publishing Co.
Music: Melody Sicilian; *The European Magazine and London Review*, 1792, alt.

87 87 87
SICILIAN MARINERS

# 438 O Jesus, I Have Promised

1 O Jesus, I have promised to serve thee to the end; be thou forever near me, my Master and my Friend. I shall not fear the battle if thou art by my side, nor wander

2 O let me feel thee near me: the world is ever near; I see the sights that dazzle, the tempting sounds I hear; my foes are ever near me, around me and within; but, Jesus,

3 O Jesus, thou hast promised to all who follow thee, that where thou art in glory there shall thy servant be; and, Jesus, I have promised to serve thee to the end! O give me

4 O let me see thy footmarks and in them plant mine own: my hope to follow duly is in thy strength alone. O guide me, call me, draw me, uphold me to the end; and then in

Text: John Ernest Bode (1816–1874).
Music: William Harold Ferguson (1874–1950). © *Oxford University Press.*

76 76D
WOLVERCOTE
*Alt. tune* THORNBURY *444, 468*

from the path - way if thou wilt be my guide.
draw thou near - er and shield my soul from sin.
grace to fol - low, my Mas - ter and my Friend.
heaven re - ceive me, my Sav - iour and my Friend.

## Blest Are the Pure in Heart   439

*Descant*

4 Lord, we thy pres - ence seek; may ours this bless - ing be:

1 Blest are the pure in heart, for they shall see our God;
2 The Lord, who left the heavens our life and peace to bring,
3 still to the low - ly soul his pres - ence doth im - part,
4 Lord, we thy pres - ence seek; may ours this bless - ing be:

give us a pure and low - ly heart, a tem - ple fit for thee.

the se - cret of the Lord is theirs, their soul is Christ's a - bode.
to dwell in low - li - ness with us, our pat - tern and our King,
and for a dwell - ing and a throne choos - eth the pure in heart.
give us a pure and low - ly heart, a tem - ple fit for thee.

Text: St. 1, 4, John Keble (1792–1866), alt.; st. 2–3, *Mitre Hymn Book*, 1836, alt.
Music: Melody Johann Balthasar König (1691–1758); adapt. William Henry Havergal (1793–1870);
desc. Derek Holman (1931– ) ©.

SM
FRANCONIA

# 440 For All Your Blessings

1 For all your blessings, Jesus, we praise you,
2 Daily around us, pain and confusion
3 We carry with us into your presence
4 Grant us, your servants, grace to work with you,

gracious in mercy, strong to console.
crumble our feeble faith into dust.
prisoners of sickness, sadness, and fear;
that in your loving task we may share

You to our need bring comfort and healing,
Yet still we find your love in the darkness,
grant them to know your peace in their suffering
mind's understanding, hands skilled for healing,

love and forgiveness, making us whole.
changing our anxious thoughts into trust.
and new life flowing, for you are near.
hearts of compassion, joined in love's care.

Text: Alan Luff (1928– ), alt. © 1989 Hope Publishing Co.
Music: Ruth Watson Henderson (1932– ) ©.

55 54D
ISLINGTON
*Alt. tune* BUNESSAN 3, 287, 445

# Thee Will I Love, My Strength, My Tower  441

1 Thee will I love, my strength, my tower; thee will I
love, my joy, my crown; thee will I love with all my
power, in all thy works, and thee a - lone; thee will I
love till sa - cred fire fills my whole soul with pure de - sire.

2 I thank thee, un - cre - a - ted Sun, that thy bright
beams on me have shined; I thank thee, who hast o - ver -
thrown my foes, and healed my wound - ed mind; I thank thee,
whose en - liv - ening voice bids my freed heart in thee re - joice.

3 Up - hold me in the doubt - ful race, nor suf - fer
me a - gain to stray; strength - en my feet with stea - dy
pace still to press for - ward in thy way; that all my
powers, with all their might, in thy sole glo - ry may u - nite.

4 Thee will I love, my joy, my crown; thee will I
love, my Lord, my God; thee will I love, be - neath thy
frown or smile—thy scep - tre or thy rod; what though my
flesh and heart de - cay, thee shall I love in end - less day.

Text: Johann Scheffler (1624–1677); tr. John Wesley (1703–1791).
Music: Henry Carey (1687?–1743), alt.

88 88 88
SURREY

# 442 Great God, Your Love Has Called Us Here

1 Great God, your love has called us here as we, by love, for
2 We come with self-inflicted pains of broken trust and
3 Great God, in Christ you call our name and then receive us
4 Then take the towel, and break the bread, and humble us, and
5 Great God, in Christ you set us free, your life to live, your

love were made. Your living likeness still we bear, though
chosen wrong; half-free, half-bound by inner chains; by
as your own not through some merit, right, or claim, but
call us friends. Suffer and serve till all are fed, and
joy to share. Give us your Spirit's liberty to

marred, dishonoured, disobeyed. We come, with all our
social forces swept along, by powers and systems
by your gracious love alone. We strain to glimpse your
show how grandly love intends to work till all cre-
turn from guilt and dull despair and offer all that

heart and mind, your call to hear, your love to find.
close confined; yet seeking hope for humankind.
mercy seat and find you kneeling at our feet.
ation sings, to fill all worlds, to crown all things.
faith can do while love is making all things new.

Text: Brian Wren (1936– ). © 1977, 1995 Hope Publishing Co.
Music: Dimitri Bortniansky (1751–1825); adapt. *Choralbuch*, Leipzig, 1825.

88 88 88
ST. PETERSBURG

# How Beauteous Are Their Feet 443

1 How beau-teous are their feet who stand on Zi-on's hill,
2 How wel-come is their voice, how sweet the tid-ings are!
3 How hap-py are our ears that hear this joy-ful sound,
4 How bless-ed are our eyes that see this heaven-ly light!

who bring sal-va-tion on their tongues and words of peace re-veal!
Zi-on, be-hold thy Sav-iour King; he reigns and tri-umphs here.
which seers and rul-ers wait-ed for and sought, but nev-er found.
Proph-ets and saints de-sired it long, but died with-out the sight.

5 The sentinels in song
their tuneful notes employ;
Jerusalem breaks forth in hymns
and deserts sing for joy.

6 The glory of the Lord
shines through the earth abroad:
let every nation now behold
their Saviour and their God.

Text: Isaac Watts (1674–1748), alt.
Music: William Amps (1824–1910).

SM
VENICE

## 444 Your Hand, O God, Has Guided

1 Your hand, O God, has guid-ed your flock from age to
2 Your her-alds brought glad tid-ings to great-est as to
3 When shad-ows, thick-ly fall-ing, en-gulfed the world in
4 And we, shall we be faith-less, shall hearts fail, hands hang
5 Your mer-cy will not fail us, nor leave your work un-

age; the won-drous tale is writ-ten, full clear, on
least; they bade them rise, and has-ten to share the
night, you sum-moned forth your ser-vants, your mes-sen-
down? Shall we e-vade the strug-gle and cast a-
done; with your right hand to help us, your peo-ple

ev-ery page. Our fore-bears owned your good-ness and
roy-al feast; and this was all their teach-ing, in
gers of light. On them and on your peo-ple your
way the crown? Not so; in God's deep coun-sels some
shall be one; and then, by all cre-a-tion, your

Text: Edward Hayes Plumptre (1821–1891), alt. *Rev. © The Sisterhood of St. John the Divine.*
Music: Basil Harwood (1859–1949).
  *Music published by permission of the executors of the late Dr. Basil Harwood.*

76 76D
THORNBURY
*Alt. setting 468*

we    their deeds re - cord,    and   both  of  this  bear  wit -  ness:
ev - ery deed and word,    to    all   a - like pro - claim -  ing
plen - teous grace was poured,   and  this was still their mes -  sage:
bet - ter gift is stored:   the  cov - e - nant of  prom - ise—
name shall  be  a - dored,    and  this shall  be  their  an -  them:

one church,        one  faith,   one        Lord.

# 445 God the Creator

*Unison*

1 God the Cre - a - tor, you in love made me
2 O Christ the Sav - iour, you in love called me
3 O God the Spir - it, you in love move me
4 And with the peo - ple sum - moned to - geth - er

who once was noth - ing but now have grown.
who once was no one lost and a - lone.
who once was no - where and felt un - known.
to be the church in which faith is sown,

I bring the best of all my life of - fers;
I pledge to go wher - ev - er you sum - mon,
I know my need of you for com - pan - ion:
I make my prom - ise to live for Je - sus

for you I share what - ev - er I own.
mak - ing your will and pur - pose my own.
all things can change when not on my own.
and let the world know all are his own.

Text: John L. Bell (1949– ).
Music: Melody Gaelic trad.; arr. The Iona Community (Scotland).
*Text and arr. © 1989 WGRG The Iona Community (Scotland).*
*Used by permission of G.I.A. Publications, Inc., exclusive agent.*

55 54D
BUNESSAN
*Alt. settings and higher key 3, 287*

# Word of God, Come Down on Earth   446

1 Word of God, come down on earth, liv - ing rain from heaven de -
2 Word e - ter - nal, throned on high, Word that brought to life cre -
3 Word that caused blind eyes to see, speak and heal our mor - tal
4 Word that speaks God's ten - der love, one with God be - yond all

scend - ing: touch our hearts and bring to birth
a - tion, Word that came from heaven to die,
blind - ness. Deaf we are: our heal - er be;
tell - ing; Word that sends us from a - bove

faith and hope and love un - end - ing. Word al - might - y,
cru - ci - fied for our sal - va - tion; sav - ing Word, the
loose our tongues to tell your kind - ness. Be our Word in
God the Spir - it, with us dwell - ing; Word of truth, to

we re - vere you; Word made flesh, we long to hear you.
world re - stor - ing, speak to us, your love out - pour - ing.
pi - ty spo - ken; heal the world by our sin bro - ken.
all truth lead us; Word of life, with one bread feed us.

Text: James Quinn, SJ (1919– ) ©. *Used by permission of Selah Publishing Co., Inc., North American Agent.*
Music: Melody Johann Rudolph Ahle (1625–1673); harm. George Herbert Palmer (1846–1926).

78 78 88
LIEBSTER JESU

# 447 Lord, We Hear Your Word with Gladness

1 Lord, we hear your word with glad - ness: you have spo - ken—
2 May we hear with un - der - stand - ing, by your Spir - it
3 You have spo - ken; yours the full - ness, ours the wealth of

we re - joice: words of love and life and free - dom—
taught and led; may the springs of all our be - ing
this your Word: debt - ors, then as liv - ing let - ters,

help us make their truth our choice! Now in ho - ly cel - e -
by your liv - ing Word be fed; may our hearts ac - cept with
we must make our gos - pel heard! By your Spir - it's power trans -

bra - tion for your Word we wor - ship you; spo - ken,
meek - ness all the grace your light makes known; may o -
form us; shed your sav - ing light a - broad till our

Text: Margaret Clarkson (1915– ). © 1987 Hope Publishing Co.
Music: William Penfro Rowlands (1860–1937) ©. Reprinted by permission of Mr. G.A. Gabe.

87 87D
BLAENWERN
*Lower key 486, 601; Alt. tune* HERMON *451*

writ - ten, known in Je - sus, ours to - day to prove a - new.
be - dience mark our foot - steps till we make each word our own!
lives by love in ac - tion show our world the truth of God!

## Jesus Lord, How Joyful You Have Made Us  448

Je - sus A, Na - he - to - tae - ta - no - me tseh - ma - no' - ee' -
*Je - sus Lord, how joy - ful you have made us to come to - geth -*

to - va - tse - me - no - to, tse - 'o - noo - me - me - no - to.
*er here with you now! In your mer - cy you have called us.*

"Na - nee - hoo - ve me - o - 'o," tsex - he - še - me - no - to. Neh - pa - ve -
*You say, "I am the way." We hear you call us. We ask you,*

a - me - otše - še - me - no ne - me - o - ne - va!
*"Come lead us day by day." We fol - low your way.*

Cheyenne text: John Heap of Birds (1894–1966); Eng. tr. David Graber (1943– ) and others;      Irregular
*Tsese-Ma'heone-Nemeototse.* © 1982 Mennonite Indian Leaders Council.      JESUS NAHETOTAETANOME
Music: Plains Indian melody.

## 449 How Shall They Hear the Word of God

1 How shall they hear the word of God unless the
2 How shall they call to God for help unless they
3 How shall the gos - pel be pro - claimed that sin - ners

truth is told? How shall the sin - ful be set free, the
have be - lieved? How shall the poor be giv - en hope, the
may re - pent? How shall the world find peace at last if

sor - row - ful con - soled? To all who speak the
pris - on - er re - prieved? To those who help the
her - alds are not sent? So send us, Lord, for

truth to - day im - part your Spir - it, Lord, we pray.
blind to see, give light and love and clar - i - ty.
we re - joice to speak of Christ with life and voice.

Text: Michael Perry (1942–1996). © 1982 Hope Publishing Co.
Music: Melody and figured bass Johann Balthasar Reimann (1702–1749);
    alt. and harm. The English Hymnal, 1906.

86 86 88
O Jesu

# You Call Us, Lord, to Be 450

1 You call us, Lord, to be a peo-ple set a-part,
2 You call us, Lord, to care for self and neigh-bour too,
3 You call us, Lord, to be good stew-ards of the earth;
4 You call us, Lord, to serve: to die that we may live,

to feel with thought-ful mind and think with ten-der heart.
to take the risk, and dare to show what love can do.
to tend it as a place of bless-ed-ness and worth.
to know we best re-ceive when joy-ful-ly we give.

Thus cho-sen, now, O Lord, we ask for faith in your un-

fail-ing grace to make us e-qual to the task.

Text: Jane Manton Marshall (1924– ). © 1992 Hope Publishing Co.
Music: John David Edwards (1806–1885).

66 66 888
RHOSYMEDRE

## 451 King of Love, O Christ, We Crown You

1 King of love, O Christ, we crown you Lord of thought and
2 King of life, you have cre-a-ted wheat in gold-en
3 King of mer-cy, you have saved us from the haunt-ing
4 King tri-um-phant, King vic-to-rious, take your throne our

Lord of will, each de-mand of your high chal-lenge ded-i-
har-vest spread: make your ser-vants strong to serve you by the
sense of loss, nail-ing in your vast com-pas-sion sin's in-
hearts with-in, lest the might of fierce temp-ta-tion snare us

cat-ed to ful-fil; we with you by grace co-work-ers,
gift of dai-ly bread. Feed us with your bod-y bro-ken,
dict-ment to the cross. Those who love, by your sore ang-uish,
in-to dead-ly sin. By the Spir-it's rich a-noint-ing,

till, where hu-man foot has trod, peo-ples, kings, do-
with your blood out-poured sus-tain, that our souls di-
from the past you cleanse and free, breath-ing words of
grant us strength life's race to run, till the power of

Text and melody: Charles Venn Pilcher (1879–1961), alt. © F.E.V. Pilcher.
Harm. Walter MacNutt (1910–1996). *Harm.* © 1973 Waterloo Music Co. Ltd.

87 87D
HERMON

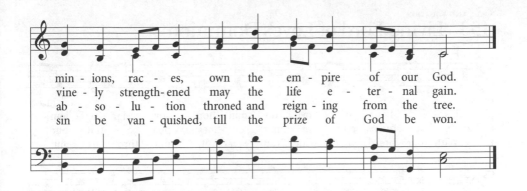

min - ions, rac – es, own the em - pire of our God.
vine - ly strength- ened may the life e - ter - nal gain.
ab - so - lu - tion throned and reign - ing from the tree.
sin be van - quished, till the prize of God be won.

## Command Your Blessing from Above  452

1 Com - mand your bless - ing from a - bove, O God, on
2 Com - mand your bless - ing, Je - sus, Lord; may we your
3 Com - mand your bless - ing in this hour, Spir - it of
4 You are our mak - er, sav - iour, guide, one true e -

all as - sem - bled here; be - hold us with your ten - der
true dis - ci - ples be. Speak to each heart your might - y
truth, and fill this place with hum - bling and with heal - ing
ter - nal God con - fessed; may naught in life or death di -

love while we your ho - ly name re - vere.
word; say to the weak - est, "Fol - low me."
power, with quick - ening and con - firm - ing grace.
vide the saints in your com - mun - ion blest.

Text: James Montgomery (1771–1854), alt.
Music: Lee Hastings Bristol, Jr. (1923–1979). © 1962 Theodore Presser Co. Used by permission.

LM
DICKINSON COLLEGE

# 453 Living Lord of Love's Dominion

1 Liv - ing Lord of Love's do - min - ion, sov - ereign Sav - iour,
2 Vis - it towns and in - ner cit - ies; pen - e - trate our
3 With your bread, your wine, your Spir - it, nur - ture us for

bless your church; call us still as your dis - ci - ples—
steel and stone with a love that melts our cold - ness,
your in - tent; let your will be our vo - ca - tion

lov - ing, serv - ing, while we search. Gath - ered: feed our
mak - ing mis - sion here our own. We will seek you,
lived as song and sac - ra - ment. May com - pas - sion

deep - est be - ing proph - et's truth and god - ly nerve; scat - tered:
love trans - fig - ured, in our neigh - bour's need un - til deep with -
lead to ser - vice till we join the saints a - bove; grant us

Text: David A. Robb (1932– ). © 1992 Hope Publishing Co.
Music: Melody *The Christian Lyre*, 1831; harm. Ralph Vaughan Williams (1872–1958).
   Harm. © Oxford University Press.

87 87D
PLEADING SAVIOUR

let our lives' fru - i - tion nour - ish oth - ers while we serve.
in our dail - y ser - vice love draws forth our ut - most skill.
hope for each to - mor - row; fill our faith with vi - brant love!

## Revive Thy Work, O Lord  454

1 Re - vive thy work, O Lord, thy might - y arm make bare;
2 Re - vive thy work, O Lord, dis - turb this sleep of death;
3 Re - vive thy work, O Lord, cre - ate soul - thirst for thee;
4 Re - vive thy work, O Lord, ex - alt thy pre - cious name;
5 Re - vive thy work, O Lord, and give re - fresh - ing showers.

speak with the voice that wakes the dead, and make thy peo - ple hear.
quick - en the smoul - dering em - bers now by thine al - might - y breath.
and hun - gering for the bread of life O may our spir - its be.
and, by the Ho - ly Ghost sent down, our love for thee in - flame.
The glo - ry shall be all thine own; the bless - ing, Lord, be ours.

Text: Albert Midlane (1825–1909), alt.
Music: Charles Lockhart (1738?–1815).

SM
CARLISLE
*Higher key 167*

# 455 Dear God, Compassionate and Kind

*Unison*

1 Dear God, com-pas - sion - ate and kind, for - give our
2 In sim - ple trust like theirs who heard, be - side the
3 O Sab - bath rest by Gal - i - lee! O calm of
4 Drop thy still dews of qui - et - ness till all our
5 Breathe through the heats of our de - sire thy cool - ness

foolish ways. Re - clothe us in our right - ful
Syr - ian sea, the gra - cious call - ing of the
hills a - bove, where Je - sus knelt to share with
striv - ings cease; take from our souls the strain and
and thy balm; let sense be dumb, let flesh re -

mind, in pur - er lives thy ser - vice find, in
Lord, let us, like them, with - out a word, rise
thee the si - lence of e - ter - ni - ty in -
stress, and let our or - dered lives con - fess the
tire; speak through the earth - quake, wind, and fire, O

deep - er rev - erence, praise, in deep - er rev - erence, praise.
up and fol - low thee, rise up and fol - low thee!
ter - pret - ed by love, in - ter - pret - ed by love!
beau - ty of thy peace, the beau - ty of thy peace.
still small voice of calm, O still small voice of calm.

Text: John Greenleaf Whittier (1807–1892), alt.
Music: Charles Hubert Hastings Parry (1848–1918).

86 886 with repeat
REPTON
*Alt. setting 466*

# He Comes to Us As One Unknown 456

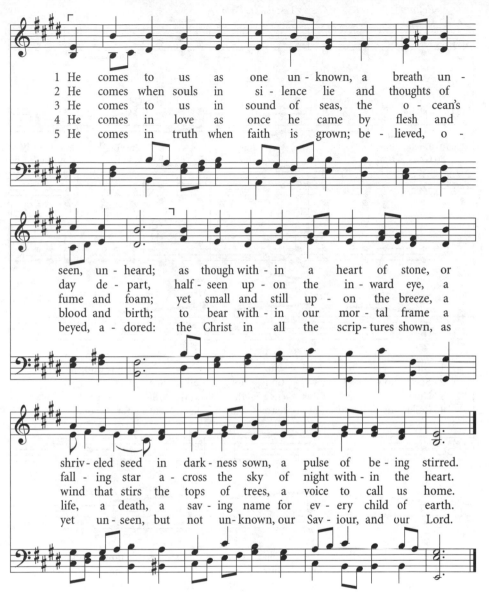

1 He comes to us as one un-known, a breath un-
2 He comes when souls in si-lence lie and thoughts of
3 He comes to us in sound of seas, the o-cean's
4 He comes in love as once he came by flesh and
5 He comes in truth when faith is grown; be-lieved, o-

seen, un-heard; as though with-in a heart of stone, or
day de-part, half-seen up-on the in-ward eye, a
fume and foam; yet small and still up-on the breeze, a
blood and birth; to bear with-in our mor-tal frame a
beyed, a-dored: the Christ in all the scrip-tures shown, as

shriv-eled seed in dark-ness sown, a pulse of be-ing stirred.
fall-ing star a-cross the sky of night with-in the heart.
wind that stirs the tops of trees, a voice to call us home.
life, a death, a sav-ing name for ev-ery child of earth.
yet un-seen, but not un-known, our Sav-iour, and our Lord.

Text: Timothy Dudley-Smith (1926– ); first line from Albert Schweitzer (1875–1965),
*The Quest of the Historical Jesus*, 1910. © *1984 Hope Publishing Co.*
Music: Melody Nikolaus Herman (1480?–1561);
adapt. and harm. Johann Sebastian Bach (1685–1750).

86 886
LOBT GOTT, IHR CHRISTEN
*Alt. tune REPTON 455 repeating last phrase of text*

# 457 Alleluia! Glory to God

*Refrain*    *Last time to Coda* ⊕

Al - le - lu - ia, al - le - lu - ia, al - le - lu - ia!

Capo 3

| Em | Bm⁷ | Em | | Bm⁷ | D | G | D | Em | Em^sus4 | Em | Em^sus4 |
| Gm | Dm⁷ | Gm | | Dm⁷ | F | B♭ | F | Gm | Gm^sus4 | Gm | Gm^sus4 |

*Unison*

Em / Gm    Em⁷ / Gm⁷    A/E / C/G    Em / Gm

1 Glo - ry to God who does won - drous things;
2 See how sal - va - tion for all has been won;
3 Now in our pres - ence the Lord will ap - pear,
4 Call us, good Shep - herd; we list - en for you,

C / E♭    D / F    Em / Gm

let all the peo - ple God's prais - es now sing;
up from the grave our new life has be - gun;
shine in the fac - es of all of us here;
want - ing to see you in all that we do;

Text: Marty Haugen, (1950– ).
Music: Melody *Airs sur les hymnes sacrez, odes et noëls*, Paris, 1623;
   adapt. Marty Haugen (1950– ). *Text and adapt. © 1986 G.I.A. Publications, Inc.*

10 10 10 with refrain
O Filii et Filiae
*Alt. setting 228*

all of cre - a - tion in splen - dour shall ring:
life now per - fect - ed in Je - sus, the Son:
fill us with joy and cast out all our fear:
we would the gate of sal - va - tion pass through:

al - le - lu - ia,

al - le - lu - ia!

5 Lord, we are open to all that you say,
   ready to listen and follow your way;
   you are the potter and we are the clay:
   alleluia!
    *Refrain*

6 If we have love, then we dwell in the Lord;
   God will protect us from <u>fire</u> and sword,
   fill us with love and the peace of his word:
   alleluia!
    *Refrain*

# 458 Seek Ye First

1 Seek ye first the king-dom of God and God's
2 Ask and it shall be giv-en un-to you; seek and

right - eous - ness, and all these things shall be
you shall find; knock and the door shall be

add - ed un - to you. Al - le - lu, al - le - lu - ia.
o - pened un - to you.

*Refrain*

Al - le - lu - ia, al - le - lu - ia,

al - le - lu - ia. Al - le - lu, al - le - lu - ia.

*This may be sung as a 2-part round or canon at the distance of 8 measures.*

Irregular with refrain
SEEK YE FIRST

# Christ Is Our Cornerstone  459

1 Christ is our cor - ner - stone, on him a -
2 O then with hymns of praise these hal - lowed
3 Here, gra - cious God, do thou for ev - er -
4 Here may we gain from heaven the grace which

lone we build; with his true saints a - lone the
courts shall ring. Our voic - es we will raise the
more draw nigh; ac - cept each faith - ful vow, and
we im - plore; and may that grace, once given, be

courts of heaven are filled. On his great love our
Three - in - One to sing, and thus pro - claim in
mark each sup - pliant sigh. In co - pious shower on
with us ev - er - more, un - til that day when

hopes we place of pres - ent grace and joys a - bove.
joy - ful song both loud and long that glo - rious name.
all who pray, each ho - ly day thy bless - ings pour.
all the blest to end - less rest are called a - way.

Text: Latin (*Angularis fundamentum,* 7th cent.); tr. John Chandler (1806–1876).  66 66 44 44
Music: Samuel Sebastian Wesley (1810–1876).  HAREWOOD
*Alt. tune GOPSAL 236 or DARWALL 323, 365, 379*

# 460 Lord, the Light of Your Love Is Shining

1 Lord, the light of your love is shin-ing, in the
2 Lord, I come to your awe-some pres-ence, from the
3 As we gaze on your king-ly bright-ness so our

midst of the dark-ness shin-ing; Je-sus, Light of the
shad-ows in-to your ra-diance; by the blood I may
fac-es dis-play your like-ness; ev-er-chang-ing from

world, shine up-on us; set us free by the truth you now
en-ter your bright-ness; search me, try me, con-sume all my
glo-ry to glo-ry, mir-rored here may our lives tell your

bring us, shine on me, shine on me.
dark-ness, shine on me, shine on me.
sto-ry, shine on me, shine on me.

Text and music: Graham Kendrick (1950– ). © 1987 Make Way Music, Ltd.
*Administered in North and South America by Integrity's Hosanna! Music (ASCAP).
All rights reserved. International copyright secured. Used by permission.*

9 9 10 10 33 with refrain
SHINE, JESUS, SHINE

# 461 Stand Up, Stand Up for Jesus

1 Stand up, stand up for Je - sus, you sol - diers of the cross!
2 Stand up, stand up for Je - sus! The trum - pet - call o - bey;
3 Stand up, stand up for Je - sus! Stand in his power a - lone,
4 Stand up, stand up for Je - sus! The fight will not be long;

Lift high his roy - al ban - ner, it must not suf - fer loss.
then join the might - y con - flict in this his glo - rious day.
for hu - man might will fail you—you dare not trust your own.
this day the noise of bat - tle, the next the vic - tor's song.

From vic - tory on to vic - tory his ar - my he shall lead
Be strong in faith and serve him a - gainst un - num - bered foes;
Put on the gos - pel ar - mour, keep watch with con - stant prayer;
To ev - ery - one who con - quers, a crown of life shall be;

till e - vil is de - feat - ed, and Christ is Lord in - deed.
let cour - age rise with dan - ger, and strength to strength op - pose.
where du - ty calls or dan - ger, be nev - er fail - ing there.
we, with the king of glo - ry, shall reign e - ter - nal - ly.

Text: George Duffield, Jr. (1818–1888); rev. *Hymns for Today's Church*. © 1982 Hope Publishing Co.
Music: George James Webb (1803–1887).

76 76D
MORNING LIGHT

# The Hidden Stream 462

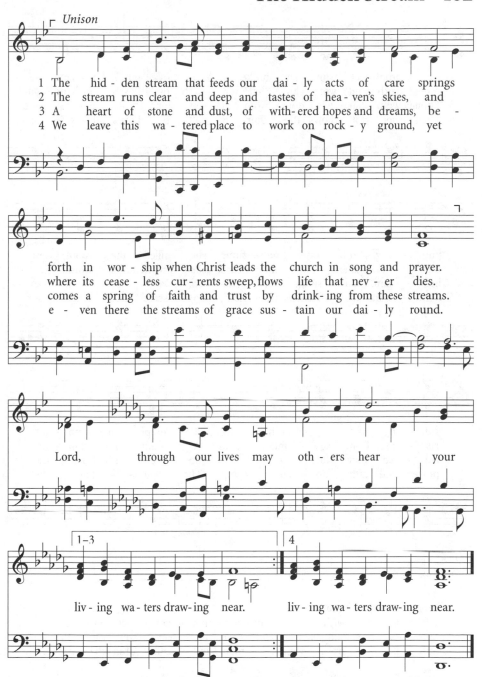

1 The hid-den stream that feeds our dai-ly acts of care springs
2 The stream runs clear and deep and tastes of hea-ven's skies, and
3 A heart of stone and dust, of with-ered hopes and dreams, be -
4 We leave this wa-tered place to work on rock-y ground, yet

forth in wor-ship when Christ leads the church in song and prayer.
where its cease-less cur-rents sweep, flows life that nev-er dies.
comes a spring of faith and trust by drink-ing from these streams.
e-ven there the streams of grace sus-tain our dai-ly round.

Lord, through our lives may oth-ers hear your

1–3
liv-ing wa-ters draw-ing near.

4
liv-ing wa-ters draw-ing near.

Text: Thomas H. Troeger (1945– ). © *1994 Oxford University Press, Inc.*
Music: John Kuzma (1946– ) ©.

SM with refrain
HIDDEN STREAM

# 463 A Prophet-Woman Broke a Jar

1 A proph-et-wom-an broke a jar by Love's di-vine ap-
2 A faith-ful wom-an left a tomb by Love's di-vine com-
3 Though wom-an-wis-dom, wom-an-truth for cen-tu-ries were
4 The Spir-it knows, the Spir-it calls, by Love's di-vine or-

point-ing. With rare per-fume she filled the room, pre-
mis-sion. She saw, she heard, she preached the word, a-
hid-den, un-sung, un-writ-ten, and un-heard, de-
dain-ing, the friends we need, to serve and lead, their

sid-ing and a-noint-ing. A proph-et-wom-an
ris-ing from sub-mis-sion. A faith-ful wom-an
rid-ed and for-bid-den, the Spir-it's breath, the
powers and gifts un-chain-ing. The Spir-it knows, the

broke a jar, the sneers of scorn de-fy-ing. With rare per-
left a tomb with res-ur-rec-tion gos-pel. She saw, she
Spir-it's fire, on free and slave de-scend-ing, can tum-ble
Spir-it calls from wom-en, men, and chil-dren the friends we

Text: Brian Wren (1936– ). © 1993 Hope Publishing Co.
Music: Walter K. Stanton (1891–1978). © Oxford University Press.

87 87D (Iambic)
MEGERRAN

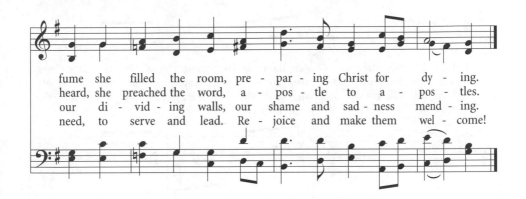

fume she filled the room, pre - par - ing Christ for dy - ing.
heard, she preached the word, a - pos - tle to a - pos - tles.
our di - vid - ing walls, our shame and sad - ness mend - ing.
need, to serve and lead. Re - joice and make them wel - come!

## Bonum est Confidere  464

Bo - num est con - fi - de - re in Do - mi - no,
*It is good to trust in the Lord our God,*

bo - num spe - ra - re in Do - mi - no.
*trust and hope in the Lord our God.*

Text: Latin; tr. Taizé Community (France).
Music: Jacques Berthier (1923–1994).
*Tr. and music © 1991 Les Presses de Taizé. Used by permission of G.I.A. Publications, Inc., exclusive agent.*

BONUM EST

# 465 Here in This Place New Light Is Streaming

1 Here in this place new light is stream-ing; now is the dark-ness
2 We are the young— our lives are a mys-tery; we are the old— who
3 Here we will take the wine and the wa-ter; here we will take the
4 Not in the dark of build-ings con-fin-ing, not in some heav-en,

van-ished a-way. See in this space our fears and our dream-ings,
yearn for your face. We have been sung through-out all of his-to-ry,
bread of new birth. Here you shall call your sons and your daugh-ters,
light years a-way, but here in this place the new light is shin-ing;

brought here to you in the light of this day.
called to be light to the whole hu-man race.
call us a-new to be salt for the earth.
now is the king-dom, now is the day.

Text and music: Marty Haugen (1950– ). © 1982 G.I.A. Publications, Inc.

Gath-er us in— the lost and for-sak-en; gath-er us in— the
Gath-er us in— the rich and the haugh-ty; gath-er us in— the
Give us to drink the wine of com-pas-sion; give us to eat the
Gath-er us in and hold us for-ev-er; gath-er us in and

blind and the lame; call to us now, and we shall a-wak-en;
proud and the strong; give us a heart so meek and so low-ly;
bread that is you; nour-ish us well, and teach us to fash-ion
make us your own; gath-er us in— all peo-ples to-geth-er,

we shall a-rise at the sound of our name.
give us the cour-age to en-ter the song.
lives that are ho-ly and hearts that are true.
fire of love in our flesh and our bone.

# 466 How Clear Is Our Vocation, Lord

*Unison*

1 How clear is our vo - ca - tion, Lord, when once we heed your
2 But if, for - get - ful, we should find your yoke is hard to
3 We mark your saints, how they be - came in hin - dran - ces more
4 In what you give us, Lord, to do, to - geth - er or a -

call: to live ac - cord - ing to your word, and
bear; if world - ly pres - sures fray the mind and
sure, whose joy - ful vir - tues put to shame the
lone, in old rou - tines or ven - tures new, may

dai - ly learn, re - freshed, re - stored, that you are
love it - self can - not un - wind its tan - gled
ca - sual way we wear your name, and by our
we not cease to look to you, the cross you

Lord of all, and will not let us fall.
skein of care: our in - ward life re - pair.
faults ob - scure your power to cleanse and cure.
hung up - on, all you en - deav - oured done.

Text: Fred Pratt Green (1903– ). © 1982 Hope Publishing Co.
Music: Charles Hubert Hastings Parry (1848–1918); arr. Michael Fleming (1928– ).
*Arr. © The Royal School of Church Music.*

86 88 66
REPTON
*Alt. setting 455*

# Forth in Thy Name, O Lord, I Go 467

1 Forth in thy name, O Lord, I go, my dai - ly
2 The task thy wis - dom hath as - signed O let me
3 Thee may I set at my right hand, whose eyes my
4 Give me to bear thy ea - sy yoke, and ev - ery
5 for thee de - light - ful - ly em - ploy what - e'er thy

la - bour to pur - sue, thee, on - ly thee, re -
cheer - ful - ly ful - fil, in all my works thy
in - most sub - stance see, and la - bour on at
mo - ment watch and pray, and still to things e -
boun - teous grace hath given, and run my course with

solved to know in all I think or speak or do.
pres - ence find, and prove thy good and per - fect will.
thy com - mand and of - fer all my works to thee.
ter - nal look, and hast - en to thy glo - rious day;
c - ven joy, and close - ly walk with thee to heaven.

Text: Charles Wesley (1707–1788).
Music: Melody and bass Orlando Gibbons (1583–1625); harm. *The English Hymnal*, 1906, alt.

LM
SONG 34

# 468 To Abraham and Sarah

1 To A - bra - ham and Sa - rah the call of God was
2 From A - bra - ham and Sa - rah a - rose a pil - grim
3 We of this gen - er - a - tion on whom God's hand is

clear: "Go forth and I will show you a
race, de - pen - dent for their jour - ney on
laid can jour - ney to the fu - ture se -

coun - try rich and fair. You need not fear the
God's a - bun - dant grace; and in their heart was
cure and un - a - fraid, re - joic - ing in God's

jour - ney, for I have pledged my word
writ - ten by God this sav - ing word,
good - ness and trust - ing in this word,

Text: Judith Fetter (1937– ) ©.
Music: Basil Harwood (1859–1949). *Music published by permission of the executors of the late Dr. Basil Harwood.*

76 76D
THORNBURY
*Alt. setting 444*

that you shall be my peo - ple and
"That you shall be my peo - ple and
"That you shall be my peo - ple and

I will be your God." (will be your God.)

# 469 Sing Praises Old and New

1 Sing prais-es old and new; past and pres-ent join in one. Old cov-e-nants re-new: new com-mit-ments have be-gun. God's soar-ing pur-pose spans all a-ges, lives, and lands. Christ's o-pen,

2 Word, from the heart of God, cost-ly, un-ex-pect-ed grace; Love, mak-ing all things good, Light of all the hu-man race; hail, Wis-dom, deep and vast, shin-ing in Is-rael's past, rais-ing the

3 Great Spi-rit, make us wise; doors of pro-mise op-en wide. Though e-vil's dead-ly lies truth and good-ness set a-side, faith nev-er stands a-lone, hope rolls a-way the stone, love makes your

4 Peo-ple of hope, be strong! Love is mak-ing all things new. Lift our u-nit-ed song, show what faith can dream and do! Come, Pres-ence, ev-er near, re-vive us year by year. Sing through our

Text: Brian Wren (1936– ).
Music: John Carter (1930– ).
*Text and music © 1992 Hope Publishing Co.*

67 67 666 7
FONDREN

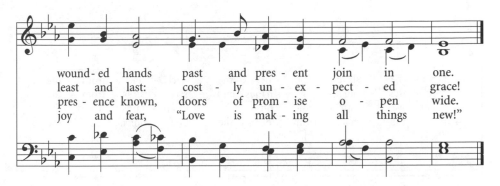

wound-ed hands past and pres-ent join in one.
least and last: cost - ly un - ex - pect - ed grace!
pres - ence known, doors of prom-ise o - pen wide.
joy and fear, "Love is mak - ing all things new!"

## Seek Not in Distant, Ancient Hills  470

*Unison*

D5   Em   Bm   Am   D

1 Seek not in dis - tant, an - cient hills the
2 A sin - gle heav - en wraps a - round this
3 To climb the tem - pled, foot - worn peak where
4 In spir - it and in truth, you'll find what

F#m7   Gsus4   G   A   D   F   D

prom - ised ho - ly land, but where you live do
whirl - ing, wa - tered stone, and ev - ery place is
pil - grims long have trod, un - lock the bolt - ed
hu - man thought can't frame: the source of breath and

G   Bm   Am7   C2   C   D5

what God wills and find it close at hand.
sa - cred ground where God is loved and known.
soul and seek the pres - ent, liv - ing God.
pulse and mind, the pri - mal wind and flame.

Text: Thomas H. Troeger (1945– ). © *1983 Oxford University Press, Inc.*
Music: Melody Brian Ruttan (1947– ) ©; harm. Roland Packer (1955– ) ©.

CM
WOODBURN
*Alt. tune* MORNING SONG *105, 219*

# 471 Let My People Seek Their Freedom

1 "From the slave pens of the Del - ta, from the
2 "From the ag - ing shrines and struc - tures, from the
3 When we mur - mur on the moun - tains for the
4 In the mael - strom of the na - tions, in the

ghet - tos on the Nile, let my peo - ple seek their
clois - ter and the aisle, let my peo - ple seek their
old E - gyp - tian plains, when we miss our an - cient
jour - ney in - to space, in the clash of gen - er -

free - dom in the wil - der - ness a - while": so God
free - dom in the wil - der - ness a - while": so the
bond - age and the hope, the pro - mise, wanes, then the
a - tions, in the hun - ger - ing for grace, in our

87 87D
OMNI DIE

spoke from out of Si - nai, so God spoke and
Son of God has spo - ken, and the storm - clouds
rock shall yield its wa - ter and the man - na
a - go - ny and glo - ry, we are called to

it was done, and the peo - ple crossed the
are un - furled, for his peo - ple must be
fall by night, and with vi - sions of a
new - er ways by the Lord of our to -

wa - ters toward the ris - ing of the sun.
scat - tered to be ser - vants in the world.
fu - ture shall we march to - ward the light.
mor - rows and the God of earth's to - days.

# 472 Eternal God, Lord of All Space and Time

1 Eternal God, Lord of all space and time,
the source of truth and righteousness and grace,
we thank thee that thy majesty sublime thou
dost reveal in every human face.

2 We thank thee, Lord, for love's deep fount of joy,
for inward peace that never can be told,
for comradeship no changes can destroy,
faith and hope that all our days enfold.

3 For love uniquely makes us one with thee,
re-moulding us according to thy will,
enabling us in true humanity
purpose of thy kingdom to fulfil.

4 Fixed deeper than the source of human strife,
may we in love a steadfast anchor find;
do thou, unchanging through the stress of life, to
thine own love our hearts forever bind.

Text: Robert Dobbie (1901–1995), alt. © Estate of Robert Dobbie.
Music: Ralph Vaughan Williams (1872–1958). © Oxford Univerrsity Press.

10 10 10 10
MAGDA

# Miren qué bueno, qué bueno es 473

Refrain is sung twice before and after each stanza.
May be sung in unison or 2 parts.

Text: Ps. 133; para. Pablo Sosa (1933– ), alt.
Music: Melody Pablo Sosa (1933– ); arr. Darryl Nixon (1952– ).
*Text and melody © Pablo Sosa. Arr. © Songs for a Gospel People, admin. Wood Lake Books.*

Irregular with refrain
MIREN QUÉ BUENO

# 474 Jesus, Where'er Thy People Meet

1 Je - sus, wher - e'er thy peo - ple meet, there they be -
2 For thou, with - in no walls con - fined, in - hab - it -
3 Here may we prove the power of prayer to strength - en
4 Lord, we are few, but thou art near; nor short thine

hold thy mer - cy seat; wher - e'er they seek thee,
est the hum - ble mind; such ev - er bring thee
faith and sweet - en care, to teach our faint de -
arm, nor deaf thine ear; O rend the heavens, come

thou art found, and ev - ery place is hal - lowed ground.
where they come, and go - ing, take thee to their home.
sires to rise, and bring all heaven be - fore our eyes.
quick - ly down, and make a thou - sand hearts thine own!

Text: William Cowper (1731–1800).
Music: Ralph Harrison (1748–1810).

LM
WARRINGTON

# Not Far Beyond the Sea 475

1 Not far be-yond the sea nor high a - bove the heavens, but
2 Root - ed and ground-ed in thy love, with saints on earth and
3 Help us to press to - ward that mark, and, though our vi - sion

ve - ry nigh thy voice, O God, is heard. For
saints a - bove we join in full ac - cord to
now is dark, to live by what we see. So,

each new step of faith we take, thou hast more truth and
grasp the breadth, length, depth, and height, the cru - ci - fied and
when we see thee face to face, thy truth and light our

light to break forth from thy ho - ly Word.
ris - en might of Christ, the in - car - nate Word.
dwell - ing place for ev - er - more shall be.

Text: George Bradford Caird (1917–1984). © *Estate of George Bradford Caird. Used by permission of Viola M. Caird.*
Music: Melody William Boyce (1710–1779); alt. and harm. William Henry Havergal (1793–1870).

886D
CHAPEL ROYAL
*Alt. tune* WILLOUGHBY NEW 289

# 476 God, You Have Caused to Be Written

*Unison*

1 God, you have caused to be writ-ten your word for our
learn-ing; grant us that, hear-ing, our hearts may be
in-ward-ly burn-ing. Give to us grace, that in your
Son we em-brace life, all its glo-ry dis-cern-ing.

2 Now may our God give us joy, and all peace in be-
liev-ing all things were writ-ten in truth for our
thank-ful re-ceiv-ing. As Christ did preach, through all the
world love must reach: grant us each day love's a-chiev-ing.

3 Lord, should the powers of the earth and the heav-ens be
sha-ken, grant us to see you in all things, our
vi-sion a-wak-en. Help us to see, though all the
earth cease to be, your truth shall nev-er be shak-en.

Text: Herbert O'Driscoll (1928– ) ©.
Music: F. R. C. Clarke (1931– ) ©.

14 14 4 7 8
CAUSA DIVINA

# Lamp of Our Feet, Whereby We Trace  477

1 Lamp of our feet, whereby we trace our path when
2 bread of our souls, whereon we feed, true man - na
3 pil - lar of fire, through watch - es dark, or ra - diant
4 word of the ev - er liv - ing God, will of the
5 Lord, grant us all a right to learn the wis - dom

wont to stray; stream from the fount of
from a - bove; our guide and chart, where -
cloud by day; when waves would whelm our
glo - rious Son; with - out thee how could
it im - parts, and to its heaven - ly

heaven - ly grace, brook by the trav - eller's way;
in we read of God's un - end - ing love;
toss - ing bark, our an - chor and our stay;
earth be trod, or heaven it - self be won?
teach - ing turn with sim - ple, child - like hearts.

Text: Bernard Barton (1784–1849).
Music: Melody Johann Crüger (1598–1662).

CM
GRÄFENBURG (NUN DANKET ALL)

# 478 Almighty God, Thy Word Is Cast

1 Al - might - y God, thy word is cast like
2 Let not the foe of right - eous - ness this
3 Let not the world's de - ceit - ful cares the
4 Oft as the pre - cious seed is sown, thy

seed in - to the ground: now let the dew of
ho - ly seed re - move: but give it root in
ris - ing plant des - troy: but let it yield a
quick - ening grace be - stow, that all whose souls the

heaven des - cend and right - eous fruits a - bound.
ev - ery heart, to bring forth fruits of love.
hun - dred - fold the fruits of peace and joy.
truth re - ceive its sav - ing power may know.

Text: John Cawood (1775–1852), alt.
Music: Francis Vincent Novello (1781–1861).

CM
ALBANO
*Lower key 479*

# O Christ, the Master Carpenter 479

1 O Christ, the mas-ter car-pen-ter, high
2 O Christ, up-on that Fri-day cross your
3 O Christ, take up your work-er's tools and
4 O Christ, the mas-ter car-pen-ter, let

on a cross you died; a wood-en cross, with
work on earth was done; yet, tru-ly, in my
shape my life a-new, that I who now ap -
beau-ty gent-ly shine with-in the work-shop

i - ron nails, a spear thrust in your side.
life to - day your work has just be - gun.
pear rough-hewn may be re - stored by you.
of my life— the praise be yours, not mine.

Text: David Mowbray (1938– ). © *1982 Hope Publishing Co.*
Music: Francis Vincent Novello (1781–1861).

CM
ALBANO
*Higher key 478*

## 480 Lord, Be Thy Word My Guide

1 Lord, be thy word my guide; in it may I re-joice:
2 thy prom-is-es my hope, thy prov-i-dence my guard,

thy glo-ry be my aim, thy ho-ly will my choice,
thine arm my strong sup-port, thy-self my great re-ward.

Text: Christopher Wordsworth (1807–1885).
Music: William Boyce (1710–1779).

66 66
KINGSLAND

## 481 May the Grace of Christ Our Saviour

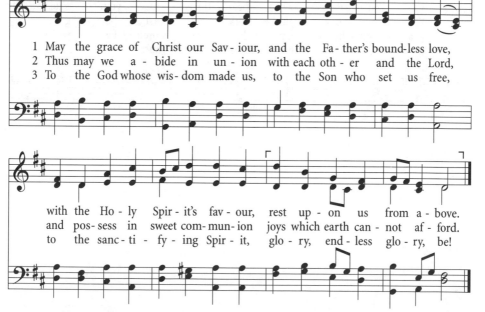

1 May the grace of Christ our Sav-iour, and the Fa-ther's bound-less love,
2 Thus may we a-bide in un-ion with each oth-er and the Lord,
3 To the God whose wis-dom made us, to the Son who set us free,

with the Ho-ly Spir-it's fav-our, rest up-on us from a-bove.
and pos-sess in sweet com-mun-ion joys which earth can-not af-ford.
to the sanc-ti-fy-ing Spir-it, glo-ry, end-less glo-ry, be!

Text: St. 1–2, John Newton (1725–1807); st. 3, *New English Hymnal*.
Music: William Boyce (1710–1779), alt.

87 87
HALTON HOLGATE (SHARON)
*Alt tune* OMNI DIE DIC MARIA *74, 657*

# Come and Journey with a Saviour 482

1 Come and jour-ney with a Sav-iour who has called us from our birth,
2 Come and jour-ney, jour-ney in - ward, come and seek him deep with - in,
3 Come and jour-ney, jour-ney out - ward, tell - ing oth - ers of his name,
4 Come and jour-ney, jour-ney out - ward, where that cross calls us to care,

who has washed us in the wa - ters, and who loved us on the earth.
where he meets us in our liv - ing, in our striv - ing and our sin.
tell - ing oth - ers of his glo - ry, of his cross and of the shame.
where in - jus - tice and where hun - ger and the poor call us to share.

*Refrain*

Come and jour - ney, come and jour - ney with a Sav - iour who has come.

We are all God's sons and daugh - ters; in the Spir - it we are one.

5 Come and journey, journey upward.
Sing his praises, offer prayer.
In the storm and in the stillness
find his presence everywhere.
*Refrain*

6 Come and journey, journey onward;
all our gifts we now shall bring
to the building of a city
that is holy, Christ its King.
*Refrain*

Text: Herbert O'Driscoll (1928– ) ©.
Music: Melody *The Sacred Harp*, Mason, 1844; attrib. to Benjamin Franklin White (1800–1879);
harm. Ronald A. Nelson (1927– ). *Harm. © 1978* Lutheran Book of Worship.
*Reprinted by permission of Augsburg Fortress.*

87 87 with refrain
BEACH SPRING
*Alt. settings 35, 585*

# 483 May the Spirit of Christ Be Our Hope

*Refrain*

May the Spir-it of Christ be our hope through the day, be our guard through the night, our com-pan-ion on the way.

*1–5* | *To stanzas* | *Last time*

Text: *St. Patrick's Breastplate*, Irish hymn; attrib. Patrick of Ireland (389?–461?);
 para. Marty Haugen (1950– ).
Music: Marty Haugen (1950– ). *Para. and music © 1986 G.I.A. Publications, Inc.*

Irregular with refrain
SONG OF ST. PATRICK

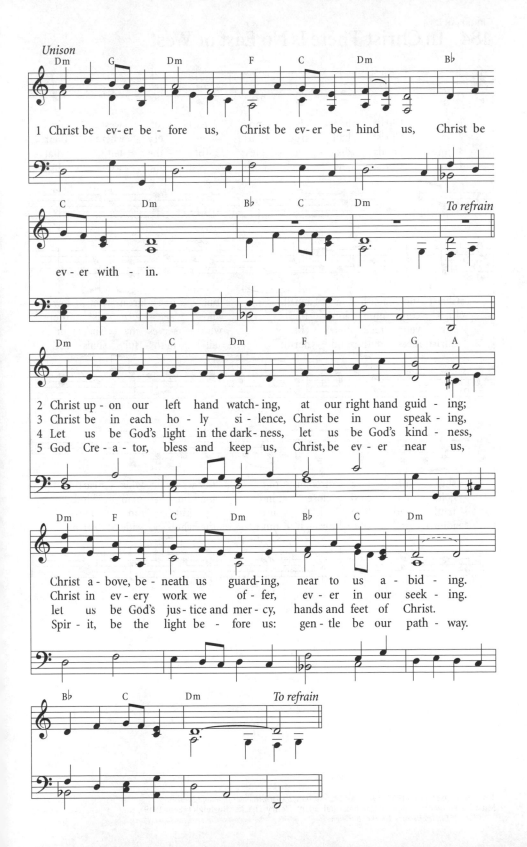

*Unison*

1 Christ be ev-er be-fore us, Christ be ev-er be-hind us, Christ be

ev-er with - in.

*To refrain*

2 Christ up-on our left hand watch-ing, at our right hand guid - ing;
3 Christ be in each ho - ly si - lence, Christ be in our speak - ing,
4 Let us be God's light in the dark-ness, let us be God's kind - ness,
5 God Cre - a - tor, bless and keep us, Christ, be ev - er near us,

Christ a - bove, be - neath us guard-ing, near to us a - bid - ing.
Christ in ev - ery work we of - fer, ev - er in our seek - ing.
let us be God's jus - tice and mer - cy, hands and feet of Christ.
Spir - it, be the light be - fore us: gen - tle be our path - way.

*To refrain*

## 484 In Christ There Is No East or West

1 In Christ there is no east or west, in
2 In Christ shall true hearts ev - ery - where their
3 Join hands, dis - ci - ples of the faith, what -
4 In Christ now meet both east and west, in

Christ no south or north, but one great fel - low -
high com - mun - ion find, whose ser - vice is the
e'er your race may be; who serves my God in
Christ meet south and north; all faith - ful souls are

ship of love through - out the whole wide earth.
gold - en cord close - bind - ing hu - man - kind.
truth and love is sure - ly kin to me.
joined in one through - out the whole wide earth.

Text: John Oxenham (1852–1941), alt., ©. *Reprinted by permission of Desmond Dunkerley.*
Music: Melody African-Amercan spiritual; adapt. Henry Thacker Burleigh (1866–1949).
*Adapt. © Estate of Henry Thacker Burleigh.*

CM
MCKEE

# Love Divine, All Loves Excelling 485

1 Love di - vine, all loves ex - cel - ling, joy of
2 Je - sus, thou art all com - pass - ion; pure, un -
3 Come, al - might - y to de - liv - er; let us
4 Thee we would be al - ways bless - ing, serve thee

heaven to earth come down, fix in us thy hum - ble
bound - ed love thou art; vis - it us with thy sal -
all thy grace re - ceive; sud - den - ly re - turn, and
as thy hosts a - bove, pray and praise thee with - out

dwell - ing; all thy faith - ful mer - cies crown.
va - tion, en - ter ev - ery trem - bling heart.
nev - er, nev - er - more thy tem - ples leave.
ceas - ing, glo - ry in thy per - fect love.

5 Finish, then, thy new creation;
   pure and spotless let us be;
   let us see thy great salvation
   perfectly restored in thee,

6 changed from glory into glory,
   till in heaven we take our place,
   till we cast our crowns before thee,
   lost in wonder, love, and praise.

Text: Charles Wesley (1707–1788).
Music: John Stainer (1840– 1901).

87 87
LOVE DIVINE
*Alt. tune* BLAENWERN *447, 486, 601*

# 486 Love Divine, All Loves Excelling

1 Love di - vine, all loves ex - cel - ling, joy of heaven to
2 Come, al - might - y to de - liv - er; let us all thy
3 Fin - ish, then, thy new cre - a - tion; pure and spot - less

earth come down, fix in us thy hum - ble dwell - ing;
grace re - ceive; sud - den - ly re - turn, and nev - er,
let us be; let us see thy great sal - va - tion

all thy faith - ful mer - cies crown. Je - sus, thou art
nev - er - more thy tem - ples leave. Thee we would be
per - fect - ly re - stored in thee, changed from glo - ry

all com - pas - sion; pure, un - bound - ed love thou art; vis - it
al - ways bless - ing, serve thee as thy hosts a - bove, pray and
in - to glo - ry, till in heaven we take our place, till we

Text: Charles Wesley (1707–1788).
Music: William Penfro Rowlands (1860–1937) ©. *Reprinted by permission of Mr. G.A. Gabe.*

87 87D
BLAENWERN
*Higher key 447*
*Alt. tune HYFRYDOL 374, 643*

us with thy sal-va-tion, en-ter ev-ery trem-bling heart.
praise thee with-out ceas-ing, glo-ry in thy per-fect love.
cast our crowns be-fore thee, lost in won-der, love, and praise.

## Where Charity and Love Prevail 487

1 Where char-i-ty and love pre-vail, there God is ev-er found;
2 With grate-ful joy and ho-ly fear his char-i-ty we learn;
3 For-give we now each oth-er's faults as we our faults con-fess;
4 Let strife a-mong us be un-known, let all con-ten-tion cease;

brought here to-geth-er by Christ's love, by love are we thus bound.
let us with heart and mind and strength now love him in re-turn.
and let us love each oth-er well in Chris-tian ho-li-ness.
be his the glo-ry that we seek, be ours his ho-ly peace.

5 Let us recall that in our midst
dwells God's begotten Son;
as members of his body joined,
we are in him made one.

6 Love can exclude no race or creed
if honoured be God's name;
our common life embraces all
whose Father is the same.

Text: Latin (9th cent.); tr. Omer Westendorf (1916– ), alt.
© 1961, 1962 World Library Publications, Inc. A division of J.S. Paluch Company, Inc.
Music: Attrib. Lucius Chapin (1769–1842).

CM
TWENTY-FOURTH (PRIMROSE)

# 488 The Tree of Life My Soul Hath Seen

1 The tree of life my soul hath seen, la - den with fruit and
2 His beau - ty doth all things ex - cel. By faith I know, but
3 For hap - pi - ness I long have sought, and plea - sure dear - ly
4 I'm wea - ry with my for - mer toil. Here I will sit and
5 This fruit doth make my soul to thrive. It keeps my dy - ing

al - ways green. The trees of na - ture fruit-less be com -
ne'er can tell the glo - ry which I now can see in
I have bought. I missed in all; but now I see 'tis
rest a - while. Un - der the sha - dow will I be of
faith a - live; which makes my soul in haste to be with

pared with Christ the ap - ple tree.
Je - sus Christ the ap - ple tree.
found in Christ the ap - ple tree.
Je - sus Christ the ap - ple tree.
Je - sus Christ the ap - ple tree.

Text: Joshua Smith (18th cent.), *Divine Hymns or Spiritual Songs*, New Hampshire, 1784.
Music: Daniel Pinkham, (1923– ). © 1990 Ione Press, Inc. Used by permission of E.C. Schirmer, Inc.

LM
PINKHAM

# From the Falter of Breath 489

1 From the fal-ter of breath, through the si-lence of death,
2 From frus-tra-tion and pain, through hope hard to sus-tain,
3 From the dim-ming of light, through the dark-ness of night,
4 From to-day till we die, through all ques-tion-ing why,

to the won-der that's break-ing be-yond,
to the whole-ness here prom-ised, there known,
to the glo-ry of good-ness a-bove,
to the place from which time and tide flow,

God has wo-ven a way, un-ap-par-ent by day,
Christ has gone where we fear and has vowed to be near
God the Spir-it is sent to en-sure heaven's in-tent
an-gels tread on our dreams, and mag-nif-i-cent themes

for all those of whom heav-en is fond.
on the jour-ney we make on our own.
is em-braced and com-plet-ed in love.
of heaven's prom-ise are ech-oed be-low.

*Best when sung unaccompanied, whether in unison or 4 parts.*

Text: John L. Bell (1949– ). © 1988 WGRG The Iona Community (Scotland).
*Used by permission of G.I.A. Publications, Inc., exclusive agent.*
Music: Melody Scottish trad.; arr. George Black (1931– ) ©.

669D
IONA BOAT SONG

## 490  God of All Being, Throned Afar

1 God of all be - ing, throned a - far, thy glo - ry
2 Sun of our life, thy quick - ening ray sheds on our
3 Source of all life, be - low, a - bove, whose light is
4 Grant us thy truth to make us free, and kin - dling

flames from sun and star; cen - tre and soul of
path the glow of day; star of our hope, thy
truth, whose warmth is love, be - fore thy ev - er
hearts that burn for thee, till all thy liv - ing

ev - ery sphere, yet to each lov - ing heart how near.
soft - ened light cheers the long watch - es of the night.
blaz - ing throne we ask no lus - tre of our own.
al - tars claim one ho - ly light, one heaven - ly flame.

Text: Oliver Wendell Holmes (1809–1894).
Music: Jeremiah Clarke (1673?–1707).

LM
UFFINGHAM

# The Head That Once Was Crowned 491

1 The head that once was crowned with thorns is
crowned with glo - ry now; a roy - al di - a -
dem a - dorns the might - y Vic - tor's brow.

2 The high - est place that heaven af - fords is
his, is his by right, the King of kings and
Lord of lords, and heaven's e - ter - nal light,

3 the joy of all who dwell a - bove, the
joy of all be - low, to whom he man - i -
fests his love and grants his name to know.

4 To them the cross, with all its shame, with
all its grace, is given, their name an ev - er -
last - ing name, their joy the joy of heaven.

5 They suffer with their Lord below,
they reign with him above,
their profit and their joy to know
the mystery of his love.

6 The cross he bore is life and health,
though shame and death to him,
his people's hope, his people's wealth,
their everlasting theme.

Text: Thomas Kelly (1769–1855).
Music: Attrib. Jeremiah Clarke (1673?–1707).

CM
ST. MAGNUS

# 492 Sing Hallelujah to Our God

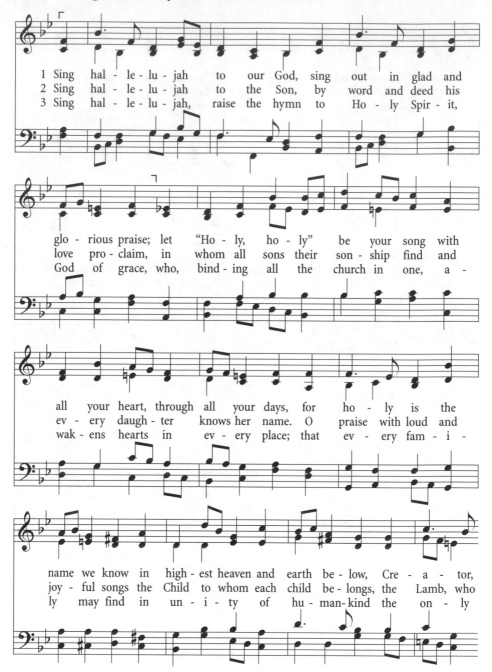

1 Sing hal - le - lu - jah to our God, sing out in glad and
2 Sing hal - le - lu - jah to the Son, by word and deed his
3 Sing hal - le - lu - jah, raise the hymn to Ho - ly Spir - it,

glo - rious praise; let "Ho - ly, ho - ly" be your song with
love pro - claim, in whom all sons their son - ship find and
God of grace, who, bind - ing all the church in one, a -

all your heart, through all your days, for ho - ly is the
ev - ery daugh - ter knows her name. O praise with loud and
wak - ens hearts in ev - ery place; that ev - ery fam - i -

name we know in high - est heaven and earth be - low, Cre - a - tor,
joy - ful songs the Child to whom each child be - longs, the Lamb, who
ly may find in un - i - ty of hu - man - kind the on - ly

Text: Rosemary Anne Benwell, SSJD (1915– ).
Music: Thelma Anne McLeod, SSJD (1928– ).
*Text and music © 1984 The Sisterhood of St. John the Divine.*

LMD
KINGSWOOD NEW

Fa - ther, Mo - ther blest in whom all par - ents end their quest.
to the Fa - ther brings all liv - ing, dy - ing, help - less things.
truth that sets us free, the love that serves e - ter - nal - ly.

## Blessed Are the Persecuted  493

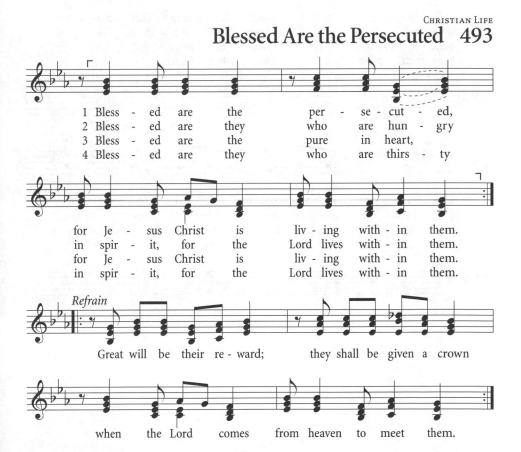

1 Bless - ed are the per - se - cut - ed,
2 Bless - ed are they who are hun - gry
3 Bless - ed are the pure in heart,
4 Bless - ed are they who are thirs - ty

for Je - sus Christ is liv - ing with - in them.
in spir - it, for the Lord lives with - in them.
for Je - sus Christ is liv - ing with - in them.
in spir - it, for the Lord lives with - in them.

*Refrain*

Great will be their re - ward; they shall be given a crown

when the Lord comes from heaven to meet them.

*Verse and refrain may be sung twice.*

Text: Esther C. Bergen (1921– ). © 1990 Mennonite World Conference.
Music: Tonga melody, Zambia.

8 10 with refrain
TONGA MELODY

# 494 Not for Tongues of Heaven's Angels

1 Not for tongues of heav-en's an-gels, not for wis-dom
2 Love is hum-ble, love is gen-tle, love is ten-der,
3 Nev-er jeal-ous, nev-er self-ish, love will not re-
4 In the day this world is fad-ing, faith and hope will

to dis-cern, not for faith that mas-ters
true, and kind; love is gra-cious, ev-er
joice in wrong; nev-er boast-ful nor re-
play their part; but when Christ is seen in

moun-tains, for this bet-ter gift we yearn:
pa-tient, gen-er-ous of heart and mind:
sent-ful, love be-lieves and suf-fers long:
glo-ry, love shall reign in ev-ery heart:

Text: Timothy Dudley-Smith (1926– ). © 1985 Hope Publishing Co.
Music: Michael Joncas (1951– ). © 1988 G.I.A. Publications, Inc.

87 87 with refrain
COMFORT
*Alt. tune* BRIDEGROOM *635 using only line 2 of refrain*

# 495 Should I Rehearse with Human Voice

1 Should I re-hearse with hu-man voice the words which
2 In love is pa-tience al-ways found, for love kind
3 Let strange and start-ling lan-guage cease, let tongues their

an - gels make their choice, de - void of love, my song re -
hearts make com - mon ground; from love, con - ceit and pride take
ec - sta - sy re - lease, let knowl-edge come and go in

sounds mag - nif - i - cent but emp - ty. And
flight and jeal - ou - sy is ban - ished. Love
peace— these things are not e - ter - nal; for

should I preach with earn - est tone and know what-ev - er
keeps no score of what's gone wrong nor sings a pes - si -
all the thought and skill we show are but a stage through

Text: I Cor. 13; para. John L. Bell (1949– ).
Music: Melody Scottish trad.; arr. John L. Bell.
*Para. and arr. © 1988 WGRG The Iona Community (Scotland). Used by permission of G.I.A. Publications, Inc., exclusive agent.*

88 87 888 7
A ROSEBUD

can be known and move the hills by faith a-
mis - tic song nor lets re - gret or guilt pro-
which we grow till, face to face with God, we'll

lone— if I lack love, I'm noth - ing.
long, for love ex - pects to - mor - row.
know that love which lasts for - ev - er.

## Teach Me, My God and King   496

1 Teach me, my God and King, in all things thee to see,
2 All may of thee par - take; noth - ing can be so mean,
3 A ser - vant with this clause makes drudg - er - y di - vine;
4 This is the fa - mous stone that turn - eth all to gold;

and what I do in an - y - thing to do it as for thee.
which with this tinc - ture, "For thy sake," will not grow bright and clean.
who sweeps a room as for thy laws makes that and the ac - tion fine.
for that which God doth touch and own can - not for less be told.

Text: George Herbert (1593–1633).
Music: William Henry Walter (1825–1893).

SM
FESTAL SONG
*Alt. tune CARLISLE 167, 454*

# 497 Eternal Ruler of the Ceaseless Round

1 E - ter - nal Rul - er of the cease - less round of cir - cling
2 We are of thee, the chil - dren of thy love, com - pan - ions
3 We would be one in ha - tred of all wrong, one in our
4 O clothe us with thy heaven - ly ar - mour, Lord, thy trus - ty

plan - ets sing - ing on their way, Guide of the na - tions
of thy well - be - lov - ed Son; des - cend, O Ho - ly
love of all things sweet and fair, one with the joy that
shield, thy sword of love di - vine; our in - spi - ra - tion

from the night pro - found in - to the glo - ry of the per - fect
Spir - it, like a dove, in - to our hearts that we may be as
ris - es in - to song, one with the grief that finds no voice in
be thy con - stant word; we ask no vic - to - ries that are not

day: rule in our hearts, that we may ev - er be
one: as one with thee, to whom we ev - er tend;
prayer, one in the power that makes thy chil - dren free
thine: give us the shield of faith that we may be

Text: John White Chadwick (1840–1904), alt.
Music: Orlando Gibbons (1583–1625).

10 10 10 10 10 10
SONG 1

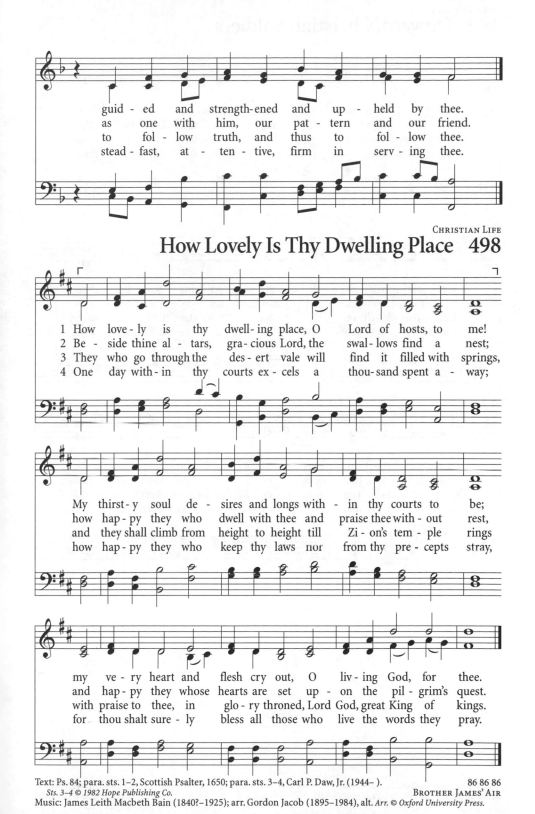

guid - ed and strength-ened and up - held by thee.
as one with him, our pat - tern and our friend.
to fol - low truth, and thus to fol - low thee.
stead - fast, at - ten - tive, firm in serv - ing thee.

## How Lovely Is Thy Dwelling Place 498

1 How love - ly is thy dwell- ing place, O Lord of hosts, to me!
2 Be - side thine al - tars, gra - cious Lord, the swal- lows find a nest;
3 They who go through the des - ert vale will find it filled with springs,
4 One day with- in thy courts ex - cels a thou- sand spent a - way;

My thirst- y soul de - sires and longs with - in thy courts to be;
how hap - py they who dwell with thee and praise thee with - out rest,
and they shall climb from height to height till Zi - on's tem - ple rings
how hap - py they who keep thy laws nor from thy pre - cepts stray,

my ve - ry heart and flesh cry out, O liv - ing God, for thee.
and hap - py they whose hearts are set up - on the pil - grim's quest.
with praise to thee, in glo - ry throned, Lord God, great King of kings.
for thou shalt sure - ly bless all those who live the words they pray.

Text: Ps. 84; para. sts. 1–2, Scottish Psalter, 1650; para. sts. 3–4, Carl P. Daw, Jr. (1944– ).
*Sts. 3–4 © 1982 Hope Publishing Co.*
Music: James Leith Macbeth Bain (1840?–1925); arr. Gordon Jacob (1895–1984), alt. *Arr. © Oxford University Press.*

86 86 86
BROTHER JAMES' AIR

# 499 Onward, Christian Soldiers

1 On - ward, Chris - tian sol - diers, march - ing as to war,
2 At the sign of tri - umph Sa - tan's host doth flee:
3 Crowns and thrones may per - ish, king - doms rise and wane,
4 On - ward, then, ye peo - ple, join our hap - py throng,

with the cross of Je - sus go - ing on be - fore.
on, then, Chris - tian sol - diers, on to vic - to - ry!
but the church of Je - sus con - stant will re - main:
blend with ours your voic - es in the tri - umph song:

Christ, the roy - al mas - ter, leads a - gainst the foe;
Hell's foun - da - tions quiv - er at the shout of praise;
gates of hell can nev - er 'gainst that church pre - vail;
glo - ry, laud, and hon - our un - to Christ the king,

Text: Sabine Baring-Gould (1834–1924).
Music: Arthur Seymour Sullivan (1842–1900).

65 65D with refrain
ST. GERTRUDE

for - ward in - to bat - tle, see, his ban - ners go.
broth - ers, lift your voic - es; loud your an - thems raise.
we have Christ's own prom - ise, and that can - not fail.
this through count - less a - ges men and an - gels sing.

*Refrain*

On - ward, Chris - tian sol - diers, march - ing as to war,

with the cross of Je - sus go - ing on be - fore.

# 500 Sister, Let Me Be Your Servant

1 Sis - ter, let me be your ser - vant, let me be as
2 We are pil - grims on a jour - ney, fel - low trav - ellers
3 I will hold the Christ-light for you in the night - time
4 I will weep when you are weep - ing; when you laugh I'll

Christ to you; pray that I may have the
on the road; we are here to help each
of your fear; I will hold my hand out
laugh with you. I will share your joy and

grace to let you be my ser - vant too.
oth - er walk the mile and bear the load.
to you, speak the peace you long to hear.
sor - row till we've seen this jour - ney through.

5 When we sing to God in heaven,
we shall find such harmony,
born of all we've known together
of Christ's love and agony.

6 Brother, let me be your servant,
let me be as Christ to you;
pray that I may have the grace to
let you be my servant too.

Text: Richard Gillard (1953– ).
Music: Melody Richard Gillard (1953– ); arr. Betty Carr Pulkingham (1928– ).
*Text and music © 1977 Scripture in Song (a div. of Integrity Music, Inc.).*
*All rights reserved. International copyright secured. Used by permission.*

87 87
SERVANT SONG

# Through All the Changing Scenes of Life   501

1 Through all the chang - ing scenes of life, in
2 O mag - ni - fy the Lord with me, ex -
3 The guard - ian hosts en - camp a - round the
4 O make but tri - al of God's love; ex -

trou - ble and in joy, the prais - es of my
alt the sa - cred name; when in dis - tress to
dwell - ings of the just; de - liv - erance they pro -
per - ience will de - cide how blest and fav - oured

God shall still my heart and tongue em - ploy.
heaven I called, God to my res - cue came.
vide to all who in God's shel - ter trust.
are they all who in this love con - fide.

5 Fear God, you saints, and you will then
    have nothing else to fear;
    let service be your life's delight;
    your wants shall be God's care.

6 To Father, Son, and Spirit blest,
    the God whom we adore
    be glory, as it was, is now,
    and shall be evermore.

Text: Ps. 34.1–9; para. Nahum Tate (1652–1715) and Nicholas Brady (1659–1726), *New Version*, 1696, alt.   CM
Music: George Smart (1776–1867).   WILTSHIRE

# 502 You Are Salt for the Earth

1 You are salt for the earth, O people: salt for the
2 You are a light on the hill, O people: light for the
3 You are a seed of the Word, O people: bring forth the
4 We are a blest and a pil - grim people bound for the

king-dom of God! Share the fla-vour of life, O people:
ci - ty of God! Shine so ho - ly and bright, O people:
king-dom of God! Seeds of mer-cy and seeds of jus - tice
king-dom of God! Love our jour-ney and love our home-land:

life in the king - dom of God!
shine for the king - dom of God!
grow in the king - dom of God!
love is the king - dom of God!

Text and music: Marty Haugen (1950– ). © 1986 G.I.A. Publications, Inc.

Irregular with refrain
BRING FORTH THE KINGDOM

# 503 Fight the Good Fight with All Thy Might

1 Fight the good fight with all thy might, Christ is thy
2 Run the straight race through God's good grace; lift up thine
3 Cast care a- side, lean on thy guide; his bound-less
4 Faint not, nor fear, his arms are near; he chang-eth

strength and Christ thy right; lay hold on life and
eyes and seek his face. Life with its path be-
mer- cy will pro- vide; trust, and the trust- ing
not and thou art dear. On- ly be- lieve, and

it shall be thy joy and crown e- ter- nal- ly.
fore us lies; Christ is the way and Christ the prize.
soul shall prove Christ is its life, and Christ its love.
thou shalt see that Christ is all in all to thee.

Text: John Samuel Bewley Monsell (1811–1875).
Music: William Boyd (1847–1928).

LM
PENTECOST

# Jesu, Jesu, Fill Us with Your Love  504

**Refrain** ⌐ Unison

Je - su,    Je - su,    fill   us   with your love,   show

*Last time* ⌐

us  how  to  serve   the  neigh-bours we have   from  you.

1 Kneels  at   the  feet  of   his   friends,   si - lent - ly  wash - es  their
2 Neigh - bours are  rich       and  poor,   var - ied  in  col - our  and
3 These   are  the  ones  we should serve,   these  are  the  ones  we should
4 Lov - ing  puts  us   on   our  knees,   serv - ing  as though we  are
5 Kneel   at   the  feet  of   our  friends,   si - lent - ly  wash - ing  their

*To refrain*

feet,     mas - ter  who acts   as     a    slave    to  them.
race,     neigh-bours are  near       and   far     a - way.
love;      all   these are neigh-bours to    us    and  you.
slaves;    this   is   the  way  we should   live   with  you.
feet;      this   is   the  way  we should   live   with  you.

*Best when sung unaccompanied.*

Text: Tom Colvin (1925– ), alt.
Music: Melody Ghanaian trad.; adapt. Tom Colvin (1925– );
   arr. Jane Manton Marshall (1924– ). *Text and melody © 1969, arr. © 1982 Hope Publishing Co.*

Irregular with refrain
CHEREPONI

# 505 Be Thou My Vision

1 Be thou my vi - sion, O Lord of my heart;
2 Be thou my wis - dom, and thou my true Word;
3 Rich - es I heed not, nor the world's emp - ty praise;
4 High King of heav - en, when vic - tory is won,

naught be all else to me, save that thou art—
I ev - er with thee and thou with me, Lord;
thou mine in - her - i - tance, now and al - ways:
may I reach heav - en's joys, bright heav - en's Sun!

thou my best thought, by day or by night,
thou my great Fa - ther; thine own may I be,
thou and thou on - ly, first in my heart,
Heart of my own heart, what - ev - er be - fall,

wak - ing or sleep - ing, thy pres - ence my light.
thou in me dwell - ing, and I one with thee.
high King of heav - en, my trea - sure thou art.
still be my vi - sion, O Rul - er of all.

Text: Irish hymn (8th cent.); tr. Mary Elizabeth Byrne (1880–1931); vers. Eleanor H. Hull (1860–1935), alt.  10 10 10 10
*Vers. © courtesy of the estate of Eleanor H. Hull and Chatto & Windus Ltd.*  SLANE
Music: Melody Irish trad.; arr. Martin Shaw (1875–1958), alt. *Arr. © Oxford University Press.*

1 Lord of all hope - ful - ness, Lord of all joy, whose
2 Lord of all ea - ger - ness, Lord of all faith, whose
3 Lord of all kind - li - ness, Lord of all grace, your
4 Lord of all gen - tle - ness, Lord of all calm, whose

trust, ev - er child - like, no cares could de - stroy, be
strong hands were skilled at the plane and the lathe, be
hands swift to wel - come, your arms to em - brace, be
voice is con - tent - ment, whose pres - ence is balm, be

there at our wak - ing and give us, we pray, your
there at our la - bours and give us, we pray, your
there at our hom - ing and give us, we pray, your
there at our sleep - ing and give us, we pray, your

bliss in our hearts, Lord, at the break of the day.
strength in our hearts, Lord, at the noon of the day.
love in our hearts, Lord, at the eve of the day.
peace in our hearts, Lord, at the end of the day.

Text: Jan Struther (1901–1953).
Music: Melody Irish trad.; arr. Martin Shaw (1875–1958), alt.
*Text and arr. © Oxford University Press.*

10 11 11 12
SLANE

## 507 Blest Be the Tie That Binds

1 Blest be the tie that binds our hearts in
2 Be - fore God's gra - cious throne we pour our
3 We share each oth - er's woes, each oth - er's
4 When for a while we part, this thought will

Je - sus' love; the fel - low-ship of Chris - tian
ar - dent prayers: our fears, our hopes, our aims are
bur - dens bear; and of - ten for each oth - er
soothe our pain; that we shall still be joined in

minds is like to that a - bove.
one, our com - forts and our cares.
flows the sym - pa - thiz - ing tear.
heart and one day meet a - gain.

5 One glorious hope revives
   our courage by the way,
   while each in expectation lives
   and longs to see the day

6 when from all toil and pain
   and sin we shall be free,
   and perfect love and friendship reign
   through all eternity.

Text: John Fawcett (1740–1817), alt.
Music: Attrib. Johann G. Nägeli (1772–1836); adapt. Lowell Mason (1792–1872).

SM
DENNIS

# I Heard the Voice of Jesus Say 508

1 I heard the voice of Jesus say, "Come unto me and rest;
2 I heard the voice of Jesus say, "Behold, I freely give
3 I heard the voice of Jesus say, "I am this dark world's light;

lay down, thou weary one, lay down thy head upon my breast."
the living water; thirsty one, stoop down and drink and live."
look unto me, thy morn shall rise, and all thy day be bright."

I came to Jesus as I was, so weary, worn, and sad;
I came to Jesus and I drank of that life-giving stream;
I looked to Jesus and I found in him my star, my sun;

I found in him a resting place, and he has made me glad.
my thirst was quenched, my soul revived, and now I live in him.
and in that light of life I'll walk till travelling days are done.

Text: Horatius Bonar (1808–1889).
Music: Melody English trad.; coll. Lucy Broadwood (1858–1929);
  adapt and harm. Ralph Vaughan Williams (1872–1958). *Harm. © Oxford University Press.*

CMD
KINGSFOLD

# 509 Precious Lord, Take My Hand

1 Pre - cious Lord, take my hand, lead me on, let me
2 When my way grows drear, pre - cious Lord, lin - ger
3 When the dark - ness ap - pears and the night draws

stand; I am tired, I am weak, I am worn;
near; when my life is al - most gone,
near, and the day is past and gone,

through the storm, through the night, lead me on to the
hear my cry, hear my call, hold my hand lest I
at the riv - er I stand; guide my feet, hold my

light: take my hand, pre - cious Lord, lead me home.
fall: take my hand, pre - cious Lord, lead me home.
hand: take my hand, pre - cious Lord, lead me home.

Text: Thomas A. Dorsey (1899–1993).
Music: Melody George Nelson Allen (1812–1877); arr. Thomas A. Dorsey (1899–1993).

669D
PRECIOUS LORD

# You Have Passed By 510

1 You have passed by, you came like fire that lights the skies;
2 You have passed by, as brief as foot-prints on the sea;
3 You have passed by, a strange and yet fa-mil-iar face,

sparks fall-ing from your name glow in our hearts like eyes.
why did you go so far? You went too far for me.
a frag-ment of our being, a flick-ering light, a trace.

In tat-ters hangs your word, draped round our world and torn;
You are for-ev-er now as deep in God as breath;
Your light is in my blood, my bo-dy is your day;

now we shall live in you; like cloth-ing you are worn.
no still-ness cap-tures you, un-think-a-ble your death.
I hope my whole life long to meet you on the way.

Text: Huub Oosterhuis (1933– ); tr. Redmond McGoldrick (19??– ). 12 12 12 12
Music: Melody Thoinot Arbeau (1520–1595), *Orchésographie*, 1589; harm. Bernard Huijbers (1922– ). PIEDS EN L'AIR
*Text and music © 1971 Gooi en Sticht, bv., Baarn, The Netherlands. Reprinted by permission of OCP Publications,*
*exclusive agent for English-language countries.*

# 511 Lord Jesus, Think on Me

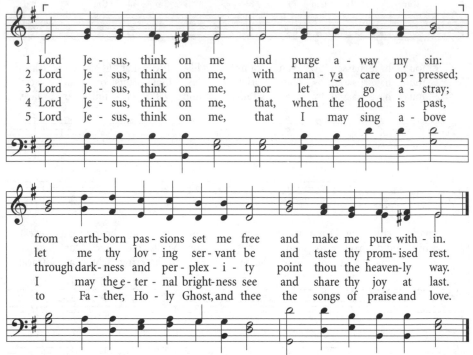

1 Lord Jesus, think on me and purge away my sin:
2 Lord Jesus, think on me, with many a care oppressed;
3 Lord Jesus, think on me, nor let me go astray;
4 Lord Jesus, think on me, that, when the flood is past,
5 Lord Jesus, think on me, that I may sing above

from earth-born passions set me free and make me pure within.
let me thy loving servant be and taste thy promised rest.
through darkness and perplexity point thou the heavenly way.
I may the eternal brightness see and share thy joy at last.
to Father, Holy Ghost, and thee the songs of praise and love.

Text: Synesius of Cyrene (365?–414); tr. Allen W. Chatfield (1808–1896).  SM
Music: William Daman (1540–1591), *Psalmes*, 1579, alt.  SOUTHWELL

# 512 I Want Jesus to Walk with Me

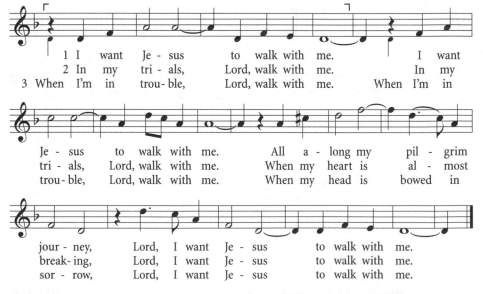

1 I want Jesus to walk with me. I want
2 In my trials, Lord, walk with me. In my
3 When I'm in trouble, Lord, walk with me. When I'm in

Jesus to walk with me. All along my pilgrim
trials, Lord, walk with me. When my heart is almost
trouble, Lord, walk with me. When my head is bowed in

journey, Lord, I want Jesus to walk with me.
breaking, Lord, I want Jesus to walk with me.
sorrow, Lord, I want Jesus to walk with me.

Text and music: African-American spiritual.  888 9
I WANT JESUS TO WALK WITH ME (SOJOURNER)

2 Hold my hand...
3 Stand by me...
4 I'm your child...
5 Search my heart...
6 Guide my feet...

Text: African-American spiritual.
Music: Melody African-American spiritual; harm. Wendell Whalum (1932–1987).
*Harm. © 1987 Estate of Wendell Whalum.*

888 10
GUIDE MY FEET

# 514 Jesus, Joy of Our Desiring

1 Je - sus, joy of our de - sir - ing, ho - ly wis - dom,
2 Through the way where hope is guid - ing, hark, what peace - ful

love most bright; drawn by thee, our souls as - pir - ing soar to
mu - sic rings, where the flock, in thee con - fid - ing, drink of

un - cre - a - ted light. Word of God, our flesh that
joy from death - less springs. Theirs is beau - ty's fair - est

fash - ioned, with the fire of life im - pas - sioned, striv - ing
plea - sure; theirs is wis - dom's ho - liest trea - sure. Thou dost

Text: Martin Janus (1620?–1682?); tr. Robert Seymour Bridges (1844–1930), alt.
*Tr. © Oxford University Press. Alt. with permission.*
Music: Melody Johann Schop (1590?–1664?); harm. Johann Sebastian Bach (1685–1750).

87 87 88 77
WERDE MUNTER

still    to    truth un-known,    soar-ing,  dy - ing round      thy throne.
ev - er  lead thine   own    in    the   love    of  joys     un-known.

## Thou Art the Way: to Thee Alone    515

1 Thou  art  the way:  to    thee a-lone from  sin  and death we    flee;
2 Thou  art  the truth: thy  word a-lone true  wis-dom can  im - part;
3 Thou  art  the life:  the   rend-ing tomb pro-claims thy  con-quering arm;
4 Thou  art  the way,  the   truth, the life: grant  us   that  way  to   know,

and   those who would the    Fa - ther seek must seek him, Lord, by    thee.
thou  on - ly canst in - form the mind and    pur - i - fy the   heart.
and   those who put their trust in  thee nor   death nor hell shall harm.
that  truth to keep, that   life  to  win, whose joys e - ter - nal   flow.

Text: George Washington Doane (1799–1859), alt.
Music: Raphael Courteville (?–1735).

CM
St. James

# 516 Dear Lord, We Long to See Your Face

1 Dear Lord, we long to see your face, to know you
2 Dear Friend, we do not know the way, nor clear-ly
3 We find it hard, Lord, to be-lieve. Long hab-it
4 You come to us, our God, our Lord. You do not

ris-en from the grave, but we have missed the joy and
see the path a-head; so of-ten, there-fore, we de-
makes us want to prove: to see, to touch, and thus per-
show your hands and side, but give, in-stead, your best re-

grace of see-ing you, as oth-ers have; yet in your
lay and doubt your power to raise the dead; yet we with
ceive the truth and per-son whom we love; yet when in
ward as in your prom-ise we a-bide. By faith we

com-pa-ny we'll wait, and we shall see you, soon or late.
you will firm-ly stay— you are the truth, the life, the way.
fel-low-ship we meet, you come your-self, each one to greet.
know and grow and wait to see and praise you, soon or late.

Text: J. R. Peacey (1896–1971). © 1991 Hope Publishing Co.
Music: Melchior Vulpius (1570?–1615).

88 88 88
DAS NEUGEBORNE KINDELEIN

# O God, Your Constant Care and Love  517

1 O God, your con - stant care and love are
2 We thank you, Lord, for dreams of youth, for
3 All time is yours, O Lord, to give; may
4 Let not the pass - ing of the years rob

shed up - on us from a - bove through - out our lives, in
wis - dom lead - ing on to truth, for mem - ories gath - ered
we, in all the years we live, find ev - ery day of
us of joy, nor cause us fears; and give us faith, O

ev - ery stage, from in - fan - cy to lat - er age.
through the years, and faith that grows from joys and tears.
life is new, a cel - e - bra - tion, Lord, with you.
Lord, that we may live with you e - ter - nal - ly.

Text: H. Glen Lanier (1925–1978), alt. © 1976 The Hymn Society in the United States and Canada.
All rights reserved. Used by permission of Hope Publishing Co.
Music: Melody Francois H. Barthélémon (1741–1808);
harm. The Church Hymnal for the Church Year, 1917.

LM
MORNING HYMN
Higher key 8; Alt. tune WAREHAM 40, 353

# 518 O Christ Who Holds the Open Gate

1 O Christ who holds the o-pen gate,
2 lo, all my heart's field red and torn,
3 and when the field is fresh and fair
4 the corn that makes the ho-ly bread

O Christ who drives the fur-row straight,
and thou wilt bring the young green corn,
thy bless-ed feet shall glit-ter there,
by which our hun-gering souls are fed,

O Christ, the plough, O Christ, the laugh-
the young green corn di-vine-ly spring-
and we will walk the weed-ed field,
the ho-ly bread, the food un-priced,

ter of ho-ly white birds fly-ing af-ter;
ing, the young green corn for-ev-er sing-ing;
and tell the gold-en har-vest's yield,
thy ev-er-last-ing mer-cy, Christ.

*"Corn" in North American parlance would be "wheat."*

Text: John Masefield (1878–1967).
  © *The Society of Authors as Literary Representatives of the Estate of John Masefield.*
Music: *Llyfr Tonau Cynulleidfaol*, 1859.

Irregular
LLEDROD (LLANGOLLEN)
*Lower key 41*

# The Lord's My Shepherd 519

1 The Lord's my shep - herd, I'll not want: he
2 My soul he doth re - store a - gain, and
3 Yea, though I walk through death's dark vale, yet
4 My ta - ble thou hast fur - nish - ed in
5 Good - ness and mer - cy all my life shall

makes me down to lie in pas - tures green; he
me to walk doth make with - in the paths of
will I fear no ill; for thou art with me,
pres - ence of my foes; my head thou dost with
sure - ly fol - low me, and in God's house for

lead - eth me the qui - et wa - ters by.
right - eous - ness, even for his own name's sake.
and thy rod and staff me com - fort still.
oil a - noint, and my cup ov - er - flows.
ev - er - more my dwell - ing place shall be.

Text: Ps. 23; para. Scottish Psalter, 1650.
Music: Melody Jessie Seymour Irvine (1836–1887); harm. Thomas C. L. Pritchard (1885–1960).
*Harm. © Oxford University Press.*

CM
CRIMOND

# 520 The King of Love My Shepherd Is

*Descant*

6 And so through all the length of days thy

1 The King of love my shep - herd is, whose
2 Where streams of liv - ing wa - ter flow, my
3 Per - verse and fool - ish oft I strayed, but
4 In death's dark vale I fear no ill with

good - ness fail - eth nev - er; good Shep - herd, may I

good - ness fail - eth nev - er; I noth - ing lack if
ran - somed soul he lead - eth, and where the ver - dant
yet in love he sought me, and on his shoul - der
thee, dear Lord, be - side me; thy rod and staff my

sing thy praise with - in thy house for - ev - er!

I am his and he is mine for - ev - er.
pas - tures grow, with food ce - les - tial feed - eth.
gent - ly laid, and home re - joic - ing brought me.
com - fort still, thy cross be - fore to guide me.

Text: Ps. 23; para. Henry Williams Baker (1821–1877).
Music: John Bacchus Dykes (1823–1876); desc. David Willcocks (1919– ).
*Desc. © Oxford University Press.*

87 87
DOMINUS REGIT ME
*Alt. tune* ST. COLUMBA 65

5 Thou spread'st a table in my sight;
  thy unction grace bestoweth;
  and O what transport of delight
  from thy pure chalice floweth!

6 And so through all the length of days
  thy goodness faileth never;
  good Shepherd, may I sing thy praise
  within thy house forever!

## Dear Shepherd of Your People, Hear 521

1 Dear Shepherd of your people, hear; your presence now display; as you have given a place for prayer, so give us hearts to pray.

2 Within these walls let holy peace and love and concord dwell; here give the troubled conscience ease, the wounded spirit heal.

3 May we in faith receive your word, in faith present our prayers, and in the presence of our Lord disburden all our cares.

4 The hearing ear, the seeing eye, the humbled mind bestow; and shine upon us from on high to make our graces grow.

Text: John Newton (1725–1807), alt.
Music: Melody Thomas Wright (1763–1829); harm. *The English Hymnal*, 1906.

CM
STOCKTON
*Alt. tune CAITHNESS 556*

# 522 Rock of Ages, Cleft for Me

1 Rock of a-ges, cleft for me, let me hide my-
2 Not the la-bours of my hands can ful-fil thy
3 Noth-ing in my hand I bring; sim-ply to thy
4 While I draw this fleet-ing breath, when mine eye-lids

self in thee; let the wa-ter and the blood,
law's de-mands; could my zeal no res-pite know,
cross I cling; na-ked, come to thee for dress;
close in death, when I soar through tracts un-known,

from thy riv-en side which flowed, be of sin the
could my tears for-ev-er flow, all for sin could
help-less, look to thee for grace; foul, I to the
see thee on thy judge-ment throne, Rock of a-ges,

dou-ble cure, cleanse me from its guilt and power.
not a-tone: thou must save, and thou a-lone.
foun-tain fly; wash me, Sav-iour, or I die.
cleft for me, let me hide my-self in thee.

Text: Augustus Montague Toplady (1740–1778).
Music: Richard Redhead (1820–1901).

77 77 77
Redhead No. 76 (Petra)

# We Sing to You, O God  523

*Unison*

1 We sing to you, O God, the rock who gave us
2 We wan- dered far from home out in a des- ert
3 You bear us through the world, an ea- gle to her
4 O God, e - ter- nal God, we hide with- in your

birth; let our re - joic - ing sing your name in
land; you shield - ed with your love our fear - ful
young, who ris - es on her wings and bears us
wings, the ev - er - last - ing arms to whom our

all the earth. To you, O God, let songs be
pil - grim band. You kept us safe with - in your
toward the sun. We ride the vaults of light and
prais - es ring. Your word is true, your way is

raised in joy - ful hymns, our feast of praise.
arms and shel - tered us a - gainst the storm.
air and trust in your un - fail - ing care.
just, you are the God in whom we trust.

Text: Gracia Grindal (1943– ). © 1990 Selah Publishing Co., Inc.
Music: Richard Proulx (1937– ). © 1980 G.I.A. Publications, Inc.

66 66 88
CAMANO

## 524 O Christ, the Great Foundation

1 O Christ, the great foun-da-tion on which your peo-ple stand
2 Bap-tized in one con-fes-sion, one church in all the earth,
3 Where ty-rants' hold is tight-ened, where strong de-vour the weak,
4 This is the mo-ment glo-rious when he, who once was dead,

to preach your true sal-va-tion in ev-ery age and land:
we bear our Lord's im-pres-sion, the sign of sec-ond birth.
where in-no-cents are fright-ened, the right-eous fear to speak;
shall lead his church vic-to-rious, their cham-pion and their head.

pour out your Ho-ly Spir-it to make us strong and pure,
One ho-ly peo-ple gath-ered in love be-yond our own;
there let your church a-wak-ing at-tack the powers of sin,
The Lord of all cre-a-tion his heaven-ly king-dom brings:

to keep the faith un-bro-ken as long as worlds en-dure.
by grace we were in-vit-ed, by grace we make you known.
and, all their ram-parts break-ing, with you the vic-tory win.
the fi-nal con-sum-ma-tion, the glo-ry of all things.

Text: Timothy Tingfang Lew (1891–1947), alt.
Music: Samuel Sebastian Wesley (1810–1876).

76 76D
AURELIA
*Higher key 434, 525*

# The Church's One Foundation 525

1 The church's one foun-da-tion is Je-sus Christ our Lord;
2 E-lect from ev-ery na-tion yet one o'er all the earth,
3 Though with dis-may and won-der we see the church op-pressed,
4 'Mid toil and trib-u-la-tion and tu-mult of our war,
5 Yet we on earth have u-nion with God the Three-in-One,

we are his new cre-a-tion by wa-ter and the word:
our char-ter of sal-va-tion one Lord, one faith, one birth;
by schis-ms rent a-sun-der, by her-e-sies dis-tressed:
we wait the con-sum-ma-tion of peace for ev-er-more,
and mys-tic sweet com-mu-ion with those whose rest is won.

from heaven he came and sought us to be his ho-ly bride;
one glo-rious name we hal-low, par-take one ho-ly food,
yet saints their watch are keep-ing; their cry goes up, "How long?"
till with the vi-sion glo-rious our long-ing eyes are blessed,
O hap-py ones and ho-ly! Lord, give us grace that we

with his own blood he bought us, and for our life he died.
and to one hope we fol-low, with ev-ery grace en-dued.
And soon the night of weep-ing shall be the morn of song.
and the great church vic-tor-ious shall be the church at rest.
like them, the meek and low-ly, on high may dwell with thee.

Text: Samuel John Stone (1839–1900), alt.
Music: Samuel Sebastian Wesley (1810–1876).

76 76D
AURELIA
*Lower key 524*

## 526 God Is Our Fortress and Our Rock

1 God is our for-tress and our rock, our might-y help in
2 Our hope is fixed on Christ a-lone, the Man of God's own
3 The Word of God will not be slow while de-mon hordes sur-

dan-ger; he shields us from the bat-tle's shock and
choos-ing; with-out him noth-ing can be won and
round us, though e-vil strike its cruel-lest blow and

thwarts the dev-il's an - ger: for still the prince of
fight-ing must be los-ing: so let the powers ac-
death and hell con-found us: for e-ven if dis-

night pro-longs his e-vil fight; he us-es ev-ery skill
cursed come on and do their worst; the Son of God shall ride
tress should take all we pos-sess, and those who mean us ill

to work his wick-ed will— no earth-ly force is like him.
to bat-tle at our side, and he shall have the vic-tory
should rav-age, wreck, or kill, God's king-dom is im-mor-tal!

Text: Martin Luther (1483–1546); rev. Michael Perry (1942–1996). © *1982 Hope Publishing Co.*
Music: Melody Martin Luther (1483–1546), alt.; harm. *Book of Common Praise*, 1938.

87 87 66 66 7
EIN' FESTE BURG
*Alt. setting and higher key 318*

# How Firm a Foundation 527

1 How firm a foundation, ye saints of the Lord,
2 "Fear not, I am with thee; O be not dismayed!
3 When through the deep waters I call thee to go,
4 When through fiery trials thy pathway shall lie,
5 The soul that on Jesus hath leaned for repose

is laid for your faith in his excellent word!
For I am thy God and will still give thee aid;
the rivers of woe shall not thee overflow;
my grace, all-sufficient, shall be thy supply:
I will not—I will not desert to its foes;

What more can he say than to you he hath said,
I'll strengthen thee, help thee, and cause thee to stand,
for I will be with thee, thy troubles to bless,
the flame shall not hurt thee; I only design
that soul, though all hell should endeavour to shake,

to you who to Jesus for refuge have fled?
upheld by my righteous, omnipotent hand.
and sanctify to thee thy deepest distress.
thy dross to consume, and thy gold to refine.
I'll never—no, never—no, never forsake!"

Text: John Rippon (1751–1836), called "K" in *A Selection of Hymns*, 1787.
Music: Melody *Genuine Church Music*, 1832; harm. *Tabor*, 1867.

11 11 11 11
FOUNDATION
Alt. tune ST. DENIO 393

# 528 O God, Our Help in Ages Past

*Descant*

6 O God, our help in a - ges past, our hope for years to come,

1 O God, our help in a - ges past, our hope for years to come,
2 un - der the shad - ow of thy throne thy saints have dwelt se - cure;
3 Be - fore the hills in or - der stood, or earth re - ceived its frame,
4 A thou-sand a - ges in thy sight are like an eve - ning gone,

be thou our guard while trou - bles last, and our e - ter - nal home.

our shel - ter from the storm - y blast, and our e - ter - nal home:
suf - fi - cient is thine arm a - lone, and our de - fence is sure.
from ev - er - last - ing thou art God, to end - less years the same.
short as the watch that ends the night be - fore the ris - ing sun.

5 Time like an ever-rolling stream
bears all our years away;
they fly forgotten, as a dream
dies at the opening day.

6 O God, our help in ages past,
our hope for years to come,
be thou our guard while troubles last,
and our eternal home.

Text: Ps. 90; para. Isaac Watts (1674–1748), alt.
Music: William Croft (1678–1727); desc. Alan Gray (1855–1935). *Desc. © Cambridge University Press.*

CM
ST. ANNE

*Plains Cree text*

1 ᑭᓴᒪᓂᑐ ᑳ ᑭ ᐯ
ᑲᓇᐍᔨᒥᔮᕽ
ᒥᓇ ᓂ ᓂᑳᓂᒥᓈᕽ
ᓂᐟ ᐊᐢᐯᔨᒧᓈᐣ

2 ᑳ ᐊᐢᐯᔨᒧᑐᑖᐢᑭᐟ
ᑕᑲᐦᑫᔨᒧᐘᐠ
ᓇᒪ ᑫᑿ ᐊᐢᑖᓯᐎᐣ
ᐁ ᓈᑕᒪᐘᒋᐠ

3 ᒷᔭᐢ ᐘᒋᔭ ᐊᔮᑭ
ᐊᐦᐳ ᒷᔭᐢ ᐊᐢᑭ
ᑳᑭᑫ ᑭ ᒪᓂᑐᐎᐣ
ᒥᓇ ᐅᑌ ᓂᑳᐣ

4 ᑭᐦᒋᒥᑖᐦᑐᒥᑕᓇᐤ
ᐊᐢᑭᔭ ᐃᔨᑯᕽ
ᑖᐱᐢᑯᐨ ᐯᔭᐠ ᑭᓯᑳᐤ
ᐁᑖᐱᓯᓂᔭᐣ

5 ᑖᐱᐢᑯᐨ ᐱᒥᒋᐘᓄᕽ
ᐁ ᐍᐹᐳᑯᔮᕽ
ᑭᔨᐸ ᑖᓂᐍᑐᑫ
ᓂ ᐍᔪᐎᓂᓈᐣ

6 ᑭᓴᒪᓂᑐ ᑳ ᑭ ᐯ
ᑲᓇᐍᔨᒥᔮᕽ
ᓂ ᓂᑳᓂᒥᓈᕽ ᒥᓇ
ᑭᐢᑭᓄᑕᐦᐃᓈᐣ

1 Kisāmunito ka ke pā
Kunuwāyimiyak"
Menu nu nekaneminak
Net uspāyimonan.

2 Ka uspāyimototaskik"
Tukukāyimoowuk
Numu kākwi ustasiwin
Ā natumuwuchik.

3 Mwuyās wucheyu uyake
Upo mwuyās uske
Kakikā ke Munitoowin
Menu otā nekan.

4 Kichimitatomitunow
Uskeyu eyikok
Tapiskoch pāyuk kesikaw
Ātapisineyun.

5 Tapiskoch pimichiwunok
A wāpapokoyak
Keyipu tani wātokā
Ne weyoowininan.

6 Kisāmunito ka ke pā
Kunuwāyimiyak
Ne nekaneminak menu
Kiskinotuhinan.

Tr. John Alexander Mackay (1838–1923).

# 529 God, My Hope on You Is Founded

*Unison*

1 God, my hope on you is found - ed; you my faith and
2 Hu - man pride and earth - ly glo - ry, sword and crown, be -
3 Dai - ly does the al - might - y Giv - er boun - teous gifts on
4 God's great good - ness lasts for - ev - er, deep - est wis - dom,
5 Still from earth to God e - ter - nal sac - ri - fice of

trust re - new: through all change and chance you
tray our trust; though with care and toil we
us be - stow; God's de - sire for us de -
pass - ing thought: splen - dour, light, and life at -
praise be done, high a - bove all prais - es

guide me, on - ly good and on - ly true. God un -
build them, tower and tem - ple fall to dust. But your
lights us, plea - sure leads us where we go. Here at
tend - ing, beau - ty spring - ing out of naught. Ev - er -
prais - ing for the gift of Christ the Son. Christ, you

Text: Joachim Neander (1650–1680); tr. Robert Seymour Bridges (1844–1930), alt.
*Tr. © Oxford University Press. Alt. with permission.*
Music: Herbert Howells (1892–1983). *© Novello & Co., Ltd. Reprinted by permission of Shawnee Press, Inc. (ASCAP).*

87 87 337
MICHAEL

known, you a - lone  call my heart to be  your own.
power, hour by hour,  is my tem - ple and  my tower.
hand, love takes stand,  joy a - waits God's sure  com - mand.
more from God's store  new - born worlds rise and  a - dore.
call one and all;  those who fol - low shall  not fall.

## De noche iremos 530

De no - che i - rem - os, de no - che, que
*By night we has - ten, in dark - ness, to*

pa - ra en - con - trar la fuen - te, só - lo la sed nos a -
*seek for the liv - ing wa - ter; on - ly our thirst lights us*

lum - bra, só - lo la sed nos a - lum - bra. De
*on - wards, on - ly our thirst lights us on - wards. By*

Text: Luis Rosales (1910–1992).
Music: Jacques Berthier (1923–1994).
Text and music © 1991 Les Presses de Taizé. Used by permission of G.I.A. Publications, Inc., exclusive agent.

DE NOCHE IREMOS

# 531 You Who Dwell in the Shelter of the Lord

1 You who dwell in the shel-ter of the Lord, who a-bide in his shad-ow for life, say to the Lord: "My
2 Snares of the fowl-er will nev-er cap-ture you, and fam-ine will bring you no fear: un-der his wings your
3 You need not fear the ter-ror of the night, nor the ar-row that flies by day; though thou-sands fall a-
4 For to his an-gels he's giv-en a com-mand to guard you in all of your ways; up-on their hands they will

Irregular with refrain
ON EAGLES' WINGS

# 532 What a Friend We Have in Jesus

1 What a friend we have in Je - sus, all our sins and
2 Have we tri - als or temp - ta - tions? Is there trou - ble
3 Are we weak and hea - vy - la - den, cum - bered with a

griefs to bear! What a priv - i - lege to car - ry
an - y - where? We should nev - er be dis - cour - aged;
load of care? Christ the Sav - iour is our ref - uge;

ev - ery - thing to God in prayer! O what peace we of - ten
take it to the Lord in prayer. Can we find a friend so
take it to the Lord in prayer. Do our friends de - spise, for -

for - feit, O what need - less pain we bear, all be -
faith - ful who will all our sor - rows share? Je - sus
sake us? Are we tempt - ed to de - spair? Je - sus'

Text: Joseph Medlicott Scriven (1819–1886), alt.
Music: Charles Crozat Converse (1832–1918).

87 87D
FRIENDSHIP

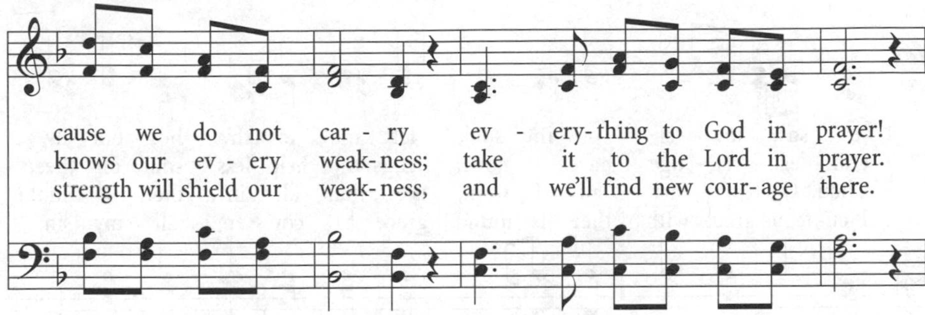
cause we do not car - ry ev - ery- thing to God in prayer!
knows our ev - ery weak- ness; take it to the Lord in prayer.
strength will shield our weak- ness, and we'll find new cour- age there.

*Eastern Cree text*

1 ᔅᑲ ᒋ ᐧᐃᒋᐃᑯᓇᐧᐊ!
ᒋᓴᔅ ᒋᑐᑖᒥᓇᐤ;
ᔅᑲ ᒥᐧᔮᔦ ᒧᐃᐧᐊᐧᐊ!
ᒥᔑᐤ ᐋᔭᒥᐋᔅᑕᑦ,
ᐧᐋ ᒥᓛᐧᑕᐤ ᐧᐊᓇᑖᔭᒃ
ᒋᔮᒫᔦᑕᒪᐧᐃᓐ
ᐋ ᐋᑳ ᐱᔑᒋᑐᐧᐊᒃ
ᒧᔥ ᐋᔭᒥᐋᒃ, ᑳ ᔦᑦ.

2 ᒋᓴᔅ, ᑳ ᐱᒫᒋᐃᑕᒃ,
ᒋ ᒋᔅᓛᔦᒥᑯᓇᐤ
ᐋ ᐧᐃ ᐧᐃᒋᐃᑯᔨᔭᒃ,
ᐧᐃᔭ ᒫᑲ ᑭᔅᒋᑕᐤ.
ᐋᑲᐧᐃᔭ ᐳᓂᐋᑕᐤ
ᒥᔖᒫᔦᑕᒪᐧᑲ
ᑲᔭ ᐋᑳ ᒋ ᑎᔭᐧᑲ
ᐋᔦᒫᔦᑖᐧᑲᓛ.

3 ᐣᑐᒫᔑᒧᔥᑐᐧᐋᑲᓐ
ᐧᐋᐧᓈᔦᑖᐧᑲᓛ,
ᒋᑐᑕᒪᒡ ᓂᐱᐧᑖᐧᐊ
ᒋᑎᒫᑎᔨᔭᓇ.
ᒧᔥ ᐋᔭᒥᐋᔅᑐ ᑲᔭ
ᐧᐃᐸᒡ ᒪᒋᐧᑖᐧᐃᓇ
ᐧᐃ ᔖᑯᒋᐃᑯᔭᓇ
ᐋᑯ ᓛ ᓵᐱᐧᐃᐃᐃᔅᑲ.

Tr. William Gladstone Walton (1867–1948) and Daisy Alice Spence Walton (1873–1948), *Common Prayer and Hymns in the Cree-Indian Language*, 1923.

# 533 Jesus, Lover of My Soul

1 Je - sus, lov - er of my soul, let me to thy bos - om fly,
2 Oth - er ref - uge have I none; hangs my help - less soul on thee.
3 Thou, O Christ, art all I want; more than all in thee I find!
4 Plen - teous grace with thee is found, grace to cov - er all my sin;

while the near - er wa - ters roll, while the tem - pest still is high.
Leave, ah! leave me not a - lone; still sup - port and com - fort me.
Raise the fal - len, cheer the faint, heal the sick, and lead the blind.
let the heal - ing streams a - bound; make and keep me pure with - in.

Hide me, O my Sav - iour, hide, till the storm of life is past;
All my trust on thee is stayed, all my help from thee I bring;
Just and ho - ly is thy name; I am all un - righ - teous - ness:
Thou of life the foun - tain art; free - ly let me take of thee;

safe in - to the ha - ven guide; O re - ceive my soul at last.
cov - er my de - fence - less head with the shad - ow of thy wing.
false and full of sin I am; thou art full of truth and grace.
spring thou up with - in my heart; rise to all e - ter - ni - ty.

Text: Charles Wesley (1707–1788).
Music: Joseph Parry (1841–1903).

77 77D
ABERYSTWYTH
*Higher key 250*

# Here, O Lord, Your Servants Gather 534

*Unison*

1 Here, O Lord, your ser-vants gath-er, hand we link with hand.
2 Man-y are the tongues we speak, scat-tered are the lands,
3 Na-ture's se-crets o-pen wide, chang-es nev-er cease.
4 Grant, O God, an age re-newed, filled with death-less love.

Look-ing toward our Sav-iour's cross, joined in love we stand.
yet our hearts are one in God, one in love's de-mands.
Where, oh where, can wear-y souls find the source of peace?
Help us as we work and pray, send us from a-bove

As we seek the realm of God, we u-nite to pray:
Even in dark-ness hope ap-pears, call-ing age and youth.
Un-to all those sore dis-tressed, torn by end-less strife,
truth and cour-age, faith and power, need-ed in our strife.

Je-sus, Sav-iour, guide our steps, for you are the way.
Je-sus, Teach-er, dwell with us, for you are the truth.
Je-sus, Heal-er, bring your balm, for you are the life.
Je-sus, Mas-ter, be our way, be our truth, our life!

Text: Tokuo Yamaguchi (1900–1995); tr. Everett M. Stowe (1897– ). © 1958 The United Methodist
Publishing House. (Administered by The Copyright Company, Nashville, TN). All rights reserved.
International copyright secured. Used by permission.
Music: Isao Koizumi (1907– ). © 1958 JASRAC; used by permission of JASRAC License No. 9800785.

75 75D
TOKYO

# 535 As Jacob with Travel Was Weary

_Unison_

1 As Ja - cob with trav - el was wea - ry one day, at
2 The lad - der is long, it is strong and well-made, has stood
3 Come, let us as - cend! All may climb it who will, for the
4 And when we ar - rive at the ha - ven of rest, we shall

night on a stone for a pil - low he lay; he
hun - dreds of years and is not yet de-cayed; man - y
an - gels of Ja - cob are guard - ing it still; and re -
hear the glad words, "Come to me, all the blest, here are

saw in a vi - sion a lad - der so high
mil - lions have climbed it and reached Zi - on's hill,
mem - ber, each step that by faith we pass o'er,
re - gions of light, here are man - sions of bliss."

that its foot was on earth and its top in the sky:
man - y mil - lions by faith now are climb - ing it still:
man - y proph - ets and mar - tyrs have trod it be - fore:
Who would not want to climb such a lad - der as this?

Text: English trad. (18th cent.).
Music: Melody English trad.; arr. Gerald H. Knight (1908–1979).
_Arr. © 1971 Walton Music Corporation._

Irregular with refrain
JACOB'S LADDER

Refrain

Al - le - lu - ia to Je - sus, who died on the tree and has
raised up a lad - der of mer - cy for me, and has
raised up a lad - der of mer - cy for me.

# 536 Singing Songs of Expectation

1 Sing-ing songs of ex-pec-ta-tion, on-ward goes the pil-grim band,
2 One the light of God's own pres-ence, o'er his ran-somed peo-ple shed,
3 One the strain the lips of thou-sands lift as from the heart of one;

through the night of doubt and sor-row, march-ing to the prom-ised land.
chas-ing far the gloom and ter-ror, bright-ening all the path we tread:
one the con-flict, one the per-il, one the march in God be-gun:

Clear be-fore us through the dark-ness gleams and burns the guid-ing light:
one the ob-ject of our jour-ney, one the faith which nev-er tires,
one the glad-ness of re-joic-ing on the far e-ter-nal shore,

trust-ing God, we march to-geth-er step-ping fear-less through the night.
one the ear-nest look-ing for-ward, one the hope our God in-spires.
where the one al-might-y Fa-ther reigns in love for ev-er-more.

Text: Bernard Severin Ingemann (1789–1862); tr. Sabine Baring-Gould (1834–1924), alt.
Music: Melody *The Columbian Harmony*, Cincinnati, 1825; acc. Marty Haugen (1950– ).
*Acc. © 1987 G.I.A. Publications, Inc.*

87 87D
HOLY MANNA

# In the Cross of Christ I Glory  537

1 In the cross of Christ I glory, tower-ing
2 When the woes of life o'er-take me, hopes de-
3 When the sun of bliss is beam-ing light and
4 Bane and bless-ing, pain and plea-sure, by the
5 In the cross of Christ I glory, tower-ing

o'er the wrecks of time; all the light of
ceive, and fears an-noy, nev-er shall the
love up-on my way, from the cross the
cross are sanc-ti-fied; peace is there that
o'er the wrecks of time; all the light of

sa-cred sto-ry gath-ers round its head sub-lime.
cross for-sake me: lo, it glows with peace and joy.
ra-diance stream-ing adds more lus-tre to the day.
knows no mea-sure, joys that through all time a-bide.
sa-cred sto-ry gath-ers round its head sub-lime.

Text: John Bowring (1792–1872).
Music: John Stainer (1840–1901).

87 87
CROSS OF JESUS

# 538 Nearer, My God, to Thee

1 Near - er, my God, to thee, near - er to thee!
2 Though, like the wan - der - er, the sun gone down,
3 There let the way ap - pear, steps un - to heaven;

Even though it be a cross that rais - eth me,
dark - ness be o - ver me, my rest a stone,
all that thou send - est me, in mer - cy given;

still all my song would be: "Near - er, my God, to thee,
yet in my dreams I'd be near - er, my God, to thee,
an - gels to beck - on me near - er, my God, to thee,

near - er, my God, to thee, near - er to thee!"
near - er, my God, to thee, near - er to thee.
near - er, my God, to thee, near - er to thee.

4 Then with my waking thoughts
bright with thy praise,
out of my stony griefs
Bethel I'll raise,
so by my woes to be
nearer, my God, to thee,
nearer, my God, to thee,
nearer to thee.

5 Or if on joyful wing
cleaving the sky,
sun, moon, and stars forgot,
upwards I fly,
still all my song shall be
"Nearer, my God, to thee,
nearer, my God to thee,
nearer to thee!"

Text: Sarah Flower Adams (1805–1848).
Music: Lowell Mason (1792–1872).

64 64 66 64
EXCELSIOR

# Come, O Thou Traveller Unknown 539

1 Come, O thou Trav-el-ler un-known, whom still I
2 I need not tell thee who I am; my mis-er-
3 Yield to me now, for I am weak, but con-fi-
4 'Tis Love! 'Tis Love! Thou diedst for me, I hear thy

hold, but can-not see! My com-pa-ny be-fore is
y and sin de-clare. Thy-self hast called me by my
dent in self - de-spair! Speak to my heart, in bless-ing
whis-per in my heart. The morn-ing breaks, the shad-ows

gone, and I am left a-lone with thee. With thee all
name; look on thy hands and read it there. But who, I
speak; be con-quered by my in - stant prayer. Speak, or thou
flee, pure, un - i - ver - sal Love thou art. To me, to

night I mean to stay and wres-tle till the break of day.
ask thee, who art thou? Tell me thy name, and tell me now.
nev - er hence shalt move, and tell me if thy name is Love.
all, thy mer - cies move; thy na - ture and thy name is Love.

Text: Charles Wesley (1707–1788).
Music: Henry Carey (1687?–1743), alt.

88 88 88
SURREY

# 540 Just As the Deer

1 Just as the deer longs for the wa-ter brooks, so longs my
2 Deep calls to deep in cat-ar-acts of thun-der; your floods and
3 All through the day my God will com-fort me, and in the

soul for you, O Lord my God. All that I am thirsts
rap-ids crash a-cross my life. My tears have been my
night my voice will raise God's song, and I will go to

for the liv-ing spring of your kind pres-ence well-ing
food both day and night; my God, why now have you for-
wor-ship in God's house. God of my life, to you I

deep with-in. Why now so full of heav-i-ness my
got-ten me? Why now so full of heav-i-ness my
raise my prayer, and when I come in-to your pres-ence,

Text: Ps. 42; para. Brian Ruttan (1947– ) ©.
Music: Jean Sibelius (1865–1957); arr. *The Hymnal*, 1933. *Music © Breitkopf & Härtel, Wiesbaden;*
*arr. © 1933, 1961 Presbyterian Board of Christian Education. Used by permission of Westminster/John Knox Press.*

10 10 10 10 10 10
FINLANDIA

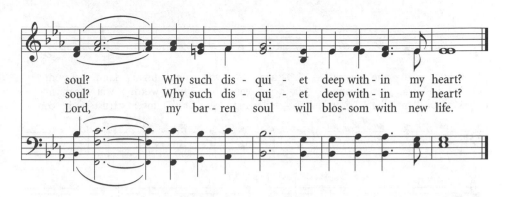

soul? Why such dis - qui - et deep with - in my heart?
soul? Why such dis - qui - et deep with - in my heart?
Lord, my bar - ren soul will blos - som with new life.

## As Longs the Hart for Flowing Streams 541

1 As longs the hart for flow-ing streams, so longs my
2 My tears have fed me day and night, while oth-ers
3 Why do I mourn and toil with-in, when it is

soul for you, O God; my soul does thirst for the liv - ing
said, "Where is your God?" But I re - call, as my soul pours
mine to hope in God? I shall a - gain sing praise to

God: when shall I come to see your face?
dry, the days of praise with - in your house.
God, who is my help, who is my God.

Text: Ps. 42; para. Danna Harkin.
*Para. © 1975 Word Music (a div. of WORD MUSIC). All rights reserved. Used by permission.*
Music: Melody English trad.; arr. Noel Tredinnick (1949– ). *Arr. © 1982 Hope Publishing Co.*

LM
O WALY, WALY

# 542 Out of the Depths

1 Out of the depths I turn to you on high; Lord, hear my
2 I wait for you, I trust your ho-ly word; you hear my
3 Hope in the Lord: un-fail-ing is God's love; trust and con-

call. Bend down your ear and lis-ten to my cry, for-
sighs. My soul still waits and looks un-to you, Lord; my
fide. Mer-cy and full re-demp-tion from a-bove does

giv-ing all. If you should mark our sins, who then could
prayers a-rise. I look for you to drive a-way my
grace pro-vide. From sin and e-vil, might-y though they

stand? But grace and mer-cy dwell at your right hand.
night— yes, more than those who watch for morn-ing light.
seem, God's sav-ing arm will all the saints re-deem.

Text: Ps. 130; para. *The Psalter*, 1912, alt.
Music: Melody Charles H. Purday (1799–1885); harm. F. R.C. Clarke (1931– ) ©.

10 4 10 4 10 10
SANDON
*Alt. setting 543*

# Unto the Hills around Do I Lift Up  543

1 Un - to the hills a - round do I lift up my long - ing
2 He will not suf - fer that thy foot be moved: safe shalt thou
3 Je - ho - vah is him - self thy keep - er true, thy change - less
4 From ev - ery e - vil shall he keep thy soul, from ev - ery

eyes: O whence for me shall my sal - va - tion come, from
be. No care - less slum - ber shall his eye - lids close who
shade; Je - ho - vah thy de - fence on thy right hand him -
sin: Je - ho - vah shall pre - serve thy go - ing out, thy

whence a - rise? From God the Lord doth come my cer - tain
keep - eth thee. Be - hold, our God, the Lord, he slum - bereth
self hath made. And thee no sun by day shall ev - er
com - ing in. A - bove thee watch - ing, he whom we a -

aid, from God the Lord, who heaven and earth hath made.
ne'er, who keep - eth Is - rael in his ho - ly care.
smite; no moon shall harm thee in the si - lent night.
dore shall keep thee hence - forth, yea, for ev - er - more.

Text: Ps.121; para. John Campbell, The Marquis of Lorne (1845–1914).
Music: Charles H. Purday (1799–1885).

10 4 10 4 10 10
SANDON
*Alt. setting 542*

# 544 Can I See Another's Woe

*Unison*

1 Can I see an - oth - er's woe, and not
2 Can I see a fall - ing tear, and not
3 Think not thou canst sigh a sigh, and thy
4 O! God give to us his joy that our

be in sor - row too? Can I see an - oth - er's
feel my sor - row's share? Can a par - ent see a
Mak - er is not by; think not thou canst weep a
grief he may de - stroy: till our pain and sor - row

grief, and not seek for kind re - lief?
child weep, nor be with sor - row filled?
tear, and thy Mak - er is not near.
leave, God doth sit by us and grieve.

Text: William Blake (1757–1827).
Music: Roland Packer (1955– ) ©.

77 77
BLAKE

# We Will Lay Our Burden Down  545

2 We will light the flame of love...
as the hands of the risen Lord.

3 We will show both hurt and hope...
like the hands of the risen Lord.

4 We will walk the path of peace...
hand in hand with the risen Lord.

Text and music: John L. Bell (1949– ).
*© 1989 WGRG The Iona Community (Scotland).*
*Used by permission of G.I.A. Publications, Inc., exclusive agent.*

777 8
LAYING DOWN

## 546 God Moves in a Mysterious Way

1 God moves in a mys-te-rious way his
2 Deep in un-fath-om-a-ble mines of
3 Ye fear-ful saints, fresh cour-age take; the
4 Judge not the Lord by fee-ble sense, but

won-ders to per-form; he plants his foot-steps
nev-er-fail-ing skill he trea-sures up his
clouds ye so much dread are big with mer-cy,
trust him for his grace; be-hind a frown-ing

in the sea and rides up-on the storm.
bright de-signs and works his sov-ereign will.
and shall break in bless-ings on your head.
prov-i-dence he hides a smil-ing face.

5 His purposes will ripen fast,
   unfolding every hour;
   the bud may have a bitter taste,
   but sweet will be the flower.

6 Blind unbelief is sure to err
   and scan his work in vain;
   God is his own interpreter
   and he will make it plain.

Text: William Cowper (1731–1800).
Music: Melody Scottish Psalter, 1635, alt.; harm. John Playford (1623–1686).

CM
London New

1 I sought the Lord, and af-ter-ward I knew he moved my
2 Thou didst reach forth thy hand and mine en-fold; I walked and
3 I find, I walk, I love; but, oh, the whole of love is

soul to seek him, seek-ing me. It was not I that
sank not on the storm-vexed sea. 'Twas not so much that
but my an-swer, Lord, to thee! For thou wert long be-

found, O Sav-iour true; no, I was found of thee.
I on thee took hold as thou, dear Lord, on me.
fore-hand with my soul; al-ways thou lov-edst me.

Text: *Holy Songs, Carols, and Sacred Ballads*, Boston, 1880, alt.
Music: J. Harold Moyer (1927– ). © *1969 Faith and Life Press/Mennonite Publishing House.*

10 10 10 6
Faith

# 548 Eye Has Not Seen, Ear Has Not Heard

*Refrain*

Eye has not seen, ear has not heard what you have rea-dy for those who love you. Spir-it of love, come, give us the mind of

Text: 1 Cor. 2. 9–10; para. Marty Haugen (1959– ), alt.
Music: Marty Haugen (1950– ).
*Para. and music © 1982 G.I.A. Publications, Inc.*

Irregular with refrain
EYE HAS NOT SEEN

*Last time*

Je - sus;        teach us your wis- dom, O  Lord.

*Last time*

G                 D/F♯  G    D/A    A⁷   G/D       D

1 When  pain and sor - row   weigh us down,   be  near  to us,    O
2 Our    lives are but  a     sin - gle breath;  we  flow - er and   we
3 To     those who see with  eyes of faith,   you, Lord, are ev - er

C                   G/B           Gm/B♭

Lord;    for - give the weak - ness  of our faith  and bear us up  with-
fade.    Yet all our days are   in your hands,  so  we re - turn  in
near,    re - flect- ed in the   fac - es  of  all  the poor  and

D/A      Bm⁷               D/F♯         C

*To refrain*

in your peace - ful    word.
love what love  has    made.
low - ly  of   the    world.

*To refrain*

4 We  sing a mys - tery  from the past   in  halls where saints have

trod,    yet  ev - er new  the   mu - sic rings  to   Je - sus, Liv - ing

Song of God.

## La ténèbre n'est point ténèbre 549

La té - nè - bre n'est point té - nè - bre de - vant toi: la
Our dark - ness is nev - er dark - ness in your sight: the

nuit com - me le jour est lu - miè - re. La té -
deep - est night is clear as the day - light. Our

Text: Ps. 139.11; Fr. and Eng. paras. Taizé Community (France).
Music: Jacques Berthier (1923–1994).
*Paras. and music © 1991 Les Presses de Taizé. Used by permission of G.I.A. Publications, Inc.., exclusive agent.*

LA TÉNÈBRE

# 550 Light's Abode, Celestial Salem

1 Light's a-bode, ce-les-tial Sa-lem, vi-sion whence true peace doth spring,
2 There for-ev-er and for-ev-er al-le-lu-ia is out-poured;
3 There no cloud nor pass-ing va-pour dims the bright-ness of the air;
4 O how glo-rious and re-splend-ent, fra-gile bo-dy, shalt thou be,

bright-er than the heart can fan-cy, man-sion of the high-est King;
for un-end-ing, for un-bro-ken is the feast-day of the Lord;
end-less noon-day, glo-rious noon-day, from the Sun of suns is there;
when en-dued with so much beau-ty, full of health and strong and free,

O how glo-rious are the prais-es which of thee the proph-ets' sing!
all is pure and all is ho-ly that with-in thy walls is stored.
there no night brings rest from la-bour, for un-known are toil and care.
full of vig-our, full of plea-sure that shall last e-ter-nal-ly!

5 Now with gladness, now with courage,
bear the burden on thee laid,
that hereafter these thy labours
may with endless gifts be paid;
and in everlasting glory
thou with brightness be arrayed.

6 Laud and honour to the Father,
laud and honour to the Son,
laud and honour to the Spirit,
ever Three, and ever One,
one in love and one in glory,
while unending ages run.

Text: Attrib. Thomas à Kempis (1379?–1471); tr. John Mason Neale (1818–1866), alt.
Music: *An Essay on the Church Plain Chant*, 1782.

87 87 87
ALLELUIA, DULCE CARMEN
*Alt. tune* REGENT SQUARE 143

# My Faith Looks Up to Thee  551

1 My faith looks up to thee, thou Lamb of Cal - va - ry,
2 May thy rich grace im - part strength to my faint - ing heart,
3 While life's dark maze I tread, and griefs a - round me spread,
4 When ends life's tran - sient dream, when death's cold sul - len stream

Sav - iour di - vine. Now hear me while I pray; take all my
my zeal in - spire. As thou hast died for me, O may my
be thou my guide; bid dark - ness turn to day, wipe sor - row's
shall o'er me roll, blest Sav - iour, then, in love, fear and dis -

guilt a - way. O let me from this day be whol - ly thine.
love to thee pure, warm, and change - less be, a liv - ing fire.
tears a - way, nor let me ev - er stray from thee a - side.
trust re - move; O bear me safe a - bove, a ran - somed soul.

Text: Ray Palmer (1808–1887).
Music: Lowell Mason (1792–1872).

664 6664
OLIVET

## 552 My Heart Looks in Faith

*Unison*

1 My heart looks in faith to the Lamb di-vine;
2 My heart looks in hope to the Son of God;
3 My heart looks in love to Je-sus my friend;
4 Faith and hope and love, all to Christ I give;

his pre-cious blood flows down for these sins of mine.
he saves me, he leads me on the road he trod.
he does my soul strength-en and my life de-fend.
his ser-vant I will be so long as I live.

Text: Tzu-chen Chao (1888–1979); tr. Frank W. Price (1895–1974), alt.
Music: Melody Chinese trad.; arr. Bliss Wiant (1895–1975).
*Text, tr. and arr. © 1977 Chinese Christian Literature Council, Hong Kong.*

55 65
SONG OF THE YANGTZE BOATMAN

## 553 Ubi Caritas et Amor

F    C    Dm    B♭    D    G    C

U - bi ca - ri - tas et a - mor,
*Live in char - i - ty and stead - fast love,*

F    C    Dm    Gm    C    F

u - bi ca - ri - tas, De - us i - bi est.
*live in char - i - ty; God will dwell with you.*

Text: 1 John 4.16b; Eng. para. Taizé Community (France).
Music: Jacques Berthier (1923–1994).

UBI CARITAS

*Eng. para. and music © 1991 Les Presses de Taizé. Used by permission of G.I.A. Publications, Inc., exclusive agent.*

# Come, People of the Living God  554

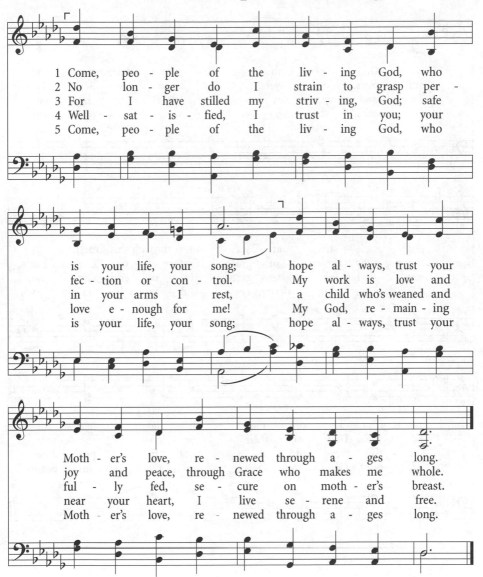

1 Come, peo - ple of the liv - ing God, who
2 No lon - ger do I strain to grasp per -
3 For I have stilled my striv - ing, God; safe
4 Well - sat - is - fied, I trust in you; your
5 Come, peo - ple of the liv - ing God, who

is your life, your song; hope al - ways, trust your
fec - tion or con - trol. My work is love and
in your arms I rest, a child who's weaned and
love e - nough for me! My God, re - main - ing
is your life, your song; hope al - ways, trust your

Moth - er's love, re - newed through a - ges long.
joy and peace, through Grace who makes me whole.
ful - ly fed, se - cure on moth - er's breast.
near your heart, I live se - rene and free.
Moth - er's love, re - newed through a - ges long.

Text: Ps. 131; para. Ruth Duck (1947– ). *Para.* © 1992 G.I.A. Publications, Inc.
Music: Jane Manton Marshall (1924– ) ©. *Used by permission.*

CM
WALDEN

## 555 O God of Bethel, by Whose Hand

1 O God of Beth - el, by whose hand thy
2 our vows, our prayers, we now pre - sent be -
3 Through each per - plex - ing path of life our
4 O spread thy cov - ering wings a - round till

peo - ple still are fed, who through this earth - ly
fore thy throne of grace. God of our fore - bears,
wan - dering foot - steps guide; give us each day our
all our wan - derings cease and in the ci - ty

pil - grim - age thy mul - ti - tudes hast led:
be the God of their suc - ceed - ing race.
dai - ly bread and rai - ment fit pro - vide.
of our God our souls ar - rive in peace.

Text: Philip Doddridge (1702–1751) and John Logan (1748–1788), alt.
Music: Johann Michael Haydn (1737–1806), alt.

CM
SALZBURG

# O for a Closer Walk with God  556

1 O for a clos - er walk with God, a
2 What peace - ful hours I once en - joyed! How
3 Re - turn, O ho - ly Dove, re - turn, sweet
4 The dear - est i - dol I have known, what -
5 So shall my walk be close with God, calm

calm and heaven - ly frame, a light to shine up -
sweet their mem - ory still! But they have left an
mes - sen - ger of rest: I hate the sins that
e'er that i - dol be, help me to tear it
and se - rene my frame; so pur - er light shall

on the road that leads me to the Lamb.
ach - ing void the world can nev - er fill.
made thee mourn and drove thee from my breast.
from thy throne and wor - ship on - ly thee.
mark the road that leads me to the Lamb.

Text: William Cowper (1731–1800).
Music: Melody Scottish Psalter, 1635; harm. *The English Hymnal*, 1906.

CM
CAITHNESS

# 557 Eternal Spirit of the Living Christ

1 Eternal Spirit of the living Christ,
I know not how to ask or what to say;
I only know my need, as deep as life,
and only you can teach me how to pray.

2 Come, pray in me the prayer I need this day;
help me to see your purpose and your will—
where I have failed, what I have done amiss;
held in forgiving love, let me be still.

3 Come with the strength I lack, the vision clear
of neighbour's need, of all humanity;
fulfilment of my life in love outpoured;
my life in you, O Christ; your love in me.

Text: Frank von Christierson (1900–1996). © 1974 The Hymn Society in the United States and Canada. All rights reserved. Used by permission of Hope Publishing Co.
Music: Alfred Morton Smith (1879–1971). © Estate of Doris Wright Smith.

10 10 10 10
SURSUM CORDA

# God, When I Stand, No Path Before Me  558

1 God, when I stand, no path before me clear,
2 When all my prayers no an-swer seem to bring,
3 When the dark lord of lone-li-ness pre-vails,
4 When, as did Thom-as, I pre-sume thee dead,

when ev-ery prayer seems pris-oner of my pain,
and there is si-lence in my deep-est soul;
and, all de-feat-ed, joy and friend-ship die,
feel-ing and faith it-self with-in me cold,

come with a gen-tle-ness which calms my fear;
when in the wil-der-ness I find no spring,
come, be my joy; such love that nev-er fails,
fresh-en my lips with wine, my soul with bread;

Lord of my help-less-ness, my vic-tory gain.
Lord of the des-ert plac-es, keep me whole.
pierce the self-pi-ty of my sha-dowed sky.
ban-ish my pov-er-ty with heav-en's gold.

Text: Herbert O'Driscoll (1928– ) ©.
Music: Frederick Cook Atkinson (1841–1897).

10 10 10 10
MORECAMBE
Alt. tune SURSUM CORDA 201, 557

## 559 Blessed Jesus, At Your Word

1 Bless-ed Je-sus, at your word we are gath-ered all to hear you. Let our hearts and souls be stirred now to seek and love and fear you. By your gos-pel pure and ho-ly, teach us, Lord, to love you sole-ly.

2 All our knowl-edge, sense, and sight lie in deep-est dark-ness shroud-ed till your Spir-it breaks our night with your beams of truth un-cloud-ed. You a-lone to God can win us, you must work all good with-in us.

3 Glo-rious Lord, your-self im-part! Light of light, from God pro-ceed-ing, o-pen lips and ears and heart, help us by your Spir-it's lead-ing. Hear the cry your church now rais-es; Lord, ac-cept our prayers and prais-es!

Text: Tobias Clausnitzer (1619–1684); tr. Catherine Winkworth (1827–1878), alt.
Music: Melody Johann Rudolph Ahle (1625–1673), alt.; harm. George Herbert Palmer (1846–1926).

78 78 88
LIEBSTER JESU

# God, Whose Almighty Word  560

*Descant*

4 Gra - cious and ho - ly Three, glo - ri - ous Trin - i - ty,

1 God, whose al - might - y Word chaos and dark - ness heard,
2 Sav - iour, who came to bring on your re - deem - ing wing
3 Spir - it of truth and love, life - giv - ing, ho - ly Dove,
4 Gra - cious and ho - ly Three, glo - ri - ous Trin - i - ty,

wis - dom, love, might, bound-less as o - cean's tide roll - ing in

and took their flight: hear us, we hum - bly pray, and where the
heal - ing and sight, health to the sick in mind, sight to the
speed on your flight! Move on the wa - ter's face bear - ing the
wis - dom, love, might, bound-less as o - cean's tide roll - ing in

full - est pride: through the world far and wide let there be light!

gos - pel - day sheds not its glo - rious ray, let there be light!
in - ly blind: now for all hu - man-kind let there be light!
lamp of grace, and in earth's dark - est place let there be light!
full - est pride: through the world far and wide let there be light!

Text: John Marriott (1780–1825), alt.
Music: Felice de Giardini (1716–1796); adapt. *Hymns Ancient and Modern*, 1875;
  desc. Craig Sellar Lang (1891–1971). Desc. © 1953 Novello & Co., Ltd.
  *Reprinted by permission of Shawnee Press, Inc. (ASCAP).*

664 6664
MOSCOW

# 561 Lord, Your Word Shall Guide Us

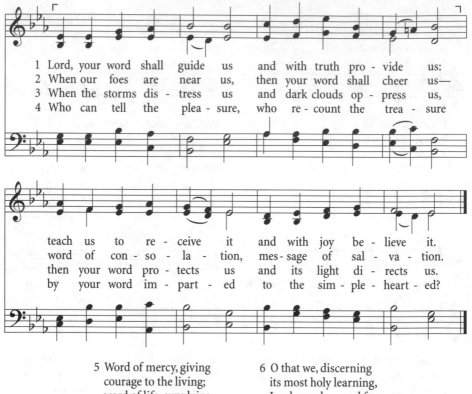

1 Lord, your word shall guide us and with truth pro - vide us:
2 When our foes are near us, then your word shall cheer us—
3 When the storms dis - tress us and dark clouds op - press us,
4 Who can tell the plea - sure, who re - count the trea - sure

teach us to re - ceive it and with joy be - lieve it.
word of con - so - la - tion, mes - sage of sal - va - tion.
then your word pro - tects us and its light di - rects us.
by your word im - part - ed to the sim - ple - heart - ed?

5 Word of mercy, giving
courage to the living;
word of life, supplying
comfort to the dying.

6 O that we, discerning
its most holy learning,
Lord, may love and fear you—
evermore be near you!

Text: Henry Williams Baker (1821–1877), rev. *Hymns for Today's Church.* © *1982 Hope Publishing Co.*     66 66
Music: Melody *Ein new Gesengbuchlen,* 1531; adapt. and harm. William Henry Monk (1823–1889).     RAVENSHAW

# 562 Dona Nobis Pacem

Do - na no - bis pa - cem, pa - cem; do - na
*Fa - ther, grant us, grant us peace; O lov - ing*

no - bis pa - cem. Do - na no - bis
*Fa - ther, grant us your peace. Grant us, grant us*

*May be sung as a 3-part round or canon.*

Text: *Agnus Dei;* tr. Ottilie Stafford (1921– ).     Irregular
Music: Composer unknown.     DONA NOBIS PACEM

## Mon âme se repose en paix 563

TRUST

Text: Ps. 62.1–2; para. Taizé Community (France).
Music: Jacques Berthier (1923–1994).
Para. and music © 1991 Les Presses de Taizé. Used by permission of G.I.A. Publications, Inc., exclusive agent.

IN GOD ALONE

# 564 Lead Us, Heavenly Father, Lead Us

1 Lead us, heaven-ly Fa-ther, lead us o'er the world's tem-
2 Sav-iour, breathe for-give-ness o'er us; all our weak-ness
3 Spir-it of our God, de-scend-ing, fill our hearts with

pes-tuous sea; guard us, guide us, keep us, feed us,
thou dost know; thou didst tread this earth be-fore us,
heaven-ly joy, love with ev-ery pas-sion blend-ing,

for we have no help but thee; yet pos-sess-ing
thou didst feel its keen-est woe; lone and drea-ry,
plea-sure that can nev-er cloy; thus pro-vid-ed,

ev-ery bless-ing if our God our Fa-ther be.
faint and wear-y, through the des-ert thou didst go.
par-doned, guid-ed, noth-ing can our peace de-stroy.

Text: James Edmeston (1791–1867).
Music: Melody Friedrich Filitz (1804–1876); adapt. Thomas Binney (1798–1874);
    harm. Lowell Mason (1792–1872), alt.

87 87 87
MANNHEIM

# Guide Me, O Thou Great Jehovah  565

1 Guide me, O thou great Je - ho - vah,* pil - grim through this bar - ren land.
2 Op - en now the crys - tal foun - tain whence the heal - ing stream doth flow;
3 When I tread the verge of Jor - dan, bid my anx - ious fears sub - side;

I am weak, but thou art might - y; hold me with thy power - ful hand.
let the fire and cloud - y pil - lar lead me all my jour - ney through.
death of death, and hell's des - truc - tion, land me safe on Ca - naan's side:

Bread of heav - en, bread of heav - en, feed me till I want no
Strong de - liv - erer, strong de - liv - erer, be thou still my strength and
songs of prais - es, songs of prais - es, I will ev - er give to

more, feed me till I want no more.
shield, be thou still my strength and shield.
thee, I will ev - er give to thee.

*or "Guide me, O thou great Redeemer"

Text: William Williams (1717–1791); tr. Peter Williams (1723–1796), alt.
Music: John Hughes (1873–1932) ©. *Reprinted by permission of Ms. C.A. Webb.*

87 87 87 with repeat
CWM RHONDDA

# 566 Great Are Your Mercies

1 Great are your mer-cies, heaven-ly Fa - ther, food and
2 Be not so anx - ious, sis - ters, broth - ers, for your
3 Birds of the air fly here and yon - der, lil - ies
4 Could Sol-o-mon in all his glo - ry match these

rai - ment you al - ways be - stow. Let me praise
dai - ly food and what you wear. Our Fa - ther
bloom, ar - rayed by na - ture thus; they sow not,
bril - liant birds and love - ly flowers? O my friends,

you al - ways, serve you all my days. You the
sees and knows all our wants and woes. Hum - bly
nor reap in, nei - ther do they spin. Yet our
do not fret: God's love fails not yet. This world

spring wind, I the grass; on me blow!
let us work and trust God's great care.
Ma - ker cares for them, more for us!
God made is your home, yours and ours.

Text: Tzu-chen Chao (1888–1979); tr. Frank W. Price (1895–1974), alt.
Music: Melody Chinese trad.; harm. W. H. Wong (1917– ).
*Text and harm. © 1977 Chinese Christian Literature Council, Hong Kong.*

99 65 73
Song of the Hoe

# Eternal Father, Strong to Save  567

1 E - ter - nal Fa - ther, strong to save, whose arm re -
2 O Christ, whose voice the wa - ters heard and hushed their
3 Cre - a - tor Spir - it, by whose breath were fash - ioned
4 O Trin - i - ty of love and power, pre - serve their

strains the rest - less wave, who bids the might - y
rag - ing at your word, who walked a - cross the
sea and sky and earth; who made the storm - y
lives in dan - ger's hour; from rock and tem - pest,

o - cean deep its own ap - point - ed bounds to keep: we
surg - ing deep and in the storm lay calm in sleep: we
cha - os cease and gave us life and light and peace: we
flood and flame, pro - tect them by your ho - ly name, and

cry, O God of maj - es - ty, for those in per - il on the sea.
cry, O Lord of Gal - il - ee, for those in per - il on the sea.
cry, O Spir - it strong and free, for those in per - il on the sea.
to your glo - ry let there be glad hymns of praise from land and sea.

Text: William Whiting (1825–1878), rev. *Hymns for Today's Church*, alt. © *1982 Hope Publishing Co.*
Music: John Bacchus Dykes (1823–1876).

88 88 88
MELITA

# 568 Nada te turbe

Na - da te tur - be, na - da te es - pan - te: Quien a Dios
*Noth - ing can trou - ble, noth - ing can fright - en. Those who seek*

tie - ne na - da le fal - ta. Na - da te tur - be,
*God shall nev - er go want - ing. Noth - ing can trou - ble,*

na - da te es - pan - te: So - lo Dios bas - ta.
*noth - ing can fright - en. God a - lone fills us.*

Text: Teresa of Avila (1515–1582); Eng. tr. Taizé Community (France).
Music: Jacques Berthier (1923–1994).

NADA TE TURBE

# Come, My Way, My Truth, My Life 569

*Unison*

1 Come, my Way, my Truth, my Life: such a
2 Come, my Light, my Feast, my Strength: such a
3 Come, my Joy, my Love, my Heart: such a

way as gives us breath, such a truth as ends all
light as shows a feast, such a feast as mends in
joy as none can move, such a love as none can

strife, such a life as kill - - eth death.
length, such a strength as makes his guest.
part, such a heart as joys in love.

Text: George Herbert (1593–1633).
Music: Ralph Vaughan Williams (1872–1958); adapt. E. Harold Geer (1886–1957). © *Stainer & Bell Ltd.*

77 77
THE CALL

# 570 Lord, Dismiss Us with Your Blessing

1 Lord, dis-miss us with your bless-ing; fill our hearts with joy and peace;
2 Thanks we give and ad-o-ra-tion for the gos-pel's joy-ful sound;

let us each, your love pos-sess-ing, tri-umph in re-deem-ing grace;
may the fruits of your sal-va-tion in our hearts and lives a-bound;

O re-fresh us, O re-fresh us, trav-elling through the wil-der-ness.
may your pres-ence, may your pres-ence, with us ev-er-more be found.

Text: Attrib. John Fawcett (1740–1817).
Music: Melody Sicilian, *The European Magazine and London Review*, 1792, alt.

87 87 87
SICILIAN MARINERS
*Alt. tune* ALLELUIA, DULCE CARMEN 550

## Shalom Chaverim 571

Sha - lom cha-ve-rim, sha - lom cha-ve-rim. Sha -
*Sha - lom, good friends, sha - lom, good friends. Sha -*
Sja - lom, chers a-mis, sja - lom, chers a-mis. Sja -

lom, sha - lom. Le - hit - ra - ot, le -
*lom, sha - lom. Till we meet a-gain, till*
lom, sja - lom. Jusqu'-au re - voir, jusqu'-

Text: Israeli trad. *Eng. and French tr.* © *1987* Songs for a Gospel People, *administered Wood Lake Books.*
Music: Israeli trad.; perc. arr. Brian Barlow (1952– ) ©.

Irregular
SHALOM

hit - ra - ot, sha - lom, sha - lom.
*we meet a - gain, sha - lom, sha - lom.*
au re - voir, sja - lom, sja - lom.

*May be sung as a 3-part round or canon.*

*Dumbek, small hand drum, or tambourine*

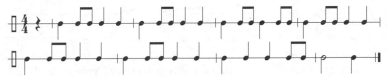

## Let There Be Light 572

1 Let there be light, let there be un - der - stand - ing,
2 o - pen our lips, o - pen our minds to pon - der,
3 per - ish the sword, per - ish the an - gry judge - ment,
4 hal - low our love, hal - low the deaths of mar - tyrs,

let all the na - tions gath - er, let them be face to face;
o - pen the door of con - cord o - pening in - to grace;
per - ish the bombs and hun - ger, per - ish the fight for gain;
hal - low their ho - ly free - dom, hal - lowed be thy name;

5 thy kingdom come,
   thy spirit turn to language,
   thy people speak together,
   thy spirit never fade;

6 let there be light,
   open our hearts to wonder,
   perish the way of terror,
   hallow the world God made.

Text: Frances Wheeler Davis (1936– ) ©.
Music: Robert J. B. Fleming (1921–1976). © 1976 Margaret Fleming.

47 76
CONCORD

# 573  O Day of Peace

1 O day of peace that dim-ly shines through all our hopes and prayers and dreams, guide us to jus - tice, truth, and love, de - liv-ered from our self - ish schemes. May swords of hate fall from our hands, our hearts from en - vy find re - lease, till by God's

Text: Carl P. Daw, Jr. (1944– ). © 1982 Hope Publishing Co.
Music: Charles Hubert Hastings Parry (1848–1918);
   arr. *The Church Hymnary*, 3rd edition, Oxford, 1973, alt.

LMD
JERUSALEM

grace   our war - ring world   shall see Christ's prom - ised reign   of

peace.

2 Then shall the   wolf   dwell with the   lamb,   nor shall the

*p*   *(p.)* Ped.

fierce de - vour   the   small;   as beasts and cat - tle calm - ly

graze,   a lit - tle child shall lead   them   all.   Then en - e -

mies shall learn to love, all creat-ures find their true ac-

cord; the hope of peace shall be ful-filled, for all the

earth shall know the Lord.

## 574 Father Eternal, Ruler of Creation

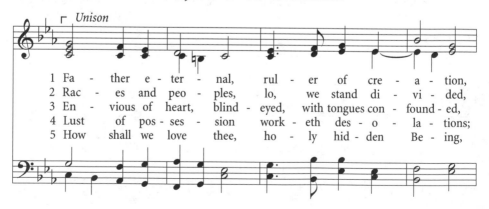

*Unison*

1 Fa - ther e - ter - nal, rul - er of cre - a - tion,
2 Rac - es and peo - ples, lo, we stand di - vi - ded,
3 En - vious of heart, blind - eyed, with tongues con - found - ed,
4 Lust of pos - ses - sion work - eth des - o - la - tions;
5 How shall we love thee, ho - ly hid - den Be - ing,

Text: Laurence Housman (1865–1959). © *Oxford University Press.*
Music: Geoffrey Turton Shaw (1879–1943). © *The United Nations Association.*

11 10 11 10 10
LANGHAM

Spir - it of life, which moved ere form was made,
and, shar - ing not our griefs, no joy can share;
na - tion by na - tion still goes un - for - given,
there is no meek - ness in the powers of earth;
if we love not the world which thou hast made?

through the thick dark - ness cov - ering ev - ery na - tion,
by wars and tu - mults love is mocked, de - rid - ed;
in wrath and fear, by jeal - ous - ies sur - round - ed,
led by no star, the rul - ers of the na - tions
O give us broad - er love for bet - ter see - ing

light to our blind - ness, O be thou our aid:
his sav - ing cross no na - tion yet will bear:
build - ing proud towers which shall not reach to heaven:
still fail to bring us to the bliss - ful birth:
thy Word made flesh, and in a man - ger laid:

thy king - dom come, O Lord, thy will be done.

# 575 Let Streams of Living Justice

1 Let streams of living justice flow down up-on the
2 For heal-ing of the na-tions, for peace that will not
3 Your ci-ty's built to mu-sic; we are the stones you

earth; give free-dom's light to cap-tives, let
end, for love that makes us lov-ers, God
seek; your har-mo-ny is lan-guage: we

all the poor have worth. The hun-gry's hands are
grant us grace to mend. Weave our var-ied gifts to-
are the words you speak. Our faith we find in

plead-ing, the work-ers claim their rights, the
geth-er; knit our lives as they are spun; on your
ser-vice, our hope in oth-er's dreams, our

Text: William Whitla (1934– ) ©.
Music: Gustav Theodore Holst (1874–1934), *The Planets*; harm. adapt. *Hymns for Church and School*, 1964. © J. Curwen & Sons, Ltd. (London). Used by permission of G. Schirmer, Inc.

13 13 13 13 13 13
THAXTED

mourn- ers long for laugh - ter, the blind- ed seek for
loom of time en - roll us till our thread of life is
love in hand of neigh - bour: our home - land bright - ly

sight. Make lib - er - ty a bea - con, strike
run. O great Weav - er of our fab - ric, bind
gleams. In - scribe our hearts with jus - tice; your

down the ir - on power; a - bol - ish an - cient
church and world in one; dye our tex - ture with your
way— the path un - tried; your truth— the heart of

ven - geance: pro - claim your peo - ple's hour.
ra - diance, light our col - ours with your sun.
strang - er; your life— the Cru - ci - fied.

## 576 For the Healing of the Nations

1 For the heal-ing of the na-tions, God, we pray with
one ac-cord; for a just and e-qual shar-ing
of the things that earth af-fords. To a life of
love in ac-tion help us rise and pledge our word.

2 Lead us, Fa-ther, in-to free-dom; from de-spair your
world re-lease, that, re-deemed from war and ha-tred,
all may come and go in peace. Show us how through
care and good-ness fear will die and hope in-crease.

3 All that kills a-bun-dant liv-ing, let it from the
earth be banned: pride of sta-tus, race, or school-ing,
dog-mas that ob-scure your plan. In our com-mon
quest for jus-tice, may we hal-low life's brief span.

4 You, Cre-a-tor God, have writ-ten your great name on
hu-man-kind; for our grow-ing in your like-ness,
bring the life of Christ to mind; that by our re-
sponse and ser-vice earth its des-ti-ny may find.

Text: Fred Kaan (1929– ), alt. © 1968 Hope Publishing Co.
Music: Henry Purcell (1659–1695), *O God, thou art my God*; adapt. *The Psalmist*, 1842.

87 87 87
WESTMINSTER ABBEY
*Higher key 300*

# God of Grace and God of Glory 577

1 God of grace and God of glo-ry, on your peo-ple pour your power;
2 Lo, the hosts of e-vil round us scorn your Christ, as-sail his ways.
3 Cure your chil-dren's war-ring mad-ness. Bend our pride to your con-trol.
4 Set our feet on lof-ty pla-ces; gird our lives that they may be

now ful-fil your chur-ch's sto-ry; bring its bud to
Fears and doubts too long have bound us; free our hearts to
Shame our wan-ton self-ish glad-ness, rich in goods and
ar-moured with all Christ-like grac-es in the fight for

glo-rious flower. Grant us wis-dom, grant us cour-age, for the
work and praise. Grant us wis-dom, grant us cour-age, for the
poor in soul. Grant us wis-dom, grant us cour-age, lest we
lib-er-ty. Grant us wis-dom, grant us cour-age, lest we

fac-ing of this hour, for the fac-ing of this hour.
liv-ing of these days, for the liv-ing of these days.
miss your king-dom's goal, lest we miss your king-dom's goal.
fail our-selves and thee, lest we fail our-selves and thee.

Text: Harry Emerson Fosdick (1878–1969), alt.
Music: John Hughes (1873–1932) ©. *Reprinted by permission of Ms. C.A. Webb.*

87 87 87 with repeat
CWM RHONDDA
*Alt. tune* RHUDDLAN 594

# 578 O Healing River

1 O heal-ing riv-er, send down your
(2 This land is) parch-ing, this land is
(3 Let the seed of) free-dom a-wake and

wa-ters, send down your wa-ters
burn-ing, no seed is grow-ing
flour-ish, let the deep roots nour-ish,

up-on this land. O heal-ing
in the bar-ren ground. O heal-ing
let the tall stalks rise. O heal-ing

*Best when sung unaccompanied.*

Text and music: Fred Hellerman (1927– ) and Fran Minkoff (19??– ).
*© 1964 (renewed) Appleseed Music, Inc. All rights reserved. Used by permission.*
Arr. Melva Treffinger Graham (1947– ) ©.

Irregular
HEALING RIVER

# 579  O Lord My God

Refrain

O Lord my God, O Lord my God, why do you seem so far from me, O Lord my God? O Lord my God, my God? O Lord, O Lord my God?

1 Night and morn-ing I make my prayer: peace for
2 Pain and suf-fering un - bound and blind plague the
3 Why, oh why do the wick - ed thrive, poor folk
4 Turn a - gain as you hear my plea; tend the

this place and help for there; wait - ing and won - dering,
pro - gress of hu - man-kind, al - ways de - mand-ing,
per - ish, the rich sur - vive; beg - ging the quest - ion,
tor - ment in all I see; lov - ing and heal - ing,

Text: Graham Maule (1958– ).
Music: John L. Bell (1949– ).
*Text and music © 1988 WGRG The Iona Community (Scotland).*
*Used by permission of G.I.A. Publications, Inc., exclusive agent.*

88 55 6 with refrain
O LORD MY GOD

waiting and wondering, does God care? Does God care?
always demanding, does God mind? Does God mind?
begging the question, is God alive? Is God alive?
loving and healing, set me free. Set me free.

## In Bethlehem a Newborn Boy 580

1 In Bethlehem a newborn boy was hailed with
2 The soldiers sought the child in vain: not yet was
3 Still rage the fires of hate today, and in no-
4 Lord Jesus, through our night of loss shines out the
5 May that great love our lives control and conquer

songs of praise and joy; then warning came of
he to share our pain. But down the ages
cents the price must pay, while aching hearts in
won-der of your cross, the love that cannot
hate in every soul, till, pledged to build and

danger near: King Herod's troops would soon appear.
rings the cry of those who saw their children die.
every land cry out, "We cannot understand!"
cease to bear our human anguish everywhere.
not destroy, we share your pain and find your joy.

Text: Rosamond Eleanor Herklots (1905–1987). © *Oxford University Press.*
Music: Melody *Antiphoner*, Grenoble, 1753; harm. Basil Harwood (1859–1949).
*Harm. published by permission of the executors of the late Dr. Basil Harwood.*

LM
DEUS TUORUM MILITUM
*Higher key 351*

# 581 Lord, Who Left the Highest Heaven

*Unison*

1 Lord, who left the high-est heav-en for a home-less hu-man birth
2 Lord, who sought by cloak of dark-ness re-fuge un-der for-eign skies
3 Lord, who lived se-cure and set-tled, safe with-in the Fa-ther's plan,
4 Lord, who leav-ing home and kin-dred fol-lowed still as du-ty led,

and, a child with-in a sta-ble, came to share the life of earth—
from the swords of Her-od's sol-diers, rav-aged homes, and par-ents' cries—
and in wis-dom, sta-ture, fa-vour grow-ing up from boy to man—
sky the roof and earth the pil-low for the Prince of glo-ry's head—

with your grace and mer-cy bless all who suf-fer home-less-ness.
may your grace and mer-cy rest on the home-less and op-pressed.
with your grace and mer-cy bless all who strive for ho-li-ness.
with your grace and mer-cy bless sac-ri-fice for right-eous-ness.

5 Lord, who in your cross and passion
   hung beneath a darkened sky,
   yet whose thoughts were for your mother,
   and a thief condemned to die—
   may your grace and mercy rest
   on the helpless and distressed.

6 Lord, who rose to life triumphant
   with our whole salvation won,
   risen, glorified, ascended,
   all the Father's purpose done—
   may your grace, all conflict past,
   bring your children home at last.

Text: Timothy Dudley-Smith (1926– ). © 1965 Hope Publishing Co.
Music: Melody Keith Landis (1922– ); harm. Jeffrey H. Rickard (1942– ). © 1992 Hope Publishing Co.

87 87 77
LATIMER

# Weary of All Trumpeting  582

1 Wea - ry of all trum - pet - ing, wea - ry of all kill - ing,
2 Cap - tain Christ, O low - ly Lord, ser - vant King, your dy - ing
3 To the tri - umph of your cross sum - mon all the liv - ing;

wea - ry of all songs that sing prom - ise, non - ful - fill - ing,
bade us sheathe the fool - ish sword, bade us cease de - ny - ing.
sum - mon us to love by loss, gain - ing all by giv - ing;

we would raise, O Christ, one song; we would join in sing - ing
Trum - pet with your Spir - it's breath through each height and hol - low;
suf - fering all, that we may see tri - umph in sur - ren - der;

that great mu - sic pure and strong, where - with heaven is ring - ing.
in - to your self - giv - ing death call us all to fol - low.
leav - ing all, that we may be part - ners in your splen - dour.

Text: Martin H. Franzmann (1907–1976). © Inter-Lutheran Commission on Worship.
*Reprinted by permission of Augsburg Fortress.*
Music: Arthur Seymour Sullivan (1842–1900).

76 76D
ST. KEVIN

# 583 When God Restored Our Common Life

1 When God re-stored our com-mon life, our hope, our lib-er-ty, at first it seemed a pass-ing dream, a wak-ing fan-ta-sy. A shock of joy swept o-ver us, for we had wept so long; the seeds we

2 We went forth weep-ing, sow-ing seeds in hard, un-yield-ing soil. With laugh-ing hearts we car-ry home the fruit of all our toil. We praise the one who gave the growth, with voic-es full and strong. The seeds we

3 Great lib-er-at-ing God, we pray for all who are op-pressed. May those who long for what is right with jus-tice now be blessed. We pray for those who mourn this day, and all who suf-fer wrong; may seeds they

Text: Ps. 126; para. Ruth Duck (1947– ). © 1992 G.I.A. Publications, Inc.
Music: Melody *The Southern Harmony*, New Haven, 1835; harm. Dale Grotenhuis (1931– ) ©.

CMD
RESIGNATION

wa - tered once with tears sprang up in - to a song.
wa - tered once with tears sprang up in - to a song.
wa - ter now with tears spring up in - to a song.

## The Church of Christ in Every Age  584

1 The church of Christ in ev - ery age, be - set by
2 A - cross the world, a - cross the street, the vic - tims
3 Then let the ser - vant church a - rise, a car - ing
4 For he a - lone, whose blood was shed, can cure the
5 We have no mis - sion but to serve in full o -

change but Spir - it - led, must claim and test its
of in - jus - tice cry for shel - ter and for
church that longs to be a part - ner in Christ's
fe - ver in our blood, and teach us how to
be - dience to our Lord: to care for all, with -

her - i - tage and keep on ris - ing from the dead.
bread to eat, and nev - er live un - til they die.
sac - ri - fice, and clothed in Christ's hu - man - i - ty.
share our bread and feed the starv - ing mul - ti - tude.
out re - serve, and spread his lib - er - at - ing word.

Text: Fred Pratt Green (1903– ). © *1971 Hope Publishing Co.*
Music: Melody Essex trad.; adapt. and arr. Ralph Vaughan Williams (1872–1958).
*Arr. © Oxford University Press.*

LM
HERONGATE

# 585 Lord, Whose Love in Humble Service

1 Lord, whose love in hum-ble ser-vice bore the
2 Still your chil-dren wan-der home-less; still the
3 As we wor-ship, grant us vi-sion till your

weight of hu-man need, who up-on the cross, for-
hun-gry cry for bread; still the cap-tives long for
love's re-veal-ing light in its height and depth and

sak-en, worked your mer-cy's per-fect deed:
free-dom; still in grief we mourn our dead.
great-ness dawns up-on our quick-ened sight,

we, your ser-vants, bring the wor-ship not of
As you, Lord, in deep com-pas-sion healed the
mak-ing known the needs and bur-dens your com-

Text: Albert Frederick Bayly (1901–1984), alt. © 1961 Oxford University Press.
Music: Melody *The Sacred Harp*, Mason, 1844; attrib. Benjamin Franklin White (1800–1879);
*arr. © 1978 Lutheran Book of Worship. Reprinted by permission of Augsburg Fortress.*

87 87D
BEACH SPRING
*Alt. settings and higher key 35, 482*

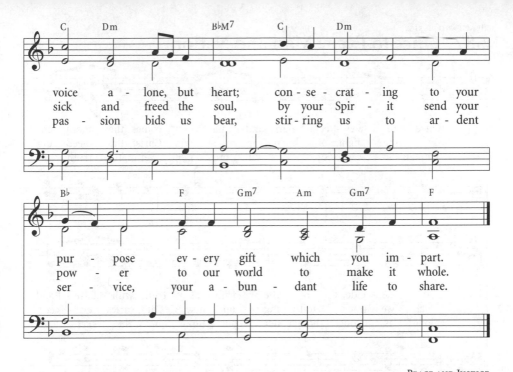

voice a - lone, but heart; con - se - crat - ing to your
sick and freed the soul, by your Spir - it send your
pas - sion bids us bear, stir - ring us to ar - dent

pur - pose ev - ery gift which you im - part.
pow - er to our world to make it whole.
ser - vice, your a - bun - dant life to share.

## Rise Up, O Saints of God 586

1 Rise up, O saints of God! From vain am - bi - tions turn;
2 Speak out, O saints of God! De - spair en - gulfs earth's frame;
3 Rise up, O saints of God! The king - dom's task em - brace;
4 Give heed, O saints of God! Cre - a - tion cries in pain;
5 Com - mit your hearts to seek the paths which Christ has trod,

Christ rose tri - um - phant that your hearts with no - bler zeal might burn.
as heirs of God's bap - tis - mal grace the word of hope pro - claim.
re - dress sin's cru - el con - se - quence; give jus - tice larg - er place.
stretch forth your hand of heal - ing now, with love the weak sus - tain.
and, quick - ened by the Spir - it's power, rise up, O saints of God.

Text: Norman O. Forness (1936– ) ©.
Music: William Henry Monk (1823–1889).

SM
ST. ETHELWALD

# 587 Once to Every Man and Nation

1 Once to ev-ery man and na-tion* comes the mom-ent
2 By the light of burn-ing mar-tyrs, Christ, thy bleed-ing
3 Though the cause of e-vil pros-per, yet 'tis truth a-

to de-cide, in the strife of truth with false-hood,
feet we track, toil-ing up new Cal-varies ev-er
lone is strong; though her por-tion be the scaf-fold,

for the good or e-vil side: some great cause, God's new Mes-
with the cross that turns not back. New oc-ca-sions teach new
and u-pon the throne be wrong, yet that scaf-fold sways the

si-ah, of-fering each the bloom or blight; and the choice goes
dut-ies; time makes an-cient good un-couth; they must up-ward
fut-ure, and, be-hind the dim un-known, stand-eth God with-

*or "Once to all, to every nation"

Text: James Russell Lowell (1819–1891);
    adapt. W. Garret Horder, *Hymns, Supplement to Existing Collections*, 1894.
Music: Thomas John Williams (1869–1944). *Music © Estate of Gwenlyn Evans.*

87 87D
EBENEZER
*Higher key 369*

by for - ev - er 'twixt that dark - ness and that light.
still and on - ward who would keep a - breast of truth.
in the shad - ow, keep - ing watch a - bove his own.

## Come Now, O Prince of Peace 588

1 Come now, O Prince of Peace, make us one bo - dy;
2 Come now, O God of love, make us one bo - dy;
3 Come now and set us free, O God, our Sav - iour;
4 Come, Hope of u - ni - ty, make us one bo - dy;

come, O Lord Je - sus, re - con - cile your peo - ple.
come, O Lord Je - sus, re - con - cile your peo - ple.
come, O Lord Je - sus, re - con - cile all na - tions.
come, O Lord Je - sus, re - con - cile all na - tions.

Text and music: Geonyong Lee (1947– ) ©; text tr. Marion Pope (1928– ), alt. ©.

65 56
O-So-So

# 589 Come, O God of All the Earth

1 Come, O God of all the earth: come to us, O
2 Come, O God of wind and flame: fill the earth with
3 Come, O God of flash-ing light, twink-ling star and
4 Come, O God of snow and rain: show-er down up-
5 Come, O Jus-tice, come, O Peace: come and shape our

right-eous one; come, and bring our love to birth
right-eous-ness; teach us all to sing your name:
burn-ing sun; God of day and God of night:
on the earth; come, O God of joy and pain,
hearts a-new; come and make op-pres-sion cease:

in the glo-ry of your Son.
may our lives your love con-fess.
in your light we all are one.
God of sor-row, God of mirth.
bring us all to life in you.

Text and music: Marty Haugen (1950– ). © 1985 G.I.A. Publications, Inc.

77 77 with refrain
SING OUT

Optional harmony

Sing out, earth and skies!

*Refrain*

Sing out, earth and skies! Sing of the God who

Sing of the God who loves you! Raise your

loves you! Raise your joy - ful cries!

dance to the life a - round you!

Dance to the life a - round you!

# 590 All Who Love and Serve Your City

Unison

1 All who love and serve your ci - ty, all who
2 in your day of loss and sor - row, in your
3 In your day of wealth and plen - ty, wast - ed
4 For all days are days of judge - ment, and the
5 Ris - en Lord! Shall yet the ci - ty be the

bear its dai - ly stress, all who cry for peace and
day of help - less strife, hon - our, peace, and love re -
work and wast - ed play, call to mind the word of
Lord is wait - ing still, draw - ing near to those who
ci - ty of de - spair? Come to - day, our Judge, our

jus - tice, all who curse and all who bless:
treat - ing, seek the Lord, who is your life.
Je - sus, "I must work while it is day."
spurn him, of - fering peace from Cal - vary's hill.
Glo - ry; be its name, "The Lord is there!"

87 87
BIRABUS

# Our Cities Cry to You, O God 591

1 Our cit-ies cry to you, O God, from out their pain and strife;
2 Yet still you walk our streets, O Christ! We know your pre-sence here,
3 Your peo-ple are your hands and feet to serve your world to-day;
4 O heal-ing Sav-iour, Prince of Peace, sal - va-tion's source and sum,

you made us for your-self a-lone, but we choose em-pty life.
where hum-ble Chris-tians love and serve in god-ly grace and fear.
our lives, the book our cit-ies read to help them find your way.
for you our bro-ken cit-ies cry— O come, Lord Je-sus, come!

Our goals are pleas-ure, gold, and power; in - jus-tice stalks our earth;
O Word made flesh, be seen in us! May all we say and do
O pour your sov-ereign Spir-it out on heart and will and brain:
With truth your roy-al di - a-dem, with right-eous-ness your rod,

in vain we seek for rest, for joy, for sense of hu-man worth.
af - firm you God in-car-nate still and turn sad hearts to you!
in - spire your church with love and power to ease our cit-ies' pain!
O come, Lord Je-sus, bring to earth the cit-y of our God!

Text: Margaret Clarkson (1915– ), alt. © *1987 Hope Publishing Co.*
Music: Alfred V. Fedak (1953– ). © *1988 Selah Publishing Co., Inc.*

CMD
HANDS OF THE POOR

# 592 Where Cross the Crowded Ways of Life

1 Where cross the crowd-ed ways of life, where cries of
2 In haunts of wretch-ed - ness and need, on shad - owed
3 From chil-dren's wound-ed help - less - ness, from men and
4 The cup of wa - ter given for you still holds the

tribe and race re - sound, a - mid the noise of
thresh - olds, dark with fears, from paths where hide the
wom - en's grief and toil, from fam - ished souls, from
fresh - ness of your grace; yet long the mul - ti -

self - ish strife, O Christ, your word of love is found.
lures of greed, we catch the vi - sion of your tears.
sor - row's stress, your heart has nev - er known re - coil.
tudes to view the strong com - pas - sion of your face.

5 O Jesus, from the mountainside
  make haste to heal these hearts of pain.
  Among these restless throngs abide;
  O tread the city's streets again,

6 till all the world shall learn your love,
  and follow where your feet have trod;
  till glorious from your heaven above
  shall come the city of our God.

Text: Frank Mason North (1850–1935), alt. © *The Sisterhood of St. John the Divine.*
Music: William Gardiner (1770–1853), *Sacred Melodies,* 1815.

LM
FULDA (WALTON)
*Higher key 629*

# O God of Every Nation 593

1 O God of ev-ery na-tion, of ev-ery race and land,
2 From search for wealth and pow-er and scorn of truth and right,
3 Lord, strength-en all who la-bour that all may find re-lease
4 Keep bright in us the vi-sion of days when war shall cease,

re-deem your whole cre-a-tion with your al-migh-ty hand;
from trust in bombs that show-er des-truc-tion through the night,
from fear of rat-tling sa-bre, from dread of war's in-crease;
when ha-tred and di-vi-sion give way to love and peace,

where hate and fear di-vide us and bit-ter threats are hurled,
from pride of race and sta-tion and blind-ness to your way,
when hope and cour-age fal-ter, Lord, let your voice be heard;
till dawns the morn-ing glor-ious when truth and love shall reign,

in love and mer-cy guide us and heal our strife-torn world.
de-liv-er ev-ery na-tion, e-ter-nal God, we pray.
with faith that none can al-ter, your ser-vants un-der-gird.
and Christ shall rule vic-to-rious o'er all the world's do-main.

Text: William Watkins Reid, Jr. (1923– ). © 1958, renewal 1986 The Hymn Society in the United States
and Canada. All rights reserved. Used by permision of Hope Publishing Co.
Music: Melody Welsh trad.; *Hymnau a Thonau*, 1865; harm. *The English Hymnal*, 1906.

76 76D
LLANGLOFFAN

# 594 Judge Eternal, Throned in Splendour

1 Judge e - ter - nal, throned in splen - dour, Lord of lords and
2 Wea - ry peo - ple still are long - ing for the hour that
3 Crown, O God, your own en - deav - our; cleave our dark - ness

King of kings, with your liv - ing fire of judge - ment
brings re - lease, and the ci - ty's crowd - ed clam - our
with your sword; cheer the faint and feed the hun - gry

purge this land of bit - ter things; com - fort all its
cries a - loud for sin to cease; and the coun - try -
with the rich - ness of your word. Cleanse the bo - dy

wide do - min - ion with the heal - ing of your wings.
side and wood - lands plead in si - lence for their peace.
of this na - tion through the glo - ry of the Lord.

Text: Henry Scott Holland (1847–1918), rev. *Hymns for Today's Church*, alt. © *1982 Hope Publishing Co.*
Music: Melody Welsh trad.; coll. Edward Jones (1752–1824), *Musical & Poetical Relicks*
of the Welsh Bards, 1800; harm. *The English Hymnal*, 1906.

87 87 87
RHUDDLAN

# And Every One 'neath Their Vine 595

And ev-ery one 'neath their vine and fig tree shall live in peace and un-a-fraid. Na-tions to plough-shares turn their swords, and they shall stu-dy war no more. war no more.

*Best when sung unaccompanied.*

Text: Shalom Altman; rev. R. Gerald Hobbs (1941– ).
*Rev. © 1987* Songs for a Gospel People, *admin.* Wood Lake Books.
Music: Melody Israeli trad.; harm. Melva Treffinger Graham (1947– ) ©.

10 8 88
SHALOM ALTMAN

# 596   O Holy City, Seen of John

*Unison*

1 O ho - ly ci - ty, seen of John, where Christ, the Lamb, doth
2 O shame on all who rest con - tent while lust and greed for
3 Give us, O God, the strength to build the ci - ty that hath
4 Al - rea - dy in the mind of God that ci - ty ri - seth

reign, with - in whose four - square walls shall come no
gain in street and shop and ten - e - ment wring
stood too long a dream, whose laws are love, whose
fair. Lo, how its splen - dour chal - leng - es the

night, nor need, nor pain, and where the tears are
gold from hu - man pain, and bit - ter lips in
crown is ser - vant - hood, and where the sun that
souls that great - ly dare— yea, bids us seize the

wiped from eyes that shall not weep a - gain!
blind de - spair cry, "Christ hath died in vain!"
shin - eth is God's grace for hu - man good.
whole of life and build its glo - ry there!

Text: Walter Russell Bowie (1882–1969).
Music: Herbert Howells (1892–1983). © 1968 Novello & Co., Ltd.
*Reprinted by permission of Shawnee Press, Inc. (ASCAP).*

86 86 86
SANCTA CIVITAS

# Lion and Lamb Lying Together  597

1 Li - on and lamb  ly - ing to - geth - er,
2 Child and snake  play - ing to - geth - er,
3 Rich and poor  shar - ing to - geth - er,
4 Strong and op - pressed  liv - ing as e - quals,

jus - tice and peace  ly - ing to - geth - er,
grow - ing in love  play - ing to - geth - er,
en - vy is gone,  shar - ing to - geth - er,
knowl - edge and trust,  liv - ing as e - quals,

li - on and lamb;
child and snake;
rich and poor;  they will not hurt nor de - stroy in all
strong and op - pressed;

Text and music: Patrick Wedd (1948– ) ©.

Irregular
LION AND LAMB

the earth, the ho - ly moun-tain of God.

1 And a lit - tle child shall
2 And the Prince of Peace will
3 And the God of love will
4 And the Cru - ci - fied re -
5 And the earth is filled with

lead them, and a lit - tle child shall
guide them, and the Prince of Peace will
chal - lenge us, and the God of love will
deems us, and the Cru - ci - fied re -
good - ness, and the earth is filled with

**Verse lines (sung text):**

F        FM⁷/A        F⁷

lead     them,      and a lit-tle child shall
guide     them,      and the Prince of Peace will
chal-lenge   us,      and the God of love will
deems     us,      and the Cru - ci - fied re-
good -    ness,      and the earth is filled with

B♭m        A♭        G♭

lead     them,    lead    them,    gent - ly
guide     them,    guide   them,    firm - ly
chal-lenge   us,    chal-lenge   us,    con-stant-ly
deems     us,    saves    us,    with his blood
good -    ness,    knowl - edge,    jus - tice,

D♭        D♭        Csus⁴    C      Csus⁴    C

lead     them    in - to God's king - dom.
guide     them    in - to God's king - dom.
chal-lenge us,    to seek her king - dom.
brings     us    in - to God's king - dom.
free -    dom,    it is God's king - dom.

*1-3: to the beginning*

*4: to 𝄋 on p. 2*

*5: Last time*

# 598 Go to the World

1 Go to the world! Go in-to all the earth. Go
2 Go to the world! Go in-to ev-ery place. Go
3 Go to the world! Go strug-gle, bless, and pray; the
4 Go to the world! Go as the ones I send, for

preach the cross where Christ re-news life's worth, bap-tiz-ing
live the word of God's re-deem-ing grace. Go seek God's
nights of tears give way to joy-ous day. As ser-vant
I am with you till the age shall end, when all the

**1-3**

as the sign of our re-birth. Al - le -
pres-ence in each time and space.
church, you fol-low Christ's own way.
hosts of glo-ry cry, "A - men!"

Text: Sylvia G. Dunstan (1955–1993). © 1991 G.I.A. Publications, Inc.
Music: Charles Villiers Stanford (1852–1924).

10 10 10 with Alleluia
ENGELBERG
Alt. tune SINE NOMINE 276, 387

## Awake! Awake! Fling Off the Night

lu - ia! Al - le - lu - ia!

1 A - wake! A - wake! Fling off the night, for God has
2 A - wake and sing, with prais - es strong, in psalm and
3 Let in the light; all sin ex - pose to Christ, whose
4 Then rise as chil - dren of the light. Be nei - ther
5 Through Christ give thanks to God, and say to oth - er

sent a glo - rious light, and we who live in
hymn and spir - it - song. Let love our words and
life no dark - ness knows. Be - fore the cross ex -
proud, nor hide from sight. Be care - ful how you
sleep - ers on the way: "A - wake, and rise up

Christ's new day must works of dark - ness put a - way.
works re - new with all that's good and right and true.
pec - tant kneel, that Christ may judge, and judg - ing, heal.
live, and wise to sift the truth from cun - ning lies.
from the dead that Christ may shine on you in - stead!"

Text: J. R. Peacey (1896–1971). © 1991 Hope Publishing Co.
Music: James William Elliott (1833–1915).

LM
CHURCH TRIUMPHANT

# 600 You Call Us Out to Praise You

**Descant**

5 Our fee - ble voic - es strug - gle to sing your jus - tice clear; the world has sunk in si - lence,

**Unison**

1 You call us out to praise you, one God for all the earth; to gath - er in com - mun - ion,
2 For var - ied hues and text - ures, new pat - terns, still you search to weave your seam - less gar - ment,
3 The church that speaks for - give - ness con - fess - es its own need; the church that feels its hun - ger
4 The church that of - fers heal - ing dis - cerns its wounds and loss; the church that fac - es dy - ing
5 Our fee - ble voic - es strug - gle to sing your jus - tice clear; the world has sunk in si - lence,

E / F / F♯m7 / Gm7 / B / C / E / F
F♯m7 / Gm7 / B / C / E / F / F♯m7 / Gm7 / B / C

Text: Anna Briggs (1947– ), alt.
Music: Patrick Wedd (1948– ); desc. Michael Capon (1963– ) ©.
*Text and melody © 1992 The General Synod of the Anglican Church of Canada; harm. © Patrick Wedd.*

76 76D
Briggs

# 601 God, Whose Giving Knows No Ending

1 God, whose giv-ing knows no end-ing, from your rich and
2 Skills and time are ours for press-ing toward the goals of
3 Trea-sure, too, you have en-trust-ed, gain through powers your

end - less store— na-ture's won - der, Je - sus' wis-dom,
Christ, your Son: all at peace in health and free-dom,
grace con - ferred, ours to use for home and kin-dred,

cost - ly cross, grave's shat-tered door— gift-ed by you,
rac - es joined, the church made one. Now di-rect our
and to spread the gos-pel word. O-pen wide our

Text: Robert L. Edwards (1915– ). © *1961, renewal 1989 The Hymn Society in the United States and Canada.*
*All rights reserved. Used by permission of Hope Publishing Co.*
Music: William Penfro Rowlands (1860–1937) ©. *Reprinted by permission of Mr. G.A. Gabe.*

87 87D
BLAENWERN
*Higher key 447*

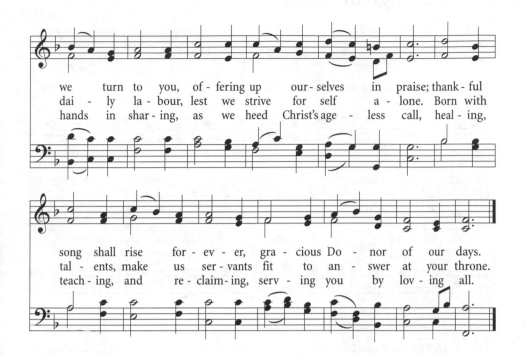

we turn to you, of - fering up our - selves in praise; thank - ful
dai - ly la - bour, lest we strive for self a - lone. Born with
hands in shar - ing, as we heed Christ's age - less call, heal - ing,

song shall rise for - ev - er, gra - cious Do - nor of our days.
tal - ents, make us ser - vants fit to an - swer at your throne.
teach - ing, and re - claim - ing, serv - ing you by lov - ing all.

# 602 Lift High the Cross

*Refrain*  *Unison*

Lift high the cross, the love of Christ pro - claim till

all the world a - dore his sa - cred name!

*Harmony*

1 Come, Chris - tian peo - ple, sing - your prais - es, shout! If
2 Je - sus, you wept to see our hu - man strife: teach
3 Peace was your plea, and peace your lov - ing theme: let
4 Great is the cost of walk - ing on this road, to
5 Worlds to be born and chil - dren yet to be, come,

*To refrain*

we are si - lent, e - ven stones cry out.
us com - pas - sion for each hu - man life.
peace be our pass - port, peace a liv - ing dream.
fol - low and suf - fer with the Son of God.
take up this song in - to e - ter - ni - ty.

Text: Refrain George William Kitchin (1827–1912); st. 1–5 Shirley Erena Murray (1931– ), alt.    10 10 with refrain
Music: Sydney Hugo Nicholson (1875–1947).    CRUCIFER
*Music © 1974, st. 1–5 © 1992 Hope Publishing Co.*

# Holy Spirit, Storm of Love  603

1 Ho - ly Spir - it, storm of love, break our self - pro -
2 Show us, in his tor - tured flesh, earth's Cre - a - tor
3 Show us how this dy - ing love en - tered, bore, and
4 Thus con - vict - ed, claimed, and called, freed, as Christ we
5 news that Je - sus is a - live, as his peo - ple

tec - tive walls. Bring us out and show us why,
on dis - play, bro - ken by af - fairs of state,
un - der - stood all our deep, un - con - scious drives,
free - ly choose, washed in love, re - born, re - named,
of the Dove, go - ing out in praise and prayer,

nak - ed - ly up - on the cross, o - pen to the
drink - ing hor - ror, pain and grief, arch - ing in the
each ex - ploit - ing, e - vil thread wo - ven through our
do - ing just - ice, know - ing God, may we wit - ness
meet the e - vils of our time and the de - mons

wind and sky, Je - sus waits and Je - sus calls.
winds of hate, giv - ing love and life a - way.
na - tions' lives, all our life a - part from God.
un - a - shamed, con - fi - dent to give good news:
of des - pair with for - giv - ing, liv - ing love.

Text: Brian Wren (1936– ). © *1986 Hope Publishing Co.*
Music: Melody Welsh trad.; coll. Edward Jones (1752–1824), *Musical & Poetical Relicks of the Welsh Bards*, 1784; harm. *The English Hymnal*, 1906.

77 77 77
ARFON MINOR

# 604 Your Word, O God, a Living Sword

*Unison*

1 Your word, O God, a liv-ing sword, re-
2 Your word, O God, a liv-ing sword, cuts
3 Your word, O God, a liv-ing sword, strikes

veals with-in each heart the love of self, the
deep, and there it finds the wall we build in
deep with-in each soul and o-pens up the

hid-den fears, that keep us far a-part; we
self-de-fence that blocks our sight and blinds; we
path by which you come to make us whole; and

seek to stand by our own strength but fail and
can-not see our neigh-bours' needs a-bove the
with your love set deep with-in we need not

Text: Christopher L. Webber (1932– ). © 1992 Hope Publishing Co.
Music: Melody George Frideric Handel (1685–1759); adapt. T. Butts, *Harmonia Sacra*, London, 1753;
   harm. David Hurd (1950– ). *Harm.* © 1985 G.I.A. Publications, Inc.

CMD
HALIFAX

fall a - lone, and still we find our -
walls and bars that we have made to
stand a - lone, for love drives out our

selves a - fraid to know as we are known.
save our - selves, and they can - not see ours.
faith - less fears and makes your peo - ple one.

## Have Mercy, Lord, on Us  605

1 Have mer - cy, Lord, on us, for you are ev - er kind;
2 Lord, wash a - way our guilt, and cleanse us from our sin;
3 The joy your grace can give, let us a - gain ob - tain;

though we have sinned be - fore you, Lord, your mer - cy let us find.
for we con - fess our wrongs, and see how great our guilt has been.
and may your Spir - it's firm sup - port our spi - rits then sus - tain.

Text: Ps. 51; para. Nahum Tate (1652–1715) and Nicholas Brady (1659–1726), alt.
Music: Samuel Howard (1710–1782).

SM
St. Bride

# 606 There's a Wideness in God's Mercy

1 There's a wide - ness in God's mer - cy like the
2 There is no place where earth's sor - rows are more
3 There is plen - ti - ful re - demp - tion in the
4 Fool - ish hearts, why will you scat - ter like a
5 For the love of God is broad - er than the

wide - ness of the sea; there's a kind - ness
felt than up in heaven; there is no place
blood that has been shed; there is joy for
crowd of fright - ened sheep? Faint - ing souls, why
mea - sure of our mind, and the heart of

in God's jus - tice which is more than lib - er - ty.
where earth's fail - ings have such kind - ly judge - ment given.
all the mem - bers in the sor - rows of the Head.
will you wan - der from a love so true and deep?
the E - ter - nal is most won - der - ful - ly kind.

Text: Frederick William Faber (1814–1863), alt.
Music: Melody Johann Ludwig Steiner (1688–1761).

87 87
GOTT WILL'S MACHEN

# Come, Let Us to the Lord Our God 607

1 Come, let us to the Lord our God with
2 His voice com-mands the tem-pest forth and
3 Long hath the night of sor-row reigned; the
4 Our hearts, if God we seek to know, shall

con-trite hearts re-turn. Our God is gra-cious,
stills the storm-y wave; and though his arm be
dawn shall bring us light. God shall ap-pear, and
know him, and re-joice; his com-ing like the

nor will leave the des-o-late to mourn.
strong to smite, 'tis al-so strong to save.
we shall rise with glad-ness in his sight.
morn shall be, like morn-ing songs his voice.

5 As dew upon the tender herb
diffusing fragrance round,
as showers that usher in the spring
and cheer the thirsty ground,

6 so shall his presence bless our souls
and shed a joyful light.
That hallowed morn shall chase away
the sorrows of the night.

Text: Hos. 6.1–4; para. John Morison (1749–1798).            CM
Music: Melody *Tochter Sion*, Köln, 1741; arr. attrib. John Richardson (1818–1879).    ST. BERNARD

# 608 Come, You Sinners, Poor and Needy

1 Come, you sin-ners, poor and need-y, weak and wound-ed,
2 Come, you thirst-y, come, and wel-come, God's free boun-ty
3 Come, you wea-ry, hea-vy la-den, lost and ru-ined

sick and sore. Je-sus, Son of God, will save you, full of
glo-ri-fy; true be-lief and true re-pent-ance, ev-ery
by the fall; if you tar-ry till you're bet-ter, you will

*Refrain*

pi-ty, love, and power.
grace that brings you nigh. I will a-rise and go to Je-sus,
nev-er come at all.

he will em-brace me in his arms; in the arms of

my dear Sav-iour, O there are ten thou-sand charms.

Text: Joseph Hart (1712–1768).
Music: *The Southern Harmony*, New Haven, 1835, alt.

87 87 with refrain
RESTORATION
*Higher key 609*

# Far, Far Away from My Loving Father  609

1 Far, far away from my loving father,
I had been wandering, wayward, wild, fearing only
lest his anger overtake his sinful child.

*Refrain I will arise and go to Jesus;
he will embrace me in his arms. In the arms of
my dear Saviour, oh, there are ten thousand charms.*

2 Fain had I fed on the husks around me,
till to myself I came, and said, "Plenty have my
father's servants; perish I for want of bread. *Refrain*

3 I will arise, though faint and weary;
home to my father I will go. Woe to me that
e'er I wandered; ah, that I such need should know." *Refrain*

4 "Father," I'll say, "I have sinned before thee;
no more may I be called thy son.
Make me only as thy servant;
pity me, a wretch undone!"
    *Refrain*

5 Then I arose and came to my father.
Mercy amazing! Love unknown!
He beheld me, ran, embraced me,
pardoned, welcomed, called me "son!"
    *Refrain*

Text: *Gospel Songs*, 1874.
Music: *The Southern Harmony*, New Haven, 1835, alt.

10 8 87 with refrain
RESTORATION
*Lower key 608*

# 610 Before I Take the Body of My Lord

*Unison*

1 Be - fore I take the bo - dy of my Lord, be-
2 The words of hope I of - ten failed to give, the
3 The nar - row - ness of vi - sion and of mind, the
4 Of those a - round in whom I meet my Lord, I
5 Lord Je - sus Christ, com - pan - ion at this feast, I

fore I share his life in bread and wine, I rec - og -
prayers of kind - ness bur - ied by my pride, the signs of
need for oth - er folk to serve my will, and ev - ery
ask their par - don and I grant them mine that ev - ery
emp - ty now my heart and stretch my hands, and ask to

nise the sor - ry things with - in— these I lay down.
care I ar - gued out of sight, these I lay down.
word and si - lence meant to hurt, these I lay down.
con - tra - dic - tion to Christ's peace might be laid down.
meet you here in bread and wine— which you lay down.

10 10 10 4
LAYING DOWN

# Our Father, We Have Wandered 611

1 Our Father, we have wandered and hidden from your face;
in foolishness have squandered your legacy of grace.
But now, in exile dwelling, we rise with fear and shame,
as, distant but compelling, we hear you call our name.

2 And now at length discerning the evil that we do,
behold us Lord, returning with hope and trust to you.
In haste you come to meet us and home rejoicing bring,
in gladness there to greet us with feast and robe and ring.

Text: Kevin Nichols (1919– ), alt. © *1981 International Committee on English in the Liturgy, Inc.*
Music: Melody Hans Leo Hassler (1564–1612);
    adapt. and harm. Johann Sebastian Bach (1685–1750).

76 76D
PASSION CHORALE

# 612 Healer of Our Every Ill

Text and music: Marty Haugen (1950– ). © 1987 G.I.A. Publications, Inc.

889 with refrain
HEALER OF OUR EVERY ILL

1 You who know our fears and sad - ness, grace us with your
2 In the pain and joy be - hold - ing how your grace is
3 Give us strength to love each oth - er, ev - ery sis - ter,
4 You who know each thought and feel - ing, teach us all your

peace and glad - ness. Spir - it of all com - fort:
still un - fold - ing, give us all your vi - sion:
ev - ery broth - er. Spir - it of all kind - ness:
way of heal - ing. Spir - it of com - pass - ion:

fill our hearts.
God of love.
be our guide.
fill each heart.

*To beginning*

# 613 We Lay Our Broken World

1 We lay our bro - ken world in sor - row
2 where hu - man life seems less than prof - it,
3 We bring our bro - ken hopes for lives of
4 We bring our bro - ken loves, friends part - ed,

at your feet, haunt - ed by hun - ger,
might, and pride: though to u - nite us
dig - ni - ty; work - less and o - ver -
fam - ilies torn; then in your life and

war, and fear, op - pressed by power and hate,
all in you, you lived and loved and died.
worked you love, and call us to be free.
death we see that love must be re - born.

5 We bring our broken selves,
   confused and closed and tired;
   then through your gift of healing grace
   new purpose is inspired.

6 Come fill us, Fire of God,
   our life and strength renew;
   find in us love and hope and trust,
   and lift us up to you.

Text: Anna Briggs (1947– ) ©.
Music: Kenneth George Finlay (1882–1974). © Broomhill Church of Scotland, Glasgow.

SM
GARELOCHSIDE

# Forgive Our Sins As We Forgive  614

1 For - give our sins as we for - give, you
2 How can your par - don reach and bless the
3 In blaz - ing light your cross re - veals the
4 Lord, cleanse the depths with - in our souls and

taught us, Lord, to pray; but you a - lone can
un - for - giv - ing heart that broods on wrongs, and
truth we dim - ly knew: what triv - ial debts are
bid re - sent - ment cease; then, bound to all in

grant us grace to live the words we say.
will not let old bit - ter - ness de - part?
owed to us, how great our debt to you!
bonds of love, our lives will spread your peace.

Text: Rosamond Eleanor Herklots (1905–1987), alt. © *Oxford University Press.*
Music: Melody *Supplement to Kentucky Harmony*, 1820; harm. Russell Schulz-Widmar (1944– ).
  Harm. © 1991 Hope Publishing Co.

CM
DETROIT

# 615 Just As I Am

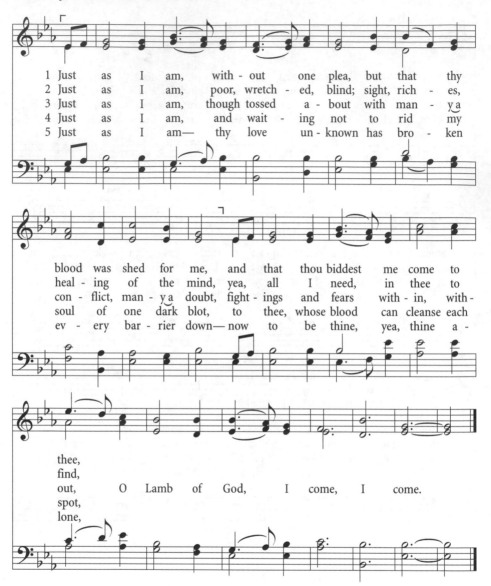

1 Just as I am, with-out one plea, but that thy
2 Just as I am, poor, wretch-ed, blind; sight, rich - es,
3 Just as I am, though tossed a - bout with man - y a
4 Just as I am, and wait - ing not to rid my
5 Just as I am— thy love un - known has bro - ken

blood was shed for me, and that thou biddest me come to
heal - ing of the mind, yea, all I need, in thee to
con - flict, man - y a doubt, fight - ings and fears with - in, with -
soul of one dark blot, to thee, whose blood can cleanse each
ev - ery bar - rier down— now to be thine, yea, thine a -

thee,
find,
out, O Lamb of God, I come, I come.
spot,
lone,

Text: Charlotte Elliott (1789–1871).
Music: William Batchelder Bradbury (1816–1868).

LM
WOODWORTH

*Moose Cree text*                 *Inuktitut text*

1 ᐅ! ᐱᑯ ᐁᐱ ᐊᔭᔭᐣ
   ᐊᒪ ᖃᐸ ᓂᒐᑐᐣ
   ᐊᔥᑕᒫ ᒫᑲ ᑭᑭ ᐃᔒᐣ
   ᐁᑯ ᓂ ᐸᒋ ᐃᑐᑕᐣ

1 O piko ashi ayayan
   Numu kakwan nitukonan
   Astum maku kikiishin
   Ako ni pachi itotan.

1 ᐃᒻᒫᕈᖅ ᐱᖃᖅᓇᖅ
   ᑕᕐᔭᐅᐸᕐᓐᔭᓐᐅᖅᒐᕐᖅ,
   ᐃᕐᐊᐃᐢ ᐊᐅᐱᐣᐠ ᐊᒃᐊᓄᕐᒃ
   ᐃᓐᖅᓄᖅ ᖁᐳᖅ (ᒫᓇ)

2 ᐅ! ᐱᑯ ᐁᐱ ᐊᔭᔭᐣ
   ᐁᖃ ᐁᐧᐅᐸᔭᐣ ᑭᒋ
   ᑭ ᑭᕐᒋᓐᑐᐧᐊᐧᐊᔭᐣ
   ᐁᑯ ᓂ ᐸᒋ ᐃᑐᑕᐣ

2 O piko ashi ayayan
   Aka apaoyan kichi
   Ke kichistapwawaloyan
   Ako ni pachi itotan.

2 ᐃᒻᒫᕈᖅ ᒍᓄᖅᓇᖅ
   ᐊᖕᒥᓄᖅ ᐱᐅᖅᓯᖅᓇᖅ.
   ᐊᐸᖅᓄᒃ ᐱᐃᐱᕐᑐᖅᓇᖅ
   ᐃᓐᖅᓄᖅ ᖁᐳᖅ (ᒫᓇ)

3 ᐅ! ᐱᑯ ᐁᐱ ᐊᔭᔭᐣ
   ᑭᑭ ᓂᒪᒋᐟᐧᐊᐧᐃᓄ
   ᔕᐧᑲᐧᓬᒧᐧᐃᐣ ᐊᓯᒋ
   ᐁᑯ ᓂ ᐸᒋ ᐃᑐᑕᐣ

3 O piko ashi ayayan
   Kiki nimuchitwawinu
   Shakwalimowin asichi
   Ako ni pachi itotan.

3 ᐃᒻᒫᕈᖅ ᐃᕐᒪᖅᑯᒃ
   ᐅᐃᒪᖅᓐᑎᑕᕈᖅ
   ᓴᖅᑮᓬᖅᒍ ᐅᐸᖅᖅᓇᕿ
   ᐃᓐᖅᓄᖅ ᖁᐳᖅ (ᒫᓇ)

4 ᐅ! ᐱᑯ ᐁᐱ ᐊᔭᔭᐣ
   ᐃᐢᐱ ᑭᓂᒪᐱᓯᔭᐣ
   ᐊᔑᐊᒪᐧᐃᐊ ᒥᑐᓂ
   ᐁᑯ ᓂ ᐸᒋ ᐃᑐᑕᐣ

4 O piko ashi ayayan
   Ispe kitimakasiyan
   Ashanumuwin nitoni
   Ako ni pachi itotan.

4 ᐃᒻᒫᕈᖅ ᐧᖅᓄᖅᔪᖅ
   ᑕᐅᔾᖅᓇᖅ, ᐧᕐᑐᖅᔪᖅ
   ᐧᖅᐸᕐᕿᐧᖅᐸᕐᓇᖅᐧᖅᓇᒪ,
   ᐃᓐᖅᓄᖅ ᖁᐳᖅ (ᒫᓇ)

5 ᐅ! ᐱᑯ ᐁᐱ ᐊᔭᔭᐣ
   ᑲ ᐱᒋ ᐊᓄᐧᐊᐸᒥᐣ
   ᑭᑕᐧᐸᑕᑎᐣ ᒥᑐᓂ
   ᐁᑯ ᓂ ᐸᒋ ᐃᑐᑕᐣ

5 O piko ashi ayayan
   Ka pachi nutuwapumin
   Kitapwatatin mitoni
   Ako ni pachi itotan.

5 ᐃᒻᒫᕈᖅ ᖁᐃᒍᐧᑮᖅᒪ
   ᐱᐅᔨᓐᔪᖅᒪ
   ᐅᕿᖅᓐᓇᒃ ᐅᐧᐱᒪ
   ᐃᓐᖅᓄᖅ ᖁᐳᖅ (ᒫᓇ)

6 ᐅ! ᐱᑯ ᐁᐱ ᐊᔭᔭᐣ
   ᐁ ᑭᓂᒪᑲᓬᒧᔭᐣ
   ᑕᐧᐸ ᓂᐢᔕᐧᐃᑯᐣ
   ᐁᑯ ᓂ ᐸᒋ ᐃᑐᑕᐣ

6 O piko ashi ayayan
   A kitimakalimoyan
   Tapwa nishakochiikon
   Ako ni pachi itotan.

6 ᐃᒻᒫᕈᖅ ᖃᐅᑐᖅ,
   ᐊᕐᒍᔭᖅᓐᖅᓄᖅ ᐃᐧᖅ,
   ᐃᓐᖅᓄᖅ ᐱᖅᑕᑎᐅᓪ,
   ᐃᓐᖅᓄᖅ ᖁᐳᖅ (ᒫᓇ)

7 ᐅ! ᐱᑯ ᐁᐱ ᐊᔭᔭᐣ
   ᑭᑭᒋ ᓴᑮᐧᐊᐧᐃᐣ
   ᑕᐧᐸ ᓂ ᐱᒫᒋᑯᐣ
   ᐁᑯ ᓂ ᐸᒋ ᐃᑐᑕᐣ

7 O piko ashi ayayan
   Kikichi sakiiwawin
   Tapwa ni pimachiikon
   Ako ni pachi itotan.

Tr.: Benjamin T. Arreak (1947– ) ©.

Tr.: *A Collection of Psalms and Hymns in the Language of the Cree Indians of North-West America*, 1887, rev. 1946; comp. John Horden (1828–1893).

# 616 Father of Heaven, Whose Love Profound

1 Father of heaven, whose love profound a ransom
2 Almighty Son, incarnate Word, our prophet,
3 Eternal Spirit, by whose breath the soul is
4 Thrice holy! Father, Spirit, Son; mysterious

for our souls hath found, before thy throne we
priest, redeemer, Lord, before thy throne we
raised from sin and death, before thy throne we
Godhead, Three-in-One, before thy throne we

sinners bend; to us thy pardoning love extend.
sinners bend; to us thy saving grace extend.
sinners bend; to us thy quickening power extend.
sinners bend; grace, pardon, life to us extend.

Text: Edward Cooper (1770–1833).
Music: John Bacchus Dykes (1823–1876).

LM
RIVAULX

# Jesus, the Very Thought of Thee 617

1 Je - sus, the ver - y thought of thee, with
2 No voice can sing, no heart can frame, nor
3 O hope of ev - ery con - trite heart, O
4 But what to those who find? Ah, this nor
5 Je - sus, our on - ly joy be thou, as

sweet - ness fills the breast; but sweet - er far thy
can the mind re - call a sweet - er sound than
joy of all the meek; to those who ask, how
tongue nor pen can show; the love of Je - sus,
thou our prize wilt be; in thee be all our

face to see, and in thy pres - ence rest.
Je - sus' name, the Sav - iour of us all.
kind thou art, how good to those who seek!
what it is none but his lov - ers know.
glo - ry now, and through e - ter - ni - ty.

Text: Latin (*Jesu dulcis memoria,* 12th cent.); tr. Edward Caswall (1814–1878), alt.
Music: Gordon Archbold Slater (1896–1979). © *Oxford University Press.*

CM
ST. BOTOLPH

# 618 Glorious in Majesty

*Unison*

1 Glo - ri - ous in maj - es - ty, ho - ly in his prais - es,
2 Vic - to - ry he won for us, free - ing us from dark - ness,
3 One in love, as fam - i - ly, liv - ing with each oth - er,

Je - sus, our Sav - iour and our King,
dy - ing and ris - ing from the dead.
glad - ly we share each oth - er's pain.

born a man, yet God of old, let us all a - dore him.
Liv - ing with the Fa - ther now, yet he is a - mong us.
Yet he will not leave us so, soon he is re - turn - ing,

Filled with his Spir - it, let us sing.
We are the bo - dy, he the head.
tak - ing us back with him to reign.

Text: Jeff Cothran (19??– ).
Music: Melody Israeli trad.; harm. Jeff Cothran (19??– ).
*Text and harm. © 1972 G.I.A. Publications, Inc.*

768 768 with refrain
SHIBBOLET BASADEH

*Refrain*

Liv - ing is to love him, serv - ing him to know his free - dom.

Come a - long with us to join the praise of Je - sus.

Come to Je - sus now; go to live his word re - joic - ing.

# 619 Fairest Lord Jesus

Descant

4 All fair-est beau-ty, heav-en-ly and earth-ly,

1 Fair-est Lord Je-sus, rul-er of all na-ture,
2 Fair are the mead-ows, fair-er still the wood-lands,
3 Fair is the sun-shine, fair-er still the moon-light,
4 All fair-est beau-ty, heav-en-ly and earth-ly,

won-drous-ly, Je-sus, is found in thee;

O thou the God-head's hu-man son:
robed in the bloom-ing garb of spring;
and fair the twink-ling, star-ry host;
won-drous-ly, Je-sus, is found in thee;

Text: *Münster Gesangbuch*, 1677; tr. *Church Chorals and Choir Studies*, 1850, alt.
Music: Melody Silesian trad.; *Schlesische Volkslieder*, Leipig, 1842;
  arr. James Hopkirk (1908–1972); desc. Kenneth Hull (1952– ) ©. *Arr. © Estate of James Hopkirk.*

568 558
CRUSADERS' HYMN

none can be near - er, fair - er, or dear - er than

thee will I cher - ish, thee will I hon - our, thou
Je - sus is fair - er, Je - sus is pur - er, who
Je - sus shines bright - er, Je - sus shines pur - er than
none can be near - er, fair - er, or dear - er than

thou, my Sav - iour, art to me.

my soul's glo - ry, joy, and crown.
makes the trou - bled heart to sing.
all the an - gels heaven can boast.
thou, my Sav - iour, art to me.

# 620 How Sweet the Name of Jesus Sounds

*Descant*

5 Weak is the ef - fort of my heart, and

1 How sweet the name of Je - sus sounds in
2 It makes the wound - ed spir - it whole, and
3 Dear name! The rock on which I build, my
4 Je - sus, my shep - herd, broth - er, friend, my
5 Weak is the ef - fort of my heart, and

cold my warm - est thought; but when I see thee

a be - liev - er's ear! It soothes our sor - rows,
calms the trou - bled breast; 'tis man - na to the
shield and hid - ing - place, my nev - er - fail - ing
proph - et, priest, and king, my Lord, my life, my
cold my warm - est thought; but when I see thee

as thou art, I'll praise thee as I ought.

heals our wounds, and drives a - way our fear.
hun - gry soul, and to the wea - ry rest.
trea - sury, filled with bound - less stores of grace.
way, my end, ac - cept the praise I bring.
as thou art, I'll praise thee as I ought.

Text: John Newton (1725–1807), alt.
Music: Alexander Robert Reinagle (1799–1877); desc. Alan Gray (1855–1935).
*Desc. © Cambridge University Press.*

CM
St. Peter

# Before the World Began 621

1 Be - fore the world be - gan, one Word was there;
2 Life found in him its source, death found its end;
3 The Word was in the world which from him came;
4 All who re - ceived the Word by God were blessed;

ground - ed in God he was, root - ed in care;
light found in him its course, dark - ness its friend.
un - rec - og - nized he was, un - known by name;
sis - ters and broth - ers, they of earth's fond guest.

by him all things were made, in him was love dis - played,
For nei - ther death nor doubt nor dark - ness can put out
one with all hu - man - kind, with the un - loved a - ligned,
So did the Word of grace pro - claim in time and space

through him God spoke, and said,
the glow of God, the shout, "I AM FOR YOU."
con - vinc - ing sight and mind,
and with a hu - man face,

Text and music: John L. Bell (1949– ).
© 1987 WGRG The Iona Community (Scotland). Used by permission of G.I.A. Publications, Inc., exclusive agent.

64 64 666 4
INCARNATION

# 622 How Bright Appears the Morning Star

1 How bright ap-pears the morn-ing star with mer-cy
2 Though cir-cled by the hosts on high, you looked on

beam-ing from a - far; the host of heaven re - joic - es.
us with pity-ing eye and saved your sin - ful crea - ture;

O right-eous Branch of Jes - se's rod, true Light of Light and
the whole cre - a - tion's head and Lord, by high - est ser - a -

Text: Philipp Nicolai (1556–1608); tr. and adapt. William Mercer (1811–1873), alt.
Music: Melody Philipp Nicolai (1556–1608);
   adapt. and harm. Johann Sebastian Bach (1685–1750).

887D 44 44 8
WIE SCHÖN LEUCHTET
*Alt. setting 648*

God of God, we, too, will lift our voic - es. Je - sus,
phim a - dored, you took our ver - y na - ture. A - men,

Je - sus, ho - ly, ho - ly, yet most low - ly, ev - er
a - men, al - le - lu - ia, al - le - lu - ia, praise be

near us, great Em - man - uel, swift to hear us.
giv - en ev - er - more by earth and heav - en.

# 623 A Mother's Labour Bears Her Child

1 A mother's labour bears her child. She shares creation's agony. The water's break anticipates the hour of her delivery.

2 A mother's body nourishes her child she comforts at her breast; and Jesus feeds us of himself, in his own life our living blessed.

And by the labour of the cross our mother Christ has brought to birth into his own eternal life the sons and daughters of the earth.

*"...our true mother Jesus, he alone bears us for joy and eternal life..."*
*Julian of Norwich (1340?–1420)*

Text and melody: Brian Ruttan (1947– ) ©; harm. Roland Packer (1955– ) ©.

LMD
JULIAN

# O Thou Who Camest from Above  624

1 O thou who cam - est from a - bove, the pure ce -
2 There let it for thy glo - ry burn with in - ex -
3 Je - sus, con - firm my heart's de - sire to work and
4 Rea - dy for all thy per - fect will, my acts of

les - tial fire to im - part, kin - dle a flame of
tin - guish - a - ble blaze, and trem - bling to its
speak and think for thee; still let me guard the
faith and love re - peat, till death thy end - less

sa - cred love on the mean al - tar of my heart.
source re - turn in hum - ble prayer and fer - vent praise.
ho - ly fire, and still stir up thy gift in me.
mer - cies seal and make the sac - ri - fice com - plete.

Text: Charles Wesley (1707–1788).
Music: Samuel Sebastian Wesley (1810–1876).

LM
HEREFORD

# 625 I Found Him Cradled

1 I found him cra-dled in a lamp-lit barn; his moth-er Ma - ry rocked
2 I heard him laugh-ing in the tem-ple court the day his par - ents lost
3 I saw him weep-ing ov - er sin and death, the sick and dy - ing round

him. The child was God they hung to-day on a big high cross and they
him. The boy was God they hung to-day and I'll nev-er know what it
him. The man was God they hung to-day on a big high cross when I

*Harmony*

mocked him there. One day on, the tomb is si - lent; one day
cost him there. Two days on, the tomb is si - lent; two days
found him there. Three days on, the tomb is o - pen! Three days

on, all heav - en weeps; one day on, and e - ven
on, all heav - en weeps; two days on, and still the
on, the loud re - frain: Christ has died, and Christ is

Text: Paul Wigmore (1925– ). © *1992 Hope Publishing Co.*
Music: David Iliff (1939– ). © *1992 Hope Publishing Co.*

10 7 8 10 87 85
Three Days On

star - light hid from Christ who sleeps.
star - light hid from Christ who sleeps.
ris - en, Christ will come a - gain!

## The Lord Almighty Spoke the Word  626

*Unison*

1 The Lord al - might - y spoke the Word; the morn - ing
2 The Lord al - might - y gave the Word that came to
3 O Lord al - might - y, liv - ing Word, and Spir - it

stars to - geth - er sang; the Word God spoke through
us in flesh to dwell; the Word God gave broke
blest, we wor - ship thee; thy Word pro - claim, and

cha - os broke, and worlds in or - der sprang.
through the grave, and van - quished sin and hell.
in thy name the king - dom that shall be.

Text: Charles E. Watson (1869–1942). © *Rodborough Tabernacle United Reformed Church.*
Music: F. R. C. Clarke (1931– ) ©.

8 8 4 4 6
SYDENHAM STREET

# 627 The Voice of God Goes Out

1 The voice of God goes out to all the world,
2 The Lord has said: "Re - ceive my mes - sen - ger,
3 The bro - ken reed he will not tram - ple down,
4 A - noint - ed with the Spir - it and with power,
5 His touch will bless the eyes that dark - ness held;

and glo - ry speaks a - cross the u - ni - verse.
my prom - ise to the world, my pledge made flesh,
nor set his heel up - on the dy - ing flame.
he comes to crown with com - fort all the weak,
the lame shall run, the halt - ing tongue shall sing,

The great King's her - ald cries from star to star:
a lamp to ev - ery na - tion, light from Light":
He binds the wounds, and health is in his hand:
to show the face of jus - tice to the poor:
and pris - oners laugh in light and lib - er - ty:

with power, with jus - tice, Christ will walk his way.

Text: Luke Connaughton (1919–1979), alt. © 1970 McCrimmon Publishing Co., Ltd.
Music: Cyril Vincent Taylor (1907–1991). © 1985 Hope Publishing Co.

10 10 10 10
SHELDONIAN

# O Love, How Deep, How Broad, How High 628

1 O love, how deep, how broad, how high! It fills the
heart with ec-sta-sy, that God, the Son of
God, should take our mor-tal form for mor-tals' sake.

2 God sent no an-gel to our race, of high-er
or of low-er place, but wore the robe of
hu-man frame for us, and to this lost world came.

3 For us he was bap-tized, and bore his ho-ly
fast, and hun-gered sore; for us temp-ta-tions
sharp he knew; for us the tempt-er o-ver-threw.

4 For us he prayed, for us he taught, for us his
dai-ly works he wrought; by words and signs, and
ac-tions, thus still seek-ing not him-self but us.

5 For us by wickedness betrayed,
scourged, mocked, in purple robe arrayed,
he bore the shameful cross and death;
for us at length gave up his breath.

6 For us he rose from death again,
for us he went on high to reign,
for us he sent his Spirit here
to guide, to strengthen, and to cheer.

7 To God whose boundless love has won
salvation for us through the Son,
to God the Father, glory be
both now and through eternity.

Text: Latin (*O amor quam*, 15th cent.); tr. Benjamin Webb (1819–1885).
Music: Melody Trier MS (15th cent.); adapt. Michael Praetorius (1571–1621);
   harm. George Ratcliffe Woodward (1848–1934).
   *Harm. © Mowbray (an imprint of Cassell plc, London).*

LM
PUER NOBIS NASCITUR

# 629 Jesus, Thy Blood and Righteousness

1 Je - sus, thy blood and right - eous - ness my beau - ty
2 Bold shall I stand in thy great day; for who aught
3 Je - sus, be end - less praise to thee, whose bound - less
4 O let the dead now hear thy voice; now bid thy

are, my glo - rious dress; 'midst flam - ing worlds, in
to my charge shall lay? Ful - ly ab - solved through
mer - cy hath for me— for me a full a -
ban - ished ones re - joice; their beau - ty this, their

these ar - rayed, with joy shall I lift up my head.
these I am from sin and fear, from guilt and shame.
tone - ment made, an ev - er - last - ing ran - som paid.
glo - rious dress, Je - sus, thy blood and right - eous - ness.

Text: Nikolaus Ludwig von Zinzendorf (1700–1760); tr. John Wesley (1703–1791).
Music: William Gardiner (1770–1853), *Sacred Melodies*, 1815.

LM
FULDA (WALTON)
*Lower key 592*

# You, Lord, Are Both Lamb and Shepherd  630

1 You, Lord, are both lamb and shep-herd. You, Lord, are both
2 Clothed in light up-on the moun-tain, stripped of might up-
3 You, who walk each day be-side us, sit in pow-er
4 Wor-thy is our earth-ly Je-sus! Wor-thy is our

prince and slave. You, peace-mak-er and sword-bring-er
on the cross, shin-ing in e-ter-nal glo-ry,
at God's side. You, who preach a way that's nar-row,
cos-mic Christ! Wor-thy your de-feat and vic-tory.

of the way you took and gave. You, the ev-er-
beg-gared by a sol-dier's toss, you, the ev-er-
have a love that reach-es wide. You, the ev-er-
Wor-thy still your peace and strife. You, the ev-er-

last-ing in-stant; you, whom we both scorn and crave.
last-ing in-stant; you, who are both gift and cost.
last-ing in-stant; you, who are our pil-grim guide.
last-ing in-stant; you, who are our death and life.

Text: Sylvia G. Dunstan (1955–1993), alt. © *1991 G.I.A. Publications, Inc.*
Music: John R. Van Maanen (1958– ) ©.

87 87 87
CHRISTUS PARADOX
*Alt. tune WESTMINSTER ABBEY 288, 300, 576*

# 631 The Kingdom of God Is Justice and Joy

1 The king-dom of God is jus-tice and joy,
2 The king-dom of God is mer-cy and grace;
3 The king-dom of God is chal-lenge and choice:
4 God's king-dom is come, the gift and the goal,

for Je-sus re-stores what sin would de-stroy.
the cap-tives are freed, the sin-ners find place.
be-lieve the good news, re-pent and re-joice!
in Je-sus be-gun, in heav-en made whole.

God's pow-er and glo-ry in Je-sus we know,
The out-casts are wel-comed God's ban-quet to share,
His love for us sin-ners brought Christ to his cross,
The heirs of the king-dom shall an-swer his call,

and here and here-af-ter the king-dom shall grow.
and hope is a-wak-ened in place of de-spair.
our cri-sis of judge-ment for gain and for loss.
and all things cry "Glo-ry!" to God All-in-All.

Text: Byrn Austin Rees (1911–1983). © *Mrs. Olwen A. Scott.*
Music: Melody German trad.; *Catholisch-Paderbornisches Gesangbuch,* 1765;
   harm. attrib. Sydney Hugo Nicholson (1875–1947), *Hymns Ancient and Modern,*
   *2nd Supplement,* 1916. *Harm. © Hope Publishing Co.*

10 10 11 11
PADERBORN

# The King of Glory Comes  632

*Refrain*   Em   *Unison*     B7    Em

The King of glo - ry comes, the na - tion re - joic - es.

B7    Em

O - pen the gates be - fore him, lift up your voic - es.

G      C    D7      G

1 Who is the King of glo - ry? What shall we call him?
2 In all of Gal - i - lee, in ci - ty or vil - lage,
3 He gave his life for us, the pledge of sal - va - tion;
4 He con - quered sin and death; he tru - ly has ris - en.

Em    CM7    G    CM7   D7    G    *To refrain*

He is Em - man - u - el, the prom - ised of a - ges.
he goes a - mong his peo - ple, cur - ing their ill - ness.
he took up - on him - self the sin of the na - tions.
And he will share with us his heav - en - ly vi - sion.

Text: Willard F. Jabusch (1930– ) ©.
Music: Melody Israeli trad.; arr. John Ferguson (1941– ).
*Arr. © 1974 The Hymnal of the United Church of Christ. Administered by The Pilgrim Press.*

12 12 with refrain
PROMISED ONE

# 633 Lord Christ, We Praise Your Sacrifice

1 Lord Christ, we praise your sacrifice,
your life in love so freely given. For those who
took your life away you prayed, that they might
be forgiven; and there, in helplessness ar-

2 Once helpless in your mother's arms,
dependent on her mercy then, at last, by
choice, in other hands, you were as helpless
once again; and, at their mercy, cruci-

3 Though helpless and rejected then,
you're now as risen Lord acclaimed; for-ever
by your sacrifice is God's eternal
love proclaimed: the love which, dying, brings to

4 So, living Lord, prepare us now
your willing helplessness to share, to give our-
selves in sacrifice, to overcome the
world's despair; in love to give our lives a-

Text: Alan Gaunt (1935– ). © 1991 Stainer & Bell Ltd. All rights reserved.
Used by permission of Hope Publishing Co.
Music: Cyril Knight (1908–1982). © Executors of the estate of Rachel Knight, deceased.

88 88 88
MEYRICK PARK

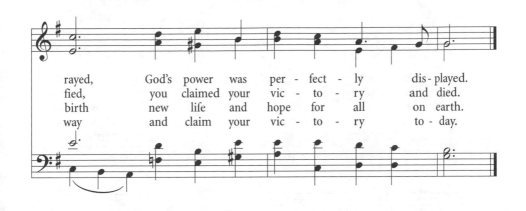

rayed,     God's power was per - fect - ly dis - played.
fied,       you claimed your vic - to - ry and died.
birth     new life and hope for all on earth.
way       and claim your vic - to - ry to - day.

## Jesus, Remember Me  634

Je - sus, re - mem - ber me when you come in - to your king - dom.

Je - sus, re - mem - ber me when you come in - to your king - dom.

Text: Luke 23.42.
Music: Jacques Berthier (1923–1994). *Music © 1978, 1980, and 1981 Les Presses de Taizé.*
*Used by permission of G.I.A. Publications, Inc., exclusive agent.*

JESUS, REMEMBER ME

# 635 Like the Murmur of the Dove's Song

*Unison*

1 Like the mur - mur of the dove's song, like the
2 To the mem - bers of Christ's bo - dy, to the
3 With the heal - ing of di - vi - sion, with the

chal - lenge of her flight, like the vig - our of the
branch - es of the vine, to the church in faith as -
cease - less voice of prayer, with the power to love and

wind's rush, like the new flame's ea - ger
sem - bled, to her midst as gift and
wit - ness, with the peace be - yond com -

might: come, Ho - ly Spir - it, come.
sign: come, Ho - ly Spir - it, come.
pare: come, Ho - ly Spir - it, come.

Text: Carl P. Daw, Jr. (1944– ). © *1982 Hope Publishing Co.*
Music: Peter Cutts (1937– ). © *1969 Hope Publishing Co.*

87 87 6
BRIDEGROOM

# Come, Thou Holy Spirit, Come 636

1 Come, thou Holy Spir - it, come, and from thy ce -
2 thou of com - fort - ers the best, thou the soul's most
3 O most bless - ed Light di - vine, shine with - in these
4 Heal our wounds, our strength re - new; on our dry - ness
5 On the faith - ful, who a - dore and con - fess thee,

les - tial home shed a ray of light di - vine;
wel - come guest, sweet re - fresh - ment here be - low;
hearts of thine, and our in - most be - ing fill;
pour thy dew; wash the stains of guilt a - way;
ev - er - more in thy seven - fold gifts de - scend:

come, De - fend - er of the poor, come, thou source of
in our la - bour rest most sweet, grate - ful cool - ness
where thou art not, we have naught, noth - ing good in
bend the stub - born heart and will; melt the fro - zen,
give them vir - tue's sure re - ward, give them thy sal -

all our store, come, with - in our bo - som shine:
in the heat, so - lace in the midst of woe.
deed or thought, noth - ing free from taint of ill.
warm the chill; guide the steps that go a - stray.
va - tion, Lord, give them joys that nev - er end.

Text: Latin (13th cent.); tr. Edward Caswall (1814–1878), alt.
Music: Samuel Webbe the elder (1740–1816).

777D
VENI SANCTE SPIRITUS

# 637 Come, Holy Ghost, Our Souls Inspire

1 Come, Ho - ly Ghost, our souls in - spire,
2 Thy bless - ed unc - tion from a - bove
3 A - noint and cheer our soil - ed face
4 Teach us to know the Fath - er, Son,

and light - en with ce - les - tial fire;
is com - fort, life, and fire of love;
with the a - bun - dance of thy grace;
and thee, of both, to be but one:

thou the a - noint - ing Spir - it art,
en - a - ble with per - pet - ual light
keep far our foes, give peace at home;
that through the a - ges all a - long

Text: Latin (9th cent.); tr. John Cosin (1594–1672).
Music: Melody Mechlin plainsong, Mode 8; harm. Healey Willan (1880–1968).
*Harm. © 1995 Waterloo Music Co. Ltd.*

LM with coda
VENI CREATOR SPIRITUS (1)

St. 1–3 to beginning

who dost thy seven - fold gifts im - part.
the dull - ness of our blind - ed sight.
where thou art guide no ill can come.
this may be our end - less song: St. 4 to Coda

St. 1–3 to beginning

*Coda*  *Last time*

praise to thy e - ter - nal mer - it,

Fa - ther, Son, and Ho - ly Spir - it.

# 638 O Holy Spirit, By Whose Breath

1 O Ho - ly Spir - it, by whose breath
2 You are the seek - er's sure re - source,
3 In you God's en - er - gy is shown;
4 Flood our dull sens - es with your light;
5 From in - ner strife grant us re - lease.

life ris - es vi - brant out of death,
of burn - ing love the liv - ing source,
to us your var - ied gifts made known.
in mu - tual love our hearts u - nite.
Turn na - tions to the ways of peace.

come to cre - ate, re - new, in - spire;
pro - tec - tor in the midst of strife,
Teach us to speak; teach us to hear;
Your power the whole cre - a - tion fills;
To ful - ler life your peo - ple bring,

Text: Latin (9th cent.); tr. John Webster Grant (1919– ) ©.
Music: Melody Mechlin plainsong, Mode 8; harm. Healey Willan (1880–1968).
Harm. © 1995 Waterloo Music Co. Ltd.

LM with coda
VENI CREATOR SPIRITUS (1)

St. 1–4 to beginning

| come, | kin - dle | in | | our | hearts | | your | fire. |
| the | giv - er | and | | the | Lord | | of | life. |
| yours | is | the | tongue | and | yours | | the | ear. |
| con - | firm | our | weak, | un - | cer - | | tain | wills. |
| that | as | one | bo - | dy | we | | may | sing: *St. 5 to Coda* |

St. 1–4 to beginning

*Coda*   *Last time*

praise to    the    Fa  -  ther, Christ    his    Word,

and    to    the    Spir  -  it:    God    the    Lord.

# 639 Come, O Creator Spirit, Come

1 Come, O Cre - a - tor Spir - it, come,
2 O Com - fort - er, that name is thine,
3 Our sens - es with thy light in - flame,
4 May we by thee the Fath - er learn,

and make with - in our hearts thy home.
of God most high the gift di - vine;
our hearts to heaven - ly love re - claim,
and know the Son, and thee dis - cern,

To us thy grace ce - les - tial give,
the well of life, the fire of love,
our bod - ies' poor in - fir - mi - ty
who art of both, and so a - dore

Text: Latin (9th cent.); tr. Robert Seymour Bridges (1844–1930). *Tr. © Oxford University Press.*
Music: Melody Plainsong, Mode 8; harm. George Black (1931– ) ©.

LM
VENI CREATOR SPIRITUS (2)

who      of thy   breath - ing         move and live.
our      souls' a -  noint - ing       from a - bove.
with     strength per - pet - ual      for - ti - fy.
in       per - fect faith for          ev - er - more.

## Come, Holy Spirit, Heavenly Dove  640

1 Come,   Ho - ly  Spir - it,   heaven - ly  dove,   with
2 In       vain  we  tune   our   for - mal  songs,   in
3 Dear     Lord! And  shall  we   ev - er   live   at
4 Come,    Ho - ly  Spir - it,   heaven - ly  dove,   with

all    thy quick - ening  powers,   kin - dle  a   flame  of
vain   we  strive  to   rise;    ho - san - nas  lan - guish
this   poor dy - ing   rate?    Our  love  so  faint,  so
all    thy quick - ening  powers;   come,  shed  a - broad  a

sa - cred  love    in   these cold  hearts  of   ours.
on    our  tongues,  and  our  de - vo - tion     dies.
cold   to  thee,   and  thine  to   us   so   great!
Sav - iour's love,   and  that  shall  kin - dle     ours.

Text: Isaac Watts (1674–1748).
Music: John Dykes Bower (1905–1981). © *Estate of John Dykes Bower.*

CM
HARESFIELD

# 641 Creator Spirit, By Whose Aid

1 Cre - a - tor Spir - it, by whose aid the world's foun - da - tions
2 O source of un - cre - a - ted light, the Fa - ther's prom - ised
3 Plen - teous of grace, de - scend from high rich in thy seven - fold
4 Im - mor - tal hon - our, end - less fame, at - tend the al - might - y

first were laid, come, vis - it ev - ery hum - ble mind; come,
Par - a - clete, thrice ho - ly fount, thrice ho - ly fire, our
en - er - gy; make us e - ter - nal truths re - ceive, and
Fath - er's name; the Sav - iour Son be glo - ri - fied, who

pour thy joys on hu - man - kind; from sin and sor - row
hearts with heaven - ly love in - spire; come, and thy sa - cred
prac - tise all that we be - lieve; give us thy - self, that
for the world's re - demp - tion died; and e - qual ad - o -

set us free, and make us tem - ples wor - thy thee.
unc - tion bring to sanc - ti - fy us while we sing.
we may see the Fath - er and the Son by thee.
ra - tion be, e - ter - nal Par - a - clete, to thee.

Text: Latin (9th cent.); tr. and vers. John Dryden (1631–1701).
Music: Dimitri Bortnianski (1751–1825); adapt. *Choralbuch*, Leipzig, 1825.

88 88 88
ST. PETERSBURG

# From the Waiting Comes the Sign  642

*Unison*

1 From the wait-ing comes the sign— come, Ho-ly Spir-it, come; from the pres-ence comes the peace—come, Ho-ly Spir-it, come; from the si-lence comes the song—come, Ho-ly Spir-it, come and be to us, in truth, the sign, the peace, the song.

2 In the burn-ing is the fire— come, Ho-ly Spir-it, come; in the spend-ing is the gift— come, Ho-ly Spir-it, come; in the break-ing is the life— come, Ho-ly Spir-it, come and be to us, in faith, the fire, the gift, the life.

Text: Shirley Erena Murray (1931– ). © *1992 Hope Publishing Co.*
Music: Michael Capon (1963– ) ©.

76 76 76 66
CHURCH HILL

# 643 Holy Spirit, Come with Power

1 Ho - ly Spir - it, come with pow - er, breathe in - to our
2 Ho - ly Spir - it, come with fire, burn us with your
3 Ho - ly Spir - it, bring your mes - sage, burn and breathe each

ach - ing night. We ex - pect you this glad hour,
pres - ence new. Let us as one might - y choir
word a - new deep in - to our tired liv - ing

wait - ing for your strength and light. We are
sing our hymn of praise to you. Burn a -
till we strive your work to do. Teach us

Text: Anne Neufeld Rupp (1932– ) ©.
Music: Rowland Huw Prichard (1811–1887).

87 87D
HYFRYDOL

fear - ful, we are ail - ing, we are weak and
way our wast - ed sad - ness and en - flame us
love and trust - ing kind - ness, lend our hands to

self - ish too. Break up - on your con - gre -
with your love. Burst up - on your con - gre -
those who hurt. Breathe up - on your con - gre -

ga - tion, give us vig - our, life a - new.
ga - tion, give us glad - ness from a - bove.
ga - tion and in - spire us with your word.

# 644 Come, Gracious Spirit, Heavenly Dove

1 Come, gracious Spirit, heavenly dove, with
2 The light of truth to us display and
3 Lead us to Christ, the living way, nor
4 Lead us to heaven, that we may share full -

light and comfort from above; be thou our guard-ian,
make us know and choose thy way; plant holy fear in
let us from his pas-tures stray; lead us to ho-li -
ness of joy for-ev-er there; lead us to God, our

thou our guide; o'er ev-ery thought and step pre-side.
ev-ery heart, that we from God may ne'er de-part.
ness, the road that we must take to dwell with God.
fi-nal rest, to be with him for-ev-er blest.

Text: Simon Browne (1680–1732), alt.
Music: Melody *Das ander Theil*, 1605; adapt. Johann Hermann Schein (1586–1630), alt.

LM
EISENACH
*Alt. setting and lower key 79*

# Come Down, O Love Divine 645

1 Come down, O Love divine, seek thou this soul of mine, and visit it with thine own ardour glowing; O Comforter, draw near, within my heart appear, and kindle it, thy holy flame bestowing.

2 O let it freely burn, till earthly passions turn to dust and ashes in its heat consuming; and let thy glorious light shine ever on my sight, and clothe me round, the while my path illuming.

3 Let holy charity mine outward vesture be, and lowliness become mine inner clothing; true lowliness of heart, which takes the humbler part, and o'er its own shortcomings weeps with loathing.

4 And so the yearning strong, with which the soul will long, shall far outpass the power of human telling; for none can guess its grace, till they become the place wherein the Holy Spirit finds a dwelling.

Text: Bianco da Siena (1350?–1434?); tr. Richard Frederick Littledale (1833–1890), alt.
Music: Ralph Vaughan Williams (1872–1958). © Oxford University Press.

66 11D
DOWN AMPNEY

# 646 Spirit Divine, Attend Our Prayers

1 Spir - it di - vine, at - tend our prayers, and make our
2 Come as the light: to us re - veal our emp - ti -
3 Come as the fire and purge our hearts like sac - ri -
4 Come as the dove and spread your wings, the wings of

hearts your home; de - scend with all your
ness and woe, and lead us in those
fic - ial flame; let our whole life an
peace - ful love; and let your church on

gra - cious powers: O come, great Spir - it, come!
paths of life where all the right - eous go.
off - ering be to our Re - deem - er's name.
earth be - come blest as the church a - bove.

5 Come as the wind, with rushing sound
and pentecostal grace,
that all of woman born may see
the glory of your face.

6 Spirit divine, attend our prayers;
make this lost world your home;
descend with all your gracious powers:
O come, great Spirit, come!

Text: Andrew Reed (1787–1862), alt.
Music: Melody Johann Crüger (1598–1662).

CM
GRÄFENBERG (NUN DANKET ALL)

# Spirit of the Living God 647

Spir - it of the liv - ing God, move a - mong us all;
*Spir - it of the liv - ing God, fall a - fresh on me;*

make us one in heart and mind, make us one in love:
*Spir - it of the liv - ing God, fall a - fresh on me;*

hum - ble, car - ing, self - less, shar - ing—
*break me, melt me, mould me, fill me—*

Spir - it of the liv - ing God, fill our lives with love!
*Spir - it of the liv - ing God, fall a - fresh on me!*

75 75 8 75
LIVING GOD

# 648 O Holy Spirit, Enter In

1 O Ho-ly Spir-it, en-ter in, and in our hearts
2 Left to our-selves, we sure-ly stray; O lead us on
3 O might-y Rock, O Source of life, let your good word

your work be-gin, and make our hearts your dwell-ing.
the nar-row way, with wis-est coun-sel guide us;
in doubt and strife be in us strong-ly burn-ing,

Sun of the soul, O Light di-vine, a-round and in
and give us stead-fast-ness, that we may fol-low you
that we be faith-ful un-to death and live in love

Text: Michael Schirmer (1606–1673); tr. Catherine Winkworth (1827–1878), adapt.
Music: Melody Philipp Nicolai (1556–1608); harm. Johann Hermann Schein (1586–1630).

887D 44 44 8
WIE SCHÖN LEUCHTET
*Alt. setting 622*

us bright-ly shine, your strength in us up-well - ing.
for - ev - er free, no mat - ter who de-rides us.
and ho - ly faith, from you true wis-dom learn - ing.

In your ra - diance life from heav-en now is
Gent - ly heal those hearts now bro - ken; give some
Lord, your mer - cy on us show - er; by your

giv - en ov - er - flow - ing, gift of gifts be - yond all know - ing.
to - ken you are near us, whom we trust to light and cheer us.
pow - er Christ con - fess - ing, we will cher - ish all your bless - ing.

# 649 Breathe on Me, Breath of God

1 Breathe on me, breath of God; fill me with life a-new, that I may love what thou dost love, and do what thou wouldst do.

2 Breathe on me, breath of God, un-til my heart is pure, un-til my will is one with thine to do and to en-dure.

3 Breathe on me, breath of God, till I am whol-ly thine, un-til this earth-ly part of me glows with thy fire di-vine.

4 Breathe on me, breath of God: so shall I nev-er die, but live with thee the per-fect life of thine e-ter-ni-ty.

Text: Edwin Hatch (1835–1889).
Music: Robert Jackson (1840–1914).

SM
TRENTHAM

# God's Spirit, As a Rising Gale  650

1 God's Spir-it, as a ris-ing gale, tear down our
2 God's Spir-it, as the breath of life, cre-a-tion's
3 God's Spir-it, as an i-cy blast, strike through the
4 God's Spir-it, as a heal-ing breeze, stream gent-ly
5 God's Spir-it, fierce and wild, and yet en-fold-ing

false tran-quil-li-ty; come surg-ing through our
source and guide and goal, breathe life in-to our
scorch-ing en-mi-ty that burns our hu-man
through our troub-led days, to set us on our
like a moth-er's womb, sur-prise us: bring us,

set-tled minds, de-mol-ish our com-pla-cen-cy!
souls a-gain; re-store our faith and make us whole.
love to ash; ex-tin-guish all hos-til-i-ty.
feet a-gain, with con-fi-dence, de-light, and praise.
new-ly born, with Je-sus leap-ing from the tomb!

Music: Melody *Beauties of Harmony*, Pittsburgh, 1814; harm. John Leon Hooker (1944– ) ©.

LM
BOURBON

# 651 God Sends Us the Spirit

1 God sends us the Spir - it to be - friend and help us.
2 Dark - ened roads are clear - er, hea - vy bur - dens light - er,
3 Now we are God's peo - ple, bond - ed by God's pres - ence,

Re - cre - ate and guide us, Spir - it - Friend.
when we're walk - ing with our Spir - it - Friend.
a - gents of God's pur - pose, Spir - it - Friend.

Spir - it who en - liv - ens, sanc - ti - fies, en - light - ens,
Now we need not fear the pow - ers of the dark - ness.
Lead us for - ward ev - er, slip - ping back - ward nev - er,

sets us free, is now our Spir - it - Friend.
None can o - ver - come our Spir - it - Friend.
to your re - made world, our Spir - it - Friend.

Text: Tom Colvin (1925– ).
Music: Melody Gonja trad.; adapt. Tom Colvin (1925– ); acc. Marty Haugen (1950– ).
*Text and adapt. © 1969, acc. © 1987 Hope Publishing Co.*

12 9 12 9 with refrain
NATOMAH

*Sing a., b., and c. after each stanza.*

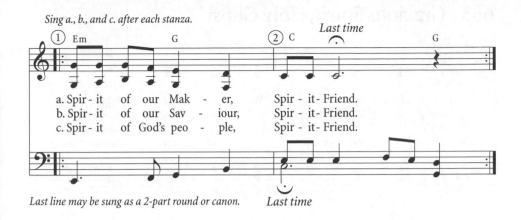

① Em ... G ... ② C ... *Last time* ... G

a. Spir - it of our Mak - er, Spir - it-Friend.
b. Spir - it of our Sav - iour, Spir - it-Friend.
c. Spir - it of God's peo - ple, Spir - it-Friend.

*Last line may be sung as a 2-part round or canon.*    *Last time*

## Fire of God, Thou Sacred Flame   652

1 Fire of God, thou sa - cred flame, Spir - it who in splen - dour came,
2 Breath of God, that swept in power in the pen - te - cost - al hour,
3 Truth of God, thy pierc - ing rays pen - e - trate my se - cret ways.
4 Love of God, thy grace pro - found know - eth neith - er age nor bound:

let thy heat my soul re - fine till it glows with love di - vine.
ho - ly breath, be thou in me source of vi - tal en - er - gy.
May the light that shames my sin guide me ho - lier paths to win.
come, my heart's own guest to be, dwell for ev - er - more in me.

Text: Albert Frederick Bayly (1901–1984). © 1988 Oxford University Press.
Music: Charles John King (1859–1934). © 1983 Hope Publishing Co.

77 77
Northampton

# 653 Gracious Spirit, Holy Ghost

1 Gracious Spirit, Holy Ghost, taught by
2 Love is kind, and suffers long; love is
3 Prophecy will fade away, melting
4 Faith will vanish into sight; hope be

thee, we covet most, of thy gifts at
meek, and thinks no wrong; love than death it-
in the light of day; love will ever
emptied in delight; love in heaven will

Pentecost, holy, heavenly love.
self more strong; therefore give us love.
with us stay; therefore give us love.
shine more bright; therefore give us love.

5 Faith and hope and love we see
joining hand in hand agree;
but the greatest of the three,
and the best, is love.

6 From the overshadowing
of thy gold and silver wing
shed on us, who to thee sing,
holy, heavenly love.

Text: Christopher Wordsworth (1807–1885).
Music: Friedrich Filitz (1804–1876); adapt. Peter Maurice (1803–1878).

77 75
CAPETOWN
Alt. tune CHARITY 654

# Holy Spirit, Gracious Guest 654

1 Ho - ly Spir - it, gra - cious guest, hear and
2 Faith that moun - tains could re - move, tongues of
3 Though I as a mar - tyr bleed, give my
4 Love is kind and suf - fers long, love is

grant our heart's re - quest for that gift su -
earth or heaven a - bove, knowl - edge, all things,
goods the poor to feed, all is vain if
pure and thinks no wrong, love than death it -

*Unison*

preme and best: ho - ly, heaven - ly love.
emp - ty prove if I have no love.
love I need: there - fore give me love.
self more strong: there - fore give us love.

5 Prophecy will fade away,
  melting in the light of day;
  love will ever with us stay:
  therefore give us love.

6 Faith and hope and love we see
  joining hand in hand agree—
  but the greatest of the three,
  and the best, is love.

Text: I Cor. 13; para. Christopher Wordsworth (1807–1885); rev. *Hymns for Today's Church.*
© *1982 Hope Publishing Co.*
Music: John Stainer (1840–1901).

77 75
CHARITY
*Alt. tune* CAPETOWN *653*

# 655 Holy Spirit, Ever Dwelling

1 Holy Spirit, ever dwelling in the holiest realms of light; Holy Spirit, ever brooding o'er a world of gloom and night; Holy Spirit,

2 Holy Spirit, ever living as the church's very life; Holy Spirit, ever striving through us in a ceaseless strife; Holy Spirit,

3 Holy Spirit, ever working through the church's ministry, quickening, strengthening, and absolving, setting captive sinners free; Holy Spirit,

Text: Timothy Rees (1874–1939), alt. © *Mowbray (an imprint of Cassell plc, London).*
Music: Melody Dutch trad.; arr. Julius Röntgen (1855–1933). © *Estate of Julius Röntgen.*

87 87D
IN BABILONE

ev - er rais - ing those of earth to
ev - er form - ing in the church the
ev - er bind - ing age to age and

thrones on high; liv - ing, life - im - part - ing Spir - it,
mind of Christ: you we praise with end - less wor - ship
soul to soul in com - mun - ion nev - er end - ing,

you we praise and mag - ni - fy.
for your gifts and fruits un - priced.
you we wor - ship and ex - tol.

# 656 She Comes Sailing on the Wind

*Unison Refrain*

She comes sail-ing on the wind, her wings flash-ing in the sun, on a jour-ney just be-gun, she flies on.

And in the pas-sage of her flight, her song rings out through the night, full of laugh-ter, full of light, she flies on.

*Last time*
(3 To a)
(5 Long)

1 Si - lent wa - ters rock - ing  on the morn-ing of our birth, like an
2 Ma - ny were the dream-ers  whose eyes were giv - en sight when the
3 gen - tle girl in Gal - i - lee  a gen - tle breeze she came, a
4 Fly - ing to the riv - er,  she wait - ed cir - cling high a -
5 af - ter the deep dark - ness  that fell up - on the world, af - ter

Text and melody: Gordon Light (1944– ); arr. Andrew Donaldson (1951– ) ©.
*Text and melody © 1987 Common Cup Company.*

Irregular with refrain
SHE FLIES ON

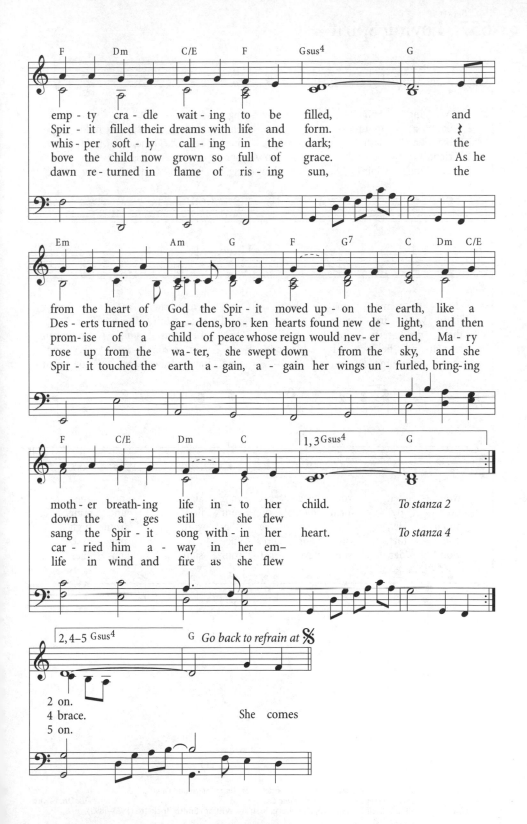

emp - ty cra - dle wait - ing to be filled, and
Spir - it filled their dreams with life and form.
whis - per soft - ly call - ing in the dark; the
bove the child now grown so full of grace. As he
dawn re - turned in flame of ris - ing sun, the

from the heart of God the Spir - it moved up - on the earth, like a
Des - erts turned to gar - dens, bro - ken hearts found new de - light, and then
prom - ise of a child of peace whose reign would nev - er end, Ma - ry
rose up from the wa - ter, she swept down from the sky, and she
Spir - it touched the earth a - gain, a - gain her wings un - furled, bring-ing

1, 3

moth - er breath-ing life in - to her child.     *To stanza 2*
down the a - ges still she flew
sang the Spir - it song with - in her heart.     *To stanza 4*
car - ried him a - way in her em—
life in wind and fire as she flew

2, 4–5          *Go back to refrain at* 𝄋

2 on.
4 brace.     She comes
5 on.

# 657 Loving Spirit

1 Lov - ing Spir - it, lov - ing Spir - it, you have
2 Like a moth - er, you en - fold me, hold my
3 Like a fath - er, you pro - tect me, teach me
4 Friend and lov - er, in your close - ness I am
5 Lov - ing Spir - it, lov - ing Spir - it, you have

chos - en me to be— you have drawn me to your
life with - in your own, feed me with your ver - y
the dis - cern - ing eye, hoist me up up - on your
known and held and blessed; in your prom - ise is my
chos - en me to be— you have drawn me to your

won - der, you have set your sign on me.
bo - dy, form me of your flesh and bone.
shoul - der, let me see the world from high.
com - fort, in your pres - ence I may rest.
won - der, you have set your sign on me.

Text: Shirley Erena Murray (1931– ). © 1987 The Hymn Society in the United States and Canada.
All rights reserved. Used by permission of Hope Publishing Co.
Melody Gross Catholisch Gesangbuch, Nürnberg, 1631; arr. William Smith Rockstro (1823–1895).

87 87
OMNI DIE DIC MARIA

# Filled with the Spirit's Power 658

1 Filled with the Spir - it's power, with one ac - cord the in - fant
2 Now with the mind of Christ set us on fire, that un - i -
3 Wi - den our love, good Spir - it, to em - brace in your strong

church con-fessed its ris - en Lord. O Ho - ly Spir - it, in the church to -
ty may be our great de - sire. Give joy and peace; give faith to hear your
care peo-ple of ev - ery race. Like wind and fire with life a - mong us

day no less your power of fel - low-ship dis - play.
call, and read - i - ness in each to work for all.
move, till we are known as Christ's, and Chris - tians prove.

Text: J. R. Peacey (1896–1971), alt. © 1978 Hope Publishing Co.
Music: Cyril Vincent Taylor (1907–1991). © 1985 Hope Publishing Co.

10 10 10 10
SHELDONIAN

# 659 O Canada

1 O Can-a-da! Our home and na-tive land! True pa-triot
1 Ô Ca-na-da! Ter-re de nos aï-eux, ton front est

love in all thy sons com-mand. With glow-ing hearts we
ceint de fleu-rons glo-ri-eux! Car ton bras sait por-ter l'é-

see thee rise, the true north, strong and free! From
pé - e, il sait por-ter la croix! Ton his-

far and wide, O Can-a-da, we stand on guard for
toire est une é-po-pé - e des plus bril-lants ex-

thee. God keep our land glo-rious and free!
ploits. Et ta va-leur, de foi trem-pé - e,

English Text: Robert Stanley Weir (1856–1926); French text: Adolphe B. Routhier (1839–1920).
  © Secretary of State for Canada.
Music: Melody Calixa Lavallée (1842–1891); arr. Frederick C. Silvester (1901–1966).
  Arr. © Estate of Frederick C. Silvester, c/o Mrs. Wendy Verduijn.

10 10 86 86 8 10 10
O CANADA

O Can - a - da, we stand on guard for thee.
*pro - té - ge - ra nos foy - ers et nos droits,*

O Can - a - da, we stand on guard for thee.
*pro - té - ge - ra nos foy - ers et nos droits.*

2 O Canada! Where pines and maples grow,
 great prairies spread and lordly rivers flow,
 how dear to us thy broad domain,
 from east to western sea!
 Thou land of hope for all who toil!
 Thou true north strong and free!
  *Refrain*

3 O Canada! Beneath thy shining skies
 may stalwart sons and gentle maidens rise
 to keep thee steadfast through the years
 from east to western sea,
 our own belovèd native land,
 our true north strong and free!
  *Refrain*

4 Ruler supreme, who hearest humble prayer,
 hold our dominion in thy loving care.
 Help us to find, O God, in thee
 a lasting rich reward,
 as waiting for the better day,
 we ever stand on guard.
  *Refrain*

2 *Sous l'oeil de Dieu, près du fleuve géant,*
 *le Canadien grandit en espérant.*
 *Il est né d'une race fière,*
 *béni fut son berceau.*
 *Le ciel a marqué sa carrière*
 *dans ce monde nouveau.*
 *Toujours gudé par sa lumière,*
 *il gardera l'honneur de son drapeau,*
 *il gardera l'honneur de son drapeau.*

3 *De son patron, précurseur du vrai Dieu,*
 *il porte au front l'auréole de feu.*
 *Ennemi de la tyrannie mais plein de loyauté,*
 *il veut garder dans l'harmonie,*
 *sa fière liberté;*
 *et par l'effort de son génie,*
 *sur notre sol asseoir la vérité,*
 *sur notre sol asseoir la vérité.*

4 *Amour sacré du trône et de l'autel,*
 *remplis nos coeurs de ton souffle immortel!*
 *Parmi les races étrangères, notre guide est la loi:*
 *sachons être un peuple de frères,*
 *sous le joug de la foi.*
 *Et répétons, comme nos pères,*
 *le cri vainqueur: "Pour le Christ et le roi,"*
 *le cri vainqueur: "Pour le Christ et le roi."*

# 660 God Save Our Gracious Queen

1 God save our gra - cious Queen, long live our
2 Thy choic - est gifts in store on her be
3 Our loved do - min - ion bless with her peace and

no - ble Queen: God save the Queen. Send her vic -
pleased to pour; long may she reign. May she de -
hap - pi - ness from shore to shore; and let our

to - ri - ous, hap - py and glo - ri - ous,
fend our laws, and ev - er give us cause
na - tion be loy - al, u - ni - ted, free,

long to reign o - ver us, God save the Queen.
to sing with heart and voice, God save the Queen.
true to her - self and thee for ev - er - more.

Text: St. 1–2, author unknown; st. 3, Robert Murray (1832?–1910).
Music: Melody *Thesaurus Musicus*, 1743; arr. Henry Walford Davies (1869–1941).
*Arr. © Estate of Henry Walford Davies. Used by permission of Oxford University Press.*

664 6664
NATIONAL ANTHEM

# May the Lord, Mighty God 661

May the Lord, might-y God, bless and

keep you for-ev - er, grant you peace, per - fect

*Last Time*

peace, cour - age in ev - ery en - dea - vour.

Lift your eyes and see God's face, full of

*Optional harmony*

Lift your eyes and see God's face, full of

grace for - ev - er. May the Lord, might - y

grace for - ev - er. May the Lord, might - y

*To beginning*

God, bless and keep you for - ev - er.

*To beginning*

God, bless and keep you for - ev - er.

Text: Num. 6.24–26.
Music: Pao-chen Li (1907–1979); adapt. Asian American Hymnal editors, 1980.
    *Adapt. © 1983 Abingdon Press (Administered by The Copyright Company, Nashville, TN).*
    *All rights reserved. International copyright secured. Used by permission.*

Irregular
WEN-TI

# 662 The Trees of the Field

You shall go out with joy and be led forth with peace.

The moun-tains and the hills will break forth be-

fore you. There'll be shouts of joy and all the trees of the

field will clap, will clap their hands. And all the trees of the

field will clap their hands, the trees of the field will

Text: Is. 55. 12; para. Steffi Geiser Rubin (1950– ).

Music: Melody Stuart Dauermann (1944– ); harm. Patrick Wedd (1948– ) ©.

*Para. and melody © 1975 Lillenas Publishing Co. (Administered by The Copyright Company, Nashville, TN).*

*All rights reserved. International copyright secured. Used by permission.*

Irregular

THE TREES OF THE FIELD

*clap their hands. The trees of the field will clap their hands,*

*while you go out with joy. You shall go*

*To beginning at %*

## Bwana Awabariki 663

Bwa - na a - wa - ba - ri - ki, Bwa - na a - wa - ba - ri - ki,
*May God grant you a bless-ing, may God grant you a bless-ing,*

Bwa - na a - wa - ba - ri - ki mi - le - le.
*may God grant you a bless-ing ev - er - more.*

U - ki - mcha Bwa - na. Bwa - na a - wa - ba - ri - ki.
*Re - vere the Lord. May God grant you a bless-ing.*

Text: Swahili hymn.
Music: Swahili trad.

Irregular
BWANA AWABARIKI

# 664 In Jesus' Name, We Pause to Pray

In Je-sus' name, we pause to pray: give
us our dai-ly bread to-day; bless us with strength, that
we may bless our neigh-bour out of grate-ful-ness.

Text: Rusty Edwards (1955– ). © 1989 Hope Publishing Co.
Music: Thomas Tallis (1505?–1585).

LM
TALLIS'S CANON
*Higher key 14, 25*

# 665 To God, with the Lamb and the Dove

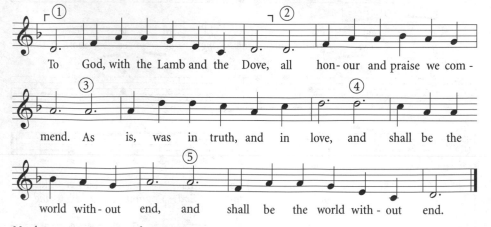

To God, with the Lamb and the Dove, all hon-our and praise we com-
mend. As is, was in truth, and in love, and shall be the
world with-out end, and shall be the world with-out end.

*May be sung as a 5-part round or canon.*

Text: Christopher Smart (1722–1771).
Music: *The Sacred Harp*, Mason, 1844.

88 88 8
EDGEFIELD

# Doxology

## 666

Praise God from whom all blessings flow;
praise him, all creatures here below;
Praise him above, ye heavenly host;
praise Father, Son, and Holy Ghost.

Text: Thomas Ken (1637–1710).

## 667

Praise God from whom all blessings flow;
praise God, all creatures high and low;
give thanks to God in love made known:
Creator, Word, and Spirit, one.

Text: Thomas Ken (1637–1710), adapt.

## 668

Praise God from whom all blessings flow,
in heaven above and earth below;
one God, three persons, we adore—
to God be praise for evermore!

Text: Thomas Ken (1637–1710); rcv. *Hymns
for Today's Church,* alt. © 1982 Hope Publishing Co.

## 669

Praise God the Source of life and birth,
praise God the Word, who came to earth.
Praise God the Spirit, holy flame.
All glory, honour to God's name.

Text: Ruth Duck (1947– ). © 1990 The Pilgrim Press.

## 670

Nous célébrons l'amour vivant:
dans le Père il est vigilant,
dans l'Esprit il est créateur,
et dans le Fils libérateur.

Texte: *Le Psautier français.* © 1995 Réveil Publications.

## 671

Gloire à Dieu notre créateur,
gloire à l'Esprit consolateur,
au Fils unique Jésus Christ,
au Dieu sauveur qui nous bénit.

Texte: *Le Psautier français.* © 1995 Réveil Publications.

## 672

Praise God from whom all blessings flow.
Praise God, all creatures high and low.
Praise God, in Jesus fully known:
Creator, Word, and Spirit one.

Text: Brian Wren (1936– ). © 1989 Hope Publishing Co.

Music: Melody Geneva, 1551.

LM
OLD 100TH

## 673

O thou in whom we move and live,
whose Spirit hovers like a dove;
we worship you in Christ and give
our praises for your steadfast love.

Text: David Beebe (1931– ). © 1990 The Pilgrim Press.

## 674

Fountain of being, you we praise,
eternal Word and Spirit blessed;
one God through everlasting days,
to you all glory be addressed.

Text: Paul Gibson (1932– ) ©.

## 675

*Mohawk text*

Ron we sen naiens ne Niio
Ron wa sen saiens ne non kwe,
Ron wa sen naiens neh ne ken
Ron wa sen naiens ro ni ha.

Tr. *Handbook for the Anglican
Indigenous Circle*, 1997.

## 676

*Inuktitut text*

ᐊᖕᒥᓂᖅ ᐱᖁᖕᕿᓇᓪᑦ
ᑦᐊᐊ ᐱᑎᑦ ᑐᓂᐊᖕᑦ,
ᐃᒻᒪᒪᑭᑉᑦ ᐃᓕᑎᐁᖅᑉᑦ
ᐅᒪᖕᒥᓄᓪᒍ ᐱᑭᖕᑦ.

Tr. Benjamin T. Arreak (1947– ) ©.

Music: Melody Geneva, 1551.

# 677 Responses to the Commandments

Lord, have mer-cy up-on us,   and in-cline our hearts to keep this law.

*After last commandment or Summary of the Law*

Lord, have mer-cy up-on us,   and write all   these thy
*both*

laws   in   our   hearts,   we   be-seech thee.

Music: John Merbecke (1510?–1585?); arr. and organ acc. Healey Willan (1880–1968).
*Arr. and organ acc. © Estate of Healey Willan.*

*May be sung in three-fold, six-fold, or nine-fold form.*

Music: John Merbecke (1510?–1585?); arr. and organ acc. Healey Willan (1880–1968).
*Arr. and organ acc. © Estate of Healey Willan.*

# 679 Gloria

Music: John Merbecke (1510?–1585?); arr. and organ acc. Healey Willan (1880–1968).
*Arr. and organ acc. © Estate of Healey Willan.*

O Lord, the on-ly-be-got-ten Son, Je-sus Christ; O Lord God,

Lamb of God, Son of the Fa - ther, that tak-est a - way the

sin of the world, have mer-cy up-on us. Thou that tak-est a -

way the sin of the world, re-ceive our prayer. Thou that sit-test at the

# Gospel Responses   680

*Before the Gospel*

Reader — The Lord be with you.

People — And with thy spirit.

Reader — The Holy Gospel of our Lord Jesus Christ according to Matthew.
Mark.
Luke.
John.

People — Glo-ry be to thee, O Lord.

*After the Gospel*

Reader — The Gos-pel of Christ.

People — Praise be to thee, O Christ.

*Best when sung unaccompanied.*

Music: Plainsong; arr. Healey Willan (1880–1968). *Arr. © Estate of Healey Willan.*

## 681   The Nicene Creed

I be-lieve in one God, the Fa-ther al-migh-ty, ma-ker of hea-ven and earth, and of all things vi-si-ble and in-vi-si-ble; and in one Lord Je-sus Christ, the on-ly-be-got-ten Son of God,

Music: John Merbecke (1510?–1585?); arr. and organ acc. Healey Willan (1880–1968).
*Arr. and organ acc. © Estate of Healey Willan.*

by the Ho-ly Ghost of the Vir-gin Ma-ry, and was made man,

and was cru-ci-fi-ed al-so for us un-der Pon-tius Pi-late.

He suf-fer-ed and was bu-ri-ed, and the third day he rose a-gain

ac-cord-ing to the scrip-tures, and as-cend-ed in-to heaven,

re - sur - rec- tion of the dead, and the life of the world to come. A - men.

# Sursum Corda 682

*Celebrant*  *People*

The Lord be with you. And with thy spir - it.

*Celebrant*

Lift up your hearts.

*People*

We lift them up un - to the Lord.

*Celebrant*

Let us give thanks un - to our Lord God.

*People*

It is meet and right so to do.

Music: Plainsong.

# 683  Sanctus

Music: John Merbecke (1510?–1585?); arr. and organ acc. Healey Willan (1880–1968).
*Arr. and organ acc. © Estate of Healey Willan.*

# The Lord's Prayer  684

Our Fa - ther, who art in heav-en, hal-low-ed be thy name,

thy king-dom come, thy will be done, on earth as it is in heav-en.

Give us this day our dai - ly bread. And for-give us our tres-pass- es,

Music: John Merbecke (1510?–1585?); arr. and organ acc. Healey Willan (1880–1968).
*Arr. and organ acc. © Estate of Healey Willan.*

# Agnus Dei   685

O Lamb of God, that tak-est a-way the sin of the world: have mer-cy up-on us. O Lamb of God, that tak-est a-way the sin of the world: have mer-cy up-on us. O Lamb of God, that tak-est a-way the sin of the world: grant us thy peace.

Music: John Merbecke (1510?–1585?); arr. and organ acc. Healey Willan (1880–1968).
*Arr. and organ acc. © Estate of Healey Willan.*

# 686  Glory to God

Music: *New Plainsong*, David Hurd (1950– ). © *1981 G.I.A. Publications, Inc.*

you a - lone are the Most High, Je - sus Christ, with the Ho - ly Spir - it,

in the glo - ry of God the Fa - ther. A - men.

## 687  Kyrie Eleison

Ky - ri - e  e - le - i - son.    Ky - ri - e  e - le - i - son.

Music: *New Plainsong*, David Hurd (1950– ). © *1981 G.I.A. Publications, Inc.*

# 688 Trisagion

Ho - ly God, holy and might-y, ho - ly im-mor - tal one,

have mer-cy on us. Ho - ly God, ho - ly and might - y,

ho - ly im-mor - tal one, have mer - cy on us.

Music: *New Plainsong*, David Hurd (1950– ). © *1981 G.I.A. Publications, Inc.*

Ho - ly God, holy and might - y,

ho - ly im - mor - tal one, have mer - cy on us.

# 689  Holy, Holy, Holy Lord

Ho - ly,  ho - ly,  ho - ly Lord,  God of pow - er and might,

hea - ven and earth are full of your glo - ry.  Ho - san - na

in the high - est.  Bless - ed is he who comes in the

name of the Lord.  Ho - san - na in the high - est.

Music: *New Plainsong,* David Hurd (1950– ). *© 1981 G.I.A. Publications, Inc.*

# Lamb of God  690

Lamb of God, you take a-way the sins of the world: have mer-cy on us. Lamb of God, you take a-way the sins of the world: have mer-cy on us. Lamb of God, you take a-way the sins of the world: grant us peace.

Music: *New Plainsong,* David Hurd (1950– ). © *1981 G.I.A. Publications, Inc.*

# 691  Glory to God

*Throughout this setting, the sections marked A could be sung by a
cantor or semi-chorus, with the congregation responding at the B sections.*

Music: *Mass of St. Denis*, Barrie Cabena (1933– ) ©.

heaven-ly king, al-migh-ty God and Fa-ther, we wor-ship

heaven-ly king, al-migh-ty God and Fa-ther, we wor-ship

you, we give you thanks, we praise you for your glo-ry.

you, we give you thanks, we praise you for your glo-ry.

Lord Je-sus Christ, on-ly Son of the Fa - ther,

Lord Je - sus Christ, on - ly Son of the Fa - ther,

Lord God, Lamb of God, you take a - way the sin of the

Lord God, Lamb of God, you take a - way the sin of the

For you a - lone are the Ho - ly One, you a -

For you a - lone are the Ho - ly One, you a -

lone are the Lord, you a - lone are the Most High,

lone are the Lord, you a - lone are the Most High,

Je - sus Christ, with the Ho - ly Spir - it, in the glo - ry of

Je - sus Christ, with the Ho - ly Spir - it, in the glo - ry of

God the Fa - ther. A - men.

God the Fa - ther. A - men.

# 693 Trisagion

Music: *Mass of St. Denis*, Barrie Cabena (1933– ) ©.

# Holy, Holy, Holy Lord   694

*The sections marked A could be sung by a cantor or semi-chorus,
with the congregation responding at the B sections.*

Music: *Mass of St. Denis,* Barrie Cabena (1933– ) ©.

name of the Lord. Ho - san - na in the high - est.

name of the Lord. Ho - san - na in the high - est.

# 695 Acclamation Christ Has Died

Christ has died. Christ is ris - en.

Christ has died. Christ is ris - en.

Christ will come a - gain.

Christ will come a - gain.

Music: *Mass of St. Denis*, Barrie Cabena (1933– ) ©.

# Acclamation Dying You Destroyed 696

Music: *Mass of St. Denis*, Barrie Cabena (1933– ) ©.

# 697 Acclamation We Remember His Death

Music: *Mass of St. Denis,* Barrie Cabena (1933– ) ©.

# Acclamation Glory to You  698

Glo - ry to you for - e - ver and e - ver.

Glo - ry to you for - e - ver and e - ver.

*Last time*

Glo - ry to you for - e - ver and e - ver. A - men.

Glo - ry to you for - e - ver and e - ver. A - men.

Music: *Mass of St. Denis*, Barrie Cabena (1933– ) ©.

# Amen  699

A - men.

A - men.

Music: *Mass of St. Denis*, Barrie Cabena (1933– ) ©.

## 700  Acclamation  We Praise You

We praise you, we bless you, we give thanks to
you, and we pray to you, Lord our God.

Music: *Mass of St. Denis*, Barrie Cabena (1933– ) ©.

## 701  Lamb of God

Lamb of God, you

*The sections marked A could be sung by a cantor or
semi-chorus, with the congregation responding at the B sections.*

Music: *Mass of St. Denis*, Barrie Cabena (1933– ) ©.

# 702

*Refrain*

Glo - ry to God in the high - est, and

peace to his peo - ple on earth.   *To st. 1–3*

*final ending*

peo - ple on earth.

Music: *Mass of Hope*, Becket Gerald Senchur (1946– ). © 1977 St. Vincent Archabbey, Latrobe, Pa. 15650.

*To refrain*

1 Lord God, heav-en-ly King, al-might-y God and
Fa-ther, we wor-ship you, we give you thanks, we
praise you for your glo-ry.

2 Lord Je-sus Christ, on-ly Son of the Fa-ther,

Lord God, Lamb of God, you take a-way the sin of the world: have mer - cy on us; you are seat - ed at the right hand of the Fa - ther: re - ceive our prayer.

*To refrain*

3 For you a-lone are the Ho - ly One, you a-lone are the

Lord, you a - lone are the Most High, Je - sus Christ, with the Ho - ly Spir - it, in the glo - ry of God the Fa - ther.

*To refrain*

A - - - men.

*May be sung unaccompanied.*

*Small notes are for organ only*

Music: *Deutsche Messe*, Franz Schubert (1797–1828); arr. Richard Proulx (1937– ).
    Arr. © 1985, 1989 G.I.A. Publications, Inc..

*Best when sung unaccompanied. May be sung three times.*

Music: Russian chant.

*Best when sung unaccompanied. May be sung three times.*

Music: *The Divine Liturgy.* © 1977, 1982 St. Vladmir's Seminary Press. Adapt. Brigid Coult (1953– ) ©.

*Items 708–717 may be sung before the Gospel, using as the*
*verse the Sentence from the Proper of the Christian year in*
*the lectionary of* The Book of Alternative Services.

## 708

Refrain: Plainsong, Mode 6.

## 709

Refrain: VICTORY; Giovanni Pierluigi da Palestrina (1525–1594); adapt. William Henry Monk (1823–1889).

Refrain: O FILII ET FILIAE; *Airs sur les hymnes sacrez, odes et noëls,* 1623.

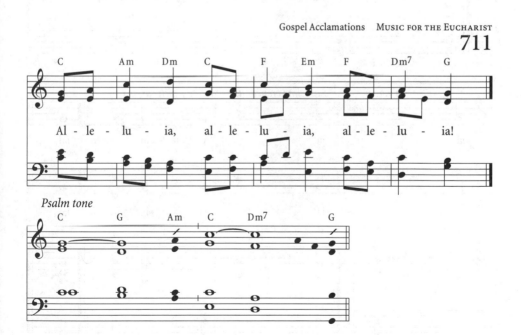

Refrain: A. Gregory Murray (1905–1992). © *McCrimmon Publishing Co. Ltd.*
Psalm tone: George Black (1931– ). © *Concacan Inc.*

*May be sung as a 3-part round or canon.*

Music: *Mass of Remembrance*, Marty Haugen (1950– ). © 1987 G.I.A. Publications, Inc.

1 Speak, O Lord, your ser - vant is lis - tening,

2 "I am the light of the world," says the Lord,

3 Bless - ed are you, O Lord of cre - a - tion, re -

4 The Word of God came and lived here a - mong us, so

you have the words of ev - er - last - ing life.

"All who fol - low me shall have the light of life."

veal - ing your king - dom to the hum - ble and weak.

all who be - lieve might be the chil - dren of God.

*To refrain*

* Choose either part.

Text and music: Fintan O'Carroll (1922–1981) and Christopher Walker (1947– ).
© 1985 Fintan O'Carroll and Christopher Walker. Published by OCP Publications.

*Verses*

1 The Word of the Lord lasts for - ev - er.
2 God brings the world to him - self,
3 The Word of the Lord is a - live, the

What is the Word that is liv - ing? It is
now through his Christ re - con - cil - ing; he has
Word of God is ac - tive— it can

*To refrain*

brought to us through his Son Je - sus Christ.
trust - ed us with the news of re - deem - ing love.
judge our thoughts, bring us clos - er to the Fa - ther.

*\* Guitar chords marked with an asterisk are to be strummed once.*

# 719 Holy, Holy, Holy Lord

Music: LAND OF REST; American trad.; adapt. Marcia Pruner (19??– ); harm. John Campbell (1950– ) ©.
*Adapt. © 1980 Church Pension Fund.*

# Acclamation Christ Has Died 720

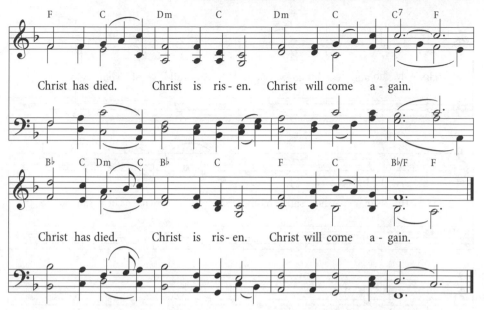

Christ has died.    Christ is ris-en.    Christ will come a-gain.

Christ has died.    Christ is ris-en.    Christ will come a-gain.

*For a shorter version, sing the first two measures and the last two measures.*

Music: Land of Rest; American trad.; adapt. Richard Proulx (1937– ); harm. John Campbell (1950– ) ©.
    Adapt. © 1986 G.I.A. Publications, Inc.

# Amen 721

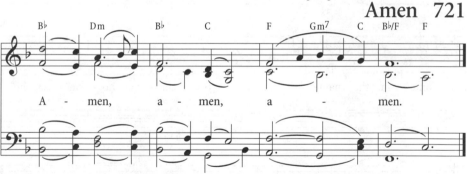

A - men,    a - men,    a - men.

Music: Land of Rest; American trad.; adapt. Richard Proulx (1937– ); harm. John Campbell (1950 ) ©.
    Adapt. © 1986 G.I.A. Publications, Inc.

# Holy, Holy, Holy Lord 722

*Unison*

Ho-ly, ho-ly, ho-ly Lord,    Lord God of power and might,

Music: Picardy; French carol (17th cent.); arr. Patrick Wedd (1948– ) ©.

heav'n and earth are full, full of your glo - ry. Ho - san - na, ho - san - na, ho - san - na, ho - san - na in the high - est. Bless - ed is he who comes, who comes in the name of the Lord. Ho - san - na, ho - san - na, ho - san - na, ho - san - na in the high - est.

## Acclamation Dying You Destroyed Our Death   723

Dy - ing you de - stroyed our death, ris - ing you re - stored our life. Lord Je - sus, come in glo - ry.

Music: PICARDY; French carol (17th cent.); adapt. George Black (1931– ) ©.

## Acclamation We Remember His Death   724

We re - mem - ber his death, we pro - claim his re - sur - rec - tion, we a - wait his com - ing in glo - ry.

Music: PICARDY; French carol (17th cent.); adapt. George Black (1931– ) ©.

## Amen   725

A - men, a - men.

Music: PICARDY; French carol (17th cent.); adapt. George Black (1931– ) ©.

## 729 Acclamation We Remember His Death

We re-mem-ber his death, we pro-claim his re-sur-rec-tion,

we a-wait his com-ing in glo - - - ry.

*Best when sung unaccompanied.*

Music: Byzantine; arr. George Black (1931– ) ©.

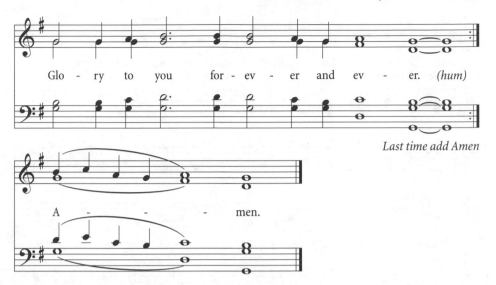

Glo - ry to you for - ev - er and ev - er. *(hum)*

*Last time add Amen*

A - - - men.

*Best when sung unaccompanied.*

Music: Byzantine; arr. George Black (1931– ) ©.

We praise you, we bless you, we give thanks to you,

and we pray to you. Lord our God.

*Best when sung unaccompanied.*

Music: Byzantine; arr. George Black (1931– ) ©.

# 732  Holy, Holy, Holy Lord

Ho - ly, ho - ly, ho - ly Lord,    God    of pow-er and might,

heav'n    and earth    are full    of your glo - ry.    Ho -

san - na in the high-est,    ho - san - na    in    the high-est.

Blessed is he who comes    in the name    of the Lord.    Ho -

Music: *Community Mass*, Richard Proulx (1937– ). *© 1971, 1977 G.I.A. Publications, Inc.*

**Acclamation** Christ Has Died **733**

*Unison* *Descant*

Christ has died; Christ is ris-en; Christ will come a-gain.

Music: *Community Mass*, Richard Proulx (1937– ). © 1971, 1977 G.I.A. Publications, Inc.

**Amen 734**

*Unison* *Descant*

A - men, a - men, a - men.

Music: *Community Mass*, Richard Proulx (1937– ). © 1971, 1977 G.I.A. Publications, Inc.

# 735  Holy, Holy, Holy Lord

Ho - ly, ho - ly, ho - ly Lord, God of power and might.

Ho - ly, ho - ly, ho - ly Lord, God of power and might,

heav - en and earth are full,    full    of your glo -

ry. Ho - san - na    in    the high - est,    ho - san - na

*Small notes are for organ only.*

Music: *Deutsche Messe*, Franz Schubert (1797–1828); arr. Richard Proulx (1937– ).
   *Arr.* © 1985, 1989 G.I.A. Publications, Inc.

in the high - est. Bless - ed is he who comes

in the name of the Lord. Ho - san - na in the

high - est, ho - san - na in the high - est.

## 741  Glory to You

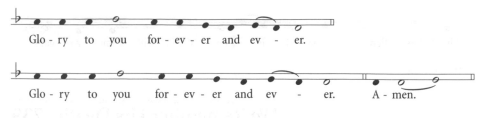

Glo - ry  to  you  for - ev - er  and  ev  -  er.

Glo - ry  to  you  for - ev - er  and  ev  -  er.  A - men.

Music: Plainsong.

## 742  We Praise You

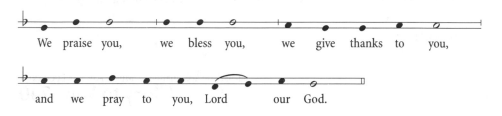

We  praise  you,  we  bless  you,  we  give  thanks  to  you,

and  we  pray  to  you, Lord  our  God.

Music: Plainsong.

## 743  We Praise Thee

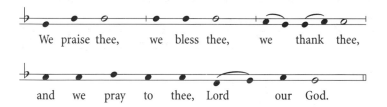

We  praise  thee,  we  bless  thee,  we  thank  thee,

and  we  pray  to  thee, Lord  our  God.

Music: Plainsong.

Text: Matt. 6.9–13. *Tr. © 1989 English Language Liturgical Consultation.*
Music: Nicholas Rimsky-Korsakov (1844–1908); arr. George Black (1931– ) ©.

Save us from the time of trial, and de - liv - er us from e - vil.

For the king - dom, the power, and the glo - ry are yours,

now and for - ev - er. A - men.

# 748  Venite (Psalm 95.1–7)

Samuel Arnold (1740–1802)

Richard Goodson (1655?–1718)

Come, let us ' sing to • the ' Lord;*
    let us shout for joy to the ' rock of ' our sal'vation.
Let us come before his ' presence • with ' thanksgiving*
    and raise a loud ' shout to ' him with ' psalms.

For the Lord is a ' great ' God,*
    and a great ' king a•bove ' all ' gods.
In his hand are the ' caverns • of the ' earth,*
    and the ' heights of • the ' hills are • his ' also.
The sea is ' his and • he ' made it,*
    and his hands have ' moulded • the ' dry ' land.

Come, let us bow down, and ' bend the ' knee,*
    and ' kneel be•fore the ' Lord our ' maker.
For he is the Lord our God,
and we are the people of his pasture and the ' sheep of • his ' hand.*
    Oh, that today you would ' hearken ' to his ' voice!

Glory to the Father, and ' to the ' Son,*
    and ' to the ' Holy ' Spirit:
as it was in the be'ginning, • is ' now,*
    and will be for'ever. A'men.

# Jubilate (Psalm 100)   749

Be joyful in the Lord, *all* you lands;
serve the *Lord* with gladness
and come before his presence *with* a song.

Know this: the Lord him-*self* is God;
he himself has made us, and *we* are his;
we are his people and the *sheep of* his pasture.

Enter his *gates* with thanksgiving;
go into his *courts* with praise;*
give thanks to him and call u-*pon* his name.

For the *Lord* is good;
his mercy is *ev*-er-lasting;
and his faithfulness endures from *age* to age.

Music: Patrick Wedd (1948– ) ©.

*Items 749, 750, 752, 756, and 758–760 use a similar method of fitting words to music. The syllable printed in bold italics is sung on the first black note after the reciting note. Subsequent words are matched individually to the remaining notes, or by syllables with hyphens indicating the divisions.*

# 750  Christ Our Passover

Al - le - lu - ia, al - le - lu - ia, al - le - lu - ia!

*A cantor sings the Alleluias. All repeat them. A cantor or choir sings the verses.*
*All repeat the Alleluias after each stanza.*

1  Christ our passover has been sacrificed for us;
2  therefore let us keep *the* feast
3  not with the old leaven, the leaven of ma-*lice* and evil,
4  but with the unleavened bread of sinceri-*ty* and truth.
    *R*  Alleluia, alleluia, alleluia!

1  Christ being raised from the dead will never die again;
2  death no longer has dominion o-*ver* him.
1  The death that he died, he died to sin, once for all;
2  but the life he lives, he lives *to* God.
3  So also consider yourselves *dead* to sin,
4  and alive to God in Jesus *Christ* our Lord.
    *R*  Alleluia, alleluia, alleluia!

1  Christ has been raised from the dead,
2  the first fruits of those who have fallen *a*-sleep.
1  For since by a man came death,
2  by a man has come also the resurrection of *the* dead.
3  For as in A-*dam* all die,
4  so also in Christ shall all be *made* a-live.
    *R*  Alleluia, alleluia, alleluia!

Text: I Cor. 5.7–8, Rom. 6.9–11, I Cor. 15.20–22.
Music: VULPIUS; Melchior Vulpius (1560?–1615); harm. and psalm tone George Black (1931– ).
   © 1986 Anglican Book Centre.

# O Gracious Light (*Phos hilaron*) 751

*Unison*

1 O gra-cious Light, pure bright-ness of the ev-er-liv-ing Fa-ther in heaven,

O Je-sus Christ, ho-ly and bless-ed! 2 Now as we come to the set-ting

of the sun, and our eyes be-hold the ves-per light,  we sing your prais-es, O God:

Fa-ther, Son, and Ho-ly Spir-it. 3 You are wor-thy at all times to be

praised by hap-py voic-es,  O Son of God,  O Giv-er of life,

and  to  be  glo-ri-fied  through all  the  worlds.

*May be sung unaccompanied with a few voices humming D as a drone throughout.*

Music: George Black (1931– ) ©.

# 752  O Gracious Light (*Phos hilaron*)

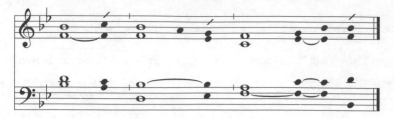

O gracious **Light,**
pure brightness of the everliving Father *in* heaven,
O Jesus Christ, ho-*ly* and blessèd!

Now as we come to the setting of the **sun,**
and our eyes behold the ves-*per* light,
we sing your praises, O God: Father, Son, and **Ho**-ly Spirit.

You are worthy at all times to be praised by happy **voices,**
O Son of God, O Giver *of* life,
and to be glorified through **all** the worlds.

Music: George Black (1931– ) ©.

Be - hold now, bless the Lord, all you servants of the Lord,*

you that stand by night in the house of the Lord.

Lift up your hands in the holy place and bless the Lord;*

the Lord who made heaven and earth bless you out of Zi - on.

Music: Plainsong, Tone I.3; arr. Patrick Wedd (1948– ) ©.

# 754 A Song of Creation (Canticle 15)

**Refrain** *Last time sing twice*

Praise him and high-ly ex-alt him for-ev-er.

Bm    Em    F#m    Em⁷    A    Dsus⁴    D

**Verses 1, 3, 6** *To refrain*

1 Glo-ri-fy the Lord, all you works of the Lord.

3 Glo-ri-fy the Lord, O moun-tains and hills.

6 Let the earth glo-ri-fy the Lord.

D    F#m    Em⁷    A⁷ *To refrain*

Text: Song of the Three 35–36, 52–60.
Music: Melody Rupert Lang (1948– ) ©; acc. Melva Treffinger Graham (1947– ) ©.

Stanzas 2, 4 · To refrain

2 In the fir-ma-ment of his pow-er glo-ri-fy the Lord.

To refrain

4 O springs of wa-ter, seas, and streams,

Bm · D/A · A · G · A⁷ · To refrain

Stanza 5 · To refrain

5 O whales and all that move in the wa-ters,

G · F · Em⁷ · To refrain

# 755 The Beatitudes (Canticle 17)

*The cantor sings the first refrain. All repeat it.*
*The cantor (or cantors) sing the verses. All sing the two refrains as indicated.*
*May be sung with either refrain or both.*

**Refrain 1**

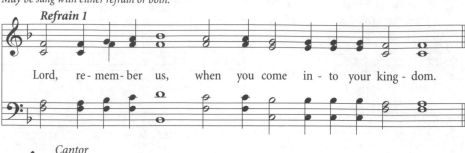

Lord, re - mem - ber us, when you come in - to your king - dom.

**Cantor**

Bless - ed are the poor in spi - rit, for theirs is the king-dom of heav - en.

Bless - ed are those who mourn, for they shall be com - fort - ed.

**Refrain 2**

Re - joice and be glad, for your re - ward is great in heav - en.

**Cantor**

Bless - ed are the gen - tle, for they shall in - her - it the earth.

Bless - ed are those who hun - ger and thirst for what is right,

for they shall be sa - tis - fied.

**Refrain 1**
Lord, remember us,
when you come into your kingdom.

Bless - ed are the mer - ci - ful, for mer - cy shall be shown to them.

Text: Matt. 5.3–12.
Music: Russian chant; adapt. George Black (1931– ) ©.

Bless - ed   are the pure in heart,   for they shall see God.

***Refrain 2*** Rejoice and be glad, for your reward is great in heaven.

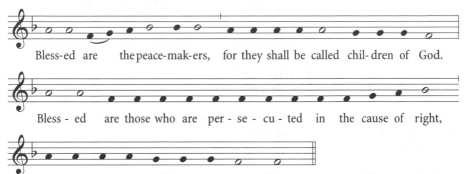

Bless-ed  are       the peace-mak-ers,  for they shall be called  chil-dren  of  God.

Bless - ed    are those who are  per - se - cu - ted   in   the cause of  right,

for theirs is   the king-dom  of  heav - en.

***Refrain 1*** Lord, remember us, when you come into your kingdom.

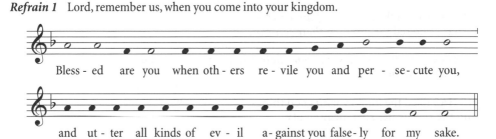

Bless - ed    are  you   when oth - ers   re - vile  you  and  per - se-cute you,

and ut - ter  all kinds of   ev - il   a- gainst you false- ly  for   my   sake.

**Refrains 2 and 1**
Rejoice and be glad, for your reward is great in heaven.
Lord, remember us, when you come into your kingdom.

*Optional harmony when choir replaces cantor:*

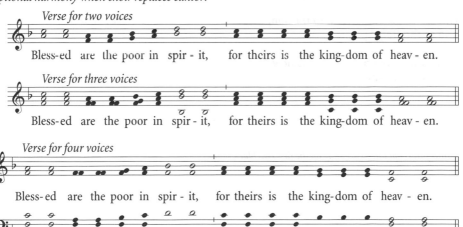

*Verse for two voices*

Bless-ed  are  the poor in  spir - it,   for theirs  is   the king-dom of heav - en.

*Verse for three voices*

Bless-ed  are  the poor in  spir - it,   for theirs  is   the king-dom of heav - en.

*Verse for four voices*

Bless-ed  are  the poor in  spir - it,   for theirs  is   the king-dom of heav - en.

# 758 The Song of Zechariah (Canticle 19a)

Thomas Attwood Walmisley (1814–1856)

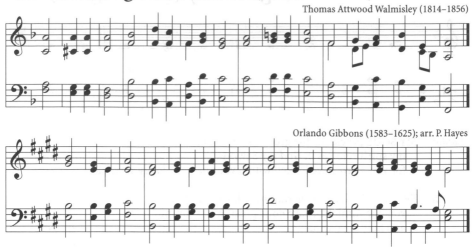

Orlando Gibbons (1583–1625); arr. P. Hayes

Blessed be the Lord, the ' God of ' Israel;*
    for he has come to his ' people • and ' set them ' free.
He has raised up for us a ' mighty ' Saviour, *
    born of the ' house of • his ' servant ' David.

Through his holy prophets he promised of old,
that he would ' save us • from our ' enemies, *
    from the ' hands of ' all who ' hate us.
He promised to show ' mercy • to our ' fathers *
    and to re'member • his ' holy ' covenant.

This was the oath he swore to our ' father ' Abraham, *
    to set us ' free • from the ' hands of • our ' enemies,
free to worship him with'out ' fear, *
    holy and righteous in his sight all the ' days ' of our ' life.

You, my child, shall be called the prophet of the ' Most ' High, *
    for you will go before the ' Lord • to pre'pare his ' way,
to give his people ' knowledge • of sal'vation *
    by the for'giveness ' of their ' sins.

In the tender compassion ' of our ' God *
    the dawn from on ' high shall ' break up'on us,
to shine on those who dwell in darkness and the ' shadow • of ' death, *
    and to guide our feet ' into the ' way of ' peace.

Glory to the Father, and ' to the ' Son, *
    and ' to the ' Holy ' Spirit:
as it was in the be'ginning, • is ' now, *
    and will be for'ever. ' A'men.

# The Song of Simeon (Canticle 20)

Lord, now you let your servant **go** in peace; *
your word has **been** ful-filled.

My own eyes have seen **the** sal-vation *
which you have prepared in the sight of **ev**-ery people;

a light to reveal you **to** the nations *
and the glory of your **peo**-ple Israel.

Glory to the Father, and **to** the Son, *
and to the **Ho**-ly Spirit:*

as it was in the begin-**ning**, is now, *
and will be for-ev-**er**. A-men.

Text: Luke 2.29–32; tr. International Consultation on English Texts ©.
Music: George Black (1931– ) ©.

# 760 Song of the Multitude in Heaven (Canticle 25)

*Cantor sings the Alleluias. All repeat them.*
*A cantor or choir sings the verses. All repeat the Alleluias after each verse.*

Al - le - lu - ia,     al - le - lu - ia!

To our God belong victory, glory, and ***power***, *
for right and just are ***his*** judge-ments.
  ***R*** Alleluia, alleluia!

Praise our God, all you who ***serve him,*** *
you who fear him, great ***and*** small.
  ***R*** Alleluia, alleluia!

Alle-***luia!*** *
The Lord God almighty has claimed ***his*** king-dom.
  ***R*** Alleluia, alleluia!

Let us rejoice and triumph and give him ***praise:*** *
the time has come for the wedding-feast of ***the*** Lamb.
  ***R*** Alleluia, alleluia!

Text: Rev. 19.1, 2, 5–7; tr. International Consultation on Common Texts ©.
Music: Plainsong, mode 1; adapt. George Black (1931– ). © *1987 Anglican Book Centre.*

# You Are God (Canticle 26)

You are God: we *praise you;*
you are the Lord: we ac-*claim you;*
you are the eternal *Father:*
all creation worships *you.*

To you all angels, all the powers of *heaven,*
cherubim and seraphim, sing in endless *praise:*
holy, holy, holy Lord, God of power and *might,*
heaven and earth are full of your *glory.*

1   The glorious company of apostles *praise you.*
2   The noble fellowship of prophets *praise you.* *(omit measure 3)*
4   The white-robed army of martyrs *praise you.*

Throughout the world the holy Church ac-*claims you:*
Father, of majesty un-*bounded,*
your true and only Son, worthy of all *worship,*
and the Holy Spirit, advocate and *guide.*

You, Christ, are the King of *Glory,*
the eternal Son of the *Father,*
When you became man to set us *free*
you did not shun the Virgin's *womb.*

You overcame the sting of *death*
and opened the kingdom of heaven to all be-*lievers.*
You are seated at God's right hand in *glory.*
We believe that you will come, and be our *judge.*

Come then, Lord, and help your *people,*
bought with the price of your own *blood,*
and bring us with your *saints*
to glory ever-*lasting.*

Text: *You Are God (Te Deum,* Latin hymn, 400?); tr. International Consultation on English Texts ©.
Music: Robert Knox Kennedy (1945– ) ©.

*Items 762–769 may be used with any psalm or canticle as appropriate.*

Give thanks to the Lord, for he is good.

Music: David Millard (1959– ) ©.

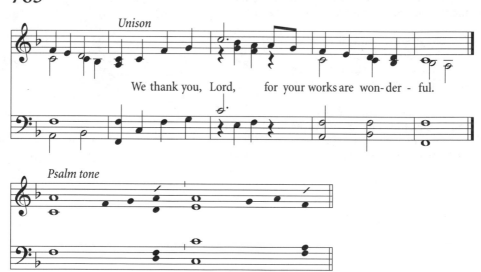

We thank you, Lord, for your works are won-der - ful.

Music: Refrain: Steven Morgan (19??– ); psalm tone: Gregory Murray (1905–1992).
© McCrimmon Publishing Company, Ltd.

Sing to the Lord a new song.

*Psalm tone*

Music: Brigid Coult (1953– ) ©.

The Lord is close to all who call him.

*Psalm tone*

Music: Brigid Coult (1953– ) ©.

*Unison*

In - cline your ear, O Lord, and save us.

*Psalm tone*

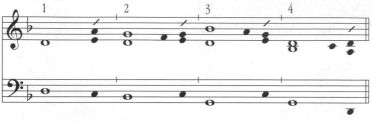

*For a shorter tone, use sections 2 and 4.*

Music: George Black (1931– ). © *1996 Anglican Book Centre.*

*Unison*

The Lord is kind and mer - ci - ful.

*Psalm tone*

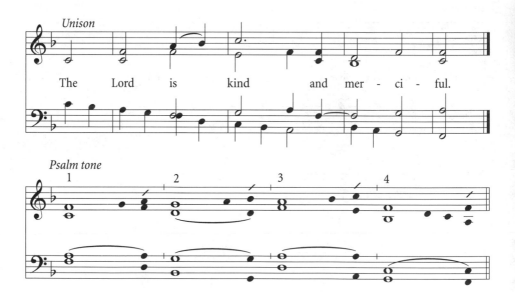

*For a shorter tone, use sections 2 and 4.*

Music: George Black (1931– ). © *1996 Anglican Book Centre.*

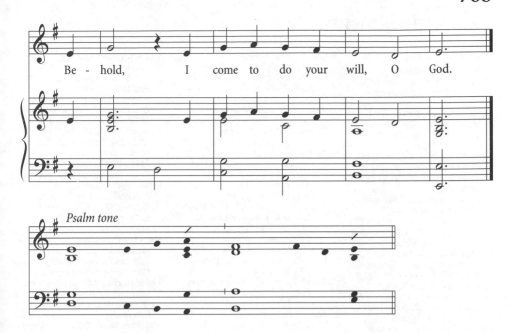

Be - hold, I come to do your will, O God.

*Psalm tone*

Music: Brigid Coult (1953– ) ©.

*Unison*

Re - mem - ber, O Lord, your faith - ful - ness and love.

*Psalm tone*

Music: Brigid Coult (1953– ) ©.

# Acknowledgments

## Alphabetical List of Copyright Holders

Owners or administrators of at least five items in this hymnal

**Anglican Book Centre**, 600 Jarvis Street, Toronto ON M4Y 2J6 Canada Ph: (416) 924-9192 Fax: (416) 968-7983.

Canon **Benjamin T. Arreak**, PO Box 154, Kuujjuaj QC J0M 1C0 Canada Ph: (819) 964-2129 Fax: (819) 964-2113.

**Augsburg Fortress**, 426 South Fifth Street, Box 1209, Minneapolis MN 55440 USA Ph: (612) 330-3300; (800) 328-4648 Fax: (612) 330-3455.

**George Black**, 21 North Sherbourne Street, Toronto ON M4W 2T3 Canada Ph: (416) 920-9506 Fax: (416) 920-9529.

**Barrie Cabena**, #1-60 Allen Street W., Waterloo ON N2L 6H5 Canada Ph: (519) 579-8827.

**Cambridge University Press**, Rights and Permissions, 40 West 20th Street, New York NY 10011-4211 Ph: (212) 924-3900 Fax: (212) 691-3239.

**John Campbell**, c/o Church of the Redeemer, 162 Bloor Street W., Toronto ON M5S 1M4 Canada Ph: (416) 922-4948

**Cassell plc**, 125 Strand, London WC2R 0BB UK Ph: 011-44-171-420-5555 Fax: 01-44-171-240-8531.

The **Church Pension Fund**, administered by Church Publishing Inc., 445 Fifth Avenue, New York NY 10016 USA Ph: (800) 223-6602 x. 786 Fax: (212) 779-3392.

**The Copyright Company**, 40 Music Square East, Nashville TN 37302 USA Ph: (615) 244-5588 Fax: (615) 244-5591.

**Brigid Coult**, 9111 Alberta Road, Richmond BC V6Y 1T7 Ph: (604) 270-4250.

**English Language Liturgical Consultation**, c/o International Committee on English in the Liturgy Inc., (International Commission on English in the Liturgy) Att. Peter C. Finn, 1522 K Street, N.W., Washington DC 20005-1202 USA Ph: (202) 347-0800 Fax: (202) 347-1839.

**G.I.A. Publications, Inc.**, 7404 S. Mason Ave., Chicago IL 60638 USA Ph: (708) 496-3800 Fax: (708) 496-3828.

**The General Synod of the Anglican Church of Canada**, 600 Jarvis Street, Toronto ON M4Y 2J6 Canada Ph: (416) 924-9192 Fax: (416) 968-7983.

**Paul Gibson**, 588 Millwood Road, Toronto ON M4S 1K8 Canada Ph: (416) 487-2008 Email: paul.gibson@ecunet.org.

**Melva Treffinger Graham**, 17 Conrad Ave., Toronto ON M6G 3G4 Ph: (416) 652-9135 Fax: (416) 488-4770 Email: cantor@interlog.com.

The executors of the late Dr. **Basil Harwood**, c/o Ms. Elizabeth Paterson, The Public Trustee M4582, Stewart House, 24 Kingsway, London UK WC2B 6JX Ph: 0171-664-7187 Fax: 0171-664-7704.

**Derek Holman**, 75 George Henry Blvd., Willowdale ON M2J 1E8 Canada Ph: (416) 494-7068.

**Hope Publishing Co.**, 380 South Main Place, Carol Stream IL 60188 USA Ph: (800) 323-1049 Fax: (708) 665-2552. All rights reserved. Used by permission.

**International Committee on English in the Liturgy, Inc.**, (International Commission on English in the Liturgy) Att. Peter C. Finn, 1522 K Street, N.W., Suite 1000, Washington DC 20005-1202 USA Ph: (202) 347-0800 Fax: (202) 347-1839.

**Novello**, see Shawnee Press, Inc.

**OCP Publications, Inc.**, Licensing Dept., P.O. Box 18030, 5536 NE Hassalo Portland OR 97218-0030 USA Ph: (800) 547-8992 Fax: (503) 282-3486.

Canon **Herbert O'Driscoll**, 1000 Jasmine Ave., Victoria BC V8Z 2P4 Canada Ph: (250) 479-9847 Fax: (250) 479-8556.

**Oxford University Press, Inc.**, New York, Attn: Brian Hill, Music Dept., 198 Madison Ave., New York NY 10016 USA Ph: (212) 726-6000 Fax: (212) 726-6444.

**Oxford University Press**, Great Clarendon Street, Oxford OX2 6DP England Ph: 011-44-186-555-6767 Fax: 011-44-186-555-6646.

**The Pilgrim Press**, 700 Prospect Ave. East, Cleveland OH 44115-1100 USA Ph: (216) 736-3700 Fax: (216) 736-3703.

**Réveil Publications**, B.P. 4464, 20 Rue Calliet, Lyon Cédex 04, France 69241 Ph: 011-33-72-00-08-54 Fax: 011-33-72-00-02-74.

**E.C. Schirmer Music Co.**, 138 Ipswich Street, Boston MA 12215 USA Ph: (617) 236-1935 Fax: (617) 236-0261.

**G. Schirmer, Inc.** (ASCAP). Att: Zoraya Mendez, Permissions, 257 Park Ave. South, 20th Floor, New York NY 10010 USA Ph: (212) 254-2100 Fax: (212) 254-2013 Email: 71360.3514@compuserve.com. Email: schirmer@mcs-qs.com.

**Selah Publishing Co., Inc.**, Rights & Permissions, 58 Pearl Street, P.O. Box 3037, Kingston NY 12401-0902 USA Ph: (800) 852-6172 Fax: (914) 338-2991.

**Shawnee Press, Inc.** (ASCAP), c/o Music Sales Corporation, 257 Park Ave. S., New York NY 10010 USA. See G. Schirmer, Inc.

**The Sisterhood of St. John the Divine**, 1 Botham Rd., Willowdale ON M2N 2J5 Canada.

**Waterloo Music Co. Ltd.**, 3 Regina St. N., Waterloo ON N2J 4A5 Canada Ph: (519) 886-4990 or 1-800-563-9683 Fax: (519) 886-4999.

**Patrick Wedd**, 3435 Hingston Ave., Montréal QC Canada Fax: (514) 843-6344.

Estate of **Healey Willan**, c/o Mary Willan Mason, 101-350 Lonsdale Rd., Toronto ON M5P 1R6 Canada Ph: (416) 481-9909.

## Credits by hymn number

1 Text: Naskapi translation © Joseph Guanish, c/o Naskapi Development Corporation, PO Box 5023, Kawawachikamach QC Canada G0G 2T0 Ph: (418) 585-2612 Fax: (418) 585-3953 Text: Inuktitut translation © Benjamin T. Arreak. Music: Descant © Godfrey Hewitt, 221 Wilshire Ave., Ottawa ON K2C 0E6 Canada Ph: (613) 225-8141 Fax: (613) 225-9008.

3 Text: © David Higham Associates Ltd., 5-8 Lower John Street, Golden Square, London UK W1R 4HA Ph: 011-44-171-437-7888 Fax: 011-44-171-437-1072. Music: Arrangement © C. Richard Hunt, 101 Rue-Les-Pins, Laval-sur-lac, QC H7R 1C8 Ph: (514) 627-3575.

4 Text: Stanza 3 © James Waring McCrady, University of the South, Sewanee TN 37375 USA Ph: (615) 598-5931.

6 Music: © 1936, Ascherberg, Hopwood and Crew Ltd., Chappell Music Ltd. London, c/o International Music Publications, Unit 15, Woodford Trading Estate, Southend Rd., Woodford Green, Essex IG8 8HN UK Ph: 011-44-181-551-6131 Fax: 011-44-181-551-1595.

9 Text and Music: © 1989 WGRG The Iona Community (Scotland). Used by permission of G.I.A. Publications, Inc., exclusive agent.

10 Text: © The Reverend Canon J.E. Bowers, 13 Bathurst, Orton Goldhay, Peterborough, Cams. PE2 5QH UK Ph: 011-44-173-336-1834. Music: Harmony © Derek Holman.

11 Text: Paraphrase © 1989 Hope Publishing Co. Music: © Dorothy Howell Sheets, Apt. 316, 145 Columbia Ave., Holland MI 49423-2984 USA Ph: (616) 394-0327.

12    Text: Paraphrase © Paul Gibson. Music: Harmony © Oxford University Press.
13    Text: Translation © Oxford University Press.
14    Text: Paraphrase © 1985 The Church Pension Fund.
15    Text: Paraphrase © Paul Gibson. Music: Harmony © Oxford University Press.
16    Text: Paraphrase © 1989 Hope Publishing Co.
17    Text: Translation © 1982 The Church Pension Fund. Text: Revision © Anne K. LeCroy, East Tennessee State University College of Arts and Sciences, Department of English, Box 70683, Johnson City TN 37614-0683 USA. Music: Harmony © Estate of Healey Willan.
18    Text: Paraphrase © 1991 G.I.A. Publications, Inc. Music: © John R. Van Maanen, 27 Foster Street, Simcoe ON N3Y 2C3 Canada.
19    Text: Translation © Oxford University Press, alt. with permission.
20    Text: James Quinn, SJ ©. Used by permission of Selah Publishing Co., Inc., North American agent.
21    Text and Music: © 1989 WGRG The Iona Community (Scotland). Used by permission of G.I.A. Publications, Inc., exclusive agent.
23    Music: Harmony © Oxford University Press.
26    Text: Stanzas 1-3 © The Church Pension Fund. Stanza 4 © James Waring McCrady, University of the South, Sewanee, TN  37375 USA Ph: (615) 598-5931. Music: Harmony © Estate of Healey Willan.
27    Text: Translation © Anne K. LeCroy, East Tennessee State University, College of Arts and Sciences, Department of English, Box 70683, Johnson City TN 37614-0683 USA. Music: © 1971 Faber Music, Ltd. Reprinted by permission from "The New Catholic Hymnal." Faber Music Ltd., 3 Queen Sq., London WC1N 3AU England Ph: 011-44-171-278-7436 Fax: 011-44-171-278-3817.
28    Text: Translation Stanzas 1-4 The Hymnal 1982 © The Church Pension Fund; Stanza 5 adaptation © Anne K. LeCroy, East Tennessee State University, College of Arts and Sciences, Department of English, Box 70683, Johnson City, TN 37614-0683 USA. Music: Harmony © Janet MacFarlane Peaker, Estate of Charles Peaker, 18 Nesbitt Drive, Toronto ON M4W 2G3 Canada.
29    Music: Descant © Kenneth Hull, c/o Department of Music, Conrad Grebel College, Waterloo ON N2L 3G6 Canada Ph: (519) 885-0220 Fax: (519) 885-0014.
32    Text: © Arthur Charles Lawson, R.R. 1 Gores Landing, ON K0K 2E0 Canada Ph: (905) 342-5302. Music: © Patrick Wedd.
33    Text: © Benedictine Nuns of Malling Abbey, The Reverend Mother Abbess and Community, St. Mary's Abbey, Swan Street, West Malling, Kent ME19 6JX UK Ph: . 011-44-173-284-3309. Music: © 1984 G.I.A. Publications, Inc.
35    Text: © 1989 The United Methodist Publishing House (Administered by The Copyright Company, Nashville, TN) All rights reserved. International copyright secured. Used by permission. The Copyright Company, 40 Music Square East, Nashville TN 37302 USA Ph: (615) 244-5588 Fax: (615) 244-5591. Music: Harmony © 1992 The Pilgrim Press.
36    Text: © Lynette Miller, PO Box 45032, 600 Winona, Winnipeg MB Canada R2C 2N9 Ph: (204) 224-4988
37    Text: © Ian Sowton, 21 Chudleigh Ave., Toronto ON M4R 1T1 Canada Ph: (416) 489-9120. Music: Arrangement © John Campbell. Melody © 1994 Hal Leonard Corp, 7777 West Bluemound Road, P.O. Box 13819, Milwaukee WI 53213 USA Ph: (414) 774-3630, Fax: (414) 774-3259, Email: halinfo@halleonard.com.
38    Text: © 1988 Jaroslav J. Vajda. Used by permission. Jaroslav J. Vajda, 3534 Brookstone S. Dr., St. Louis MO 63129-2900 USA Ph: (314) 892-9473. Music: © Barrie Cabena.
39    Text and Music: © 1988 G.I.A. Publications, Inc.
41    Text: © Mary E. Arthur, c/o Mary Feldman, 2050 Sharon Rd., Menlo Park CA 94025 USA.

42    Text: © 1991 G.I.A. Publications, Inc. Music: © J. Curwen & Sons, Ltd. (London). Used by permission of G. Schirmer, Inc. (ASCAP).
43    Text: © 1988 Hope Publishing Co. Music: © Mowbray (an imprint of Cassell plc, London).
44    Text: Paraphrase © 1991 G.I.A. Publications. Music: Harmony © George Black.
45    Text: © 1991 G.I.A. Publications. Music: Harmony © 1959 Concordia Publishing House, 3558 South Jefferson Ave., Saint Louis MO 63118-3968 USA Ph: (314) 268-1000 Fax: (314) 268-1329.
46    Text: Paraphrase and Music: © S.C. Ochieng Okeyo, Kenyatta University, Faculty of Arts, P.O. Box 43844, Nairobi, Kenya Ph: 011-254-810-902.
47    Text: © Judith Beatrice O'Neill, Lonsdale Terrace, Edinburgh EH3 9HN Scotland. Music: Harmony © 1991 Hope Publishing Co.
50    Music: Harmony © Oxford University Press.
52    Text: Revision Hymns for Today's Church, 1982. © 1982 Hope Publishing Co.
53    Text and Music: © 1969 Hope Publishing Co.
54    Music: Harmony © Oxford University Press.
55    Text: St. 1 © The Church Pension Fund. Music: © 1985 G.I.A. Publications, Inc.
56    Text and Music: © 1988 Hope Publishing Co.
57    Text: © 1983 Hope Publishing Co.
58    Text: © Ian Sowton, 21 Chudleigh Ave., Toronto ON M4R 1T1 Canada Ph: (416) 489-9120.
59    Text and Music: Arrangement © 1989 WGRG The Iona Community (Scotland). Used by permission of G.I.A. Publications, Inc., exclusive agent.
60    Text: © 1971, 1995 Hope Publishing Co. Music: Harmony © 1989 The United Methodist Publishing House (Administered by The Copyright Company, Nashville, TN). All rights reserved. International copyright secured. Used by permission.
61    Text: © 1989 Hope Publishing Co. Music: © 1990 Selah Publishing Co., Inc.
62    Text: Stanzas 1-3 and Music: Melody © The Lutheran World Federation, General Secretariat, 150 route de Ferney, CP 2100, 1211 Geneva 2, Switzerland Fax: 011-41-22-798 8616; Stanza 4 and Music: Harmony © Augsburg Fortress. Reprinted by permission.
63    Text: Paraphrase and Music: © 1984 Les Presses de Taizé. Used by permission of G.I.A. Publications, Inc., exclusive agent.
65    Text: © Estate of F.E.V. Pilcher, c/o Mrs. Isabel F. Pilcher, 94 Willingdon Blvd., Toronto ON M8X 2H7 Canada Ph: (416) 231-3022. Music: Flute descant © Melva Treffinger Graham.
67    Text: © 1991 Hope Publishing Co. Music: © Oxford University Press.
68    Text and Music: © 1983 G.I.A. Publications, Inc.
69    Text: © 1989 WGRG The Iona Community (Scotland). Used by permission of G.I.A Publications, Inc., exclusive agent. Music: Harmony © George Black.
71    Music: Harmony © The Society of St. John the Evangelist, 22 Great College Street, Westminster, London UK SW1P 3QA Ph: 011-44-171-222-9234.
73    Text and Music: © 1978 John B. Foley, SJ and New Dawn Music. Admin. by Oregon Catholic Press. OCP Publications.
75    Text: © 1989 Hope Publishing Co. Music: © 1973 Waterloo Music Co. Ltd.
76    Music: Harmony © Margaret Drynan, 589 Pinewood St., Oshawa ON L1G 2S2 Canada Ph: (905) 576-9851.
77    Music: © Basil E. Bridge, 124 Linacre Ave., Sprowston, Norwich NR7 8JS UK Ph: 011-44-160-348-6638.
78    Text: Revision, Hymns for Today's Church, 1982. © 1982 Hope Publishing Co.
79    Text: © The Sisterhood of St. John the Divine.
81    Text: Translation © 1985 The Church Pension Fund.

82    Text and Music: © 1984 Utryck. Used by permission of Walton Music Corp., Att: Sherry Halpern, Auditor, 170 N.E. 33rd Street, Ft. Lauderdale FL 33334 USA Ph: (954) 563-1844 Fax: (954) 563-9006.
83    Music: Harmony © The Society of St. John the Evangelist, 22 Great College Street, Westminster, London UK SW1P 3QA Ph: 01-71-222-9234.
84    Music: © 1994 Waterloo Music Co. Ltd.
86    Text and Music: Melody © 1993 Common Cup Company, c/o Ian Macdonald, 7591 Gray Ave., Burnaby BC V5J 3Z4 Ph: (604) 434-8323 Fax: (604) 430-3697. Music: Arrangement © 1997 Andrew Donaldson, Seraph Music 14 Hambly Ave., Toronto ON M4E 2R6 Canada Ph: (416) 691-1158 Fax: (416) 690-9967 Email: seraph@pathcom.com.
87    Text: Translation and Adaptation © Oxford University Press from The English Hymnal, 1906.
88    Music: Descant © 1983 Hope Publishing Co.
89    Music: Arrangement © 1996 Concordia Publishing House. Used with permission, 3558 South Jefferson Ave., Saint Louis MO 63118-3968 USA Ph: (314) 268-1000 Fax: (314) 268-1329; Music: Refrain descant and alternative harmony © Oxford University Press.
90    Text: © Anna Briggs, 26 Beverley Terrace, North Shields NE30 4NT UK
91    Text: © David Higham Associates Ltd., 5-8 Lower John Street, Golden Square, London UK W1R 4HA Ph: 011-44-171-437-7888 Fax: 011-44-171-437-1072. Music: Harmony © Oxford University Press.
92    Text: © 1988 Emmanuel College, Toronto, Principal's Office, Rights & Permissions, 75 Queen's Park Cres. E., Toronto ON M5S 1K7 Canada Ph: (416) 585-4539 Fax: (416) 585-4516. Music: © Estate of James Hopkirk, c/o Arthur E.B. Armstrong, 131 Brenda Cres., Scarborough ON M1K 3C8 Canada Ph: (416) 261-2539.
94    Text: Paraphrase and Music: © 1991 Les Presses de Taizé. Used by permission of G.I.A. Publications, Inc., exclusive agent.
95    Music: © Estate of Godfrey Ridout, c/o Michael Ridout, 22 Enderby Road, Toronto ON M4E 2S3 Canada Ph: (416) 690-7833.
96    Music: Harmony © Oxford University Press.
100    Music: Revision © 1995 Réveil Publications, B.P. 4464, 20 Rue Calliet, Lyon Cédex 04 France 69241 Ph: 011-33-7-200-0854 Fax: 011-33-7-200-0274.
102    Text: Adaptation © Charles P. Price, 605-1250 S. Washington Street, Alexandria VA 22314 USA.
104    Music: Arrangement © Patrick Wedd.
105    Text: © Brian Ruttan, 94 Lake Ave. Drive, Stoney Creek ON L8G 3N4 Canada Ph: (905) 662-7607. Music: Harmony © 1940, renewed 1981, The Church Pension Fund.
106    Music: © Estate of Henry Hugh Bancroft. Used by permission of Eldred Bancroft. Executor: Brian Burrows, 11331-75 Ave., Edmonton AB T6G 0H6 Canada Ph: (403) 434-0790.
107    Text: Paraphrase and Music: © 1982, 1983, 1984 Les Presses de Taizé. Used by permission of G.I.A. Publications, Inc., exclusive agent.
108    Music: Descant © Cambridge University Press.
109    Text: © 1982 Hope Publishing Co.
110    Text: Translation © 1982 Hope Publishing Co.
111    Text: © Estate of Moir A.J. Waters. Used by permission of Margaret Waters, 134 St. Lawrence Blvd., London ON N6J 2X1 Canada Ph: (519) 685-1714.
113    Text and Music: © 1976 North American Liturgy Resources (NALR). Reprinted by permission of OCP Publications.
115    Text: © 1980 Augsburg Publishing House. Reprinted by permission of Augsburg Fortress. Music: © Max B. Miller, 45 Hunnewell Ave., Newton MA 02158 USA Ph: (617) 244-7621.
118    Music: Alternative refrain setting © 1961 Oxford University Press.

119   Text: Naskapi translation © Joseph Guanish, c/o Naskapi Development Corporation, PO Box 5023, Kawawachikamach QC Canada G0G 2T0 Ph: (418) 585-2612 Fax: (418) 585-3953. Text: Kwak'wala translation © U'mista Cultural Society, PO Box 253, Alert Bay, BC V0N 1A0 Canada Ph: (250) 974-5403 Fax: (250) 974-5499 E-mail umista@north.island.net

121   Music: Harmony © Oxford University Press.

122   Music: © Oxford University Press.

124   Text and Music: © 1992 Hope Publishing Co.

125   Music: Harmony © 1955, 1983 John Ribble. Used by permission of Westminster/John Knox Press, 100 Witherspoon Street, Louisville KY 40202-1396 USA Ph: (502) 569-5060 Fax: (502) 569-5113.

127   Text: Translation and Music: Harmony © 1958 Basilian Fathers, Willis Music Co., 7380 Industrial Road, Florence KY 41042 USA Ph: (606) 371-5050.

128   Text and Music: © 1945 Boosey & Co., Ltd., copyright renewed. Used by permission of Boosey & Hawkes, Inc., 35 East 21st Street, New York NY 10010-6212 USA Ph: (212) 358-5300 Fax: (212) 358-5301.

129   Text: © St. Luke's Anglican Church, Winnipeg. Used by permission, Estate of Frieda Major, St. Luke's Anglican Church, 130 Nassau Street, N. Winnipeg MB R3L 2H1 Canada Ph: (204) 452-3609. Music: © 1976 Margaret Fleming, 57-8889 212th Street, Langley BC V1M 2E8 Canada Ph: (604) 888-9302 Fax: (604) 534-0781.

130   Text and Music: © 1964 Stainer & Bell Ltd. All rights reserved. Used by permission of Hope Publishing Co.

131   Text: Revision *Hymns for Today's Church*, 1982. © 1987 Hope Publishing Co. Music and Harmony adaptation: © Oxford University Press.

132   Music: Harmony © Estate of Healey Willan.

133   Text: Stanzas 3-6 © 1978 *Lutheran Book of Worship*. Reprinted by permission of Augsburg Fortress.

135   Text: Translation © Mowbray (an imprint of Cassell plc, London). Music: Arrangement © Oxford University Press.

136   Music: Descant © Novello & Co., Ltd.

138   Music: Alternative setting © Oxford University Press.

139   Music: Alternative refrain harmony and Descant © 1926 Oxford University Press Inc.

142   Text and Music: © 1980 Waterloo Music Co. Ltd.

143   Music: Descant © Novello & Co., Ltd.

144   Text: © 1992 G.I.A.Publications, Inc. Music: © John S. McIntosh, 49 Nelson Street W., Goderich ON N7A 2M4 Canada Ph: (519) 524-2901.

146   Text: Translation © The Frederick Harris Music Co., Ltd. Unit 1, 5865 McLaughlin Road, Mississauga ON L5R 1B8 Canada Ph: (905) 501-1595 Fax: (905) 501-0929. Music: Harmony © 1978 *Lutheran Book of Worship*. Reprinted by permission of Augsburg Fortress.

147   Text: Stanzas 2-3 © 1989 Hope Publishing Co.

150   Text and Music: Harmony © 1924 (renewed) J. Curwen & Sons, Ltd. (London). Used by permission of G. Schirmer, Inc. (ASCAP).

151   Text: Stanza 1 © 1928 Oxford University Press. Stanza 2 © Estate of William T. Pennar Davies, Mrs. Rosemary Pennar Davies, 10 Grosvenor Rd., Sketty Swansea, Wales UK SA2 0SP Ph: 011-44-179-229-9534. Music: Arrangement © Oxford University Press.

152   Music: Melody © 1969, Arrangement © 1982, Flute descant © 1998 Hope Publishing Co.

155   Music: Harmony © Mowbray (an imprint of Cassell plc, London).

157   Text: Paraphrase © 1990 Hope Publishing Co. Music: © 1990 Selah Publishing Co., Inc.

159   Music: © 1994 Waterloo Music Co. Ltd.

161   Text: © 1982 Hope Publishing Co.

162   Text: © 1990 Hope Publishing Co.

163   Music: Harmony © Hope Publishing Co.

164   Text and Music: 1987, 1991 Oxford University Press, Inc.

165   Text: © 1990 Hope Publishing Co. Music: Harmony © 1977 Hope Publishing Co.

166   Text: © 1988 Hope Publishing Co.

168   Text: © 1991 Stainer & Bell Ltd. All rights reserved. Used by permission of Hope Publishing Co.

169   Text: © 1977, 1995 and Music: © 1985 Hope Publishing Co.

170   Text: © Oxford University Press.

171   Text: © Oxford University Press. Music: © 1969 Hope Publishing Co.

172   Text: © James Quinn, SJ. Used by permission of Selah Publishing Co. Music: Harmony © John Leon Hooker, Episcopal Divinity School, 99 Brattle Street, Cambridge MA 02138 USA Ph: (617) 868-3450.

173   Text: © J. Donald P. Hughes, 4 Northmead, Prestbury, Cheshire SK10 4XD UK.

174   Text: © 1982 Thomas H. Cain, Walnut Hill Farmhouse, R.R.#1, Jerseyville ON L0R 1R0 Canada Ph: (905) 648-1070. Music: © 1988 G.I.A.Publications, Inc.

175   Text: Revision *Hymns for Today's Church*, 1982. © 1982 Hope Publishing Co.

176   Text: © Estate of Gertrude Hollis. Current information sought.

177   Text: © 1985 Oxford University Press, Inc. Music: © 1990 Selah Publishing Co.

178   Text: © 1989 Hope Publishing Co. Music: © The Estate of James Hopkirk, c/o Arthur E.B. Armstrong, 131 Brenda Cres., Scarborough ON M1K 3C8 Canada Ph: (416) 261-2539.

179   Text: © 1984 G.I.A. Publications, Inc. Music: © 1984 G.I.A. Publications, Inc.

181   Music: Descant © The Society of St. John the Evangelist, 22 Great College Street, Westminster, London UK SW1P 3QA Ph: 01-71-222-9234.

183   Text: © 1990 Hope Publishing Co. Music: Percussion arrangement © Brian Barlow, 414 St. Clair Ave. E., Toronto ON M4T 1P5 Canada Ph: (416) 482-3538.

184   Music: © The John Ireland Trust, c/o Mr. P.B.A.Taylor, 35 St. Mary's Mansions, London UK W2 1SQ.

185   Text: Translation © Oxford University Press.

186   Text: Translation © Oxford University Press. Music: Harmony © Estate of Healey Willan.

187   Text: Translation © 1991 Stainer & Bell Ltd. All rights reserved. Used by permission of Hope Publishing Co. Music: © Oxford University Press.

189   Text: Translation © The Church Pension Fund.

191   Text: © 1973 Hope Publishing Co.

194   Text and Music: Arrangement © 1991 Les Presses de Taizé. Used by permission of G.I.A. Publications, Inc., exclusive agent.

196   Text: Translation © Oxford University Press. Alt. and used with permission.

197   Text: © Mowbray (an imprint of Cassell plc., London).

198   Text: Revision *Hymns for Today's Church*, 1982. © 1982 Hope Publishing Co.

199   Text and Music: Arrangement © 1988 WGRG The Iona Community (Scotland). Used by permission of G.I.A.Publications, Inc., exclusive agent.

200   Music: © 1939 Hope Publishing Co.

201   Text: © 1991 Stainer & Bell, Ltd. All rights reserved. Used by permission of Hope Publishing Co. Music: © The Estate of Doris Wright Smith, c/o Gerald R. Spall, 817 East Landis Ave., CN 1501 Vineland NJ 08360 USA Ph: (609) 691-0100 Fax: (609) 692-4095; (609) 691-3302.

203   Text: Nisga'a translation © George Nelson Sr., 1727 Volunteer Dr., Kincolith, BC V0V I80 Ph: (250) 326-2384 Fax: (250) 326-4208 (Gingolx Band Office). Music: Descant © Derek Holman.

204   Text: Translation © 1991 Stainer & Bell Ltd. All rights reserved. Used by permission of Hope Publishing Co.

206   Music: Descant © 1987 Concordia Publishing House, 3558 South Jefferson Ave., Saint Louis MO 63118-3968 USA Ph: (314) 268-1000 Fax: (314) 268-1329.

207   Music: Alternative harmony © Derek Holman

209   Text: © 1965, renewal 1993 The Hymn Society in the United States and Canada. All rights reserved. Used by permission of Hope Publishing Co. Music: © F. Alan E. Reesor, Cathedral Church of St. Peter, Rochford Square, P.O. Box 713, Charlottetown PEI C1A 7L3 Canada, Ph: (902) 566-2102 Email: stptepub@isn.nte

210   Text: Revision *Hymns for Today's Church*, 1982. © 1982 Hope Publishing Co. French text from *Cantate Domino* © World Student Christian Federation, 5, Route des Morillons, Grand Saconnex, Switzerland CH-1218 Ph: 011-41-22-798-8953 Fax: 011-41-22-798-2370.

211   Text: © 1958, renewal 1986 Hope Publishing Co. Music: Harmony © Estate of Sir Ernest MacMillan, Ross A. MacMillan, executor, 1671 Lakeshore Road, Sarnia ON N7X 1B7 Canada Ph: (519) 542-4572 Fax: (519) 542-4754 Email: rmacmill@ebtech.net.

213   Text: Paraphrase and Music: Adaptation © 1976 Hope Publishing Co.

214   Music: Harmony © Hope Publishing Co.

217   Music: Descant © Stephen A.Crisp, 60 Lambton, Ormstown QC J0S 1G0 Canada Ph: (514) 829-2904.

218   Text: Paraphrase © 1978 *Lutheran Book of Worship*. Reprinted by permission of Augsburg Fortress.

219   Text: © Margaret Beatrice Cropper, administered by Stainer & Bell Ltd. on behalf of the successor to the deceased. Reprinted by permission of Hope Publishing Co. Music: Harmony © The Church Pension Fund.

221   Music: © Burns & Oates Ltd. and Search Press Ltd., Rights & Permissions, Wellwood North Farm Road, Tunbridge Wells, Kent, TN2 3DR UK. UK Ph: 011-44-189-251-0850.

222   Text: © 1984 Hope Publishing Co.

223   Text: © 1986 Hope Publishing Co. Music: Harmony © 1955, 1983 John Ribble. Used by permission of Westminster/John Knox Press, 100 Witherspoon Street, Louisville KY 40202-1396 USA Ph: (502) 569-5060 Fax: (502) 569-5113

225   Music: Harmony © Jack W.Burnam, Immanuel Episcopal Church, Highlands, 2400 W. Seventeenth Street, Wilmington DE 19806 USA Ph: (302) 658-7326.

226   Text: © Burns & Oates, Ltd., Search Press Ltd., Rights & Permissions, Wellwood North Farm Road, Tunbridge Wells, Kent, TN2 3DR UK Ph: 011-44-189-251-0850.

227   Text: Paraphrase and Music: Melody: © Paul W. Quinlan, 98 Cherry Street, West Newton, MA 02165 USA Ph: (617) 964-5170. Accompaniment: © Patrick Wedd

228   Music: Harmony © Estate of Edmund W. Goldsmith. Current information sought.

229   Text: © 1984 Hope Publishing Co. Music: Harmony © Oxford University Press.

230   Text: © 1991 G.I.A.Publications, Inc.

231   Music: Adaptation © Oxford University Press, London; Music: Harmony © Derek Holman.

232   Text and Music: © 1989 WGRG The Iona Community (Scotland). Used by permission of G.I.A.Publications, Inc., exclusive agent.

233   Text: Adaptation and Music: Arrangement: © 1989 The United Methodist Publishing House (Administered by The Copyright Company, Nashville, TN). All rights reserved. International copyright secured. Used by permission.

234   Music: © 1983 Hope Publishing Co.

235   Text and Music: © 1990 Selah Publishing Co., Inc.

236   Text: © The Sisterhood of St. John the Divine.

237   Text and Music: Harmony: © 1928 Oxford University Press.

238   Text: © Ian Sowton, 21 Chudleigh Ave., Toronto ON M4R 1T1 Canada Ph: (416) 489-9120.

240   Text: © 1987 The Shadyside Presbyterian Church, 5121 Westminster Place, Pittsburg PA 15232-2116 USA Ph: (412) 682-4300. Music: Melody © 1977 Hinshaw Music, Inc. Used with permission, P.O. Box 470, Chapel Hill NC 27514-0470 Ph: (919) 933-1691 Fax: (919) 967-3399; Music: Adaptation © 1980 W. Thomas Jones, 508 South 5th Street, Mebane NC Email: tomi@netpath.net.

241   Music: Harmony: © Patrick Wedd.

242 Text: Paraphrase and Music: © 1978 *Lutheran Book of Worship*. Reprinted by permission of Augsburg Fortress.

243 Text and Music: © Patrick Wedd.

244 Music: © 1984 G.I.A. Publications, Inc.

245 Text: Stanzas 1-3 Revision © 1982 The Church Pension Fund. Music: © Oxford University Press.

246 Music: Descant © Kenneth Hull, c/o Dept. of Music, Conrad Grebel College, Waterloo, ON N2L 3G6 Canada Ph: (519) 885-0220 Fax: (519) 885-0014.

248 Text: © Morehouse Publishing, reprinted by permission, Morehouse Publishing, 811 Ethan Allen Hwy., Suite 204, Ridgefield CT 06877-2801 USA Ph (203) 431-3927 Fax( (203) 431-3964.

249 Text: © 1983 Oxford University Press, Inc.

250 Text: © 1990 Hope Publishing Co.

251 Music: © 1993 The Pilgrim Press.

253 Text: © 1991 Hope Publishing Co.

254 Music: Harmony from *Songs for the People of God*. Harmony © 1994 Selah Publishing Co., Inc.

255 Text: © 1991 Stainer & Bell Ltd. All rights reserved. Used by permission of Hope Publishing Co. Music: © Oxford University Press, London.

256 Text: © Estate of Elliot Rose, c/o Peter Turner, 175 Brunswick Ave., Toronto ON M5S 2M4 Canada Ph: (416) 964 5940. Music: Harmony © Oxford University Press, London.

258 Music: Trumpet descant for refrain © Melva Treffinger Graham.

259 Text: © 1970 Hope Publishing Co.

260 Text: © 1961, renewal 1989 The Hymn Society in the United States and Canada. Used by permission of Hope Publishing Co.

261 Text: © The Estate of John Arlott. Reprinted by permission of the Trustees, Mrs. B.P. Arlott, Pear Tree Cottage, 5 Queen Elizabeth II St., Alderney, Channel Islands, GY9 3TB UK. Music: Harmony © Oxford University Press, London.

263 Music: Harmony © Derek Holman.

264 Text: Translation © 1996 Concordia Publishing House, 3558 South Jefferson Ave., Saint Louis MO 63118-3968 USA Ph: (314) 268-1000 Fax: (314) 268-1329. Music: © 1989 Selah Publishing Co., Inc.

265 Text: © 1991 Stainer & Bell Ltd. Used by permission of Hope Publishing Co. Music: Melody © Herbert G. Hobbs, 2808 Mount Vernon Lane, Blacksburg VI 24060 USA Ph: (540) 552-9617; Harmony © Jan Helmut Wubbena, 410 E. Jefferson Street, Siloam Springs AR 72761-3634 USA Ph: (501) 524-9500.

266 Text: Paraphrase © Paul Gibson.

267 Music: Harmony published by permission of the executors of the late Dr. Basil Harwood.

268 Music: Harmony © Melva Treffinger Graham.

269 Text: © Paul Gibson. Music: Harmony © Patrick Wedd.

271 Text: Stanza 3 and Music: © Richard Wayne Dirksen, 3824 Garfield Street, N.W., Washington DC 20007-1383 USA Ph: (202) 338-2095.

272 Text: Translation and Music: Harmony © Oxford University Press.

273 Text: © 1987 Hope Publishing Co. Music: © 1942, renewal 1970 Hope Publishing Co.

274 Text: © 1973 Hope Publishing Co.

276 Music: © Oxford University Press.

277 Text: © 1991 Stainer & Bell Ltd. All rights reserved. Used by permission of Hope Publishing Co.

282 Text: Revision *Hymns for Today's Church*, 1982. © 1982 Hope Publishing Co.

283 Text: Revision *The Hymnal 1982* © 1982 Church Pension Fund. Stanza 2a © Walter W.G. Deller, Diocese of Toronto Office, 135 Adelaide St. East, Toronto, ON M5C 1L8 Canada Fax: (416) 363-7678. Music: Arrangement © Oxford University Press.

284 Music: Arrangement © 1987 G.I.A.Publications, Inc.

285 Music: Harmony © 1975 Elizabeth Whitehead Lang, 2008 Prince Albert Dr., Riverside CA 92507 Ph: (909) 683-5616.

286 Music: Descant © 1982 Hope Publishing Co.

287 Text: © 1992 Hope Publishing Co. Music: Arrangement and descant © 1983 Hope Publishing Co.

288 Text: © 1989 WGRG The Iona Community (Scotland). Used by permission of G.I.A.Publications, Inc., exclusive agent.

289 Text: © 1991 Stainer & Bell Ltd. All rights reserved. Used by permission of Hope Publishing Co. Music: Harmony from *Songs for the People of God*. Harmony © 1994 Selah Publishing Co., Inc.

291 Text: © 1969 Hope Publishing Co.

292 Text and Music: Arrangement © 1989 WGRG The Iona Community (Scotland). Used by permission of G.I.A.Publications Inc., exclusive agent.

295 Text: Paraphrase © 1982 Hope Publishing Co.

296 Text: © 1989 WGRG The Iona Community (Scotland). Used by permission of G.I.A.Publications, Inc., exclusive agent.

297 Text and Music: © 1989 WGRG The Iona Community (Scotland). Used by permission of G.I.A.Publications, Inc., exclusive agent.

298 Music: Harmony © Estate of Sir Ernest MacMillan, Ross A. MacMillan, executor, 1671 Lakeshore Road, Sarnia ON N7X 1B7 Canada Ph: (519) 542-4572 Fax: (519) 542-4754 Email: rmacmill@ebtech.net.

299 Text: © 1992 Hope Publishing Co. Music: Descant © Gerald Manning, R.R. 1, Puslinch ON N0B 2J0 Canada Ph: (519) 836-0153.

300 Music: Descant © Barry Rose, 31 Abbey Mill Lane, St. Albans, Herfordshire, AL3 4HA, UK Ph. & Fax: 011-44-172-785-1810. Written for the Wedding of the Prince of Wales and the Lady Diana Spencer, July 29, 1981.

301 Text: Stanzas 1-3 © Board of Publication, Lutheran Church in America; Stanza 4 © 1958 *Service Book and Hymnal*. Reprinted by permission of Augsburg Fortress. Music: © John Beaver, 105 Gatesview Dr., Hamilton ON L9C 1B1 Ph: (905) 383-6762.

302 Text: © 1990 Hope Publishing Co. Music: © 1915 (renewed) J. Curwen & Sons, Ltd. (London). Used by permission of G. Schirmer, Inc. (ASCAP).

305 Text: © 1976 Hope Publishing Co.

306 Music: Descant © Novello & Co., Ltd.

307 Text and Music: Melody © The Reverend Dr. Peter Davison, All Saints Anglican Church, 3205-27th Street, Vernon BC V1T 4V8 Canada Ph: (250) 542 3179 Fax: (250) 542-5139; Music: Harmony © George Black.

309 Text and Music: © 1976 Hinshaw Music, Inc. Used with permission, P.O. Box 470, Chapel Hill NC 27514-0470 Ph: (919) 933-1691 Fax: (919) 967-3399.

311 Text and Music: © 1975 Choristers Guild, 2834 Kingsley Road, Garland TX 75041 USA Ph: (214) 271-1521 Fax: (214) 840-3113.

312 Text and Music: © 1972, 1974, 1979 Daniel L. Schutte and New Dawn Music. Administered by Oregon Catholic Press, OCP Publications.

313 Text: English paraphrase and Music: © 1991 Les Presses de Taizé. Used by permission of G.I.A.Publications, Inc., exclusive agent.

314 Text: English paraphrase and Music: © 1991 Les Presses de Taizé. Used by permission of G.I.A.Publications, Inc., exclusive agent.

315 Text: © 1969 Oxford University Press.

316 Text: English paraphrase © 1974 Hope Publishing Co. French paraphrase © 1995 Réveil Publications, B.P. 4464, 20 Rue Calliet, Lyon Cédex 04 France 69241 Ph: 011-33-72-00-08-54 Fax: 011-33-72-00-02-74. Music: Harmony © 1977 Hope Publishing Co.

320 Text: © Oxford University Press. Music: Harmony © Oxford University Press. Descant © Kevin Mayhew Ltd. Used by permission, c/o Jane Rayson, Rattlesden, Bury-St.-Edmunds, Suffolk UK IP30 0SZ Ph: 011-44-144-973-7978 Fax: 011-44-144-973-7834.

321 Music: Descant © 1979 G.I.A.Publications, Inc.

323 Music: Descant © Hope Publishing Co.

324 Music: © Dumisani Abraham Maraire, PO Box MP 167 Mount Pleasant, Harare, Zimbabwe Ph: 011-263-4-303211 Fax: 011-263-4-333407 Email: dmarai@zimbix.uz.zw.

325 Music: Descant © 1982 Hope Publishing Co.

326 Music: Descant © Oxford University Press.

329 Music: © Estate of Edward W. Naylor. Current information sought.

331 Text: Paraphrase © 1982 Hope Publishing Co.

335 Music: © 1973 Waterloo Music Co. Ltd.

336 Text, Music, and Arrangement: "Masithi" from the *Lumko Hymnbook* © 1991 Lumko Institute, P.O. Box 5058, 1403 Delmenville, 59 Cachet Road, Lambton, Germiston 1401, Republic of South Africa Ph: (011) 827-8924 or (011) 824-2689 Fax: (011) 827-5774.

338 Text and Music: © 1991 Les Presses de Taizé. Used by permission of G.I.A.Publications, Inc., exclusive agent.

339 Music: © Oxford University Press.

340 Text and Music: © 1997 Claude Fraysse, Chanteur évangéliste; Animateur musical, Allée de la grande Muzenne, 26750 Genissieux, France 26760 Ph: 011-33-75 02 71 93 Fax: 011-33-75 02 71 93. Text: Translation © 1989 The Hymnal Project, c/o Church of the Brethren General Board, 1451 Dundee Ave., Elgin IL 60120 Ph: (708) 742-5100.

344 Music: Harmony © Oxford University Press.

347 Text: Stanza 4 Revision, *Hymns for Today's Church*, 1982. © 1982 Hope Publishing Co.

349 Text: French paraphrase © 1995 Réveil Publications. Text: Inuktitut translation © Benjamin T. Arreak.

351 Text: Paraphrase © 1992 G.I.A.Publications, Inc. Music: Harmony published by permission of the executors of the late Dr. Basil Harwood.

352 Text: Plains Cree translation: © James Settee, PO Box 37, RR1, Christopher Lake, SK S0J 0N0 Ph: (306) 763-2455 (Anglican Church of Canada, Synod of Saskatchewan Office). Text: Inuktitut translation © Benjamin T. Arreak. Music: Harmony © John Campbell.

353 Music: Descant © Royal School of Church Music, Cleveland Lodge, Westhumble, Dorking, Surrey RH5 6BW UK Ph: 011-44 1306 877676 Fax: 011-44 1306 887260.

355 Text: © 1923 (renewed) by J. Curwen & Sons, Ltd. Reprinted by permission of G. Schirmer, Inc. (ASCAP). Music: Harmony © Oxford University Press.

357 Music: Music published by permission of the executors of the late Dr. Basil Harwood.

358 Text and Music: © 1968 Augsburg Publishing House. Reprinted by permission of Augsburg Fortress. Music: Descant for refrain © Melva Treffinger Graham.

359 Text and Music: © 1980 G.I.A. Publications, Inc.

360 Text : Paraphrase and Music: © 1991 Les Presses de Taizé. Used by permission of G.I.A.Publications, Inc., exclusive agent.

361 Text: © 1982 Hope Publishing Co. Music: © 1990 Selah Publishing Co., Inc.

362 Text: Paraphrase © 1962, renewal 1990 Hope Publishing Co. Music: Melody and Harmony © Oxford University Press. Descant © 1982 Hope Publishing Co. Alternative harmony © Derek Holman.

363 Text: Paraphrase © Paul Gibson.

364 Text: Paraphrase © 1990 Hope Publishing Co. Music: Harmony © Estate of Healey Willan.

365 Text: Paraphrase © Paul Gibson.

366 Text: Paraphrase © Paul Gibson. Music: Revision © 1995 Réveil Publications.

367 Music: © 1978, 1980, 1981 Les Presses de Taizé. Used by permission of G.I.A. Publications, Inc. exclusive agent.

368 Music: Arrangement © 1990 WGRG The Iona Community (Scotland). Used by permission of G.I.A.Publications, Inc.

369 Text: © 1969 Concordia Publishing House, 3558 South Jefferson Ave., Saint Louis MO 63118-3968 USA Ph: (314) 268-1000 Fax: (314) 268-1329. Music: © Estate of Gwenlyn Evans. Used by permission of Dilys Evans and Eluned Crump, representatives, c/o Miss Dilys Evans, Uxbridge Square Caernarfon, Gwynedd North Wales UK LL55 2RE Ph: 011 44 128 667-3740

371 Text: Revision *The Book of Praise*, 1997; revision © 1996 The Presbyterian Church in Canada, 50 Wynford Drive, North York ON M3C 1J7 Canada Ph: (416) 441-1111 Fax: (416) 441-2825.

375   Music: © Oxford University Press.

376   Text: Paraphrase and Music: © 1991 Les Presses de Taizé. Used by permission of G.I.A. Publications, Inc., exclusive agent.

377   Music: Descant © Gerald Manning, R.R. 1, Puslinch ON N0B 2J0 Canada Ph: (519) 836-0153.

380   Music: Fauxbourdon © Faith Press, Faith House, Ceased Publishing, 7 Tufton Street, London SW1P 3QD UK (current information sought); Descant © Cambridge University Press.

381   Music: Descant © Gerald Manning, R.R. 1, Puslinch ON N0B 2J0 Canada.

382   Text: Paraphrase and Music: © Ron Klusmeier, 345 Pym Street, Parksville BC V9P 1C8 Canada Ph: (250) 954-1785 Fax: (250) 954-1683 Email: musiklus@island.net.

384   Music: Descant © 1953 Novello & Co., Ltd.

386   Music: Descant © David R. Riley, 1202 Lake Falls Rd., Baltimore, MD 21210 USA Ph: (410) 377-7251.

387   Text: Paraphrase © 1985 The Church Pension Fund, administered by Church Publishing Inc. Music: © Oxford University Press.

389   Text: © 1990 Hope Publishing Co. Music: Arrangement © Oxford University Press. Music: Harmony adaptation © Patrick Wedd.

390   Text: © 1992 G.I.A.Publications, Inc. Music: © 1971 Walton Music Corp., Att: Sherry Halpern, Auditor, 170 N.E. 33rd Street, Ft. Lauderdale FL 33334 USA Ph: (954) 563-1844 Fax: (954) 563-9006.

391   Text: © 1988 Emmanuel College, Toronto, Principal's Office, Rights & Permissions, 75 Queen's Park Cres. E., Toronto ON M5S 1K7 Canada Ph: (416) 585-4539 Fax: (416) 585-4516. Music: Harmony © George Black.

392   Text: © 1989 Hope Publishing Co. Music: Arrangement © 1991 Hope Publishing Co.

394   Text: © 1988 Emmanuel College, Toronto, Principal's Office, Rights & Permissions, 75 Queen's Park Cres. E., Toronto ON M5S 1K7 Canada Ph: (416) 585-4539 Fax: (416) 585-4516. Music: © 1994 Waterloo Music Co. Ltd.

395   Text: © 1989, 1994 Hope Publishing Co. Music: © Patrick Wedd.

396   Text and Music: © 1985 Oxford University Press, Inc.

397   Text: © 1987 Hope Publishing Co.

400   Music: Harmony *The New Century Hymnal*, 1995. Harmony © 1993 The Pilgrim Press.

401   Text: Stanza 3 © 1957 (renewed) by Sanga Music, Inc. All rights reserved. Used by permission. Harold Leventhal Management, 250 West 57th Street #1218 New York NY 10107 USA Ph: (212) 586-6553 Fax: (212) 459-9035.

402   Text: English paraphrase and Music: © 1991 Les Presses de Taizé. Used by permission of G.I.A. Publications, Inc., exclusive agent.

403   Text: © 1939 E.C. Schirmer Music Co. Music: Harmony © 1978 *The Lutheran Book of Worship*. Reprinted by permission of Augsburg Fortress.

404   Text and Music: © 1989 Make Way Music. Administered in North and South America by Integrity's Hosanna! Music (ASCAP). All rights reserved. International copyright secured. Used by permission, Integrity Music, Inc., 1000 Cody Road, Mobile AL 36695 USA Ph: (334) 633-9000 Fax (334) 633-5202.

405   Text and Music: © 1973 Word of God Music (Administered by The Copyright Company, Nashville, TN). All rights reserved. International copyright secured. Used by permission.

406   Text: Paraphrase and Music: © 1979, 1991, Order of St. Benedict Inc., The Liturgical Press, St. John's Abbey, Collegeville MN 56321 USA Ph: (612) 363-2213.

407   Text: Oji-Cree text © Stan McKay, c/o Dr. Jessie Salteaux Social Centre, Box 210, Beauséjour, MB R0E 0C0 Canada Ph: (204) 268-3919 Fax: (204) 268-4463. Text: Paraphrase © South Dakota Conference, United Church of Christ, 3500 S. Phillips Ave, Suite 121, Sioux Falls SD 57105 USA Ph: (605) 338-8738 Fax: (605) 338-9422. Music: Percussion arr. © Brian Barlow, 414 St. Clair Ave. East, Toronto ON M4T 1P5 Ph: (414) 482-3538.

408   Text and Music: © 1986 G.I.A. Publications, Inc.

409   Text: © Herbert O'Driscoll. Music: © David M. Young, Estate of David M. Young, c/o Jo Young, 1619 Lancaster Ave., Sarnia ON N7V 3S7 Canada Ph: (519) 524-1129.

410   Text: © 1979 The Hymn Society in the United States and Canada. All rights reserved. Used by permission of Hope Publishing Co.

411   Text: © Oxford University Press. Music: Harmony and revision © 1995 Réveil Publications.

412   Text: © Herbert O'Driscoll.

413   Text: Paraphrase © 1981 Hope Publishing Co. Music: © Patrick Wedd.

414   Text: © Jaroslav J. Vajda, 3534 Brookstone S., Dr., St. Louis MO 63129-2900 USA Ph: (314) 892-9473. Music: © 1983 G.I.A. Publications, Inc.

416   Music: Arrangement © 1921 (renewed) by J. Curwen & Sons Ltd. (London). Used by permission of G. Schirmer, Inc. (ASCAP).

417   Text: Translation © 1983 The United Methodist Publishing House (Administered by The Copyright Company, Nashville, TN). All rights reserved. International copyright secured. Used by permission. Music: Melody © 1976 Resource Publications, Inc., Rights & Permissions, Att: Susan Marquez, 160 E. Virginia St., #290, San Jose CA 95112-5876 USA Ph: (408) 286-8505 Fax: (408) 287-8748; Music: Accompaniment © Melva Treffinger Graham.

418   Text and Music: © Common Cup Company.

419   Text: Paraphrase © 1989 Hope Publishing Co.

421   Music: © Estate of Doris Wright Smith, Mrs. Alfred Morton Smith, c/o Gerald R. Spall, 817 East Landis Ave., CN 1501 Vineland NJ 08360 USA Ph: (609) 691-0100 Fax: (609) 692-4095; (609) 691-3302.

422   Text: © Estate of Mary Susannah Edgar, Estate Executor, c/o Mr. John W. Gilchrist, 10 Wychwood Park, Toronto ON M6G 2V5 Canada Ph: (416) 656-3403. Music: © Estate of Henry Walford Davies. Used by permission of Oxford University Press.

423   Text and Music: Harmony © 1953, renewed 1981, Stuart K. Hine, assigned to Manna Music, Inc. All Rights Reserved. Used by permission, Manna Music, P.O. Box 218, 35255 Brooton Road, Pacific City OR 97135 USA Ph: (503) 965-6112 Fax: (503) 965-6880.

424   Text and Music: © 1989 WGRG The Iona Community (Scotland). Used by permission of G.I.A. Publications, Inc., exclusive agent.

426   Music: Trombone arrangement © Melva Treffinger Graham.

427   Music: Harmony © Oxford University Press.

428   Text: © Walter Henry Farquharson, Box 126, Saltcoats SK S0A 3R0 Canada Ph: (306) 744-2214. Music: © 1942, renewal 1970, Hope Publishing Co.

429   Music: Harmony © Oxford University Press.

430   Text and Music: Arrangement © 1987 WGRG The Iona Community (Scotland). Used by permission of G.I.A. Publications, Inc., exclusive agent.

431   Music: Descant © Cambridge University Press.

433   Text: © 1978 Hope Publishing Co. Music: © 1942, renewal 1970 Hope Publishing Co.

434   Text: © Herbert O'Driscoll.

437   Text: © 1982 Hope Publishing Co.

438   Music: © Oxford University Press.

439   Music: Descant © Derek Holman.

440   Text: © 1989 Hope Publishing Co. Music: © Ruth Watson Henderson, 23 Birchview Blvd., Etobicoke ON M8X 1H4 Canada Ph: (416) 231-8338.

442   Text: © 1977, 1995 Hope Publishing Co.

444   Text: Revision © The Sisterhood of St. John the Divine. Music: Music published by permission of the executors of the late Dr. Basil Harwood.

445   Text and Music: Arrangement © 1989 WGRG The Iona Community (Scotland). Used by permission of G.I.A. Publications, Inc., exclusive agent.

446   Text: © James Quinn, SJ. Used by permission of Selah Publishing Co., Inc., North American agent.

447   Text: © 1987 Hope Publishing Co. Music: © William Penfro Rowlands. Reprinted by permission of Mr. G.A. Gabe, "Seaward," Lambswell Close, Langland Swansea SA3 4HJ UK Ph: 011-44-179-236-6183.

448   Text: © 1982 Mennonite Indian Leaders Council, c/o Willis Busenitz, Busby MT 59016 USA Ph: (406) 592-3643.

449   Text: © 1982 Hope Publishing Co.

450   Text: © 1992 Hope Publishing Co.

451   Text and Music: Melody © F.E.V. Pilcher, Estate of F.E.V.Pilcher c/o Mrs. Isabel F. Pilcher, 94 Willingdon Blvd, Toronto ON M8X 2H7 Canada Ph: (416) 231-3022. Music: Harmony © 1973 Waterloo Music Co. Ltd.

452   Music: © 1962 Theodore Presser Co. Used by permission, 1 Presser Place, Bryn Mawr PA 19010-3490 USA Ph: (610) 525-3636 Fax: (610) 527-7841.

453   Text: © 1992 Hope Publishing Co. Music: Harmony © Oxford University Press.

456   Text: © 1984 Hope Publishing Co.

457   Text and Music: Adaptation © 1986 G.I.A. Publications, Inc.

458   Text and Music: © 1972 Maranatha! Music (Administered by The Copyright Company, Nashville, TN). All rights reserved. International copyright secured. Used by permission.

460   Text and Music: © 1987 Make Way Music, Ltd. Administered in North and South America by Integrity's Hosanna! Music (ASCAP). All rights reserved. International copyright secured. Used by permission, Integrity Music, Inc., 1000 Cody Road, Mobile AL 36695 USA Ph: (334) 633-9000 Fax (334) 633-5202.

461   Text: Revision *Hymns for Today's Church*. © 1982 Hope Publishing Co.

462   Text: © 1994 Oxford University Press, Inc. Music: © John Kuzma, 1648 Krameria Street, Denver CO 80220-1553 USA Ph: (303) 322-3920.

463   Text: © 1993 Hope Publishing Co. Music: © Oxford University Press.

464   Text: Translation and Music © 1991 Les Presses de Taizé. Used by permission of G.I.A. Publications, Inc., exclusive agent.

465   Text and Music: © 1982 G.I.A. Publications, Inc.

466   Text: © 1982 Hope Publishing Co. Music: Arrangement © The Royal School of Church Music, Cleveland Lodge, Westhumble, Dorking, Surrey RH5 6BW UK Ph: 011-44 1306 877676 Fax: 011-44 1306 887260.

468   Text: © Judith Fetter, 3450 Cook Street, Victoria BC V8X 1B1 Ph: (250) 920-9935 Fax: (250) 479-8243. Music: Music published by permission of the executors of the late Dr. Basil Harwood.

469   Text and Music: © 1992 Hope Publishing Co.

470   Text: © 1983 Oxford University Press, Inc. Music: Melody © Brian Ruttan, 94 Lake Ave. Drive, Stoney Creek ON L8G 3N4 Canada Ph: (905) 662-7607; Music: Harmony © Roland Packer, 29 Blackwood Cresc., Hamilton ON L8S 3H6 Canada.

471   Text: © 1971 The United Methodist Publishing House (Administered by The Copyright Company, Nashville, TN). All rights reserved. International copyright secured. Used by permission.

472   Text: © Estate of Robert Dobbie, c/o Charles Dobbie, 65 Tidefall Drive, Agincourt ON M1W 1J1 Canada Ph: (416) 497-5885. Music: © Oxford University Press.

473   Text and Music: Melody © Pablo Sosa, Camacuá 282, 1406 Buenos Aires Argentina. Music: Arrangement © *Songs for a Gospel People*, administered by Wood Lake Books, 10162 Newene Rd., Winfield BC V4V 1R2 Canada Ph: (250) 766-2778 Fax: (250) 766-2736.

475   Text: © Estate of George Bradford Caird. Used by permission of Viola M. Caird, The G.B.Caird Memorial Trust, Mansfield College, Oxford OX1 3TF UK Ph: 011 44 186 527 0999.

476   Text: © Herbert O'Driscoll. Music: © F.R.C. Clarke, 260 Indian Road, Kingston ON K7M 1T7 Canada Ph: (613) 548-7470.

479   Text: © 1982 Hope Publishing Co.

482   Text: © Herbert O'Driscoll. Music: Harmony © 1978 *Lutheran Book of Worship*. Reprinted by permission of Augsburg Fortress.

483 Text: Paraphrase and Music: © 1986 G.I.A. Publications, Inc.

484 Text: © John Oxenham, deceased. Reprinted by permission of Desmond Dunkerley, 23 Haslemere Rd. Southsea-Portsmouth, Hants. P0B 8BB UK Ph: 011-44-170-573-5264. Music: Adaptation © Estate of Henry Thacker Burleigh. Current information sought.

486 Music: © William Penfro Rowlands. Reprinted by permission of Mr. G.A. Gabe, "Seaward," Lambswell Close, Langland Swansea SA3 4HJ UK Ph: 011-44-179-236-6183.

487 Text: © 1961, 1962 World Library Publications, Inc. A division of J.S. Paluch Company, Inc., 3825 N Willow Road, Schiller Park IL 60176 USA Ph: (847) 678-0621 Fax: (847) 671-5715.

488 Music: © 1990 Ione Press, Inc. Used by permission of E.C. Schirmer Music Co.

489 Text: © 1988 WGRG The Iona Community (Scotland). Used by permission of G.I.A. Publications, Inc., exclusive agent. Music: Arrangement © George Black.

492 Text and Music: © 1984 The Sisterhood of St. John the Divine.

493 Text: © 1990 Mennonite World Conference, 50 Kent Ave., Kitchener ON N2G 3R1 Canada Ph: (519) 571-0060 Fax: (519) 571-1980.

494 Text: © 1985 Hope Publishing Co. Music: © 1988 G.I.A. Publications, Inc.

495 Text: Paraphrase and Music: Arrangement © 1988 WGRG The Iona Community (Scotland); used by permission of G.I.A. Publications, Inc., exclusive agent.

498 Text: Stanzas 3-4 © 1982 Hope Publishing Co. Music: Arrangement © Oxford University Press.

500 Text and Music: © 1977 Scripture in Song (a div. of Integrity Music, Inc.). All rights reserved. International copyright secured. Used by permission, Integrity Music, Inc., 1000 Cody Road, Mobile AL 36695 USA Ph: (334) 633-9000 Fax (334) 633-5202.

502 Text and Music: © 1986 G.I.A. Publications, Inc.

504 Text: © 1969 Hope Publishing Co. Music: Melody © 1969 and Arrangement © 1982 by Hope Publishing Co.

505 Text: Versification © courtesy of the estate of Eleanor Hull and Chatto & Windus Ltd., Random House, 20 Vauxhall Bridge Road, London SW1V 2SA UK Ph: 011-44-171-973-9000 Fax: 011-44-171-233-8791. Music: Arrangement © Oxford University Press.

506 Text and Music: Arrangement © Oxford University Press.

508 Music: Harmony © Oxford University Press.

509 Text and Music: © 1938 Hill and Range Songs. Copyright renewed, Unichappell Music, Inc. c/o Hal Leonard Corporation, 7777 West Bluemound Road, P.O Box 13819 Milwaukee WI 53213 USA Ph: (414) 774-3630 Fax: (414) 774-3259 Email: halinfo@halleonard.com.

510 Text and Music: © 1971 Gooi en Sticht, bv., Baarn, The Netherlands. Reprinted by permission of OCP Publications, exclusive agent for English-language countries.

513 Music: Harmony © 1987 Estate of Wendell Whalum, c/o Mrs. Clarie G. Whalum, 2439 Greenwood Circle, East Point GA 30344 USA Ph: (404) 349-7475.

514 Text: Translation © Oxford University Press. Altered with permission.

516 Text: © 1991 by Hope Publishing Co.

517 Text: © 1976 by The Hymn Society in the United States and Canada. All rights reserved. Used by permission of Hope Publishing Co.

518 Text: The Society of Authors as Literary Representatives of the Estate of John Masefield. 84 Drayton Gardens, London SW10 95B Ph: 011-44-171-373-6643 Fax: 011-44-171-373-5768 E-mail: authorsoc@writers.org.uk

519 Music: Harmony © Oxford University Press.

520 Music: Descant © Oxford University Press.

523 Text: © 1990 Selah Publishing Co., Inc. Music: © 1980 G.I.A. Publications Co.

526 Text: © 1982 Hope Publishing Co.

528 Music: Descant © Cambridge University Press.

529 Text: Translation © Oxford University Press. Altered with permission. Music: © Novello & Co., Ltd.

530 Text and Music: © 1991 Les Presses de Taizé. Used by permission of G.I.A. Publications, Inc., exclusive agent.

531 Text: Paraphrase and Music: © 1979, 1991 New Dawn Music. Administered by Oregon Catholic Press.

534 Text: © 1958 The United Methodist Publishing House (Administered by The Copyright Company, Nashville, TN). All rights reserved. International Copyright Secured. Used by permission. Music: © 1958 JASRAC; used by permission of JASRAC License No. 9800785, JASRAC, Jasrac House, 7-13 1-Chome Nishishimbashi, Tokyo, Japan 105.

535 Music: Arrangement © 1971 Walton Music Corporation, Att: Sherry Halpern, Auditor, 170 N.E. 33rd Street, Ft. Lauderdale FL 33334 USA Ph: (954) 563-1844 Fax: (954) 563-9006.

536 Music: Accompaniment © 1987 G.I.A. Publications, Inc.

540 Text: Paraphrase © Brian Ruttan, 94 Lake Ave. Drive, Stoney Creek ON L8G 3N4 Canada Ph: (905) 662-7607. Music: © Breitkopf & Härtel, Walkmühlstr. 52, Wiesbaden, D-65195 Germany Ph: 011-49-611-45008-0 Fax: 011-49-611-45008-59 or 60. Arrangement © 1933, 1961 Presbyterian Board of Christian Education. Used by permission of Westminster/John Knox Press, 100 Witherspoon Street, Louisville KY 40202-1396 USA Ph: (502) 569-5060 Fax: (502) 569-5113.

541 Text: Paraphrase © 1975 Word Music (a div. of WORD MUSIC). All Rights Reserved. Used By Permission, c/o Darlene K. Abbott, 3319 West End Ave, Suite 200, Nashville TN 37203 Ph: (615) 385-9673 Fax: (615) 386-9696. Music: Arrangement © 1982 by Hope Publishing Co.

542 Music: Harmony © F. R.C. Clarke, 260 Indian Road, Kingston ON K7M 1T7 Canada Ph: (613) 548-7470.

544 Music: © Roland A.H.Packer, 29 Blackwood Cresc., Hamilton ON L8S 3H6 Canada.

545 Text and Music: © 1989 WGRG The Iona Community (Scotland). Used by permission of G.I.A. Publications, Inc., exclusive agent.

547 Music: © 1969 Faith and Life Press/Mennonite Publishing House, 616 Walnut Ave., Scottdale PA 15683-1999 USA Ph: (412) 887-8500; Faith and Life Press, P.O. Box 347, Newton KS 67114 USA Ph: (316) 283-5100.

548 Text: Paraphrase and Music: © 1982 G.I.A. Publications, Inc.

549 Text: French and English paraphrases and Music: © 1991 Les Presses de Taizé. Used by permission of G.I.A. Publications, Inc., exclusive agent.

552 Text: Translation and Music: Arrangement © Chinese Christian Literature Council Ltd., Att: Rev. S.Y.So, Chairman Block A H/F, 138 Nathan Rd., Tsim Sha Tsui, Kowloon, Hong Kong Ph: (852) 2367 8031-3 Fax: (852) 2739 6030.

553 Text: English paraphrase and Music: © 1991 Les Presses de Taizé. Used by permission of G.I.A. Publications, Inc., exclusive agent.

554 Text: Paraphrase © 1992 G.I.A. Publications, Inc. Music: © Jane Manton Marshall. Used by permission, 4077 Northaven Road, Dallas TX 75229 USA Ph: (214) 351-1960.

557 Text: © 1974 The Hymn Society in the United States and Canada. All rights reserved. Used by permission of Hope Publishing Co. Music: © The Estate of Doris Wright Smith, c/o Gerald R. Spall, 817 East Landis Ave., CN 1501 Vineland NJ 08360 USA Ph: (609) 691-0100 Fax: (609) 692-4095; (609) 691-3302.

558 Text: © Herbert O'Driscoll.

560 Music: Descant © 1953 Novello & Co., Ltd.

561 Text: Revision Hymns for Today's Church, © 1982 by Hope Publishing Co.

563 Text: Paraphrase and Music: © 1991 Les Presses de Taizé. Used by permission of G.I.A. Publications, Inc., exclusive agent.

565 Music: © John Hughes, deceased. Reprinted by permission of Ms. C.A. Webb, 4 Nant Walla, Heol y Felin, Rhiwbina, Cardiff CF4 6NT UK Ph: 011-44-122-261-1495.

566 Text and Music: Harmony © 1977 Chinese Christian Literature Council, Ltd., Att: Rev. S.Y.So, Chairman Block A H/F, 138 Nathan Rd., Tsim Sha Tsui, Kowloon, Hong Kong Ph: (852) 2367 8031-3 Fax: (852) 2739 6030.

567 Text: Revision Hymns for Today's Church, 1982. © 1982 Hope Publishing Co.

568 Text: English translation and Music: © 1991 Les Presses de Taizé. Used by permission of G.I.A.Publications, Inc., exclusive agent.

569 Music: 1911 © Stainer & Bell Ltd., P.O. Box 110, Victoria House, 23 Gruneisen Road, Finchley, London UK N3 1DZ Ph: 0181-343 3303 Fax: 0181-343 3024 Internet: http:// www.stainer.demon.co.uk email: post@stainer.demon.co.uk

571 Text: English and French translations © 1987 Songs for a Gospel People, administered by Wood Lake Books, 10162 Newene Rd., Winfield BC V4V 1R2 Canada Ph: (250) 766-2778 Fax: (250) 766-2736. Music: Percussion arrangement © Brian Barlow, 414 St. Clair Ave. East, Toronto ON M4T 1P5 Ph: (416) 482-3538.

572 Text: © Frances Wheeler Davis, 5205 Belmore Ave., Montréal PQ H4V 2C7 Canada Ph: (514) 484-7646. Music: © 1976 Margaret Fleming, 57-8889 212th Street, Langley BC V1M 2E8 Canada Ph: (604) 888-9302 Fax: (604) 534-0781.

573 Text: © 1982 Hope Publishing Co.

574 Text: © Oxford University Press. Music: © The United Nations Association, Peter Dyson, United Nations Association of Great Britain and Northern Ireland, 3 Whitehall Court London SW1A 2EL UK Ph: 011-44-171-930-2931.

575 Text: © William Whitla, 76 Evans Ave., Toronto ON M6S 3R8 Ph: (416) 766-6393. Music: © J. Curwen & Sons, Ltd. (London). Used by permission of G. Schirmer, Inc. (ASCAP).

576 Text: © 1968 Hope Publishing Co.

577 Music: © John Hughes, deceased. Reprinted by permission of Ms. C.A. Webb, 4 Nant Walla, Heol y Felin, Rhiwbina, Cardiff CF4 6NT UK Ph: 011-44-122-261-1495.

578 Text and Music: © 1964 (renewed) by Appleseed Music Inc. All rights reserved. Used by permission c/o Sanga Music Inc. Harold Leventhal Management, 250 W. 57th St. #1218, New York, NY 10107 USA Ph: (212) 586-6553 Fax: (212) 459-9035 Music: Arrangement Melva Treffinger Graham.

579 Text and Music: © 1988 WGRG The Iona Community (Scotland). Used by permission of G.I.A.Publications, Inc., exclusive agent.

580 Text: © Oxford University Press. Music: Harmony published by permission of the executors of the late Dr. Basil Harwood.

581 Text: © 1965 and Music © 1992 Hope Publishing Co.

582 Text: © Inter-Lutheran Commission on Worship. Reprinted by permission of Augsburg Fortress.

583 Text: © 1992 G.I.A. Publications, Inc. Music: Harmony © Dale Grotenhuis, 2299 Aimie Ave SW, Byron Center MI 49315 USA Ph: (616) 878-3733.

584 Text: © 1971 Hope Publishing Co. Music: Arrangement © Oxford University Press.

585 Text: © 1961 Oxford University Press. Music: Arrangement © 1978 Lutheran Book of Worship. Reprinted by permission of Augsburg Fortress.

586 Text: © Norman O.Forness, 38 East Stevens Street, Gettysburg PA 17235 USA Ph: (717) 334-6893.

587 Music: © Estate of Gwenlyn Evans. Used by permission of Dilys Evans and Eluned Crump, representatives, c/o Miss Dilys Evans Uxbridge Square Caernarfon, Gwynedd North Wales UK LL55 2RE Ph: 011 44 128 667-3740

588 Text and Music: © Geonyong Lee, Korean National Institute of Arts, 700 Seocho-dong Seocho-gu, Seoul, Korea; Text: Translation © Marion Pope, 135 - 211 College St., Toronto ON M5T 1R1 Canada Ph: (416) 351-0904.

589 Text: © 1985 G.I.A.Publications, Inc. Music: © 1985 G.I.A.Publications, Inc.

590 Text: © 1969 Stainer & Bell Ltd. All rights reserved. Used by permission of Hope Publishing Co. Music: © 1969 Hope Publishing Co.

591 Text: © 1987 Hope Publishing Co. Music: © 1988 Selah Publishing Co., Inc.

592 Text: © The Sisterhood of St. John the Divine.

593 Text: © 1958, renewal 1986 The Hymn Society in the United States and Canada. All rights reserved. Used by permission of Hope Publishing Co.

594 Text: Revision *Hymns for Today's Church*, 1982. © 1982 Hope Publishing Co.

595 Text: Revision © *Songs for a Gospel People*, administered by Wood Lake Books, 10162 Newene Rd., Winfield BC V4V 1R2 Canada Ph: (250) 766-2778 Fax: (250) 766-2736. Music: Harmony © Melva Treffinger Graham.

596 Music: © 1968 Novello & Co., Ltd.

597 Text and Music: © Patrick Wedd.

598 Text: © 1991 G.I.A.Publications, Inc.

599 Text: © 1991 Hope Publishing Co.

600 Text and Music: Melody © 1992 The General Synod of the Anglican Church of Canada. Music: Harmony © Patrick Wedd. Music: Descant © Michael Capon, 130 Connaught St., Apt. 8, Fredericton, NB E3B 2A9 Canada Ph: (506) 450-8500.

601 Text: © 1961, renewal 1989 The Hymn Society in the United States and Canada. All rights reserved. Used by permission of Hope Publishing Co Music: © William Penfro Rowlands. Reprinted by permission of Mr. G.A. Gabe, "Seaward," Lambswell Close, Langland Swansea SA3 4HJ UK Ph: 011-44-179-326-6183.

602 Text: Stanzas 1–5 © 1992 and Music: © 1974 Hope Publishing Co.

603 Text: © 1986 Hope Publishing Co.

604 Text: © 1992 Hope Publishing Co. Music: Harmony © 1985 G.I.A. Publications, Inc.

610 Text and Music: © 1989 WGRG The Iona Community (Scotland). Used by permission of G.I.A.Publications, Inc., exclusive agent.

611 Text: © 1981 International Committee on English in the Liturgy, Inc.

612 Text and Music: © 1987 G.I.A. Publications, Inc.

613 Text: © Anna Briggs, 26 Beverley Terrace, North Shields NE30 4NT UK. Music: © The Reverend William B. Ferguson, Broomhill Church of Scotland, 228 Queen Victoria Drive, Glasgow G13 1TN Scotland Ph: 041-959 7182.

614 Text: © Oxford University Press. Music: Harmony © 1991 Hope Publishing Co.

615 Inuktitut translation © Benjamin T. Arreak.

617 Music: © Oxford University Press.

618 Text and Music: Harmony © 1972 G.I.A. Publications, Inc.

619 Music: Arrangement © Estate of James Hopkirk, c/o Arthur E.B. Armstrong, 131 Brenda Cres., Scarborough ON M1K 3C8 Canada Ph: (416) 261-2539; Descant © Kenneth Hull, c/o Department of Music, Conrad Grebel College, Waterloo ON N2L 3G6 Canada Ph: (519) 885-0220 Fax: (519) 885-0014.

620 Music: Descant © Cambridge University Press.

621 Text and Music: © 1987 WGRG The Iona Community (Scotland). Used by permission of G.I.A.Publications, Inc., exclusive agent.

623 Text and Music: Melody © Brian Ruttan, 94 Lake Ave. Drive, Stoney Creek ON L8G 3N4 Canada Ph: (905) 662-7607. Music: Harmony © Roland A.H.Packer, 29 Blackwood Cres., Hamilton ON L8S 3H6 Canada Ph: (416) 978-7751.

625 Text and Music: © 1992 Hope Publishing Co.

626 Text: © Rodborough Tabernacle United Reformed Church, Rev. R.E.Francie, The Manse, Tabernacle United Reformed Church, Tabernacle Walk, Rodborough, Stroud, Glos. GL5 3UJ England Ph: 01453 758179 Fax: 171 916 2021. Music: © 1971 F.R.C.Clarke, 260 Indian Road, Kingston ON K7M 1T7 Canada Ph: (613) 548-7470.

627 Text: © 1970 McCrimmon Publishing Co., Ltd., State Mutual Bk. & Periodical Service Ltd., 10-12 High Street Great Wakering, Southend-on-Sea SS3 0EQ UK Ph: 011-44-170-221-8956 Fax: 011-44-170-221-6082. Music: © 1985 Hope Publishing Co.

628 Music: Harmony © Mowbray (an imprint of Cassell plc, London).

630 Text: © 1991 G.I.A.Publications, Inc. Music: © John R. Van Maanen, 27 Foster Street, Simcoe ON N3Y 2C3 Canada.

631 Text: © Mrs. Olwen A. Scott, 4 Anthony Close, Colchester, Essex CO4 4LD, UK Ph: 011-44-120-684-3477. Music: Harmony © Hope Publishing Co.

632 Text: © Willard F. Jabusch, Catholic Student Center at the University of Chicago, Calvert House, 5735 S. University Ave., Chicago IL 60637 USA Ph: (773) 288-2311. Music: Arrangement © 1974 The Hymnal of the United Church of Christ. Administered by The Pilgrim Press.

633 Text: © 1991 Stainer & Bell Ltd. All rights reserved. Used by permission of Hope Publishing Co. Music: © The executors of the estate of Rachel Knight, deceased, 23 Regent Road, Downham Market, Norfolk PE38 9TN UK.

634 Music: © 1978, 1980, and 1981 Les Presses de Taizé. Used by permission of G.I.A. Publications, Inc., exclusive agent.

635 Text: © 1982 and Music: © 1969 Hope Publishing Co.

637 Music: Harmony © 1995 Waterloo Music Co.Ltd.

638 Text: Translation © John Webster Grant, Emmanuel College, 75 Queen's Park Crescent, Toronto ON M5S 1K7 Canada Ph: (416) 585-4539 Fax: (416) 585-4516. Music: Harmony © 1995 Waterloo Music Co.Ltd.

639 Text: Translation © Oxford University Press. Music: Accompaniment © George Black.

640 Music: © Estate of John Dykes Bower, c/o Lee, Bolton & Lee, 1 The Sanctuary, London SW1P 3JT UK Ph: 011-44-171-222-5381.

642 Text: © 1992 Hope Publishing Co. Music: © Michael Capon, 130 Connaught St., Apt. 8, Fredericton, NB E3B 2A9 Canada Ph: (506) 450-8500.

643 Text: © Anne Neufeld Rupp, 13844 Sycamore, Olathe KS 66062 USA Ph: (913) 782-1793.

645 Music: © Oxford University Press.

647 Text: © 1982 Hope Publishing Co. Alternative text and Music: © 1935, 1963 Birdwing Music, div. of Sparrow Corp. All rights reserved. Used by permission of CMC Ltd.

650 Text: © 1991 Stainer & Bell Ltd. Used by permission of Hope Publishing Co. All rights reserved. Music: Harmony © John Leon Hooker, Episcopal Divinity School, 99 Brattle Street, Cambridge MA 02138 USA Ph: (617) 868-3450.

651 Text and Music: © 1969 Hope Publishing Co. Music: Adaptation © 1969 and Accompaniment © 1987 Hope Publishing Co.

652 Text: © 1988 Oxford University Press. Music: © 1983 Hope Publishing Co.

654 Text: Revision *Hymns for Today's Church*, 1982 © 1982 Hope Publishing Co.

655 Text: © Mowbray (an imprint of Cassell plc, London). Music: Arrangement © Estate of Julius Röntgen, c/o F.E.Röntgen. Current information sought.

656 Text and Music: Melody © 1987 Common Cup Company, c/o Ian Macdonald, 7591 Gray Ave., Burnaby BC V5J 3Z4 Ph: (604) 434-8323 Fax: (604) 430-3697. Music: Arrangement © Andrew Donaldson, Seraph Music, 14 Hambly Ave., Toronto ON M4E 2R6 Canada Ph: (416) 691-1158 Fax: (416) 690-9967 Email: seraph@pathcom.com

657 Text: © 1987 The Hymn Society in the United States and Canada. All rights reserved. Used by permission of Hope Publishing Co.

658 Text: © 1978 and Music: © 1985 Hope Publishing Co.

659 Text: © Secretary of State for Canada. Music: Arrangement © Estate of Frederick Silvester, c/o Mrs. Wendy Verduijn, 385 Walkers Line, Burlington ON L7N 2C9 Canada Ph: (905) 634-6852.

660 Music: Arrangement © Estate of Henry Walford Davies. Used by permission of Oxford University Press.

661 Music: Adaptation © 1983 Abingdon Press. (Administered by The Copyright Company, Nashville, TN). All rights reserved. International copyright secured. Used by permission.

662 Text: Paraphrase and Music: Melody: © 1975 Lillenas Publishing Co. (Administered by The Copyright Company, Nashville, TN). All rights reserved, International copyright secured. Used by permission.

664 Text: © 1989 Hope Publishing Co.

668 Text: Revision *Hymns for Today's Church*, 1982. © 1982 Hope Publishing Co.

669 Text: © 1990 The Pilgrim Press.

670 Text: *Le Psautier français*, 1995. © 1995 Réveil Publications.

671 Text: *Le Psautier français*. © 1995 Réveil Publications.

672 Text: © 1989 Hope Publishing Co.

673 Text: © 1990 The Pilgrim Press.

674 Text: © Paul Gibson.

676 Text: Inuktitut translation © Benjamin T. Arreak.

677 Music: Arrangement and organ accompaniment © Estate of Healey Willan.

678 Music: Arrangement and organ accompaniment © Estate of Healey Willan.

679 Music: Arrangement and organ accompaniment © Estate of Healey Willan.

680 Music: Arrangement © Estate of Healey Willan.

681 Music: Arrangement and organ accompaniment © Estate of Healey Willan.

683 Music: Arrangement and organ accompaniment © Estate of Healey Willan.

684 Music: Arrangement and organ accompaniment © Estate of Healey Willan.

685 Music: Arrangement and organ accompaniment © Estate of Healey Willan.

686 Music: © 1981 G.I.A. Publications, Inc.

687 Music: © 1981 G.I.A. Publications, Inc.

688 Music: © 1981 G.I.A. Publications, Inc.

689 Music: © 1981 G.I.A. Publications, Inc.

690 Music: © 1981 G.I.A. Publications, Inc.

691 Music: © Barrie Cabena.

692 Music: © Barrie Cabena.

693 Music: © Barrie Cabena.

694 Music: © Barrie Cabena.

695 Music: © Barrie Cabena.

696 Music: © Barrie Cabena.

697 Music: © Barrie Cabena.

698 Music: © Barrie Cabena.

699 Music: © Barrie Cabena.

700 Music: © Barrie Cabena.

701 Music: © Barrie Cabena.

702 Music: *Mass of Hope*, © 1977 St. Vincent Archabbey, 300 Fraser Purchase Road, Latrobe PA 15650-2690 USA Ph: (412) 539-9761.

703 Music: © C.T. Andrew. Current information sought.

704 Music: © Geoffrey Chapman (an imprint of Cassell plc, London).

705 Music: Arrangement © 1985, 1989 G.I.A. Publications, Inc.

707 Music: Melody © 1977, 1982 St. Vladimir's Seminary Press, 575 Scarsdale Rd., Crestwood, NY 10707 USA Fax: (914) 961-4507; Adaptation © Brigid Coult.

711 Music: Refrain © McCrimmon Publishing Co. Ltd., State Mutual Bk. & Periodical Service Ltd., 10-12 High Street, Great Wakering, Southend-on-Sea SS3 0EQ UK Ph: 011-44-170-221-8956 Fax: 011-44-170-221-6082; Psalm tone: © Concacan Inc. Conférence des Évéques catholiques du Canada, 90 Parent Ave. Ottawa ON K1N 7B1 Canada Ph: (613) 241-9461

712 Music: *Mass of Remembrance*, © 1987 G.I.A. Publications, Inc.

713 Music: © Patrick Wedd.

714 Music: © 1984 Les Presses de Taizé. Used by permission of G.I.A. Publications, Inc., exclusive agent.

715 Text and Music: © 1985 Fintan O'Carroll and Christopher Walker, Published by OCP Publications.

716 Music: © 1975 G.I.A. Publications, Inc.

717 Music: © 1975 G.I.A. Publications, Inc.

719 Music: Harmony © John Campbell. Music: Adaptation © 1980 Church Pension Fund.

# Authors, Composers, and Sources

# Hymns in Languages other than English

# Hymns for Use with Children and Youth

The music in this index reflects the wide range of musical tastes and abilities of children and youth, and includes music from each season of the church year.

Some of the characteristics that make hymns appropriate for use with young people include: images, situations, or stories that will be familiar or otherwise readily understood; poetry that is appealing to youth, even while it may not be easily understood; simple or repetitive tunes and rounds (such as the music of Taizé); tunes which are engaging because of their varying rhthyms, or their influence from different cultures; some hymns in languages other than English (children will often learn these quite readily).

Because it is most important for young people to learn the service music that is used by their parish, all of the service music has been included in this index.

# Subject Index

The following table provides a list of hymns and some service music by subjects. The list of subjects includes liturgical elements, such as canticles and psalms, for which paraphrases and substitutes are suggested. This flexibility is in accordance with directions provided in the *Book of Alternative Services* of the Anglican Church of Canada where it is suggested that other translations of the canticles may be used (p. 74) and that, "Those responsible for planning worship should be free to choose translations [of the psalms] appropriate to the liturgical needs and abilities of a congregation. The metric translations of the Reformed tradition should not be forgotten" (p. 703).

# Biblical Index

The following index is supplied to assist worship planners in choosing hymns that complement biblical readings. Not every reading identified by the Revised Common Lectionary appears in this list, and some biblical texts are included which do not appear in that particular lectionary but which may be used in other circumstances.

The index is intended to suggest hymns which will round out the themes of biblical readings used in a liturgy, giving them voice in praise and supplication. It is not necessary for each reading to be preceded or followed immediately by a hymn containing one or more of its themes—a communion hymn, for instance, may have been chosen from among those linked by the index with the Old Testament reading. It is sufficient for the whole liturgy to expand and reflect in thought, feeling, and prayer the subjects suggested by one or more of the readings of the day. Hymns are used in a liturgy in a poetic pattern, enriching the total environment of worship in its various moments of gathering, proclamation, intercession, thanksgiving, and dismissal for mission.

The choice of hymns will be affected not only by their relationship to the readings and their place within the liturgy but by seasonal, local, and pastoral concerns.

## John

## Acts of the Apostles

## Romans

# Metrical Index

# Tune Name Index

# First Lines and Common Titles